For over thirty years, A
interviewing the world's t
and finding out just what n
the first time in book f
philosophies and advice (_____, ____
world-famous names as Sebastian Coe, Don
Quarrie, Lillian Board, Ed Moses and Debbie
Flintoff-King. Their initial impulse to take up
athletics, their struggles and dedication to make it
to the top, their great races and championships and
their hopes for the future are all featured in a series
of remarkably frank interviews.

As a runner of many years' standing, the author is
well placed to bring out the best in his subjects:
what comes over, above all else, is the sheer
exhilaration of athletics and competing, against
oneself as well as against others. Again and again,
the household names and relatively unknown club
members stress the friendship and sense of fulfilment they have gained from their chosen sport;
even the heartbreak of injury and below-standard
performances cannot dampen the spirits of these
sportsmen and women who have thrilled us with
their rivalry, across the world and across the years.
Photographs by top athletic photographer, Mark Shearman.

☆　　☆　　☆

Alastair Aitken was born in Edinburgh in 1940, and
educated at Langley School in Norfolk.

His first article on athletics was published when
he was eighteen; since then, he has had many
articles and interviews published in among others,
*Modern Athletics, Athletics Weekly, Athletics Arena,
Marathon and Distance Runner,* as well as being a listed
contributer to *Athletics Today* (since 1989) – has done
work for radio stations from London to North East
England. In 1972, he married Joanna; they have one
son, Andrew, who chose the title for this book.
Alastair Aitken lives in South London.

*(cover photograph is of Ron Clarke leading Gammoudi, Keino and Temu in
Mexico 1968)*

MORE THAN WINNING

Interviews with Great Athletes

Alastair Aitken

Foreword by

Peter Hildreth

Temple House Books
Sussex, England

Temple House Books
is an imprint of
The Book Guild Ltd.

Temple House Books
25 High Street,
Lewes, Sussex.

First published 1992
Second printing 1992
© Alastair Aitken 1992
Set in Baskerville

Typesetting by Kudos Graphics
Slinfold, Horsham, West Sussex
Printed in Great Britain by
Antony Rowe Ltd.,
Chippenham, Wiltshire.

A catalogue record for this book is
available from the British Library

ISBN 0 86332 741 9

CONTENTS

FOREWORD

During the years I have known him, Alastair Aitken has always demonstrated an estimable ability to go the distance. Whether on track, road or country, and sometimes in conditions which defeated better runners, he has never failed to finish.

This steadfast quality comes through in *More Than Winning*, the product of more than twenty-five years of patient research and tireless leg-work in many parts of the world.

In what must be a unique collection of interviews he has coaxed into eloquence stars who often prefer to let their legs do the talking.

It is a tribute to his tact and perseverance, and will be of lasting value to readers of this book, that when their legs stopped moving Alastair was on hand to tape their words.

Peter Hildreth

Sunday Telegraph Athletics Correspondent, who represented the United Kingdom as a hurdler in the Olympics of 1952, 1956 and 1960, and gained a bronze in the European Games of 1950.

INTRODUCTION

The pleasure I have derived from talking to so very many people in athletics since 1961 made it a daunting task to select from hundreds of interviews.

The main thing was that I wanted to compile a book of spontaneous conversations I had with those that made it to the top.

My imagination was captured first of all by the atmosphere of the White City Stadium when the leading athletes of the day competed in front of a packed crowd; also at that time, I started to enjoy running and jumping more than any other sports events, and the motivation to compete at school was much the same as it was for my first subject in the book. European Champion for 1500 in 1969 John Whetton:

'I think primarily one takes part in athletics because one can do it. It all begins at school really, at least it did in my case. It was something that I could do. I was hopeless at football and other sports, and at that time I was quite an insecure person with something of an inferiority complex. Athletics gave me a lot of pleasure, not least because it gave me some supremacy over the other boys in the class. From there it grew, so that I was able to express in one form a superiority over others and, deep down, I think that has been my prime reason for being an athlete'.

Having run the last twelve London Marathons, with a best of 2:47:58 in Highgate Harriers' colours in 1982, at forty-two, I have trained in many places, but again the actual enjoyment for the sport dates back since one first runs about as a child, and here Rod Dixon, who was third in the Olympic 1500 in 1972 and won the New York Marathon in 1983 (2:8:59) has something to say: 'As a kiddy on the farm which my grandparents had back in New Zealand, I used to run barefoot along the river banks, through the farm, in the grass and the lovely fresh clover. It was fantastic. I think from those early days I really developed my love for the sport and it carried right through. A good thing that has come out of it is that I have retained my love of the countryside and my basic love for running, even though obviously I have had hard days training.

'Even when I get so frustrated with the whole thing something is still within me to get out the next day and run to express myself. There is nothing better than running through the hills and along the forest trails, the river beside you and the birds singing with the sun coming down. Sometimes I would be running along a lonely road and would have my arms in the air and say, "Isn't this just absolutely fantastic." and I look down at my feet pounding along the road and I become so excited by the whole atmosphere; this is real enjoyment.'

1

QUALITIES THAT MAKE A STAR

The difference between reaching the top and being near to achieving high quality performances has a lot to do with mental attitude, and that is something Derek Ibbotson, the 1956 Olympic bronze medallist for 5000 and ex-World mile record holder with 3min 57.2, backed up:

'When you are young, the main thing is not to be worried by the reputation and physique of others. World champions come in all shapes and sizes. Youngsters are inclined to feel that they can be beaten by a bigger lad, but learn as they get older that lots of things come into it. What you have in the heart and mind counts most. The mind can plan training and racing well; the heart will carry you through and that will make up for any lack of physical make-up.'

From that wonderful, hard but good school for PE, Loughborough, came Robbie Brightwell, who was the European 400 gold medallist in 1962 as well as 4 × 400 silver at the Olympics of 1964; he also imparts good commonsense:

'The main thing is that you must first have some potential, but it is not always the athlete with the greatest potential who reaches the top, more often perhaps the athlete with the greatest perseverance. This is the thing that counts, you must never give in. Sometimes you have scrubber years, others will be good ones, but keep on racing, have faith in yourself and you will eventually come through.'

An interesting point was brought up by Bruce Tulloh, the European 5000 Champion back in 1962, when he said: 'A most essential thing for a runner and the reason why Britain produces a depth of middle distance specialists, is because of cross-country racing. It toughens the mental attitude. A

11

man capable of up to nine miles of heavy country will not be afraid of twelve laps on the track.'

Miruts Yifter was the Olympic Champion for 5/10k in 1980, and his coach, Nigusie Roba, who was then the National coach of Ethiopia, illustrated the qualities of his outstanding runner: 'When his coach gives him a pro- gramme he always fulfils it – and that is his first quality. Secondly, Yifter is not worried about any competition or afraid of any athlete. Another quality is the fact that when his friends are running with him in the big competitions he always tells them not to be nervous.'

A National coach to the Moroccan team, Aziz Daouda, who advises 1984 Olympic 5000-metre champion Said Aouita spells it out: 'The first quality Said has is that he can work very hard and accept that work. In fact I don't think there is anyone working as hard as he does. He enjoys his running, but does not have a favourite event. It is more that he likes the challenges of running against people.'

Turning the question on qualities back on the coaches' influence for the athlete to achieve success, Simon Mugglestone, a European Junior Champion of the 1980s and a rising star of the 1990s who was firstly shown the ropes as a youngster by Irish veteran International, George Blackburn, and went on to be coached by Harry Wilson (the man behind Steve Ovett's Olympic and World record achievements): 'My coach Harry Wilson is an inspiration to me, and the main thing is he is not frightened to try new ideas and methods with his coaching.'

Daley Thompson has been the outstanding decathlete in the history of the event, but in the case of Bill Toomey, who won the Olympic decathlon in 1968 in Mexico City and achieved new World record figures of 8417 in 1969, had almost insurmountable problems that made him a very special inspiration on those coming after. He ripped open his hand as a kid, having five operations on it. The median nerve in his wrist was sliced, and 'In the beginning I thought I would never be able to throw the shot properly.'

In 1965 he pierced open his leg while achieving a personal best of thirteen feet in the pole vault, and had forty stitches!

On 24 December 1965 to 1 April 1966, he contracted

hepatitis and mononucleosis: 'Boy, was I weak! I thought I would never make it back again.' It was much later in 1966 that he achieved a World Record of 8234 points, but the record was disallowed that July because the meeting organizers had not got the proper equipment.

Then, to cap it all, in early 1967 he did something to his knee and had to have an operation. The day after he started weight training in the basement of the hospital to rebuild the muscle. 'The hospital staff regarded me as somewhat mad, but I had a lot of work to do rebuilding my weakened legs, and did a lot of leg lifts whilst wearing a plaster cast. Then after I came off the crutches I discovered that I was an inch smaller. During the year I had cortisone injections for injuries on six occasions.' It is that type of resolve that makes a star. It was the year after that he became Olympic Champion with an Olympic record of 8193pts, and the most praiseworthy result was at the end of the first day he achieved a 45.6 in the 400. He was followed home in the medals by Hans-Joachim Walde (8111) and Kurt Bendlin (8064).

Bill Toomey's advice about the best way to approach the event: 'Reading, watching and understanding. Some of the best practise I have had was mental practising, working things out, experimenting.'

Without a doubt in the 1980s, Mike Conley, the World Cup winner of 1989, was the best combination long and triple jumper in the world, and his advice on whether he would encourage a young person to come into athletics or not, with all the problems that have been well-publicized: 'The thing about athletics is it is more of an individual sport. It takes a lot of hard work, and for that reason a lot of self-discipline as well. But it is a sport you can always improve on. If you can't win you can still improve your performance, whereas with some sports you really don't know. Take soccer or basketball or football – you can be overshadowed and never know whether you have improved. But in a sport like athletics you have always got something to shoot at.'

2

SYDNEY WOODERSON

Born London, 13 August 1914; 5'6"/125lbs.
It was an easy task to choose Sydney Wooderson as a subject for the book because his range at Championship events was second to none. He was world record holder at 800/880, European 1500 and 5000 Champion.

Blackheath Harrier club mate Jack Braughton, who he coached for a place in the 5000 Olympic team in 1948 'Sydney Wooderson was a great athlete at any distance on any course and a true amateur.'

Interview in 1979

How would you compare the champions of yesteryear to the world-class athletes of today?

'I think that you have to judge a runner by the time he runs, and therefore it is very difficult to compare runners then to now, but I would think anybody who did well before the war would similarly have done well after the war, and at the present time. Nurmi and Zatopek were champions; they were champions in their day, they would be champions today!'

Who were the hardest runners you raced against?

'Now this again is rather difficult, because I think if you are running at your best you can beat your rivals fairly easily, but if you are not running well then you can't. Take, for instance, Jack Lovelock. He was a great competitor, but I beat him; yet when I ran in the 1936 Olympics and I had something wrong with my leg, of course he easily beat me. In the half-mile I ran against Mario Lanzi, and that was a very hard race when I beat him in the international meeting at the White City, but I never met Rudolf Harbig, the great German runner. I am quite sure if I had run against him over half a mile he would have beaten me, because I think he is one of the greatest half-milers there has ever been.'

People must look back and think Jack Lovelock was an athlete who had superb timing for getting right for the medal race. I see you as more of a racer over many years and, although you gave careful thought to your races, you appeared to race purely because you enjoyed athletics.

'I was a racer, but I used to start at the beginning of the season in March, April, May, and work gradually up to what I felt was the greatest race I would run in and then put everything in there. Afterwards I felt I would be going down gradually, so up until that time of my peak I really enjoyed racing, but afterwards I did not. I think to a certain extent that is the difference between those days and today; as I say, they never seem to stop running. As regards to myself, anyway, I don't think I could do that sort of racing. I would have to carry on as I did before, come up to a peak, have a great race and then gradually slacken off and do cross-country in the winter months.'

I am not quite so sure that the club these days means quite so much to the 'class' athlete, whereas your club, Blackheath, appeared to mean a great deal to you and was a motivating force to keep you running?

'Definitely! I do feel a bit upset about that, as far as cross-country is concerned. In my day we used to have packs that went out – the fast pack, slower pack and slow pack, and everybody was put in the pack and kept with the pack leader. But today they come up to run out on a Saturday afternoon from the club headquarters, going out in their ones and twos just as they like, and they sometimes don't come up at all if they are racing on the Sunday or whatever!'

You excelled at the half-mile, mile, 5000m, cross-country, but I would have thought you would prefer to be thought of as an outstanding miler. Do you consider that your best event?

'Yes, I felt that it was my distance as I enjoyed it. It was not too short like the half-mile, and was not too long like the three miles. It was just right for me. I found racing cross-country a little bit boring, especially with these lap courses. I used to enjoy cross-country training and racing cross-country, provided I was not out to win. If I knew I could come in second or third but came fifth, I really enjoyed cross-country, but when I went out with the idea of say, winning the National or the Southern, I did not enjoy it.'

How much training did you do?

'What training I did I thought was more than most people did, but of course compared with the training of today it was very little, and therefore I could combine my work and my racing and the training. We used to train about five or six times a week, but only once a day. I used to do the usual warm-up, about two or three miles. It was very similar training throughout the week but mixing the fast stuff with a 600-yards, three-quarters of a mile, mile, mile and a half, and two miles. That sort of training to me was quite a lot, but today it probably sounds nothing at all.'

It depends at what intensity you were doing it. What was the duration of your training when you went out the door to finishing your session?

'I suppose it would be a matter of one to two hours. As for the sort of pace I did, let us say I was aiming to do a mile in 4.20 on the Saturday. Probably on a Wednesday I would do a three-quarter mile in 3.15, knowing that on the Saturday I could carry on at the same pace for the full distance. Of course that sort of training is very mild compared to the training they do today, isn't it?'

Yes and no, because you have not burned up all reserves in training, which may possibly be done if people do too much intensive training?

'That is my opinion too, but it is difficult really for me to be objective on that because I have not done the training. But I do feel they tend to do too much training today! With so much competition these days, it seems very difficult to have a proper job and to give up your job completely and concentrate on your training or, otherwise, cut down your racing so that you can do your job as well.'

When you were eighteen you ran 4:29.8, for the mile which was then the fastest on record for a schoolboy. Did you think you had a good chance of getting to the top?

16

'I enjoyed running, but I just took it as it came, and when I left school I ran for the club and actually went in for the County Championships, then the Southern and then on to the next thing and so forth. It gradually came along, and I did not think much about it.'

Was it a turning point for you when Albert Hill, the 1920 Olympic gold medallist for the 800 and 1500, met you?

'Albert Hill was a very nice man. He is the only great athlete I have known who has carried on his training ability. A lot of people, myself included, would not have been a good trainer or coach – but he was and, of course, he was the club coach too.'

In the 1938 European Championships you met the 1934 European Champion from Italy, Luigi Beccali. Did you think you might have a few problems beating him in the 1500 final?

'Yes, as he had won before, I definitely thought Beccali was going to be the danger. It was a bit of a mix-up really, as no-one wanted to take the lead and everybody was cutting in, getting spiked and all sorts of things. I think to a certain extent the others were a little afraid of me so that was why I won, as I don't think I was quite at my best at that time; I went in the home straight, if I remember rightly.'
(5 September, 1938. 1. Sydney Wooderson, 3:53.6, 2. Joseph Mostert, (Bel.) 3:54.5, 3. Luigi Beccali, (Italy) 3:55.2.)

In 1937 you set a world record for the mile (4:06.4) and in 1938, before the European Championships, you also achieved at Motspur Park 800 (1:48.4) and 880 yds (1:49.2) world records. Did the fact that they were handicap races help you break the records?

'I would like to point out that over a mile there were six or seven seconds between my time and the next man's time in the country. But for the fact that it was company for me in the race, I don't think really they helped me whatsoever. In fact in some ways they hindered me, because for the first lap they made me run too fast, whereas if I had been on my own I would have settled for a more even pace. I think it was just the fact of having company in the attempt that was the help rather than they were strung out round the track, which I did not think helped me at all.'

You took Glen Cunningham's world mile record off the

books with your 4:06.4. Was that the most satisfying world record of the three for you?

'Definitely. I did not go out with the intention of breaking the world record, only with the intention of breaking my own British record of 4:10.8.'

You did have a couple of major disappointments in your career: the race in Princeton, USA, when you were knocked off the track, and being badly injured at the 1936 Olympic Games. Did that persuade you to atone for those performances and to carry on longer?

'Yes; also the fact that I failed in 1939 spurred me on to carry on after the war. Of course I am pleased to say I did.'

Did you get a chance to train during the war?

'I used to keep up my running, but of course on very bad tracks and with very little competition, and I could not train properly. It was only in 1945 that I really started getting back into trim. Right at the start of the war I was medically graded C3 and put in an inferior regiment, but I always tried to train wherever I was stationed, whether it was over the country or in a field or on an army track.'

You ran against Arne Anderson in front of a 54,000 crowd at the White City in 1945, where you were a close second, and also you ran your fastest ever mile of 4:04.2 in Sweden behind him. That must have really pleased you.

'Specially as it was without proper training, so obviously I was very, very pleased. I thoroughly enjoyed my race with Anderson at the White City.'

You turned from the mile to the 5000 in 1946. Was that your coach's idea or yours?

'During the war I had not had any contact with my coach, and I really took over myself, training on his lines, but I was self-coached from 1940. I think there were two reasons why I changed over to the long distance. Perhaps I had not got the speed of a younger man like Lennart Strand, who was the top miler or 1500 man of those days.'

In the 1946 European 5000 you had Gaston Reiff, Emil Zatopek and Willem Slijkhuis among your opponents. Whom did you consider your most dangerous rival?

'I obviously went to Oslo for those championships with the sole idea of winning, and I knew my chief opponent again was going to be Slijkhuis, and he was. In some ways it was a very similar race to the AAA three miles I had at the White City, but he started his sprint in the European much earlier – with 400 to go, whereas before it was with 200 left. In the European I shot him in the beginning of the back straight and found it much easier to win than I had done at the White City. In the AAA, I had led most of the way until the last bend, but on the last lap I eased slightly and he shot past me; then, coming into the straight, I sprinted past him and won by a few yards. At Oslo, with the great number of first-class competitors, it was really that they were leading most of the way and I gradually eased up from the back of the field to tenth, third, and then second behind Slijkhuis and, as I say, on the last lap I shot past him on the back straight.'

(23 August, 1946, – 1. Sydney Wooderson, 14:08.6, 2. Willem Slijkhuis (Hol.), 14:14.0, 3. Evert Nyberg (Swe.), 14:23.2).

Finally, you won the Southern and National cross-country titles in 1948, but were unplaced in the International. Why was that?

'I was fairly light in weight, and racing cross-country, hard, took a lot out of me. I really had not got anything left in the International!'

Modest and bespectacled, Sydney Wooderson, who will be remembered running in his famous black strip, went on to become President of his club and a good official.

19

3

HERB McKENLEY

Born Clarendon, Jamaica, 10 July, 1922.

Herb McKenley, who was known as 'Hustling Herb', was the most versatile sprinter of the late 1940s and early 1950s. Besides breaking the World one lap record he went on to gain a silver in the Olympics of 1948.

In 1952 he obtained two individual silvers for the 100/400 in the Olympics in Helsinki, only losing by inches in each case, and was the most significant factor (with his 44.6 penultimate leg) in the outstanding victory of the Jamaican team over the strong USA quartet and therefore won himself a coveted, well-deserved gold medal.

What brought you into athletics?

'It was the spectacle of Arthur Wint, who used to go to the same high school as me in Jamaica. I saw him in action, and I thought he looked really tremendous and graceful. Then a year later (1938), he was selected for the Jamaican team for the Caribbean Games, and he came to the school dressed in his uniform, which at the time was a cream suit with a maroon tie, white shoes and a Panama straw hat. I thought, 'Boy, this is really great; one day I must wear that uniform.'

When did you begin to feel you could yourself be a world-beating athlete?

'I remember in the fall of 1945 my coach at the University of Illinois, Leo Johnson, saying to me, 'How would you like to be the greatest quarter-miler in the world?' I just could not think of it. Then, one night, I dreamt I was running . . . I was sweating so much that when I woke up and realized I was in bed I couldn't believe it, because the memory of it was so vivid and real. In the dream I broke the world record.

20

There was the headline in the *Chicago Tribune* 'Herb McKenley creates new world record'. After I woke up I wondered why I should dream about that, and then I remembered my coach saying I could be the best in the world. The next day I told Leo about it, and after three days of trying to pin him down and get some answers, he said to me, "It seems as if you have realized that this is a possibility." When he had first broached the matter I had said, "Leo, how can I, from little Jamaica, be better than everybody else in the world?" I had just laughed it off. Now, when we started to discuss the dream, he said: "You know, Herb, a lot of the great things that happen in this world first started with a dream like the one you just had. What you are telling me now is that your subconscious has accepted the idea."

'I asked him what I should do, and he said, "Herb, you are going to have to prepare for it." I said I was preparing, and he replied: "Yes, you are training like the other seventy-five boys out there. But you want to be the champion of the world, so your preparation has to be so much better and so much more exact and more refined. Also your commitment has to be even more pronounced. Whatever you want in life, there is a price tag to it. You have to give something to receive. It might mean giving up a trip to Chicago, it might be giving up a date with your best girl, and that sort of thing. It's a matter of whether your commitment is strong enough. At this point in time I cannot tell you that your goal will definitely be achieved; you will have to go on faith and your belief in what I am advising you is correct."

'Leo asked me if I thought I was ready to go for it. I said yes, and his reply to that was, "Okay, let's begin with your programme." We went inside his office, and he brought out some foolscap on which he wrote – HERB McKENLEY TRAINING PROGRAMME – WORLD RECORD? Then he wrote CROSS-COUNTRY, and I said, "Cross-country, Leo?" You must remember that in 1945, when you thought of cross-country you were thinking of the training for milers or distance runners. I must have been the first sprinter to do that type of work in the fall. I was doing three or four miles. I questioned Leo about it and he said, "Herb, this is

21

the first instalment of that payment."

'At first it did not make sense to me. I remember running through the cornfields of Champaign, Illinois, my feet blistered and aching, but the funny thing was that throughout those runs – and probably when the pain was greatest – I kept hearing in my mind the cheers of the crowd, and that kept me going. A year later I ran 46.2 for 440 y. on a very wet day on cinders at Champaign, and that broke the world record 46.4 which was held by Ben Eastman and Grover Klemmer.'

At the 1948 Olympics in London you were the favourite to win the 400, but you were beaten by Arthur Wint. What went wrong?

'Although Arthur was my idol, it just never occurred to me at that time that he could beat me. I remember I never felt better in my life running a 400. I ran 21.1 at 200, and I felt as though I was just coming out of the blocks, I said to myself, "McKenley, go for 45", and so my whole running pattern changed. Somebody told me later that I was through 300 in 32.8. It was just at that time that Arthur started to move. I knew something was happening because I was getting tired. If I had held my form I would probably have just made it, but . . . I don't feel I failed as much, as he ran 46.2 and I ran 46.4. In those days 46.4 would have won most races.'

Four years later at the Helsinki Olympics, you – a quarter-miler – came second in the 100 in a very close finish. What was the background to your competing in that event?

'Six weeks earlier I came down with the mumps, and I had given up all hope of going to the games. I lost fifteen or twenty pounds in weight. I was in the States at the time and cabled Jamaica to scratch me from the team. The then president, Sir Herbert Macdonald, cabled back to say that there was no-one else for the 4×400 team, and that if I didn't go it meant the whole team would be scratched. I worked out an arrangement with them that other than the relay, I would not be asked to run an individual race, because I had run last in my heat in the 400 at the American Championships in 49.2 and vowed I would never allow that sort of thing to happen to me again.

'I went to a friend of mine, Dr John Coleman, in Los Angeles for tests, and when he had finished he told me I was anaemic. I had lost a lot of weight and needed to build calcium. He gave me various prescriptions and told me not to train for eight or ten days. I followed his advice to get back into it slowly, and after two weeks I started running twice a day, and by the time we left for Europe, about three weeks before the Games, I had picked up a little bit.

'At Middlesborough, on a grass track, I won a quarter-mile race in 47.1. Evaluating the performance, I felt 47.1 was equal to 46.8 for 400, and on a cinder track it would possibly be two or three-tenths better, so a week or so before the Games I changed my programme and prepared seriously. Until then I never thought I would have been ready.

'I went into the 100 at the Olympics only because I wanted to improve my start so that I could develop my speed for the 400. I had no thought of winning the race; I did not think I was physically ready for it. I did not run very well in the heats (10.7), but I did successfully in the second round (10.5) and semi-finals (10.4). Up till then no-one, including myself, thought I had a chance – but then I went to the final with a tremendous desire to win. I was too eager, and in my anxiety to start well I came straight up, and after 30 m I was three or four or five metres behind, so my whole run was a catch-up. This was how really I lost the race; I was too far back from the beginning! At 90 m I must still have been two metres back, but at the finish I was given the same time (10.4) as the winner.'

1. Lindy Remigino (USA), 10:4, 2. Herb McKenley, 10:4, 3. Emmanuel McDonald Bailey (GB), 10:4, 4. Smith (USA), 10:4, 5. Soukharev (USSR), 10.5, 6. Treloar (Australia), 10.5.

You were a close second also in the 400, behind your team-mate George Rhoden. How did you run that race?

'I thought I need not try to run away from the crowd; I thought I could hold my own in the kick home, so in the final I ran 22.9 at 200, more than a second slower than I had ever run on the way, followed by a 23.0 second 200. I was in lane 4, Ollie Matson (USA) in 5 and Rhoden in 6, with Arthur Wint in lane 2. I decided I would stay with Matson, and as long as I stayed with him I would be in contention at the crucial moment. Just as we entered the turn for home after the 200 mark, I heard this heavy pounding. I thought that must be Wint, but what is he doing here so early? Then I did something I don't remember ever having done before: I turned round and looked.

'At that point in time I think I had the race won right there, but by the time I turned back Rhoden was six or seven metres up. Immediately I went after him. I don't know if I went after him too hard initially or what – I know I was catching him – but with about ten or fifteen metres to go I was reaching so far and could not go any further. I caught him but could not get past him, both of us being timed in 45.9. Although I lost, I felt I had vindicated myself, as most people thought I did not have a chance.'

1. George Rhoden (Jamaica), 45:9, 2. Herb McKenley, 45:9, 3. Ollie Matson (USA), 46:8.

And then came that memorable 4×400 relay, in which your third leg was crucial to the team.

'Very crucial. I remember I ran against Charlie Moore, who had just won the 400 hurdles.

'I ran 44.6 for my leg to pull back a deficit of about thirteen metres. I caught Charlie but did not really pass him, but because I was coming in faster than he was, the exchange to Rhoden gave us about a metre. Mal Whitfield, anchoring for the US, came up on Rhoden at one time, just going into the turn, and of course Rhoden was able to hold him off because Whitfield could not get around him on the turn, and that was the difference. It was a tremendous race.'

1. Jamaica, 3:03.9, 2. USA 3:04.3, 3. Germany, 3:06.6. Herb McKenley has been Jamaica's national coach, an IAAF representative and manages a branch of the First Life Insurance Company. He is often in athletics on a consultancy basis.

4

CHRIS CHATAWAY

Born Chelsea, 31 January 1931.

Christopher John Chataway, the red-haired Oxford blue, was one of the exciting middle distance runners of the 1950s. He was the main pacemaker of the first ever sub-four-minute mile achieved by his friend Roger Bannister, broke the World 5000 metres record (13:51.6), and was the Commonwealth Games three mile Champion in 1954.

He became very well-known outside the sport, both in the media and as a Cabinet Minister in Prime Minister Edward Heath's Government. He is currently the Chairman of Crown Communications Group plc.

Interview 1986

Few of us who are old enough to remember it will have seen a more gripping race than that over 5000m in 1954, when Christopher Chataway took on Vladimir Kuts under the floodlights of the old White City.

Also in that race – which established the hold that televised track and field has on the British sports fan – was Peter Driver of South London Harriers, the 1954 Commonwealth six miles champion, who was reputed to have said before the race: 'Whoever wins this, is made for life.' Sadly, both Kuts and Driver died prematurely. It is interesting to note that, after my interview, I was talking about Chris Chataway with a city newspaper-seller, and the vendor remembered there was a capacity crowd of 60,000 that October night at the White City. He had been turned away at the gate, and had to 'make do' with watching the race on television.

Chris Chataway was a charismatic runner presented by the media as a cigarette-smoking playboy who only trained lightly. In 1954, his best year, even though he appeared to have a thirst for the good life, Chataway ran to many exciting and important victories. He wrote an article headed 'I Believe' in a 1954 *World Sports*, about his attitude towards training. 'The period since the war has seen the rise of what I would call the "steamroller" approach to distance training – the reliance upon sheer quantity. This system is based, broadly speaking, upon the belief that it does not matter too much what you do as long as you do more of it than anybody else. This attitude has produced some really remarkable performances – particularly in the very long races.

'There remains, however, a large number of amateur athletes who either cannot or will not train every day throughout the year, and who are not prepared to devote three hours to each training session. I must admit to being one of these. But I believe that a much more limited programme (allowing, perhaps, an hour four days a week during the training months) can produce good results.

'A careful balance between speed and stamina training, the maintenance of a fresh aggressive attitude to racing, with a steadily graded increase in the intensity of workouts to produce peak form at the correct time, must be the characteristic of such a programme.

'It will never give the recovery rate nor the physical indifference to fatigue achieved by a full-time devotion to training. But it may produce a fresher approach on the day of the big race and that can, I think, be surprisingly important.' Perhaps these views are a little outdated, but many top athletes are breaking down from intensive workouts and the answer may be found in Chataway's statement. How does he now feel about the training he did then?

'I am sure I would have done better if I had trained more. I did honestly take it much more seriously than some of the newspaper articles would imply. In part it was an act, a game. One liked to give the impression of effortless superiority, that was rather fashionable at the time. I did smoke, but one did not realize then how bad smoking was for you. I did not smoke all that many cigars. If I had known that if I had trained much more I would have been much better, I would have done more. I suppose that one was frightened of getting stale. 1954 was my best year in athletics simply because I raced much more. The long season started when I paced Roger Bannister in his first four-minute mile; then I had lots of races and by October I did my best 5000 metres. I am sure now that the mistake I made was not to train or race enough, and the fact that I did so badly at the Olympics in 1956 was not that I did not want to do well but that I simply had not raced enough and trained enough.'

Athletics as a spectator sport in the 1950s was very popular, and people were hungry for good performances after the war years. 'I admired Sydney Wooderson. One of the first athletics meetings I ever saw was at Motspur Park where I saw Sydney running the half-mile. He was a great man whom I never met.'

A contemporary of Chris Chataway was Gordon Pirie (South London Harriers) who set world records at 3000 m, 5000, and six miles, and won the National CC championship three times. Did Chataway think Pirie would have held his own against the top runners of today?

'It is difficult to tell, isn't it? I suppose he could. We ran much faster than Paavo Nurmi ever did, but I am sure Nurmi would probably have beaten us all. It is terribly difficult to know whether Gordon Pirie could have been as good if he had run thirty years later. I think he would have been there or thereabouts.'

Chris Chataway first started to excel as a runner when he was around fifteen to sixteen years old at Sherborne School. He first ran the quarter mile, but considered he only did quite well at that. At Sherborne they only competed at sprints until they were about sixteen. He ran the half-mile in 2:05 for an intermediate school record, and then 4:42, a senior record, in 1947 for the mile. Chataway also played rugby at school. 'The school was very keen on rugby and I played hooker for the first team, but I did not like it very much, especially having my head banged on top every time the two scrums came together. I never played again after I

27

left the school. I did my National Service as a Gunner, and I started to run seriously because I got a forty-eight-hour pass every time I went to an athletics meeting, which was really a major incentive for me. Track was what I wanted to do; at Oxford University I had my eye on the three-miles event. Although I had not done a three-mile before I went to Oxford, I thought I would probably be better at three than one mile, and I did cross-country through the winter. I was really mostly training for the track, but I did win the Oxford v Cambridge cross-country race.'

In 1951, Chris Chataway was narrowly beaten by Roy Beckett (14:02.6) in the AAA three miles championship at the White City. 'I remember him well,' recalled Chris, 'and I often think about him because later that summer, in my first internationals against Yugoslavia, Greece and Turkey, we were both in the three miles. I ran three three-mile races in a week, which was a fantastic amount; at the time, three miles was something I rarely did. I think I beat Roy every time, and I don't think he ever appeared again. I have often thought, with some guilt, of the gamesmanship I applied then, which I think in part accounted for it. he rather thought I was as devil-may-care about the whole thing as I used to pretend to be. I think Wally really did stay up in nightclubs and so on throughout the entire tour. Whereas, whatever I said, I was going to be in bed at nine o'clock every night. I don't know what happened to him. I certainly remember him beating me in the AAA Final, only by a short margin, but I knew I was beaten all right.'

In 1952, Chris Chataway came up against a loaded field of world-class runners in the Olympic 5000 metres. Herbert Schade led early on, with Chris in second place and multi-distance phenomenon Emil Zatopek further back in the field. Alain Mimoun was well up from the start, but his crowning achievement was to come four years later when he won the Olympic Marathon in Melbourne. Gordon Pirie was also in the field.

Pirie idolized Zatopek, who had decided to grind everyone into the dust if he possibly could. Chris led at one stage late in the race and stuck to Zatopek well, but in a moment of fatigue fell over the curb on the last bend, leaving Zatopek, Mimoun and Schade to battle up the home straight. Zatopek claimed the second of his three gold medals at those Games.

In fourth place, just passing Chataway and sharing the same time (14:18) at the finish was Gordon Pirie. Zatopek claimed the second of his three gold medals at those Games.

'Zatopek was stronger,' Chataway remembered. 'I always kicked from the beginning of the back straight, so that was what I did. I overtook Zatopek right at the beginning of the back straight, and led the way up the straight and round the bend. I was pretty tired by then, and I hit my foot against the raised kerb on the inside of the track and fell. By the time I got up, Mimoun, Schade and Pirie had gone past me, but I think I certainly would not have won it. If I had left my kick until the home straight, which I probably ought to have done, and had I not fallen over, I would certainly have got third and might even have got second, I suppose. But I would not have beaten Zatopek.'

Then came 1953. 'I took it off really, because I was doing my final exams at Oxford. I went to America with a combined Oxford and Cambridge team after finishing my exams, and we ran against some American universities but it was very low-level stuff – I may have only had one race. I did not take part in the AAA Championships. (He had won the 1952 AAA three miles with 13:59.6) I took several months completely off. I think I hardly ran at all in 1953.'

But Chataway had already come a long way since his third place in the London Athletic Club schools mile at Motspur Park. That winter he joined his friends Roger Bannister and Chris Brasher for training sessions, sometimes under the eye of Franz Stampfl.

Then on the 6 May 1954, a Thursday evening, at 5 p.m. on the Iffley Road cinder track, Oxford, came the attempt to break four minutes for the mile. Chris Brasher was the early leader, and then Chris Chataway took over. At the bell, Chataway still led in 3:00.4; Bannister came up to Chataway's shoulder and, lengthening his stride, went away. The tall man forced himself over the last yards to win the race in 3:59.4, the first man to run inside four minutes for the mile. Chris Chataway was second in 4:07.2, and W.T. Hulatt third in 4:16.0. Bannister collapsed into the arms of his helpers, 'like an exploded flash bulb.'

On 21 June, Chataway met John Landy of Australia over one mile at Turku. The result was a new world record for John Landy of 3:58.00, and the man who ran strongly earlier in the race, Chris Chataway, was second in 4:04.4, with Olavi Vuorisalo third in 4:07.0. The fact that Chris still maintained his form to come second in both Bannister's and Landy's records interested me.

'I don't know why I finished in Roger's race, but I did. The other one, with Landy – I was not pacing him in Turku, I was not helping him at all. I was really trying to compete against him. Then with the two miles later on, where Roger was trying to help me to the world record – it was not a good one at the time, only 8:40 – I missed that by a fifth of a second. Roger tried to help me, but was not really good at anything over a mile. His intention had been to pace me over the first six laps, but he slowed after the first mile.'

In that year's AAA Championships, Chataway decided to run in the three miles. Freddy Green fought him every inch of the way on the last lap and, although both runners were credited with new world record figures of 13:32.2, Green managed to win on the tape.

The two next met at the Commonwealth Games in Vancouver, where Roger Bannister defeated John Landy in the mile, running a British record of 3:58.8, the second fastest time ever. Landy went on to take a bronze in the 1956 Olympic 1500 while Bannister completed the 1954 season with the 1500m gold at the European Championships, and then retired to concentrate on his career.

At the Commonwealth Games, Chataway gained revenge for his AAA defeat. 'Yes, I had lost again at the AAA and had been beaten by Freddy Green, just like "Wally" Beckett had beaten me. There such a world of difference between being number one and number two. Freddy Green's win in the AAA was quite a shock, because I don't remember coming across him before. The Commonwealth Games three miles was therefore a major challenge. I was pleased to win that. It shows the ups and downs – within a few weeks the roller coaster that is athletics and international competition . . . at one moment, there I was nearly getting the world two-mile record and the next moment – I am not even the best in the UK, and the next moment the best in the Commonwealth, and the next, I have got the world record. All within a few months.'

Chataway's time for the Commonwealth three miles was 13:35.2, a new Games record. Freddy Green was some fifteen yards behind, with Frank Sando third.

The summer ended on a high note for Chataway. In the European championships at Berne on 29 August, Chris lined up in the 5000 m final against some very formidable opposition. The field included the great Emil Zatopek, the Belgian Franz Herman and a promising newcomer. A Russian ex-sailor, what little was known about Vladimir Kuts was only that he tended to start too fast and be unable to hold his pace.

Zatopek was obviously the man to beat; in May he had broken the world 5000 m record, and two days later, on 1 June, he had also broken his own world 10,000 m record. At the opening of the Championships, he won the 10,000 in a time that was only four seconds slower than his world record.

'But we were both, Emil and I, looking at the wrong man. I remember going into that race, and it never occurred to me that there was anybody else except Zatopek. I made up my mind that I would follow him. We had never heard of this Russian, so it was a most appalling shock when he did not come back.'

The times of the first three were: Vladimir Kuts, 13:56.5 (world record), Christopher Chataway 14:08.8, Emil Zatopek 14:10.2.

On 13 October, in the London v Moscow match, Chataway again met Vladimir Kuts over 5000 m. The supporting cast was Peter Driver and Vladimir Okorov, who had filled fourth spot in the European 5000 m (14:20.0).

With five and a half laps left, Kuts put in a devastating burst, slowed and then quickened the pace again. 'I had never come across anybody who had put in sprints like that before, and I don't think anybody else had in those days. I just made up my mind that I would stick with him for as long as I could, and it hurt awfully. I suppose, because of the small amount of training that we used to do, the races hurt us much more than they do for people now, who are

31

better trained and tougher. We used to run on our nerves to a much greater extent because we thought we would get stale. We did relatively little training.

'To run to one's limit was terrible agony, and those bursts were simply appalling, even years later – more than three decades – I can remember it very, very vividly. Really, on the last two laps I had more or less given up hope. I was just living second by second. I thought that if I can hang on another ten yards and go on, perhaps another ten . . . The final lap was terrible. Terrible! Until the moment of hope in the last fifty yards.

'I don't know whether he did slightly falter or whether I just discovered some last reserve, but I can still recall the feeling of madness as I threw myself into that last fifty yards. It might have been that one was seeking oblivion. One really expected to expire. I could not have felt more stretched to the extremity than I did at that moment.

'In a way it was a very satisfying experience, but I absolutely know that I could not have drawn out another inch that day, that once in my life I had the experience of knowing that I had tested myself absolutely to my limit. I could have gone faster if we had run it more evenly, if we had not had those appalling bursts. It could have been a faster time, but I could not have got any more out of myself than I did that day.'

The time was a world record of 13:51.6, which Kuts improved to 13:51.2 ten days later.

The following year, on 28 May at the White City, in the *News of the World* British Games, three men who were advised at some time by Franz Stampfl, Alan Gordon, Brian Hewson and Chris Chataway, took part in the mile race. Gordon led in the early stages, and behind him at the halfway stage the young Hewson was running alongside Chataway. Lurking in the rear was Hungarian Laslo Tabori, coached by the enigmatic Mihaly Igloi. Hewson and Chataway raced into the last lap, but at 1500 m Tabori was looking menacing.

Tabori pulled away over the last 100 yards for a Hungarian record of 3:59.0; Chataway ran 3:59.8, finally cracking four minutes. Brian Hewson was also timed at 3:59.8; it was to be another three years before he broke four minutes again. It was the first race in which three men ran under four minutes, and fourth in the six man field was steeplechaser John Disley with 4:09.0.

Chataway recalled, 'That was the only time I broke four minutes. I can remember the finish of that race. Brian was a bit younger than me, a beautiful runner, wasn't he? Very elegant.'

In 1955, Chataway won the AAA three miles title from rising star Derek Ibbotson in 13:33.6. On 2 July Chris won a mile, an attempt on the world record, in 4:00.8, from Ken Wood in 4:01.6. Over one mile again in August, a great battle took place between Sandor Iharos, Laslo Tabori, Ken Wood and Chris Chataway. The Hungarians on that occasion outgunned the 'Red Fox', to win in 4:05 to Chataway's 4:06.4 and Ken Wood's 4:08.2. Hungary had briefly come to the top of the middle distance world, but the Australians were waiting.

That same month, Chris set a world record of 13:23.2 for three miles during the match between Germany and Great Britain. 'That was just a record attempt. I think it was the only time I ever succeeded in getting a record more or less cold-bloodedly. I did have somebody (Derek Ibbotson) pacing me or at least running with me, and he helped me set a fast pace. Then I ran the last two laps on my own. That was about all I did that season, as I started work in television as a newscaster. Robin Day and I were the first two newscasters when commercial television started in the summer of 1955, so I stopped fairly early in the season.'

In 1956, Chris Chataway, after finishing a close second to Derek Ibbotson (13:32.6) in the AAA three miles, had stomach cramp in the Melbourne Olympic 5000 m final and came eleventh in 14:28.8, with only old rival Herbert Schade behind him (14:31.8). The winner was Kuts in 13:39.6, 2.8 seconds slower than Gordon Pirie's world record, from Pirie himself (13:50.6) who had come back after a traumatic battle with Kuts in the 10,000 m three days beforehand. Derek Ibbotson won the bronze (13:54.4), and had his great year of 1957 before him.

'I don't know why . . . (Chataway suffered from cramp). I was over the peak of my enthusiasm because I was deep into television, working very hard at it and spending a certain amount of nervous energy, but I had taken quite a lot of time off to go to Australia. I went out there two or three weeks before the games. I had done one international race when I beat Sandor Iharos in Hungary, so I felt I was fit and trained, but it was not to be. I had made up my mind that I was not to go on beyond then. I stopped there.

'I deliberately put it out of my mind and changed my way of life when I gave up running in 1956 and threw myself into other activities. From my mid-thirties on, I came back to running purely for personal recreation, and I have kept it up since. I really regret it now if I have to go a whole week without taking any exercise. I travel a certain amount in my present job and I run wherever I am, the desert in Saudi Arabia or through the streets of New York, wherever I happen to be.'

As I left, Chris Chataway was about to go to Battersea Park for an easy run. The snow was falling on the city.

5

GORDON PIRIE

Born Leeds, 10 February 1931.

One of the most extraordinary and controversial characters of the 1950s was Gordon Pirie, the man who brought the crowds back to athletics. I can remember being at the British Whitsun Games on the Saturday, out came 'Puff! Puff!' Pirie to finish nearly last in the 800. On the Monday, along came Gordon again, and with a whithering burst up the home straight, won the international two miles, right on the tape!

There was always drama when Gordon was in the race; take the time his shoe was half-wrenched off at the first bend of a 3000 race, won by the current world record holder of the time, Sandor Iharos. Gordon threw his shoe away and carried on, but eventually had to drop out. A short time after, he went off to Malmoe and tore apart the best field available in the world over 3000 metres and sliced three seconds off the existing World mark by Iharos. (1. Gordon Pirie, 7:52.08, 2. Istvan Rozsavolgyi, 7:53.04, 3. Sandor Iharos, 8:5.08, 4. Laslo Tabori, 8:16.08, 5. Roger Dunkley)

Basil Heatley and his friend Roy Fowler were amongst the first three UK cross-country runners in 1963, and Fowler won the bronze in the European 10,000 in 1962. He told me at his home: 'I think Gordon Pirie was a great runner, and I think all the English athletes owe Gordon a thank you because he was the first Englishman, in my opinion, to prove that the foreigner could be beaten. Where in England, we used to sit back, reading the books on how to do it, the foreigner was getting out there and doing the training. He had the know-how and was coming to the White City and rubbing our noses in it, then along came

Gordon Pirie with his fantastic training schedules, pushing himself and also using his brain, and eventually he got there and took them on. I think men like Pirie need to be admired.'

Gordon Pirie has also been a successful coach of many aspiring athletes, has a knack of treating injuries and is a strong advocate of natural foods nowadays, which he only wished he had been when he was in his prime.

Interview 1989

Gordon, you are now fifty-eight years old and have run double the amazing mileage of Ron Hill during your lifetime. What have you learned from all that running?

'I have run a phenomenal mileage, and the only thing I have learned from that is DON'T, because when you do your greatest mileage you have the worst results. At a conservative estimate I think I have run about 280,000 miles but, allowing for possible error, I claim to have run around 265,000 miles. When I was in Scandinavia I ran for five hours a day, and when I read articles by the McWhirters at the time of how Jim Peters did fifteen to eighteen miles a day I realized I was doing twice as much running as him when I won the National cross-country in 1953, 1954 and 1955. In one year, I ran over 12,000 miles. I have done more than 365 marathons. They are a load of cissies nowadays. A grown man in the prime of his life runs a marathon and tells me a month later that he has not recovered from it. I recovered the next day.'

Although you are best known for your achievements, from 3000 m upwards, you beat many of the world's best milers – men like Laslo Tabori, Wes Santee and Derek Ibbotson – during the 1950s. Looking back now, do you think you could have done well in the 1956 Olympic 1500 m?

'I wanted to run in the 1500 m at the 1956 Games; my big fight was with the British Board, and Jack Crump in particular. Before Melbourne I ran against Klaus Richtzenhain (who came second in the Olympic 1500 m), and I beat him once in my personal best of 3:42.5. I reckon I was in with a chance to get in the top six, or even the top three in the 1500 m, and that was what I wanted to do.'

How fast were you running in training those days?

'Here I am training some guys, really fast runners, and they do 8×200 in 25.5. I used to do ten, twice a day, in 24.0! When I was at my best, I was incredible. I used to go and run thirty miles in training at Tooting Bec. One of the things I did in the thirty miles was to run 330 yards and jog the bend. A lot of good runners like Peter Driver, who won the Empire Games six miles in 1954, used to say, "Where is the interval?", and I used to say, "This is it". They would say, "This is too fast for the interval," and I used to say, "Hell, there is no interval; you just take a bit of a breather here." I would do forty of them like that. In races I set out with the idea of getting hold of the other runners like a terrier with a bone. I would smash them, destroy them.'

Your attitude was always to go for victory at all costs . . .

'In the Olympic 10,000 m in Helsinki, 1952, I went with Emil Zatopek and Alain Mimoun. There were just three of us left in the front at four miles, and then I was put in a coffin athletically and I don't know what I did to complete the race. If I had wanted to disregard Zatopek I could have been third in that race, but my attitude is that if I am going to run against somebody I am going to slug it out with them. Of course many people have said down the years, "You are crazy: you started too fast," but I said, "Later on, I am going to run the whole way like that," – which I did when I beat Vladimir Kuts and the Hungarians.'

In 1952, in the Olympic 5000 you finished fourth, passing Chris Chataway who had fallen at the last bend, and were strongly criticized. What are your memories of that race?

'I did not know he had fallen, but when we were staggering across the middle to get our gear I saw he had this terrible graze. It was only then that I found out he had tripped over. I was running in oblivion; all I saw was him in front of me and I just nipped him on the tape. That nearly caused me to give up athletics, because the British press never spoke to me but slammed me and criticized me as a bad sportsman for passing Chataway when he had tried so hard. I had tried hard, too. Chataway himself and Geoff Dyson, the National coach, advised me not to take notice of the press, and they soothed me down. To this day, I have not had justice from the press in this country.'

What was your score against Chataway?

'Including cross-country, we are thirteen all. But what annoyed me about Chataway was that I never ran a race with him where he did any work. I would say that if I had walked he would still have walked behind me.'

Did you ever train with him?

'I've run with Chataway, Brasher and those guys, and we would run ten quarters in 61, 62, 63 sec., I found it so boring at that speed that I would pass them in the back straight and go out and run a 55–56 with a 25 last 200 m. It was like being in a dream-world when I struck that form. I would run 8 × 880 in 1:58 with a short interval. When you are running like that, you can't lose a race!

'At Motspur Park in 1956, on a Sunday morning, I ran a 1:56.4 half-mile with the guys, then I jogged a lap and did two miles in 8:45, jogged a lap and ran four 880s between 2:03 and 2:01. Then I came back at tea-time and did 10 × 440 in an average of 58. When you're running like that, you say to yourself as you line up for a race, "Hard luck, you guys, I am going to kick the arse off you, and you can't do anything with me."

'I remember one of my thirty mile sessions round the track at Tooting Bec. Bill Nankeville was there, and he came down to run a couple of miles and a couple of sprints. He shouted out to me, "You will kill yourself, Pirie." I said "No, I am going to kill you," – which I did in the Emsley Carr Mile!

'If you could see the training I did, you would say I was completely nuts. I would go to places like the Catford track at 9.30 in the morning, do twenty minutes of hard weights, run an hour in the park and then do something like 10 × 600 or 8 × 1000, and leave at 1.30. I did that sort of training every day. Today people are cissies, and there's all this rubbish they write about recovering and taking it easy.'

In over forty years of watching athletics, the most exciting race I have ever seen in the United Kingdom was not a race with a world record, or anything like that, but a race of unusual quality. Wes Santee, who was the top miler in the world in 1953 for a short while, came to the White

City for the Emsley Carr Mile, and Gordon Pirie had the temerity to take him on, along with a field of more noted milers. There were three times AAA mile champion Bill Nankeville, and Chris Chataway, to mention two. Gordon takes up the story.

'Nobody has seen my training books, but if they did they would say, "You are a complete lunatic. It is physically impossible to do that." So, when I went to a race I knew that going around the track, even for twenty-four laps, was a kind of a sprint – that "National" cross-country was a sprint, because when you run five hours a day, that running half an hour to forty-five minutes is a joke. You just go full out; as for the mile, it is a sprint, but the other factor in the mile was the intelligence to run the race properly. In the Emsley Carr Mile I knew, if we all sat around there were some real good little sprinters off the bend, so I went, as you know, with 600 to go, and ran the 200 to the bell in twenty-nine seconds. They all looked a bit green with me at the bell, but I decided that was what I was going to do, and I had the machinery to do it. I would say, when Santee passed me in the back straight I was just about unconscious and my body had lost the race, but my mind kept my body going, and he faded and I took him. The speed we went round there was fantastic. We went this phenomenal pace – he was just drawing away from me. I was running so hard my vision was lost in jumps. I was hanging on, and then I realized I had got a gap and it stayed the same.'
(1. Pirie, 4:6.8, 2. Santee, 4:7.2, 3. Nankeville, 4:13.8)

Which of the athletes you ran against did you most admire?

'Zatopek. I beat him three times; he beat me three times. I think I was the only one who beat him so many times. Herb Elliott was the epitome of a competitor. With him, you could go home, throw your spikes in the corner and say "Forget it".'

And today's athletes?

'Aouita, although I have run a 53.8 last 440 yards, which is quicker than Aouita was running at the World Championships where Buckner could not keep up with him. I am a great admirer of Cram, Coe and Ovett because they have been phenomenal runners, but there again, jogging round three laps is pretty easy, and we know that Ovett is a failure at 5000. As for Daley Thompson, if he could run a decent 1500 m he would get a fantastic score, but he is absolutely pathetic in the 1500 m. I have trained fourteen year-old girls to run miles faster than him. They would beat him by 100 metres.'

What would you change if you had your time over again?

'I wish I knew when I was running what I know now. I did some terrible things in training, and I got away with murder. I used to do enormous training and then go out and run a world record straight on top of it, whereas now I know I need ten days to freshen up. I would have done some really good times then!'

6

GASTON ROELANTS

Interview 1964 and, based on interview, story in 1985.

Gaston Roelants was born at Opvelp, Belgium, on 5 February 1937, and started competing at cross-country running at Louvain Technical School. His steeplechasing career began at the age of eighteen when he challenged a friend, who had previously clocked 10.27, to a race and beat him. Two weeks later he took fifth place in the Belgian Championships in 9:57. 1962 was a golden year for Gaston, as he won the first of his International Senior Cross-Country Championships, then later at Belgrade, his first European Gold Medal, winning the steeplechase by five seconds from Zoltan Vamos in 8:32.6. A year later he became the first man ever to beat the 8:30 barrier, with 8:29.6 at Louvain.

All this was leading up to his greatest ever triumph, the gold medal at the Tokyo Olympics in 1964. How did Gaston train in the winter immediately preceding the Games?

'In the winter I always do a lot of cross-country racing. But in that important winter I also did a lot of interval training. Two days a week long distance, running up to fourteen miles, three times a week hurdling, and one time a week practising at the water jump.'

A great man for the 'theatrical', Roelants was very expressive about his difficulties immediately before the Olympic final. Pointing to his leg he stated 'At 11 o'clock the day before the final, I hit the hurdle hard with my upper leg and was in bed for four hours, with two doctors applying ice packs. It was not until 3 p.m. that I was able to put my foot on the ground again.'

Although because of another leg injury, he was unable to start his really hard training until one week before the Belgian team left for Tokyo, he won the final in 8:30.8 – 1.6 seconds ahead of Britain's Maurice Heriott, with Russian Ivan Belyayev third. Gaston again quotes:

'In the final I felt no pain at all, but just to make sure I hurdled very high and managed to clear them all. I always like to take the lead, so that I can see the distance between hurdles. The first kilometre was a slow 2:52, so I just took off after that point.'

The Belgian also has a fair range of personal bests outside his favourite events. These include 3:44.4 for 1500, 7:48.6 for 3000, 13:34.6 for 5000, 28:03.8 for 10,000, 57:44.4 for twenty kilometres and 20,784 for the hour, the latter two being world records when he set them in 1972. He got down to 8:26.4 for the steeplechase and 2:16.30 for the Marathon.

Regarding the latter, who can forget his epic battle with Ron Hill in the event at Athens in the 1969 European Championships, when he led for most of the race, only to be caught by Hill in the last couple of miles, to turn his gold into silver?

(1. Ron Hill, 2:16.47.8, 2. Roelants, 2:17.22.2, 3. Jim Alder, 2:19.05.8)

Gaston Roelants was runner-up in the 'World' international Cross-Country Championships in 1960, 1963, and 1970, and represented Belgium in the annual event no less than seventeen times! To add to that, he had three wins – 1967 (1. Roelants, 36:03, 2. Tim Johnston, 36:20, 3. Barry Rose (NZ), 36:27), 1969 (1. Roelants, 36:25, 2. Dick Taylor, 36:44, 3. Ian McCafferty, 36:57, and 4. Mike Tagg, (who won in 1970) 36:57), 1972 (1. Roelants, 37.43, 2. Mariano Haro, 38:01, 3. Ian Stewart, 38:20). They were at Barry, Clydebank and Cambridge respectively.

The incident that epitomises for me the extrovert character of the man came in the 1972 race at Cambridge. Here Gaston was leading along with Ian Stewart, Jaddour and Mariano Haro, when he suddenly clutched his leg and gesticulated to his supporters. By this time his challengers were forty metres ahead, but he pulled himself round and made a grandstand finish to win.

Gaston became a Vet. just before the second Master's

Games in Gothenberg. In the first Master's Games at Toronto in 1975, Roy Fowler, one of the few Englishmen to beat Roelants in the Cross-Country International, had swept the board, convincingly winning the 5000, 10,000 and cross-country in fine style. We looked forward in anticipation to a great renewal of rivalry between these two all time greats. We weren't disappointed.

At Brugge, the week before Gothenberg, the Belgian won the IGAL ten km by nearly a minute from Gunter Schmitt of Germany, with Alfons Ida, also of Germany third. The next day he completed his double by winning the twenty-five km by forty-four seconds from Britain's Cyril Leigh, with Schmitt third in the excellent time of 79.59. On to Sweden, where the first event after the opening ceremony was the 5000 metres and the long-awaited clash between Roelants and Fowler. This was something of an anticlimax, as the Belgian took the race by the scruff of the neck to win by twenty-six seconds in 14:03.

Gaston never contested the 10,000 metres, which was won by Roy Fowler by fourteen seconds from his compatriot Ron Gomez in 31:45.7.

Then on to the cross-country where, despite Fowler's greater effort, he still finished nineteen seconds down to his great Belgian rival, despite being over a minute up on Gomez. But it was in the steeplechase that Roelants gave us the greatest exhibition of his skill as he cruised round in an unpressed 8:41.5 in Oslo, which, when you consider that Taff Davies is the only other Veteran to remotely approach nine minutes, is truly sensational.

At the time of the Tokyo Olympics, he was a public relations officer for a large brewing company.

7

JANIS LUSIS

Born Jelga, Latvia, USSR, 19 May 1939.

Janis Lusis's record as a javelin thrower will be hard to match in the future, as he was on the podium to receive Olympic medals three times and also to be decorated four times as European Champion, besides breaking the world record on two occasions.

His Olympic record reads – 1964, 1. Pauli Nevala (Fin), 271'2/82.66, 2. Gergely Kulcsar (Hun), 270'0½/82.32, 3. Janis Lusis (USSR), 264'2/80.57. 1968, 1. Janis Lusis, 295'7/90.10. 2. Jorm Kinnuen (Fin), 290'00/88.58, 3. Gergely Kulcsar, 285'7½/87.06. 1972, 1. Klaus Wolfermann (W.G.), 90.48, 2. Janis Lusis, 90.46, 3.Bill Schmidt (USA), 84.62.

European titles for Janis were 1962: 82.02, 1966: 84.48, 1969: 91.52, and 1971: 93.80.

These are the facts, but what of the man? Ron Silvester, who competed at National and International level for the UK in the 1970s before injuries stopped his career short, met Janis and made the following comment: 'For me, Janis Lusis must be the greatest javelin thrower ever, having held the World record twice, won four consecutive European titles and Olympic gold, silver and bronze medals. He has shown the supreme competitive temperament and the ability to stay at the top for such a long period in such a highly technical event. With this, he sports an incredibly modest and almost shy exterior. An admirable combination.'

My interview with Janis was in London's Lancaster Gate in 1966, before he won his second European title. At the time he was in the Army at Riga and working in a sports club. He later went on to marry Elvira Ozolina, the women's Olympic gold medallist for the javelin in 1960.

1966 Interview

When did you first take up athletics?

'It was in 1957, when I was eighteen years old. It was in secondary school at Kandava in the Latvian Republic. It was in the summer that I started to throw the javelin, but before that I was doing a little long, triple and high jumping, but no throwing at all. My first competition in the javelin was in the schoolboy Championships of the Soviet Union. It was a competition for boys between seventeen and eighteen. It was a surprise for me to take first place in that with a throw of 146 feet. I can remember it was in August of 1957 at Riga.'

Were you inspired by any particular champion?

'After taking first place in that competition at Riga, I talked with a man called Krouze, who was at that time Champion of the Latvian Republic for throwing the javelin, and he said "You will never be a good javelin thrower", and this made me determined to prove him wrong, and in only two years after that, I was throwing much further than him, as he threw 223 feet. He was my coach, but I then started with another coach who is my coach now, his name is Valentin Mazzalitis. It was after I was a student at secondary school that Valentin suggested, after a long talk, that I should continue throwing and concentrate a lot less on the long jump.'

(May I interject here by saying Janis high-jumped 1.92, long-jumped 7.22, triple-jumped 14.41 and even did a decathlon, scoring 7,483 pts.)

How did you find throwing in the rain in your first Olympic Games in Tokyo, when you came third?

'My condition at those Olympic Games was not good, because that year I injured my shoulder, so naturally my technique was bad. I improved my technique in 1965. I was pleased with my performance overall in Tokyo, because I could not have done better with my injuries. One of the days before the Olympics I had been throwing the javelin when I was tired, and it was after about thirty practice

45

throw I injured the muscles in my shoulder. Then again in the competitions in Niminsky I injured my shoulder for the second time. It was only due to my good physical condition that I threw as far as 80.00 metres in Tokyo. In training, I could only manage 79.00 just before that.'

What has been your most satisfying performance up to now (middle 1966)?

.'When I established the USSR record in 1962 in Tashkent, when I threw 86.02 metres. I then became European Champion, but it was not difficult around that time as I was injury-free.'

You threw 86.56/284ft odd at Tbilisi in 1965, which put you second to Kinnunen's 289'2/88.14 in the World rankings.

'Last year I was in good condition all year round as I did over 85.00 four times, and I established a new Soviet record. I beat the best in the world in Oslo, that included Jorma Kinnunmen and Janusz Sidlo, all in the same competition too.'

What are your ambitions now in the middle of 1966.

'I am going to do my best this year in the European Games in Budapest. Already this year I have twice done over 85.00 metres.'

Were you happy with your 85.28/279'9½ at the White City on 17 June, which was an 'All Comers Record'?

'I thought I would throw 272 feet about, but not more, so I did better!'

What training have you been doing this season?

'I do javelin throwing three times a week. Also, I do weight lifting, running, and jumping. I actually train four or five times a week. I use different weights. I do two days a week weight training in the winter. I do classical exercise for the first session, and for the second session I do different varied exercises with small light weights. In the summer I do one day only of heavy weights.'

What are your favourite hobbies outside of athletics?

'I read Jack London, Galsworthy, Tolstoy, and I very much like going to the theatre and the cinema.'

How long would you like to continue in athletics?

'It is hard to say. Last year and this year I am in very good condition, so I hope to continue till after Mexico.'

46

Of course the rest is history, as he won his gold in Mexico and broke the World record in 1972.

Finally, I asked him about his advice to young javelin throwers.

'First of all, he must do regular training, year by year. He must not just train, but know what to do and how to do it. So, he must plan his training with his coach year by year. It is only by constant practice that he will reach the top. To begin with, he must do all forms of athletics to improve. For instance, he must do weight training, running, and jumping, as he must make his body strong, and of course you must be advised properly. Mazzalitis, who is a professor at the Latvian Physical Culture Institute in Riga, has helped me and another group of young throwers that sometimes train with me.'

In 1976, Miklos Nemeth, son of 1948 Olympic hammer throwing champion Imre Nemeth, was a clear winner in Montreal, lunging the spear out to 94:58 in the very first round of the final. That surprised his rivals from Finland, a country that has always had a strong tradition in the event and claimed the next three Olympic javelin titles!

Tony Issacs explained, in the *International Track and Field Annual* of 1987, that an era in the history of throwing the javelin ended on 1 April, 1986, when, quite uniquely in terms of athletic prowess, the IAAF imposed a change to the design of the men's javelin, with the deliberate intention of reducing the distances achieved at the top level of the event. It would have been interesting to see what World record holders of 1980 and 1984 – Ferenc Paragi (Hun.), who threw 96:72, and Uwe Hohn (GDR), 104:80, would have done with the new javelins!

Regarding those who have come to the top as great performers with the new-style implement, undoubtedly Stephen Backley, the Cambridge Harrier, headed the field in 1989 and the start of the 1990s, but he would have found it was a long way to achieve the incredible consistency at world level that Janis Lusis managed or, in fact, as did his fellow countrymen, three times Olympic Champion Viktor Saneyev in the triple jump and latterly by pole vaulter Sergei Bubka.

8

HENRY CARR

Born Montgomery, Alabama, 27 November 1942, 6ft 3ins/
185lbs

Looking back now to the weeks I spent in Tokyo in 1964,
the 'Man of the Games' for me was Henry Carr.

Like Tommie Smith in 1968, he was a phenomenal 200/
400 combination sprinter, and yet he retired after the
Olympics at the age of twenty-two, with an awesome ability
for the 'individual' one lap event, to a great extent,
untapped.

My memory of him was not his good individual gold in
the 200 in 20.3, but his anchor leg in the 4 × 400 relay for
the USA team that smashed the World record with 3.00.7
(Ollan Cassell, Mike Larrabee, Ulis Williams, and Henry
Carr – 44.5). The next two teams were inside the old figures
– Great Britain (anchor Robbie Brightwell, 44.8) 3:01.6, and
Trinidad & Tobago – Wendell Mottley (45.00), 3:01.7.
Henry was caught by Mottley and Kerr on the back straight
and then he accelerated, and it was all over when he sped
clear.

In 1963, Henry Carr ran the second equal fastest over the
100 yards in the World that year, and topped the lists with
the fastest ever 200 time of 20.2, having beaten the old
World best mark of 20.5 no fewer than five times. His time
for 400 of 45.4 placed him third on the World lists for 1963
as well.

In 1964 he won the AAU Championships over 200, the
preliminary Olympic trial, and did the double for USA v
USSR – 100/200 – 10.3/20.4.

He takes up the story of his life in athletics.

'I first started in athletics whilst at the Northwestern

High School, Detroit, Michigan. My coach at the time had me doing time trials, and I then converted from being a high jumper to a sprinter. I always thought I could jump pretty good so, at the start, I figured I would be all right at that event. It was in the same year at High School that I was doing the high jump and running, and in fact I jumped 5ft 6ins for the high jump then. We had athletics teams at school and I was always interested, and so, as I was doing pretty good, I stayed with it.

'At first my parents took no interest in athletics, but as I improved the more interested they became.'

I then asked Henry what qualities did he think you should have to improve to his level?

'Desire is the main thing, coupled with a little ability. You must discipline yourself if you want to make a breakthrough and get anywhere in this sport. As a sprinter, I cannot rely on anyone else to help me sprint, and therefore ability helps. In big competitions there is always a strain and pressure not experienced in lesser competitions, and I was a little more than worried in the AAU Championships (1964) because I had laid off for a month previously, and only just came back to competition a few days earlier. Also I thought that the sudden tempo of big racing so soon after a lay-off would upset me in more ways than one, but as it turned out, I came through very well indeed, and certainly much better than I had expected.'

In the 1963 AAU Championships, Henry tied with Paul Drayton in 20.4.

It was not a hard race; what happened was that I was a bit inexperienced at the time, and had counted him out of the race, so when I was ten yards from the tape I "let up" and he came through, there was nothing I could do about it.' An interesting point was made by Paul Drayton to me in 1963, regarding the main events like the National Championships: 'Being able to meet the competition is more important than running fast times. If you run a fast time in April against some hams and then cannot perform when you meet the purer competition in the National Championships later, then you are in trouble. A good athlete can meet the occasion and be able to do the best times at the right time. Armin Hary proved this point when, after doing a so-called illegal 10.00 World record, he still came through to win the Olympic gold medal.' (1960)

Looking ahead to the Olympic Games later in the year, this was how Henry viewed things: 'I have always had the desire to win. I have been training and running all the time to win a gold medal; since I am the AAU 200 metres Champion, I would like to win in Tokyo. I think speed and strength will be the two main factors in Japan, because there are so many races to run in the Olympic Games.'

Regarding the training he did, he remarked: 'Every athlete is different, so perhaps my training schedule will not help any other sprinter, and in fact it might do him more harm than good. In the early part of the season I do a considerable amount of distance work – for me as a sprinter, that means 550 and 660 yards repetitions, and 'pyramid' type sessions of 100 up to 660 yards and down again. As the season progresses my heavy work decreases, and I pile in much more speed work. I do not do any weight training, for I think that for myself weights would affect me adversely because I am so tall and bulky.

'I feel that weight training would shorten my muscles rather than build them up. I think that in fact weight training is better for small sprinters or those athletes not necessarily strong enough and already well built, to make them stronger. Training itself is rather like a job of work. I really enjoy my competition as something vastly different from training. The shorter distances in training are much more pleasurable for me, there is not the 'agony' prevalent in long training sessions. Since we race so much in the States, the number of days upon which I train vary from week to week although, discounting races, I usually like to get out for at least five days' training each week. Off-season, I always take my training easily, and am very strict on this and do not overdo the sessions. I find this helps to combat strain and fatigue. Some athletes train fairly heavily and continuously around the calendar, and of course it helps them, though this varies widely depending on the particular individual. I generally start sessions or regular training in about mid-February and, by the time the season proper comes along, I am usually in good form, so therefore I personally do not have to do a large amount of winter buildup training and so forth. Early season, I use my competition as sharpening up training, as far as getting really fit and acquiring that necessary edge is concerned.'

How then did he look at his future in the sport prior to the Tokyo Games?

'After Tokyo, I hope to retire and turn professional as a footballer so that I can carve out a decent living for my wife of five months and myself. I play quite a bit of football at school – in season, of course. Although athletics has given me fame, popularity and a chance to travel the world and see how the other half lives, it does not put bread in your stomach. You can win a gold medal in the Olympics; you can beat the best in the world; you can win all your races – but it takes a great deal of time, trouble and money to achieve one's athletic ambitions, no matter where one stands on the scale of ability and performance, so perhaps the biggest change to come about in athletics – and it's not far-off a possibility – is for track and field athletics to become a professional sport! Cash apart, I realize how better off I am being an American, especially after seeing the way that people live – and die – in other countries.'

Interview in the Olympic Village after 200 Final in 1964

What sort of training have you been doing up to the Games?

'440s, 660s and 330s. In fact, I have followed my usual pattern of training.'

You said to me you thought you would retire from the sport after the Olympics. Do you still intend to do that?

'It really does not matter, as I have a gold medal and a World record. I am a "Frontiersman", opening the path for other 200 metre men.'

You won the Olympic preliminary trials over the 200 and the AAU, but at the Olympic trials you only came fourth behind winner Paul Drayton (20.4). You were one-tenth behind Bob Hayes, who was third in that. It would have been fatal if they had stuck rigidly to first three past the post with no exceptions, but then Hayes was already in the 100 and would be picked for the 4 × 100. What was the

51

problem in the final trial?

'In Los Angeles at the trials I had a bad back and a little cold. I overcame my injuries, so that it was okay for Tokyo.'

In the semi-final in Tokyo, Paul Drayton equalled the Olympic record with 20.5, but you did 20.6 winning the other heat. Did that worry you at all?

'No, I never worry about another person running a fast trial, as long as they are not running against me. Having said that, I think Paul is about the toughest competitor in the world today over the 200. You can never leave him out, but I had not changed my style, and I knew I would maintain my speed this year and comeback after the trials, as long as I had overcome my injuries.'

In the Olympic final you were in lane 7, which is not the best place to be in a 200.

'At first I was quite disappointed about the lane, but the more I concentrated I became aware that the lane was to my advantage. I knew if I got out in front and held my speed it was to my advantage to have lane 7.'

I thought you would win from Paul Drayton, with either Commonwealth double gold medallist Seraphino Antao, Harry Jerome or Ewin Roberts filling the third spot. Did you think you could be beaten?

'Well, I knew from the start, if I was to get out and maintain my speed of relaxation no-one was going to beat me.'

(October 17 in sunny weather: 1. Henry Carr, 20.3, 2. Paul Drayton, 20.5, 3. Edwin Roberts (Trinidad), 20.6, 4. Harry Jerome (Canada), 20.7, 5. Livio Berruti (Italy), 20.8, 6. Marian Foik (Pol), 20.8, 7. Richard Stebbins (US), 20.8, 8. Sergio Ottolina (Italy), 20.9)

Finally, what do you enjoy doing outside of athletics these days?

'I enjoy playing football, reading James Baldwin, fishing, although I have not had much time to do that during the last few years. I like listening to Frank Sinatra and Dionne Warwick, in fact the appropriate music for the time and place. I am not very hard to please in that respect.'

9

LILLIAN BOARD

Born Durban, South Africa, 13 December 1948. 5ft 7ins/9st 12lbs. Lived in Ealing, West London.

Lillian Board will probably be remembered as a 'Golden Girl' of athletics in the 1968–69 seasons. Like Mary Toomey, *née* Rand (1964 Olympic long jump Champion from the same club, London Olympiads), she was an attractive blonde, with a likeable personality, matched well with an athletic talent that was never totally fulfilled as she died of cancer before she had a chance of adding the 1970 Commonwealth gold to her silver in the 1968 (400) and two golds in the European of 1969 (4×400 and 800).

Back in 1969, some people still thought of athletics mainly as a 'man's sport'. What did Lillian think about that?

'I have said many times that I think this line of thinking is absolutely unjustified. Take the British girls for example; most of them are good-lookers with enviable figures, and almost all have that man-trapper, a good pair of legs. I am quite serious about this, and I feel looking at it objectively rather than from a biased point of view.

In recent interviews with some of Lillian's male contemporaries, I have come to the conclusion that when one trains around the streets, one has to put up with cat-calling and corny comments from passers-by, so I wondered how Lillian fared in this respect.

'Funnily enough,' she told me, 'I don't find this happens. When I was quite young and no-one knew me from Adam, to run around the streets used to be more of an embarrassment to me than anything else; now, I have no inhibitions about road-running. I can remember though, when I was about fifteen years of age, I used to hear such comments as, "Look at her, silly thing,' and rather than wear a tracksuit I would merely go out wearing a jumper and pair of slacks – and carry a letter in my hand; if anybody happened to pass by, I could just stop and walk a bit until they had gone past, pretending that I was on my way to post a letter in a hurry.

'In other countries, to see runners on the roads, whether they be boys or girls, provokes no comment. I can remember one day not so long ago however, when I was out on a road run, and several times had to stop for the traffic; it must have looked rather funny I suppose, to see a girl running along, stop in the midle of the road, hitch up her trousers and then continue when the traffic had passed. Anyway, a mini-car pulled up alongside me, and the young man inside wound his window down and shouted, "Come on, get your knees up," wound his window up again and carried on. This sort of thing, and the cat-calling and so on, is something that many road runners do complain about, I know. You have only got to walk down the road in a tracksuit in England, and draw some comment or other.'

Many athletes, when starting out in the sport, mention on looking back that they had some inspiration from an outstanding athlete that they admired, someone who instilled in them the desire to be just as good. Who were Lillian Board's heroines, I wondered.

'When I started, there were two names that I knew: Mary Rand and Anita Lonsbrough. This was after the Rome Olympic Games. I can remember one girl at school saying of Mary, "She's the one they called the 'Golden Girl', but she didn't do so well in the Olympics, did she?" I joined a club of which Mary Rand was a member, and I was thrilled, especially when I met her; I was still very young.

'Mary and I became very good friends, and we used to meet and talk a lot. Ann Packer was another outstanding athlete whom I admired; she was a tremendous athlete.'

Lillian has been the winner of several outstanding awards, not least the special award in Athens for the most outstanding woman athlete of the European Championships (1969). The award surprised many, not least Miss Board herself: 'It was a tremendous atmosphere in the old stadium that night; I love marching and all the pomp of such occasions. The music was so exhilarating, and the British team looked smart in their outfits, and were marching really well. I wanted to be down there with them in the parade, and felt a bit out of it waiting to collect my trophy. The 800 metres then, was probably the 'glamour' event of the Games; for one thing the spectators can see you for two minutes, instead of a few seconds. Again it was another 'glamour' event that probably clinched my nomination for the award – the anchor leg in the 4 × 400 metres relay.

'I do not consider myself that I was the outstanding woman competitor of the Championships. I felt that Nicole Duclos was superb, and that she should have got the award. Had they sent her up there to collect the trophy I would have said, "Great, she deserves it," and personally, I did not therefore feel justified in collecting the award; standing there, I wondered just how many people were thinking, "She does not deserve that," – and I felt rather guilty, believe me.'

I asked Lillian what her reaction would be to a question that has probably been asked of her many times – why was it that it was you who gained most publicity from the Athens 4 × 400 metres relay win, when your time was only third fastest of the quartet?

'This sort of question really makes my blood boil, and I just have to take a deep breath – and say nothing.'

Do you feel that people try to antagonize you?

'Oh, yes. This is another thing. People seem to think it much more fun to try and antagonize than praise an athlete, and I get my fair share of the former. I suppose I don't really mind, actually. It puts my back up and makes me want to do even better than I have done previously, and I would think that perhaps I would not have won a European Championships gold medal had I won a gold in the Olympic Games in Mexico.

'There is one important thing to bear in mind when one runs a 400 metres – you are in a lane all the way, your lane; you've got to concentrate on running your own race within those two white lines; if someone wants to speed round the first 200 metres in 23.0, then let them, you must not worry about what they are doing. One has to run one's own race according to one's own plan. In the Olympic Games, for example, when I was really bang on form, my time for the first 200 metres was spot-on, 24.5 seconds.'

(1968 – Mexico Olympic 400 metres: Lillian Board was in lane one. 1. Colette Besson (France), 52.00, 2. Lillian Board, 52.1, 3. Natalya Pechenkina (USSR), 52.2. Fastest semi-final, Lillian Board, 52.5.)

1969

'In Athens, of course, running the last leg I didn't have to run in a lane. I had to run a tactical race against Besson; Collette went through the first 200 metres in 23.6 seconds, which is murder, believe me. At that mark she had started to pull away from me and was a good four to five metres ahead of me; my time was about 24.2, which means that it is the fastest that I have ever gone through a half-way mark in a 400 metres race (I had not run many last year), and as far as my sprinting power was concerned then, I was not at peak speed fitness-wise, so she would obviously pull away from me at that pace – and pulling all the effort out of me. At 200 metres I was quite tired, and that is why I had to ease off: I could not have kept going without that "breather". In an individual 400 metres race, I would not try to blow myself up like that; I would, as I have said earlier, run a much more even-paced race and aim for a better overall time.

'My time in the 4 × 400 was third-fastest of our foursome, and naturally the clever know-alls screamed, "What went wrong?" Nothing went wrong; nothing at all – I ran the race tactically, as I would have done under the same conditions anywhere. Collette was faster over shorter distance work than I was myself, so obviously she was able to pull away; she had been running and sprinting faster than me at that time, and was therefore capable of running the race as she did. In the end however, she almost ran herself to a standstill, and make no mistake about it – she was pulling everything out of me; I don't suppose either Janet Simpson or Pat Lowe went through any faster at 200 metres than I did, 24.2.

'Although in the home straight I seemed to be miles behind Collette, I felt I was going to win. I just sensed it, that's all I will say, I will not go into any technical detail. You can sense when you are pulling back on someone ahead of you, and I know too that the crowd could see that I was pulling her back; they would have seen, if I had come second in the race, that at least I was running strongly. I felt that I was running at 100% effort – as fast as I could go; I knew I was pulling her back, but just for a fraction of a second I thought, "You've left it too late." A few metres further on, my thoughts continued: "Maybe it's not too late; I think I can do it."

'People make some stupid remarks sometimes. One chap said to me: "You should have a good publicity agent." This upset me very much. I thought how catty, how horrible. Take away the 4 × 400 metres, and the other girls would go home finalists and I would still take home a gold medal. That is not to sound conceited, I am just stating a fact. It is because of the introduction of the 4 × 400 metres race that we all go home gold medallists, but people choose to forget that I had run an individual 800 metres, simply because it suits them to do so; it is their form of antagonism.'

The British girls did, of course, get a world-record timing for the 4 × 400 metres, and it must have been a terrific thrill to Lillian: 'Yes, it was, Alastair. It was tremendous, but then again, I would have felt a lot happier with a World record in my individual event, I would have been overjoyed. There would have been no holding me. It's nice to have a World record; for one thing, the public are going to think, "Oh, a World record. Good for our girls." The main thing in athletics, though, is to win. If a World record, or any other record, goes with the performance, that is a bonus.

'I suppose, as far as that particular World record was concerned, we were all very pleased, because we had beaten a terrific team, and only just by the skin of our teeth. The French girls were great, but they had not thought we could win. The sheer pleasure was in wanting to say, "Well, we told you so." especially as the West German team had broken the record the night before. Even Arthur Gold (British *Chef de Mission*) said to me: "Quite honestly, I thought you were in there for a bronze medal." But, to have

57

beaten the French . . .

'It makes me laugh when I think that we won that race. I did not even want to run in it; I was having a bit of back trouble, and my back was really beginning to ache, but anyway I thought, well, only two more races, and in the 4 × 400 heat I merely played at it, it was – as far as I was concerned – just one of those races where it was four to qualify for the final; not much pressure for us. I went out to run with just enough effort needed to qualify – and that's how it happened. We finished third, quite comfortably. I had plenty left at the end, and so had the other British girls.'

4 × 400 Athens – 1. GB (Rosemary Stirling, Pat Lowe, Janet Simpson and Lillian Board), 3:30.8 new World record, 2. France, 3:30.8, 3. West Germany, 3:32.7.

Lillian takes up the story of the 800 European Final in Athens: 'The heats of any big event always worry me. You go in to tackle the best at an event, and all you have got to back you up is the year's fastest times list. I was ranked ninth on that list; the top was 2:02.3, and my time was 2:04.8, way down, really. There were about six girls between 2:03.2 and 2:03.9. As far as the competitive pressure in Athens was concerned, I was in ninth place on the ranking list, in just the right place. I knew that I was worth more than 2:04.8, but I did not know how much better, and in fact I did not think that I would get below 2:02.0 out there. I didn't think I would do a personal best, but would try for 2:02.0 if I could. I was ranked ninth, and what had I got to lose? There was no real pressure on me, the press and public just put a big question mark against my name, with the general comment that I would "Make the race a bit more interesting."'

So what about the final?

'The person who worried me most was Vera Nikolic. I knew that if she went out fantastically fast – if she covered the first 200 metres in 26-27 – she would probably not win, but would certainly play havoc with the pace. One would be running, and wondering, supposing we do let her get away, one has those races where you say, oh let her go, and you find that she – whoever she might be – has been allowed to get too far away, and she could win. I made up my mind not to think about that, and just let the race unfold – that was my big problem. I still thought, please God, don't let Vera go off like a rocket, because if she goes too fast, I won't know what to do about the pace, then shall I sit tight with the others or shall I wait until Silai goes; will she go after Nikolic, or shall I go after Vera myself? So, you see, you can have three different races going through your mind.

'Well, the gun went for the start of the final – Vera did not go off fast, she stayed in the bunch, and that thrilled me no end. We were all in a bunch and I was sitting on Vera's shoulder, and – it doesn't matter who it is – I just like to be sitting in on the shoulder of the leader, helping her, and sharing the lead – if she doesn't mind, of course. That's how the race went then, until the end of the first lap. Silai came up, and I faltered momentarily over someone (I can't remember who it was), I don't know why, and let her get a couple of metres ahead of me – we all have such long strides, and it is easy to get a spiking without knowing it, and I did get a slight spiking, or felt something – and so on round to the 600 metres mark. I thought, suddenly, I am feeling fatigued, or else the pace is quickening, so I started to move a bit faster, too. All the time now, with just that 200 metres left of the race my mind was ticking away . . . Keep with the leaders, and if you are with them with 100 metres to go, you'll win . . . Yes, that sound so easy . . .

'On that last 200 metres, Nikolic and Silai began to pull away slightly, and I put in that extra effort, quickening my pace to stay with them . . . I must stay with them, I must. Then we were there – 100 metres to go, and all the differing pieces of advice I had had thrown at me became a jumble in my head. A little voice said, "You're with them; there's 100 metres to go; it's all over." I made a move out into the third lane, dropping back slightly as I made the move – and then I went. I waited for a retaliation, which did not come, and thought, where are they? Please don't catch me before I get to the tape, and they didn't!'

800m final in Athens – 1. Lillian Board, 2:01.4, 2. Annelise Damm-Olesen, 2:02.6, 3. Vera Nikolic, 2:02.6, 4. Barbara Wieck, 2:02.7, 5. Ileana Silai, 2:03.0, 6. Pat Lowe, 2:03.4.

Did Lillian have special advice when she started, I

wondered?

'No, I joined the club, as I said, and there were club athletes there, but Daddy was extremely keen for me to do well at sport because we are a sporting family, and whatever we did he would take an interest. He was keen on swimming, and people have asked me why I became keen on athletics instead, and my answer is that, whatever my sport was to be, my Father would be interested, but, as it transpired, he was keen on athletics too, so he took it up and knew exactly what the score was; he knew all about the four-minute miles, but not what a girl of twelve should be doing, so he had practically every athletics book out of the library.'

George Board, Lillian's father, has obviously had great influence over her athletics. I asked, has it been of help?

'Yes, and I am glad for it. There were so many parents who used to go down to the track week in and week out, and yet they didn't ask – why, how or what? – about what their children were doing. For instance, 8×220 yards for such and such an event; they didn't know quite why their children were doing a thing, and I feel that such parents are simply handing out schedules. But Daddy went into all the ins and outs of it all, and this has rubbed off on me. As I have said on a couple of occasions – if a coach does well enough, he eventually works himself out of a job to a certain extent. Daddy was working away in Birmingham for at least three weeks before Athens, and my last three weeks in England before the Championships were done without a coach; virtually I just saw Father at weekends, but it worked out fine, because I had remembered all that he had told me, and it got to a stage where for a short period of time I could manage virtually on my own, and I could write and tell him all I had done, and at weekends he could see me.'

10

KIP KEINO

Born Kipsamo on 17 January 1940. 5ft 9ins/9st 9lbs (62k).

Double Olympic gold medallist Kipchoge Keino was really Africa's first world-class distance runner; many followed in his footsteps over the years.

In 1962 he progressed to eleventh in the Commonwealth three miles and in 1964 he was a good fifth in the final of the 5000 metres in Tokyo, but it was in 1965 that he started to set the athletics fraternity buzzing with interest as he had two wins over that great runner Ron Clarke over 5000 and achieved a 3000 World record, on 27 August with 7:39.6. I first had the chance to talk to Kip when we travelled in a rattling minibus to the reception for the athletes who had been competing in the AAA's Championships at the White City Stadium on 30 August, 1965. It was after he defeated the strongest field he had ever encountered to that date, though still far from experienced in the event. The results were: 1. Kip Keino in an 'all comers' record of 3:54.2 (only 1/10th outside Peter Snell's World record of the year before); 2. Olympic silver medallist Josef Odlozil in a Czech record of 3:55.6; 3. Alan Simpson (GB) 3:55.7 (UK National and AAA's record); and 4. Jorgen May (GDR) 3:55.9 (German record).

Interview 1965

About the Morley mile, Kip explains: 'I was not intending winning. I was just running to get under four minutes. As I say, I was just running, but no-one passed me in the final lap. It was a surprise for me, as I had never run under four minutes for a mile before! I thought Alan Simpson or Jorgen May would win.'

Twenty-five year old Kip continued about his life in general: 'I am married to Jenny, and have a little daughter. I have three sisters and no brothers. My father was keen on sport and won his company's four-mile race back in 1933, and he encouraged me to run. In school I used to run barefoot, but not now, when I am running track races around the world.' It was interesting to note whether he had anybody helping him with his progress in the sport and the training he did prior to the European tour of 1965. Here is what he said: 'My physical training instructor at Police training school did give me some things to do to improve my times. Another influence was Malvyn Whitfield (USA Olympic 800 Champion of 1948 and 1952), when he came to Kenya, and he has been giving me programmes which I have used.

'About my training; I used to train with some people, but not now usually, because they are no longer taking part in athletics. I take physical training classes in the Police training school, so I am actively doing other sports on Tuesday and Friday, and I must say that I enjoy athletics, basketball, hockey, badminton and volleyball.

'My weekly training for athletics consists of: Monday at 6 a.m., a six miles run. Afternoon, eight quarter-miles in around 63 to 65 seconds, then rest about three minutes, start again and do another 440, then rest for three minutes and do exercises. Tuesday, no athletics. Wednesday, five miles run. Afternoon, 5×880 in about 2.14 each. Rest five minutes, then another 880. Friday, six miles. Afternoon, sprints – 330s, 220s, 80s and even 50s. Saturday and Sunday, rest. As a Corporal, I have to nearly always use my own time to train between Police duties.'

Now, what advice would he give to an aspiring distance runner?

'If you like something, you must work hard at it. If you take part in any event, do not worry about people beating you, as long as you do a good time. Train hard, and ask somebody how you can set out a training programme.'

Wise words from the man who had only that year entered the top ranks in middle-distance running. Kip Keino went on to achieve the double in the Empire Games of 1966 at Kingston Jamaica: 3.55.3 for the mile, with Alan Simpson, 2nd., 3:57.1. His time winning the three miles was 12:57.4, with Ron Clarke running 12:59. England's Allan Rushmer third in 13:06.6 (a UK National record).

In 1968, Kip Keino won the 1500 at the Mexico Olympics with 3:34.9, from Jim Ryun (USA), 3:37.8, and Bodo Tummler (WG) 3:39.0. In the 5000 at the same Games, Kip Keino was second in the 5000, just 2/10s behind winner Mohammed Gamoudi of Tunisia. In 1970, Kip won the 1500 at the Commonwealth Games in Edinburgh in 3:36.6, with Dick Quax (NZ) and Brendan Foster picking up the other medals. In 1972, Kip Keino won the 3000 steeple-chase in Munich in an Olympic record time of 8:23.6, with Ben Jipcho (Kenya) 8:24.6, and Tapio Kantanen (Fin) 8:24.8; and that was not all, as he was placed second in the 1500 metres at the same Games, one in which all the major Nations were present. The first three were: 1. Pekka Vasala (Fin), 3:36.33, 2. Kipchoge Keino, 3:36.81, 3. Rod Dixon (NZ), 3:37.46.

11

TOMMIE SMITH

Born Acworth, Texas, 12 January 1944. 6ft 3ins/185lbs.

Tommie Smith had the ability in his prime of taking his 19.82/44.55 World records of 1967–8 to well below those times, of that I feel certain. Like with Henry Carr, Tommie Smith found the 400 a very hard event to enjoy doing, so he raced mainly over 200. As a point of interest, not a lot of people know that when Tommie ran 440 yds in 44.8 (also recorded at 400, as a World record of 44.5) at San Jose on 25 May, 1967, the man who finished just behind him in 45.3 was none other than Lee Evans. Lee, of course, ran the devastating time of 43.8 the following year in the Olympic Final. In 1968, Tommie (20.00) was second to John Carlos (19.7) in the Olympic trials at Lake Tahoe, and went on to achieve the official World record of 19.8 in the Mexico Olympic Final on 16 October 1968 (1. Tommie Smith, 19.8, 2. Peter Norman (Aus), 20.00, 3. John Carlos, 20.00, 4. Edwin Roberts (T & T), 20.3, 5. Roger Bambuck (Fr), 20.5, 6. Larry Questad (USA), 20.6, 7. Mike Fray (Jam), 20.6, 8. Joachim Eigenherr (WG), 20.6).

Those who are more interested in headline news than in athletics itself would recall Tommie Smith's 'Black Power' salute on the rostrum in Mexico, but in defence of his actions, Steve Williams, the 1977 World Cup 100 metres champion spoke out: 'I think I was doubly impressed by Tommie Smith's build, which was pretty close to mine, and his style, which was flawless, and which I would aspire to be like. Pretty much also, he was someone I really admired because of his black pride and Olympic demonstration. I think that what he and John Carlos did was timely. It was a necessary demonstration for black people at the time, a sort of strength and virility which needed to be demonstrated to the young impressionable black people of the United States. I remember reading what Tommie said, that it was odd that he could compete for America as America's best but then live as a second class-American; I think that sums it up.'

In 1966, Tommie Smith first came to the United Kingdom and took on the man who was a close-up second to Mike Larrabee in the 1964 Olympic 400 final, Wendel Mottley, the Commonwealth 400 champion. It was at the White City, and Tommie Smith was the victor over one lap.

Interview 1966

At that time, Tommie was a student teacher at San José College, California. How did it all begin for him?

'I am the smallest in my family of five brothers and seven sisters. All of them are athletic: my father was a baseball player – and so was my mother; all my sisters are baseball players too. One of my brothers was, until recently, a boxer; two others are football players, and one of these is a student at Oregon State University.

'At school, basketball was always my favourite sport, due probably to my height and speed on court. There were quite a lot of other guys around, just as big and tall as myself, and just as fast, and one of the challenges was to stay in the team. This meant I had to do a lot of really hard work, because, as the basketball coach said, it was a difficult task to separate the team players from the rest; only those with endurance necessary to keep up the pressure of play were able to stay on the team. As a runner, I was able to concentrate on a buildup of sustained speed on the track; the others in the basketball team didn't have this, so I stayed in the side.

'The school coach first introduced me to quarter-miling, and I clocked 47.7 for my first one, so that was probably my first step towards concentrating, as I now do, on the event. However, I still like the 220 yards better as a race, although I like training for 440 and 220 equally.

'As a junior at High School, the thought kept returning

65

that if I were to concentrate more on track and field athletics, the door would be open to me to attend any college I wanted to, on an athletic scholarship. Don't get me wrong, I didn't just want it for sport, but at least my sporting ability could get me into college, where I would be able to study to be a teacher, whereas probably I could not enter academically. Above all, I wanted to become a teacher – and the way was open for me if I succeeded. I was offered many scholarships later, but I accepted the San José one because it seemed to be a good curriculum, and they had a good record for sport, especially track and field.'

Tommie was not inspired into modelling himself on any of the all-time greats, such as Jesse Owens: I didn't really pattern myself on anybody else, I wanted to make a path of my own so that if other sprinters wanted to follow me, they could. Right now, athletics is a means to an end: a big part of my life. A means to an end in that, as long as I am doing it, I will always do my best, and I want to attempt to do my best all my life, whether in track and field or teaching, or whatever else I might eventually take part in. If I was doing my best and not getting a great deal of personal satisfaction out of it, I would stop: if this occurred while I was an athlete, then I would retire, without hesitation.' To be able to stay at San José for two years is important to Tommie Smith: 'It is important for me, in that I am aiming well ahead to the Olympic Games in Mexico, although they do not seem to be very far away now, and if I am in the US team in 1968, I will need a lot more training and coaching and competition. The training and coaching at San José is good. An athlete needs the incentive of coaching, I feel, and although my coach Bud Winter tells me what to do (sets the training sessions but leaves me to do the work), he is always there at the right moment and, once he has given me the session to do, and talked with me about it, I have the incentive to get right on with it, no matter how hard it may be.

'As a college student, I get plenty of the right kind of competition on the college circuits. Every athlete needs this, so this is another reason why my two years in college before the Olympics is so important. All my plans are geared towards Mexico, and after the Games I shall go back to school and work for my degrees, so that I can get on with the next phase of my life as a teacher.

'My coach Bud Winter is very good but, as any other coach, he can only tell you what to do; correct your faults: plan your training. He can't do the work for you. A coach is someone who is trying to help you, not tear you down. Bud tells me what to do, and then leaves me to get on with it. He will just quietly watch, and comment from time to time. With the feeling of someone like him watching, I think anybody will have the incentive to train.'

One of Tommie's most important attributes is his ability to relax, and I asked him how in fact he acquired this ability: 'Relaxation is something that has to be worked on a great deal. It is not natural with many people, and believe me it needs a lot of perseverance to learn to relax whilst running at top speed. That many athletes cannot relax is more often than not the cause of pulled muscles ten to twenty yards from the tape. For example, although I gave the appearance of relaxation at the White City – it probably appeared that I was loafing along – I was still working hard. But I must repeat that it is very difficult to stay relaxed at maximum speed.

'Relaxation is the key to success in a race. If you relax, it helps movement of the limbs. If you do not, then every muscle in your body will contract, and you will become tense. You must give your muscles plenty of room to move in, or you will automatically tie up. When you reach top speed and relax, it helps you to maintain that speed. This goes for any athlete, whatever the event.'

Besides relaxation, Tommie Smith seemed to be able to change gear in a race, in a dramatic fashion!

'This is no secret. It just comes back to relaxing. In the race at the White City against Wendell Mottley for example, I ran his race for the first 180 to 200 yards, then I ran it my way. It was a highly tactical race, in fact. I knew Wendell would use tactics on me, and I was speculating as to just what tactics I would use on him, before the race started. Somebody had to win, and I count myself fortunate it was me. Mottley had a best time of 45.0 before the race, whilst my best was 45.6, so I ran the first 200 metres his way, so that it would obviously be the best man who would win over the second 200. You always wonder what a guy is going to do when you draw level with him, and I wondered whether Mottley would draw ahead again or stay with me.'

The race was at the White City on 20 August 1966. The result was: 1. Tommie Smith in 45.3, 2. Wendell Mottley, 45.7, and 3. Martin Wimbolt Lewis, 46.8. He explains: 'I was after power in the first half, and Mottley's run enabled me to use it. I came out of the blocks at medium speed, not as I would have done in a 100 or 200 metres. I kept up this same momentum until going into the final bend, then all I did was relax with the momentum I had. This is why I am able to sustain the same speed during a race. If I had applied more power in the first half of the race, I would have tensed up.

'Regarding my training, there's no secret in what I do, but then I would not necessarily advise others to copy my training to the letter; it is designed for me, and because of that, suits my physique and mental attitude, and fits in with my work as a student. During the winter months, plenty of light weight training is done most days, and usually once a week cross country running is included, not racing, merely an easy run for enjoyment and relaxation. For endurance training on the track I do series of 660-yard runs. I never do actual repetition 440 yards, but either go under or over 350s or 660s. Calisthenics – stretching and suppling exercises – form an important part of my daily routine. A faster track session contains a mixture of distances, from 350 yards down to 220 yards. In season, starting practice is included in every session. Repetition 110s are also brought in during mid-season, and often a whistle stop session, where a whistle is blown at intervals, so that we sprint 50 yards then jog 50 yards. The intervals are irregular so that the whistle is not anticipated.'

To finish up with Tommie Smith's philosophy:

'An awful lot of people tend to lose their identity when they are blessed with success; they lose self-control, poise, and just become gushing and big-headed. I believe that athletics is a real test of mental attitude, not just to training, but to a person's attitude to life; to people and things. If you succumb to the rigorous self-control needed, and follow the advice of your coach, who is not training to create a big-head, then you will succeed as an athlete – but more importantly as a person. Some of those I admire for their naturalness, people unspoiled by their great success, are Wendell Mottley and Andrezej Badenski, who apart from being very hard people to run against, are extremely nice people, and Ron Clarke, a very likeable and interesting individual.

'The sooner a youngster can learn his art as an athlete, the better. This is one of the reasons I want to be a school teacher so much. I want to be in a position to start people off on the right road – from the beginning. The effect of building the personality and attitude of a person is greater felt, and seen to be felt whilst he is growing up at school.

'The would-be athlete needs to understand the common-sense in eating the foods that are going to be the most nourishing, and the importance of sleep in an active life; he needs to develop the right attitude towards his chosen sport, and should take notice of those trying to help. He should best be one who does not just go out there to please the crowd, but rather one to please himself. When he is satisfied with his performance he will have achieved the ultimate at that stage, and will then go to better and higher aims – to get that feeling of great self-satisfaction.

'For my own part, I am never satisfied until I have pleased myself. Yes, it may well have pleased the crowd, but, unless I feel self-pleasure, I never feel satisfied. The incentive to please himself is born within a person, whatever his ultimate calling in life, and it is thus important that the teacher or coach endeavours to bring this out in the individual at an early stage.

'I am intrigued by youngsters, and have been for a long time, that is why I want to be a teacher. I like to know how the child's mind works, and my hobby is childcare, which has already given me a good insight into my ultimate profession as an elementary school teacher.'

12

JIM RYUN

Born August 29, 1947, at Wichita, Kansas. 6ft 2ins/160lbs.

Jim Ryun was the last runner to hold the World mile record on cinders, before the days of fast rubberized tracks, with a time of 3:51.1 in 1967, but perhaps even more amazing was the fact that he was nineteen when he first took a huge chunk off Michel Jazy's world best (3:53.6) with 3:51.3 at Berkeley (57.9, 1:55.5, 2:55.3 and 3:51.3). His other official world mark was 3:33.1 for the 1500 on 8 July 1967. The purple patch in his career came in the 1966–67 seasons, and it was in 1967 that I saw him burst away from Kip Keino at the White City to win a mile race in 3:56.0 to Keino's 3:57.4 (on 12 August); I was extremely lucky to talk to him afterwards because he had not been available for interviews.

Interview 1967

Jim Ryun: 'I started in Wichita East High School at the age of fifteen with cross-country over two miles, and then went into the spring for the track, where the longest race for me was the mile. I fell into the event which was something completely new to me, and I knew very little about anybody's accomplishments. Bob Timmons was my coach, and I would not have come so far as fast without him. I started training quite hard very young and, as I say, without him I would not have matured physically as fast.

'In the Fall (7.9.62), I ran 5min 38sec for a mile, which was not anything great then; I went for my first competition in the spring and ran second in a race in 4:26.0, and I had

70

only been running a year then! If Timmons had not given me all the work he did, I could not have done it. It was just plain work, because I had not done any kind of distance running.

'My senior year at High School I went more towards sprinting – but I did a lot of road work too. What helped was the 440s, 330s and 660s, plus cross-country work.'

Regarding his race at the White City in London in August 1967, when he beat Kip Keino: 'I thought Keino would take the pace; he did not, so I simply took the pace on myself because I felt a little heavy and tired, and when I feel that way I would rather be in front and control the race.'

It was in the interview of 1967 that I wondered which of his World records did he feel were the hardest to achieve: 1:44.9 – 880yds (800 1:44.2) in 1966, 1500m – 3:33.1, or the mile of 3:51.1 (both in 1967).

'They have not accepted the half-mile one. I can't say either one of them was harder than the other, because they were all different situations, after which I felt tired but not exhausted. Herb Elliot's 3:35.6 in Rome in 1960 was a very good record for 1500 and, I thought, it would be another year or so before it would be removed from the books. To take it out with such a big margin was a very big surprise to me.' (Los Angeles, US v British Commonwealth meet, with Kip Keino second in 3:37.2 and Alan Simpson third in 3:41.7). As a matter of interest, second in the Bakersfield world record of 3:51.1 on 23 June 1967, was Jim's racing friend Jim Grelle in 3:56.1, and Dave Wilborn ran third in 3:56.2.

Roger Bannister, who was the first man ever to break 4 minutes for the mile, made an interesting comment on the phone to me in June 1979 regarding great milers from different eras:

'A mile clash between Ryun and Filbert Bayi would obviously have produced a very fast time, perhaps bringing the mile record down to around 3:46.0.'

Did Jim Ryun's coach advise other athletes of note?

'Bob Timmons trained Archie San Romani, Junior, he was a very fine athlete, and he has had a number of swimmers and other track men too, but they never made it to world level, he developed them from nothing into great athletes, but not good enough to be at the world level. Regarding myself, I took up athletics because I could not make the team at anything else.'

How did he look at the weeks and years ahead? 'I live towards the future, I play it loosely, you might say, because you never know what is going to happen. There are too many things that do happen, especially in my life.'

Without a doubt Jim Ryun will go down in the history books as one of the best milers of all time, but there were two important races he did not win or break a record in. They both had magic in them, purely because 'Jim Ryun' was taking part! Firstly, in 1968, was the Olympic final, when Kip Keino won in Mexico in 3:34.9, with Jim Ryun second in 3:37.8. In that race, John Whetton, who ran fifth (3:43.8) and was a finalist in the 1964 Olympic 1500 that Peter Snell of New Zealand won, had something important to say about Ryun's defeat in Mexico. 'Ryun is undoubtedly one of the greatest milers that has ever lived. In 1968, he undoubtedly lost the confidence he once had, following illness. I am convinced that the result might still have been the same at sea level, with Keino the winner, but only because Ryun lacked this confidence, more especially at altitude where he thought it was impossible to run any faster than 3:39.0 for 1500. If Ryun had showed with the same tactics that I did going with them then, he would have won and beaten Keino hands down. With 300 yards to go in that race, Ryun was still behind me – but by that point Keino was close on just 200 metres from the line.'

On 16 May, 1971, Marty Liquori, who eventually moved up to the 5000 metres, won an enthralling mile in Philadelphia. The result: 1. Marty Liquori, 3:54.6. 2. Jim Ryun, 3:54.8. 3. Byron Dyce (Jam), 3:59.6. Liquori takes up the story in 1975.

'They did give Ryun the same time as me, then a week later they amended it to 3:54.8 for him, as it was obvious that it was not the same time: he was two to three yards behind. I have a lot of memories of that race: it was probably the biggest mile race in twenty years to be held in America, because of the amount of publicity it received. Not since Bill Bonthron and Glen Cunningham were running at Princeton were there races like that! We had 25,000 people come to the race on a rainy day and 56 degrees, and we probably would have had about 50,000, which in America would be unbelievable for track. Jim Ryun had been the best, then he retired, and in the two years since, I had come of age and was the top miler in America and in fact ranked number one in the world. So it was like the champion coming back to reclaim his title, and we were such diverse personalities that there was so much material there for journalists.

'It was a very strange race. The first lap was very slow, about 61 sec, then 2:03 for the half-mile. With about 700 yards to go, Ryun worked his way into the lead and I got right on his shoulder, and he only led for about 100 yards. I passed him from 650 or so out, we were neck and neck really, running as fast as we could. We ran the last half in 1:51, which at the time was one of the fastest last half-miles ever run, and it was a great race to watch. We were really sprinting for a long time.'

13

LYNN DAVIES

Born 20 May, 1942, Nantymoel, near Bridgend, Wales. 6ft 1in/12½st (174lbs).

Interviews in 1964, 1968 and 1970

Of all the interviews I have conducted since the 50s, if I were asked which athlete combined the qualities of mental toughness for major competitions blended with an engaging personality, a sense of humour on and off the track and the classical features to look the part, the person I would first think of would be Lynn Davies. I know from experience that some of the United States athletic magazine critics didn't consider him to be as great as Ralph Boston or Bob Beamon, but if you recognize his medal tally in major championships, those critics could be forced to see the error of their judgement.

Lynn's long jumping career included an Olympic title in 1964, 1966 European and Commonwealth golds, plus a win in the European indoors of 1967 and a Commonwealth gold in 1970. His long-standing UK long jump record stands at 27'0/8.23, and he was a good competitive sprinter, with times of 9.5/10.4 for the 100 yds/100 metres; and, besides other minor medals in major Chmpionships, he was an uncompromising performer who would be prepard to 'break his legs' to win.

Lynn, who has been a teacher, coach and technical director as well as a National team manager, told me prior to the Tokyo Olympics, it was sheer luck that brought him into athletics. Before moving on to Cardiff City Training

College, he attended Ogmore County Grammar School, where he captained the school rugby team, played soccer, cricket and tennis. It was there that he clocked 10.3 for 100 yards, high jumped 5'8" and did around 22 feet for the long jump. After a bash in the 1960 Welsh championships he realized his potential, setting a Welsh triple jump record of 46'11¼", and cleared 23'5" for new Welsh long jump figures. Lynn takes up the story.

'I first took it up for fun when I entered the school sports in the long jump at the age of eighteen. I ran down, not knowing which leg I was going to jump off with. My first ever jump was 21'2½", and from that they gathered that I had some potential, so from there I went on to both the area and Welsh Schools Championships, where I met Ron Pickering. That was when the training really started. In Wales we have a great rugby tradition, so for most schools in the valleys it is either that or soccer, with athletics the poor relation, mainly because we don't have the facilities. The PE master at Ogmore was very enthusiastic about rugby and gymnastics, so I indulged myself in the latter. I was a great enthusiast for all sports before the age of eighteen. Soccer was my favourite game, and I played rugby for the school on Saturday mornings and soccer for the local team in the afternoon. However, I also enjoyed gymnastics, so if I were to offer advice to young athletes it would be not to specialize too soon. If you start at fifteen, by the time you are twenty, five years seems a long time, and I think this is one of the reasons that a lot of athletes leave the sport early.'

Ron Pickering, the coach, played a great part in Lynn's early development. 'He took up his coaching appointment as Welsh National Coach in 1960, and that coincided with my commencement in athletics, and he saw me jumping 23'5" without training. He moved back to London before taking up the post, where he wrote me two or three letters to give me some idea of what a long jumper should be doing. I had no idea what training was about, previously relying upon natural ability and my fitness from rugby and soccer. Prior to the age of eighteen, I had no specialist preparation for the long jump. The triple jump was my first event, and my first ever long jump was made without any

75

training at all. The season after my first I improved to 50'7" and 24'9", and decided I would have to specialize to achieve World class. The following winter, my long jump improved to 25'4".'

At the time of the start of the Commonwealth Games at Perth in 1962, Ken Wilmshurst held the British long jump record with 24'8¾". Lynn finished fourth behind Mike Ahey of Ghana (26'5"), with new figures of 25'4"/7.72 metres. A month earlier, he had gone to Belgrade for the European Championships and finished ninth with 24'6".

Lynn was full of admiration for the Commonwealth Games gold medallist. 'Looking back, I feel Mike Ahey had the ability to jump 27'6", if he had coaching. He did 26'5" out there, and somebody described his style as a string of sausages flying through the air. I like Mike very much, but he had no technique, and I often wonder what he could have achieved with even the minimum of coaching from Ron.' It was at Belgrade that Lynn first met the man he hoped to emulate. 'My first impression of great long jumping was watching Igor Ter-Ovanesyan from the side of the pit, where the great Russian won in 26'9½". It was obvious from what I had seen there, that I would have to improve upon my basic qualities of both speed and spring. I did things through good coaching by Ron Pickering, film analysis, relating the visual impression to the calisthenic impression, the feel of it going out on the track and back to the film.

'I spent two years on changing my style from a hang to a hitchkick technique. I had a tremendous winter in 1963. This was the third year at teacher training college, which involved a lot of fitness work as well as gymnastics, swimming etc, so I reached a very high level and was also able to work on my specialist event, with everything laid on.'

As 1964 emerged with the Olympics at Tokyo, it is interesting to again record Lynn's thoughts prior to the Games.

'I get a great deal of satisfaction and a sense of achievement from athletics, and it has more or less become my life now, with high ambitions. Looking forward to Tokyo, I hope to finish in the first four and clear 27 feet.

Unless one aims high and has such ambitions, there is really no point in competing. That is my philosophy. When I began I was not interested to the same extent, but now I have to some degree modelled my performance on Ralph Boston and Igor Ter-Ovanesyan.'

Lynn's build up for the Games began in the winter of 1963 with strength building. Weight training and running hard into the wind were essential sessions for the determined Welshman. 'It may surprise you to know that I have lifted upwards of an estimated 280 tons of weight during the twelve months prior to the Games. Apart from this, I do a tremendous amount of gym work, to take away the monotony that can creep into training after a period of time. I took part in swimming, rugby and soccer.'

Then after his fantastic gold in the games – 'I hoped to take the bronze,' remarked Lynn and went on, 'I could not beat either Boston or Igor, it was just not on the cards. Ralph had averaged 26'11" in the Olympic trials and Ter-Ovanesyan was the co-World record holder, while I had jumped only 26'4" before going out there. So I reckoned I had an outside chance of a third place, if things went my way. As at Mexico four years later, it took me three jumps to even qualify. Then on the day of the final, the rain started to come down. I could see during the competition that both Ralph and Igor were badly affected by the weather. This was my opportunity, so I grabbed it with both hands; I was better prepared and able to adapt to the conditions better than they were. Of course I was beginning my career then and was not so particular what I trained on, now unless it is tartan – we are spoilt, and the longer you compete in different countries, the more you see. But in Tokyo, a really good cinder track was a luxury, as was the privilege of living in the Olympic Village for six weeks. Boston had seen all this before, so the novelty had worn off for him. Both he and Igor were less excited by the glamour of it and therefore less happy to adapt to the wet conditions, whereas it was no different to me than British conditions.' On 18 October, in a temperature of 55 degrees, Lynn's final series was 7.45, 7.59, 8.07 and 7.74. Boston's best jump was 8.03, and Ter-Ovanesyan 7.99. On his return to Nantymoel, the entire population of 3000 gave him a hero's welcome home, with the Lord Mayor's car from Cardiff threading through a route lined with people waving flags.

1965 couldn't have been anything other than an anti-climax. Lynn wanted to achieve his ambition of Olympic, European and Commonwealth gold medals, so gave up his teaching job at Bridgend Grammar School, where he had been for eighteen months. In the winter of 1966 he went to California for six weeks, and trained at UCLA in the best possible climatic conditions among the most competitive people. From there he went to South Africa in March 1967, so enjoyed excellent conditions right up to the Commonwealth Games at Kingston, Jamaica, in July.

Knowing Ralph Boston had jumped 27'2" there, Lynn had hoped for a World record. However the ground staff over watered the runway prior to the competition, and in something like quagmire conditions, he had to be satisfied with a winning games record of 26'2¾".

Then on to Budapest in September, where Lynn achieved his great ambition with the Grand Slam, winning the European with his last jump. Conditions were again similar to Tokyo, with the rain coming down halfway through the competition, so 26'2½" sufficed to win the gold medal. 1967 was another good year, climaxed with the mini-Olympics in Mexico City. Lynn jumped 27'10" in training, but only managed 26'8" in the actual competition, whereas Ter-Ovanesyan equalled the world record of 27'5". Nevertheless, that 27'10" had given the Welshman the confidence he needed in a pre-Games year, and he returned to train really hard throughout the winter.

However, as the world now knows, Bob Beamon's opening jump of 8.90 metres shattered everyone's illusions of a gold medal at Mexico City. Lynn said after the games: 'Boston and Igor had been jumping for eleven years under every condition on earth, if it had been possible to jump 28', they would have done it somewhere, and suddenly along comes this man and jumps over 29', a foot and half longer than the world record. I think a nice analogy is drawn from a letter that an actor wrote to me after the games. He compared it with going on to the stage for a first night, to find that you have rehearsed for the wrong play.'

Klaus Beer was second with 8.19, Boston third with 8.16

and Davies ninth with 7.94, which he did in the qualifying rounds. The Welshman came in for a lot of stick from the national press on his return to Britain, the same critics who had applauded him four years earlier. Their cries of 'no guts', however made him determined to make amends at Athens in 1969, the target this time being the European Games. He came up against an inspired Ter-Ovanesyan though, whose 8.17 in the wind was just 4″ too good for Lynn. He was not pleased with his silver medal, but the difference between Athens and Mexico was that he was fighting again.

And so on to Edinburgh for 1970, in what proved to be his last major games success. At these Commonwealth Games, Lynn was honoured to be made captain of the Welsh team, and here are his feelings on that: 'I was pleased to win another gold medal, but not just for myself. I have said before that when you compete for yourself, you are alone and nobody else can help you, but being captain of the team is a special responsibility, and you feel that the whole team is behind you. It helps being the captain, because I felt this responsibility and it did contribute towards my perform- ance.' In the event, he did exactly the same distance as in Tokyo with Phil May, whose best jump of 26′4″ was in the qualifying rounds. Alan Lerwill achieved third place with 26′1½″/7.78.

Finally, what benefit did athletics give him, besides the competition and training?

'The places I have been to. You are in a different society when you are in the athletics world. There are lots of people with a common aim, but you too have to learn to understand them to live with them. How many people apart from sportsmen get this opportunity to live in a village, with a lot of people with different temperaments and different attitudes and ideologies? It definitely broadens your hori- zons. How else could I travel to America, Germany, Switzerland and France all in one season? In what other sphere (apart from either being born rich, or becoming rich) can you do this and still improve your education?'

As a point of interest Bob Beaman's record was not erased till Mike Powell beat Carl Lewis on the 30th August 1991 in Tokyo and jumped 8.95/29′ 4¾″.

14

LEE EVANS

Born 25 February, 1947, Madeira, California.

When powerfully-built Lee Evans broke the 400 metres World record on 18 October, 1968, in Mexico City, in an event that had always been well-contested world-wide, little did one realize at the time that his 43:86 would stand for very nearly twenty years till Butch Reynolds ran 43:20 in Zurich on 17 August, 1988!

It was only two days after Lee's World one-lap record that the United States team smashed the 4x400 relay best in Mexico City, with a runaway victory in 2:56.1 (still the current record on the books) – In order: 1. Vince Mathews, the 1972 Olympic 400 Champion, 45:2; Ron Freeman, 43:2; Larry James, 44:2; and Lee Evans, 43:5.

Earlier in the year, Lee Evans had won the final Olympic trials in the United States in 44:06, from Larry James, 44:19.

Interview 1968

Were you inspired by anyone to take up athletics, or did you just start thinking about athletics at school itself?

'It was in Junior High School when I was twelve years old when we would run fifty-yard dashes. It was in sixth grade at Madison elementary school (in Fresno, California) when I ran in the parks. In seventh and eighth grade we would have about two meets a year. I can remember running the quarter then for the first time, between 62 and 72 seconds. We would just come out and race each other, and the coach who took us out might say, 'Okay Evans, you run the 440 today.'

'I was really inspired by my older brother who ran very well in High School, and his name was Doug Evans, that was in 1958–59. He ran 48.5 for 440 and 1.55 for the half at college, and then he quit to play football.

'I ran in my first year in High School, but I was sort of slow as I was very small. I ran the 660 yards dash in the C division and I won all my races, but in the big meets I would take second or third. I ran 1:29.2 for 660, which I guess was all right as I was only 14 then, so I was very happy with it. In my sophomore year in High School, I gained a little speed and gained a little weight. I ran the 330 yards dash in the C class again. I ran 36:00 flat which was the San Joaquin Valley record. That year my family moved to Oregon for the summer, and I gained thirty pounds between track seasons, and all of a sudden I ran 48.2 for the 440. My biggest disappointment was, that although I had run a 46.3 relay leg, I thought I had a possible chance to make the US team to go to Russia. Ollan Cassell won the National in 1965 (46.1), but the reason I could not go to the nationals was because I had a muscle injury in the High School State meet. Then I went to Salinas City College for a year, and that was where I ran 45.2 for 400 in 1966 and won the AAU Championships in New York (Evans, 45.9, Theron Lewis, 46.2. Bob Frey, 46.3). In 1967, I went to San José State College.'

What then were your memories of Tommie Smith at that period in your career?

'We came from the same area. In High School I did not run against him. We would run in the same meet, and I would always watch him run as I admired the way he ran. I was very small, and he was running big kinda stuff!'

You then did weights to improve, and you must have had coaches who advised you over the years, too?

'I did squats and pole raises which helped me gain weight, and so I got stronger and better. As for coaches, I started with Bud Winter, then I was advised by Frank Olsen and Stan Dowell.'

You must have started to look like moving towards the Olympics with great speed in 1967?

'In the Junior year in San José State College I did run

81

44.9, I won the Pan American Games 400' (1. Lee Evans, 44.9. 2. Vince Mathews, 45.1. 3. Don Domansky (Can), 45.8, Winnipeg, July).

What was your essential training for the Olympics, then?

'Every year my schedule is to train mainly for 800 metre races during the year to gain strength. I ran 600 yards indoors and 800s – David Hemery does the same type of training to get ready for the 400 metres hurdles. You have got to do a lot of over-distance work. At altitude, I normally jog between my intervals but, at altitude, you have to walk a lot more slowly and take a lot more rest between; if you don't you won't be able to function well.

'Let's say on a Monday I do 3×550 – time the first and last, do about 67', and come by the quarter in 52 to 53.

'Tuesday, I would do 6×220s in about 23 sec., with 220 walk (at altitude).

'Wednesday, I run 4×330 at a good pace, sometimes I don't get a watch, but I try to run them in about 36 seconds.

'Thursday, I would do about 6×150 for speed.

'If I have to run Saturday, I rest Friday. Sometimes I would jog on Friday.'

How about the heats in Mexico?

'Well, I think the heats helped me, because I think I am a lot stronger than most of the other guys so the heats tire them out, which helps my chances. In my first race I ran 45.3, so I sort of strolled in. If I had got going I could have run in the lower 44s' he chuckled.

How about the quarter-finals?

'I was in the 7th lane, and I went out very fast, but I did not want to win by a big margin, so I slowed up, I just got tired, so I slowed up and took second' (Amos Omolo, 45.3. Lee Evans, 45.5)

The semi-final?

'I ran great, I ran 44.8, I toodled along!' (Olympic record, with Larry James, 44.9, and Martin Jellinghaus of West Germany, 44.9).

In the final, he was in lane 6, with Larry James, his biggest rival, in 2. Lee ran the first 110 very hard, relaxed after that, before running hard again in the back straight. He kicked on the bend with a good finish in the home stretch. Full result on 18 October: 1. Lee Evans, 43.8. 2.

Larry James, 43.9. 3. Ron Freeman, 44.4. 4. Amadou
Gakou, 45.0. 5. Martin Jellinghaus, 45.3. 6. Tegegne
Bezabeth (Ethiopia), 45.4. 7. Andrez Badenski (Poland),
45.4, and 8. Amos Omolo (Uganda), 47.6.

15

MADELINE MANNING-JACKSON

Born Ohio, 11 January, 1948. 5ft 9ins/128lbs.

There have been faster 800 metre runners than Madeline Manning-Jackson, but few could claim they were amongst the best in the world in 1967 and still amongst the best thirteen years later in 1980. The highlights of her career include Pan-American Champion in 1967 (2:02.3), first in the Olympic final of 1968 (2:00.9 – Olympic record), ran a personal best in an American record of 1:57.09 in 1976, and set an American Championships best performance of 1:58.8 in 1980.

When I spoke to her, she had a charming way of expressing herself.

Interview 1968

When did it all start for Madeline Manning-Jackson?

'I started in 1965 in Cleveland, Ohio, under my coach, Alt Ferenzzy. He coached me for about one and a half years till I got out of High School, and he coached me when I went to the Olympics in Mexico. I got a scholarship down to Tennessee State University, but before that I was at John Hay High School in Cleveland. It was at Tennessee 'A' that I was under Edward Temple, who coaches me back home.

'Regarding athletics, I always liked it as well as basketball, volleyball and baseball, but I was running in High School. Alt Ferenzzy saw me doing that and asked me to run for his club. From there I went to the Women's National, and I won the girls division as a seventeen-year-old. I set a new record for my age group in the quarter, so I continued to run. I was always on the team that year,

84

running against Russia, Poland and West Germany.'

Going straight on to Mexico and the Olympic Games:

'I won both my heats in the trials and the semis, and they were quite relaxing.' Fastest heat was by Vera Nikoloc, who ran 2:05.7, Madeline running 2:08.7 to win heat 4. Semifinal, the fastest was Maria Gommers of Holland in 2:05.9.

How about the final?

'I was out in the eighth lane which is a blindman's lane, and I could not tell what my competitors were doing, but I knew I had to run out, so I did that, and by the time I could go down the straight at the back I found I was ahead. I just stayed there. The pace was very comfortable for me, and they did not pick it up any. Silai of Rumania came up on the side of me and we ran the first quarter together (59.1), and with 300 to 320 to go, I started picking it up. I started sprinting coming off the curve, and it was comfortable.'

'That was my third time in Mexico, as I came there in 1965 for the little Olympics. At that time I was running the quarter, and I won that, then we came back when we were invited down by one of the teams of Mexico. My team, the "Tennessee Tigerbells" came down in April of this year (1968), but I was kinda sick because the plane ride was very up and down!'

Did the altitude make any difference to her?

'Well, I think if we had not trained in it for a while we would have felt it even more. We were in Los Alamos from 15 September, and we left on the 30th, so we were practising up in the hills in Mexico.'

What training did she do for the Mexico 800?

'Distance, intervals and sprints.'

About her interests and family, she remarked: 'My brothers were into boxing and track and field, and I was the youngest of the family. I am studying sociology, which I find very interesting, and into all kinds of music. If I had not gone into track, I would be in music right now.'

Regarding the Olympic 800 metres final on 19 October, the full result was: 1. Madeline Manning, 2:00.9. 2. Ilona Silai, 2:02.5. 3. Maria Gommers, 2:02.6. 4. Sheila Taylor-(Carey) (UK), 2:03.8. 5. Doris Brown (US), 2:03.9. 6. Pat Cropper (neé Lowe) (UK), 2:04.2. 7. Abigail Hoffman (Canada), 2:06.8. 8. Maryvonne Dupreur (France), 2:08.2.

16

RALPH DOUBELL

Born 11 February, 1945. 63kls/141lbs; 5ft 11ins.

Ralph Doubell was undefeated over 800/1000 indoors in the 1967/68 winter season before he had injury problems, then peaked absolutely correctly for the Olympic final in Mexico City, equalling the World record of 1:44.3, which had been set by Peter Snell in 1962.

Two-lap racing is one of the hardest events to judge tactically, and many potential champions or proven world-class runners have failed on the big occasion. Americans Morgan Groth (1964) and Wade Bell (1968) did not get through the Olympic heats. In 1990, Sebastian Coe and Tom McKean were surprisingly out of the medals in the Commonwealth Games, as was our subject in 1966 and 1970.

Interview 1968

How did it all begin for the Australian two-lapper?

'I used to play football, cricket and athletics. I did sprints at school in the first two years of High School. I never won, so they never took a time. In the fifth and sixth form I started running quarter-miles and half-miles. As a sixteen-to-seventeen-year-old, I remember that I did 53 for a quarter and 2.4 to 2.5 for a half, but in my first year of track racing I got down to 1:49.8 for 800 metres. I started to run the 440 at Melbourne University, with 49.8 and 49.9. (I first started training properly for four to five months during one winter, and I ran a half mile in 1:54.8, and my previous best had been 1:59.6, so it was at that point that I thought – we

86

can start running half-miles!)

'In the 1965–67 season I ran 1:47.5 for the Victorian Championships and went to America just before the Commonwealth Games, where I came sixth in the final in 1:48.3 (880 yards). I had an injury, so I had penicillin before. The next season after that, I did not do all that much. I was not running very well, just concentrating on mainly beating Noel Clough (the 1966 Commonwealth Champion)! I ran 1:48.9 at the end of 1967. There was the USA v Commonwealth meet which I was not picked for, but after that came the World University Games in September when I won in 1:46.7, beating Franz Joseph Kemper of West Germany, in the same time in Tokyo. I was very fit then, as I had run a 74.7 660 yds just before I left for the Games, which is quite fast, then I went to America for four or five weekends to run indoors (1968). I won six races out of six, but I did not have much background behind me.

'I was living in Sydney for three months before Christmas, as I was transferred by Shell Company, and I was not training all that well, so when I came back I was beaten on two occasions. I still had not qualified for our Olympic team till after the 'Nationals': I got beaten in the National by Preston Davis of America, who ran 1:49.0 to my 1:49.3. I just ran out of puff that day. I was rather worried four days later when we had a meet. I managed 1:47.2 (Melbourne 28/3), mainly because I rested those four days and I had completely recovered, and I knew it was all or nothing for me so, that 1:47.2 qualified me, and four weeks after that I ran 1:47.9, and from there I just worked for the Games under my coach Franz Stampfl.

Mexico

'We arrived there on 16 September, and that is when I started altitude training. For the first week we were a bit puffed, but regarding altitude, a lot depends on how you react to it. There is no way of telling whether a person will or will not adapt to it. Lajos Mecser (13:05/13:29.2, 3 miles/5k runner in 1968 from Hungary) is the prime example. He had trained at altitude, but does not adapt to high altitude

87

running. Fortunately, I adapted, even though running 800 is not affected all that much by altitude. It's usually over two minutes that you start worrying. The greatest worry I had was having three races in a row, as the recovery rate is a bit slow.'

Olympic heats. Heat 4. 1. Ralph Doubell, 1:47.2.

'After the heat I did not know what to feel, as it was the first 800 I had run for about six months. I felt reasonably comfortable, but I did not know how much I had left in me.'

The semi final, heat 2. Easily the fastest, Ralph Doubell 1:45.7, and the man who was third in Tokyo, Wilson Kiprugut of Kenya, 1:45.8, and third Josef Plachy, 1:45.9, which was a European Junior record.

'It was a very hard semi compared to the other one (Walter Adams, 1:46.4); I started very slowly. I did not feel very good, but I moved up, and coming into the straight I was running fifth or sixth and I thought I would try to get up to second or third, and all of a sudden I found I was leading and it felt very easy.'

In the final: 'It was more or less how I had planned it. To take the first lap in either fifth or sixth place, take it easy then move up, down the back straight and be on the shoulders of the leaders with 200 to go, then, coming into the straight, make a break for it; it just worked out, and fortunately no-one got in the way.'

1. Ralph Doubell, 1:44.3. 2. Wilson Kiprugut, 1:44.5. 3. Tom Farrell (USA), 1:45.4. 4. Walter Adams (WG) 1:45.8. 5. Josef Plachy (Cze), 1:45.9. 6. Dieter Fromm (EG), 1:46.2. 7. Thomas Saisi (Kenya), 1:47.5, and 8. Benedict Cayenne (Trinidad), 1:54.3 (1:46.8 in the semi).

The Training Prior to Mexico

'It was going quite normally up till July/August, doing normal interval work, say 20 × 400, 10 × 800, 30 × 220, 50 × 100. In one session I would run three miles in the morning, very slow jogging, then in the evening jog, three miles, then do the work like 20 × 400 or 10 × 800 or so, but then I ran into some problems with achilles tendon trouble, and I had to do a bit longer stuff, plus I was doing the weights and swimming. My achilles was very bad and I did not train for about two weeks, and I was getting treatment twice a day for about the last four weeks before I left for Mexico, so I could not run in spikes for the last six weeks before I left for the Games, except the day before we left, with a time trial over 440 yards in 49.9 seconds, and it felt very easy; but the week prior to that, I ran a three-quarter-mile time trial in warm-up shoes in 3:1.8, so we thought everything had worked out okay, but we were fortunate it had clicked! When I landed from the airplane, the achilles was blown up to twice its normal size, but it went down and it was not sore, and I had no trouble at all.'

The obvious comment to any half-miler was that it is an event that requires stamina and a lot of speed now, and Ralph then added to that.

'It is becoming more of a sprint, as Kiprugut ran the first lap in the final in 50.8, and I did 51.50. That is fairly fast, and you have to put another 52 or 53 on top of that, so it is more of a sprint. You must have that strength and stamina to keep sprinting, and this is where interval work helps, and also the weights.'

17

AL OERTER

I feel Al Oerter is definitely one of those athletes who have done more for field events than anybody in the history of athletics, not just because he is such an incredible athlete but for the fact that he has continued to love competing, long after most world-class athletes in their day had put away their implements and hung up their spikes.

It was amazing that he was forty-three when he achieved his furthest discus mark on 31 May, 1980, at Wichita, with 69.46/227'11", which placed him second only in distance to 1976 Olympic champion Mac Wilkins, who threw 70.98 that year.

In 1989 in Oregon, he won the event in the World Veteran championships, hurling the discus (1.5 kg) to a new over-fifties World best of 62.74 m.

He achieved three world records: 1963, 62.45; 1964, 62.62; and 1965, 62.94.

His almost unbelievable Olympic record comprised of four gold medals. 1956 – 184'11"/56.36, 1960 – 194'1¾"/59.18, 1964 – 200'1½"/64.78 and, 1968 – 212'6"/61.78 (on his third throw of the competition).

Interview 1981

So which Olympic title meant most to him?

'They are all so different. The first at Melbourne in 1956 was the most unexpected.' In this he went out as second string to Fortune Gordien, but managed to beat his compatriot by over five feet, with 184'11".

The second, at Rome in 1960, was difficult. 'Expecting to

win, I had placed myself in a position of complete confidence. When something went wrong in the competition, it was hard to recover my composure and win.' But win he did with 194'1¾", nearly four feet further than Richard Babka.

The third, at Tokyo in 1964, was physically the most difficult and painful. 'I pulled quite a bit of cartilage off my ribcage, which hampered my movement somewhat.' Nevertheless he won, with a throw 1½" above the magic 200'. Ludvik Danek of Czechoslovakia was creeping up, and achieved 198'6½" for second place.

The fourth, at Mexico, he rates his most satisfying.

'The World record at that time was over seventeen feet longer than my best throw of the year hitherto. There I was in competition with not only that thrower, but two others who had already set previous World records that year. So I was not expected to be a great threat, but I was absolutely confident that I would be successful and win some kind of medal. To start with, I didn't expect it to be gold, but in the last competition of 1968 I knew I would be at my best, and had put together a programme spanning several years that had worked.

'I was able to develop the plan first, then adapt it to whatever the circumstance was – injury, increased levels of strength, throwing difficulties or whatever. The whole plan seemed to work and I peaked on the day of the Olympic final, which was most satisfying.'

The net result of that co-ordination was a new Olympic record of 212'6½". Luther Milde was second in 206'11½", and Danek third with 206'5".

How important a part of your life is athletics?

'I have always considered athletics to be one of the most important things in my life, but I have never allowed it to consume my life to a great extent. If it became a profession or a semi-profession, I would have to drop out because I could no longer enjoy the training, and the competition would be something different. Instead of competing with oneself you would then be competing against other people . . . that is hostile, and I could not do that. Athletics was always a thing that I did, it was almost recreational. I only became very intense immediately prior to the Olympic

Games in order to compete effectively.

'I have just completed raising a family. One daughter is now twenty-two, and on her own out teaching; my youngest daughter has two years to go in college, and that has consumed a great part of my time – that is, in fact, why I dropped out of sport. The main thing by far from 1968 to 1976 was to experience the growth of my daughters, as, if I had missed that, I would have regretted that loss for the rest of my life.

'One of the things I am most interested in doing right now is writing. I am preparing my first book, on fitness and training. What I am most interested in is a book on motivation, which I can write fairly well about. I have already completed a great portion of it, and that perhaps will come out before the 1984 Games. I think writing about motivation and using the Olympics as an experience, for example, is something people can relate to. They can relate to a person who has obviously had to be highly motivated to continue competing over long periods of time. What I would eventually like to get into is fiction. I find that the discipline required in a sport like track and field is absolutely transferrable to a writing career, because you establish a certain amount of time each day where you must be productive within that period.

'By profession I am involved in the computer field, but quite frankly I have become somewhat tired of being in the advanced stage of computer art for over twenty years. I started in the 1959/60 era, when computers were just becoming commercially useable, and I have gone through all the transitions, the software and the innovations that have happened. I have finally come to a realization that innovation is taking place primarily for profit purposes, and as it's no longer right for me to continue in that environment, I am going to leave. What I am going to replace it with is writing.'

Of the people who have coached or advised you over the years, who sticks out in your mind?

'I have never had a coach in my life. I have never had a physician, psychologist or any other kind of "ologist" that has understood athletics. I learned at the outset that you get out of the sport what you put into it. If I were to be the

92

kind of person who worked with a psychologist to keep my head straight, physicians to keep me totally fit all of the time, a coach to keep me training and provide some external motivation, then – if I won anything or did anything – it would be a cumulative effort. I would then have to turn round from the winner's stand and say it was not me, it was this collection of people behind me that really did that, and I was then merely the executor of all these instructions, and, in a sense, a robot. I could never do that. Win or lose or draw, it has to be on my own, and the reason perhaps I think that way is that I won my Olympic gold medal very early on in life, and it has always allowed me, from that moment, not to have to prove myself. I never had to set a World record, even though I did several times after that. I never had to win another gold medal, even though I won several more. I never had to do anything in the sport to prove myself, therefore my continuing participation was always an enjoyment. The only reason I would compete was that I would continue to enjoy the elevating environment that I find in track and field.'

Has making so many friends throughout the world helped you stay in athletics?

'Yes, I guess it has been one of the nice things that happen in track and field, as you get to travel quite a bit and you get to understand about different societies. You meet people who have chosen to do exactly the same thing that you are doing, and we all face somewhat the same problems.'

What brought you into discus throwing?

'I competed in baseball and American football because of my size, and I could throw a ball very hard. I entered track and field after a football season, and I was attracted to the individual aspect – I found it interesting, as the result you obtained was through your individual effort, not a composite effort of eight, or ten or twelve members of a team, where the individual effort is really not known. With track and field you put it on the line, and that I enjoy. I enjoy testing myself for myself.'

Have you ever imitated anyone else's technique?

'I would love to imitate John Powell's technique, but I can't do it. John is, I think, the most efficient thrower in the world right now. He gets the most out of his body in the throw. There is something unique about John . . . he is a good competitor, and is able to bring it out in very good competition, even under difficult circumstances. John is just very confident in his technique. He knows exactly where he is going to be within the ring at any time, and all he does is work on his intensity for the throw. Now if I can learn that and be that confident of the turn – not even consider the throw itself, or how I am going to throw once I enter the ring, but just work on the intensity required to throw long distances – making the 1984 Olympic team would not be a simple matter, but it would certainly be a much simpler matter than it is with my current technique.'

What is your advice to a person taking up the discus and hoping to do well?

'Obviously if a person has a need to win, that has to be determined very early on, and if a person does not like losing he had better not become a discus thrower if he is fairly small. You can't just go on winning if you are less than six foot and less than 200 lb, because it is then going to be a very difficult environment. You may enjoy it, but if you have that intensity that needs to win, it is just not for you. Discus throwers also have to be able to work with a certain amount of solitude.'

It must have been a surprise to you to go into the World Veterans Championships in Gothenberg in 1977 and find you were up against such a celebrated performer as Ludvik Danek, who at the time was still in world class?

'Ludvik is a very good friend and was somewhat ambivalent about my beating him that day, because he was working at that moment for the World Cup. To beat him after only two years' training when he was actively training over all those years to retain not only his Olympic title but his World Cup status was not so good. He should have beaten me very easily.'

So was becoming a Vet a physical and mental barrier to Al?

'No, because when I decided to return to competition I was determined to become as good as I possibly could and compete in both Open and Masters competition. When I went for my first Masters championship in the States, the

94

question was not so much "who was there" as "why weren't they there". I competed against only one other Olympian, and he was a decathlete. It was an environment that many elite athletes apparently found degrading. They could not think of competing at a lower level than they were used to. Evidently elite athletes have this sense of retiring at their peak, and to accept anything less is very difficult. But why weren't they out there, enjoying something that they had been involved in so long?

'Probably because the enjoyment was never really there. They found that the training was part of a very hard regime. It was a forced environment, with coaches and physicians keeping them in shape when they really preferred to rest when injured. It was hard for them to get back into Masters competition in a comfortable way. However, as I had always enjoyed it and nobody had ever forced me to do anything that I didn't want to do, it became more normal for me to commence Masters Athletics. Veteran athletes are beginning to test their capabilities more and more, they are starting to train sensibly, and that is providing a different avenue in their lives. For the first time, they are testing themselves in competiton, not necessarily against their opponents, just against themselves to see how much they improve.

'I am sure that when I was young I established barriers that I mentally could not go beyond. I thought I could not become stronger or throw further or work with more intensity when I turned forty, but that has obviously been proved to be untrue. I had the best result of my life at age forty-three.

What would be a reasonable week's training for competition?

'When I am working at my best, I work no more than one and a half hours a day, and that would be about six days a week. That is as much energy as I have ever put in from my teens.'

What specific training has, you feel, helped?

'It's standard, there are no secrets. There are so many little ploys that are used right now. There is the computer analysis of the discus thrower, which I have used; there is instant film available to me right now so that I can film a throwing session. I will use every innovation that I think has value, so I stay abreast of what is going on. My week is very typical of almost any athlete. I pay attention to detail . . . strength levels, technique of the throw, intensity of the throw, resting for competition and trying to get as mentally prepared for competition as you possibly can.'

Over the years, which competitors have been the hardest to beat?

'The most difficult, obviously, are the competitors that I am throwing against right now, because they are very good. People like Mac Wilkins, even though Mac is not throwing so well in 1981. In 1982 he will be back. John Powell is a very, very fine competitor. He can bring the best out of himself in almost any throw, and that is very difficult.'

His weight/height ratio, allied to his tremendous technical ability, is remarkable. He must be one of the finest technicians at the event?

'Exactly. He is the most efficient discus thrower that we have in the United States, perhaps in the world. Obviously, the most capable thrower in the world is Wolfgang Schmidt, as I think he has the tools. If anyone is going to throw 240 of 245 feet (73/74 m), it is going to be Wolfgang. When Ben Plucknett comes back to competition, he can be very formidable. He is erratic at times, but just his sheer size, the mass, and the intensity he works within the competition is awesome sometimes. I don't remember that same intensity, or the same quality of throwers, back in the 1950s.'

Was Jay Silvester a very talented thrower?

'Jay Silvester was very good, but he was also erratic in the big competitions. Jay could be rattled.'

You were fourth in the 1980 USA Olympic trials. Do you think that if you had been certain of going to the Olympics if you achieved a place in the first three, that vital motivation would have made you that much hungrier?

'It would definitely have been different, and I would have been more hungry.'

Al narrated to me one of his most satisfying recent performances.

'It was a little competition in Massachusetts where I was travelling with a friend. We saw a sign posted up pointing to a high school field, announcing that there would be a track and field meet there, and that those wishing to compete should show up at six o'clock. The entry fee would be fifty cents. Somebody loaned me a discus, and I just happened to have some jogging shoes with me. I used them and won the competition with something approaching 181 feet (about 55 metres). I won a little trophy for my fifty cents, and it was one of the most satisfying feelings I have ever had. I really felt at last I knew what track and field was all about. The whole thing just happened. It made me realize that the Olympics were not the be-all and end-all any longer. I really enjoyed an evening of competing with a gathering of people who wanted to throw as far as possible, enjoy the competition, and at the same time try to encourage each other to throw further. It was the kind of environment that I totally enjoyed.'

18

IRENA SZEWINSKA

Born Leningrad, 24 May 1946. 1.76/63kg.

Irena Szewinska first entered the bracket of track and field world-class athletes as an eighteen-year-old, Under her maiden name Kirszenstein, she obtained a silver medal in the long jump in the Olympics of 1964, as well as being in Poland's World record-breaking 4×100 team (43.6). Yet Irena was still gaining honours in the top flight in 1978, when she achieved European bronze medals in the 400 and 4×400 relay. Amongst her many successes was being the first woman ever to run inside 50.0 seconds for 400 metres.

Interview 1977

It was at her Warsaw High School at the age of fourteen, that her physical education teacher conducted a class competition over 60 metres. Irena surprised everybody, including herself, by winning in 8.3. Her teacher encouraged her to train and, as her school co-operated with one athletic club, the coach from that club visited the school and arranged afternoon training two or three times per week. One year she trained in the winter as her first competition had been in the autumn. She was fifteen when she high jumped 1.50 metres and clocked 13.6 for 100 metres. The following season she improved to 1.56 for a new Polish Junior record and 12.6 for the 100 metres.

And so to 1964 and the Tokyo Olympics. Joint co-favourites were Mary Rand and Tatyana Schelkanova of Russia, who had progressively upped the world record from 6.48 in 1961 to 6.70 in July 1964. In the event, the Somerset

98

girl won the gold with a new world record of 6.76, but the eighteen-year-old Pole easily defeated the previous World record holder for the silver with 6.60. She followed this up with another silver behind Edith McGuire (USA) in the 100, then anchored the Polish team to a gold in the sprint relay.

In 1965 Irena came to the White City for the British Games in June, and although Mary again beat her by the smallest possible margin in the long jump, she won the 100 yards in a new European record of 10.6. On 9 July she broke Wyomia Tyus's 100 metres World record with 11.1 at Prague, and then on 8 August, Wilma Rudolph's 200 metres record, with 22.7 at Warsaw.

At Budapest in the European Games one year later, she won three golds and one silver, the only defeat being to her compatriot Ewa Kobukowska in the short sprint. She went on to win the 200 in 23.1, the long jump in 6.55, before teaming up with Ewa and two other Poles to win the sprint relay.

1967 was a quieter year, although Irena did win a 'statuette' at the Europe v USA match at Montreal on 9 August for winning the 200 metres.

1968 and the Mexico Olympics. Irena was surprisingly eliminated from the long jump in the preliminary rounds, but made amends with a bronze in the 100 won by Tyus, then a magnificent World record of 22.58 for the gold in the 200. In 1969, she took a sabbatical for the very good reason that she was expecting her first child, then followed two relatively lean years until she re-emerged as a contender at the Munich Games of 1972. The East Germans had improved to a world force by now, and Renate Stecher won the 200 in 22.4, with Australia's Raelene Boyle second in 22.45, with Irena third in 22.74. She also considered 1973 to be a quiet year, yet managed a 11.1 100, 22.7 200, and 52.00 in the 400 metres, a distance she was experimenting with. How successful her experimenting was can be judged by what followed in 1974. On 13 June, she broke the 200 in Potsdam with an automatic timing of 22.20, then nine days later became the first woman to break 50 seconds for 400 metres, with 49.9 at Warsaw. Later in the year at Rome, she regained her 100 and 200 European titles from Renate

Stecher in 11.13 and 22.51.

Another comparatively quiet year followed before the next Olympics at Montreal. Here Irena concentrated on the 400. Christine Brehmer had reduced her World record to 49.77 at Dresden on 9 May, which Irena had further reduced to 49.75 at Bydzoszcy on 29 July. From lane 4, the Polish strider blasted to a scintillating 49.29 to take the gold by over a second in yet another World record. This time it stood for two years, until Marita Koch emerged to break it. Still her great career continued, as in 1977 she won both the 200 and 400 in the first World Cup at Dusseldorf, the former in 22.72 ahead of Barbel Eckert, and the latter in 49.52, with Marita Koch second.

Even this was not the conclusion. She placed third in the European Games at Prague in 1978, before anchoring the Polish team to a bronze in the sprint relay.

She wasn't as tall as either Wilma Rudolph, Fanny Blankers-Koen or Jutta Heine, but she had the ability to use every inch of her stride. A couple of quotes from when I intereviewed her at Dusseldorf in 1977. I asked her who she considered hardest to beat. 'At the beginning of my career, the best were Tyus and McGuire from the USA. Renate Stecher was a very good athlete. When we ran against each other, she was first sometimes and I was first sometimes, which made it very interesting.' I then asked her when she accelerated in the 1977 World Cup 200. Her reply was typically brief: 'From start to finish.' I think that aptly sums up the attitude of a very great athlete.

And for the last time in a major games in 1979 (sixteen years amongst the best), Irena took third place in the 400 in Montreal in 51.15, and was part of the European team that came fourth in the 4 × 400 relay in that World Cup!

19

DAVID HEMERY

When I interviewed Alan Pascoe for the first time in 1969, before he gained a bronze medal that year in the European high hurdles in Athens and went on to become 1974 European and Commonwealth 400 hurdles champion, he said: 'To be quite honest, David Hemery is the main spur, he has been the incentive. He's a tremendous competitor. I don't mind at all really being beaten by David, but my one ambition at the moment is to beat him. I want to be number one.'

One who had definite thoughts on the revolutionary aspect of David Hemery's ideas on training and his World record of 48.1 at the Olympics of 1968 was coach Malcolm Arnold, who advised John Akii-Bua of Uganda, the Olympic intermediate champion of 1972. Arnold said that in 1972, after the AAA's Championship, where David Hemery had a very narrow victory over Akii-Bua at Crystal Palace: 'From then we worked towards the Olympics doing training sessions that included hurdle-by-hurdle practice, working on David Hemery's Mexico touch-downs.' Those comments show the respect people had for the man.

Interviews from 1968 to 1975

David Hemery is one of the finest ambassadors for Great Britain's international athletes. Not only because of his magnificent 1968 Olympics gold medal at 400 metres hurdles, but also his general attitude to those less gifted than himself.

In 1970 David expounded his philosophy to me.

101

'It is not specifically allied to athletics, but the fact that I am a Christian means that it should permeate through whatever I do. I don't like the way some people say, "He is a Christian", as they would say, "He is a doctor", or "He is a lawyer". To me it means simply that I believe in God and happen to think that Christ's philosophy couldn't be bettered. His was a positive attitude towards life.

'My beliefs are not geared to standing up on a soapbox and saying that I am a Christian – that means nothing. I think that if you are living a constructive life and trying to get along with people, you are doing as much as anybody else; the motivation has to come from within, and it's the same with athletics. You can't force someone to train or to try and compete well. It has to come from within, and you can draw it out of them.

'I think everybody has at least one talent. It becomes one's responsibility to develop it, and for me it proved to be athletics. My other interest and I hope talent, is in education. If I don't develop these interests and put myself out to consolidate them, I am letting down myself, my creator, my friends, my coach and the general public. You are put on this Earth for a short time, and it is up to you to make the best of it. Whatever your concept of yourself is, is the way you are. If you see yourself as a prize twit then it is likely that you will start acting that way, but if you see yourself as being helpful to others, it is really fantastic how friendly they are in return. It is just by acting naturally and being friendly to other people.'

It was his father Peter and his brother John who sowed the seeds of his athletic prowess. John was also a Southern Counties hurdler, but ultimately became more interested in all-round fitness than specialization. David's first actual recollection of racing was at the age of ten while at school in Frinton, where he won the 80 yards hurdles. Peter also encouraged both boys to run over the breakwaters at Frinton, which proved invaluable training later in their careers.

The family moved to the USA in 1955, and David won both the 50 and 100 yards in his age group at the Colorado Spring sports meeting. A year later he moved to Thayer Academy High School at Braintree, Massachusetts, and continued to improve athletically and academically. He returned to England in 1962, and met Fred Housden, his coach, confidante and mentor from then on. That year he took sixth place in the Senior AAA 120 hurdles championship, clocking 14.7, almost a second faster than his best performance in the States.

On his return to America, he did virtually no training for twelve months, spending every spare moment studying for his examinations. Then he passed his entrance exam to Boston University, and started running and hurdling again.

David found it very difficult to get going again, after the long lay-off: 'I used to jog around the streets, but felt very sick after a couple of miles. I was certainly on the verge of giving up athletics altogether, and it might have been the end of my athletics career there and then. I didn't know why I felt so bad. Anyway, I kept at it, pushing a little harder each time out, until I began to feel that at last I was getting into shape.

'The most enjoyable part of that period was running along the beach in about a foot of surf. This was a double exercise, and caused me to lift my knees when running. Eventually I could hold a good pace for about 600 yards. The University coach, Billie Smith, felt that with my long stride, good knee lift and background of high hurdling, the 440 yards low hurdles would be my best event. However, the majority of my races that year were over the highs and indoors.'

David and Billie built up an athlete/coach rapport for stamina training, while Fred still advised him on technique by post. Unlike most inter-coach rivalries, Billie and Fred had great respect for each other, and corresponded regularly. David returned to England to win the AAA Junior 120 hurdles title in 1963, then back to the States for more stamina training.

In 1967, David's autumn training prior to the games: 'Our training then included a tremendous variety of work, and I think this made it far easier to assimilate. For example, I used to run about three to five miles in the morning. In the afternoon, either cross-country or very heavy repetition work such as 20×220, 30×200 or 30×220. Every weekend we would go down to the sand

103

dunes or nearby hills, and even tackled a ski slope. Sometimes it took three minutes to run up this mound, and that was some stamina work. From there we progressed to running a 660 and 1000 yards double in indoor meetings.

'On one occasion I can remember running the 600, 1000 and the relay. This work, interspersed with 440 yard relay legs, sharpened me up, and I got down to 48.0 indoors after a flying start on a 160 yards lap track. That, more or less, was the only speed work that I did. More quality work came in the spring, such as 5 × 220 over hurdles, or 3 × 660 flat in around 85.00.

'At times I did just a 2 × 660 in 82.00, or maybe one 660 in 78.00. Another variation was 2 × 550 over hurdles as over-distance stamina work. 660s in fact were almost my whole training, and I would not do any other work on the flat, while any sprint workouts would be over 220 hurdles.'

David's big Olympic pointer was in winning the AAA Championships at White City in 1968. As he indicated then:

'I had been working on the chop-down between thirteen and fifteen strides between hurdles with Fred. This work was done at Crystal Palace, although the Championships were at White City that year, which was very different. The heat was extremely easy, and the thirteen strides were no bother.' After the seventh hurdle David coasted, and if he had run harder would probably have broken 50 seconds. In the final, he started slowly and had to stretch a bit to get the thirteens, though they came in all right. It was not perfect, and he knew that Fred was watching and timing him. The chop-down went fairly well, and the fifteens came in much better than he had hoped (440 yds, 50.2).

'I felt that we had mastered the difficulties, and looked forward to Mexico City. I didn't predict my time there, but naturally hoped to beat 49 seconds, which would be a World record.'

David spent four weeks in Mexico before the Games, so naturally left his speed work until he arrived there. After a week, he had an over-distance run of 660 for acclimatization, but really it was just a stride. One other 660 in the middle of his second week there, but the rest was speedwork of 200 metres over hurdles and a sudden acceleration to the finish.

David takes up the Mexico Olympics story:

'I had a preconceived plan for the heats, semifinal and final, and I hoped they would all work. I aimed for 24.4 at 200 metres, which is fairly slow for a thirteen stride pattern, and managed to hit that exactly in the heat. From there I coasted to the last hurdle, and hoped I would be far enough ahead to qualify. I had to let Frinolli go and, on looking right at the last hurdle, saw there were four men there, with four to qualify. I really had to run hard for the last 150 yards, which was the only real effort I made for 50.3.

'In the semifinal, I hit the first 200 in 23.3 and found myself just with them, so held on and watched from the middle of the ninth hurdle onwards. Whitney had gone out very fast in his heat, and he was in the outside lane. He was the one I was worried about, although Hennige had done a lot of consecutive three-day runs, and was very strong. He was on my right, so I watched Skomarokhov and Knoke fight it out for fourth place out of my left eye, and just made sure that they didn't come past me.

'I was quite surprised that Knoke lost this duel, but Skomarokhov ran very well in the final to prove his point. Incredibly, Garry Knoke's non-qualifying time of 49.6 would have won him the gold medal at Tokyo four years earlier. I think the altitude probably made a difference of about half a second.'

In the final, David ran his own race with his own stride pattern, and in a way was quite isolated.

'I ran it that way throughout the year; it was not that much different, except that I ran the 200 metres a little bit faster. It might have been even faster if it had been a warm day and a dry track. I knew I was under contol, but I had no idea where the others were. I ran very hard, using thirteen strides to the sixth hurdle. I might have continued with thirteens to the seventh hurdle if there had been a wind blowing, a dry track, a warm day, or all three. I was quite surprised with the time, a new world record, 48.1. The only part of the race I criticize myself for was the last 50 yards. I tried to get into a sprint but couldn't, and was waiting for someone to catch me.'

History now records that Gerhard Hennige, John

Sherwood and Geoff Vanderstock were the next to finish in that order, all clocking 49.0. Skomarokhov was 1/10th slower, Whitney and Schubert clocked 49.2, and only Frinolli was tailed off in 50.1.

David Hemery had lane 6 and John Sherwood had the outside lane 8, and Sherwood, who went on to gain a Commonwealth gold in 1970 gives his personal account. 'I decided to go off faster than I had done. Ron Whitney (USA) in lane 7 was very strong in the finishing straight, so I had to get as far away from him as possible. I went fairly fast over the first six in thirteen strides which I had never done before, then cut down to fifteens to take them on the good leg, and I had no idea where I was placed. When someone asked me after the race where I was, I said I was third, fourth or fifth. I had no idea I was so close to second. I could not tell where I was, but I was very pleased with third.'

In 1969, David reverted to 110 hurdles, and straightaway he achieved many things and was rated eighth in the world by the end of the year in *Track and Field News*.

He won races in London, Leicester then London again in 14.1/14.2, then he won with 13.6 in the match v Czechoslovakia, 13.9 in Ostrava, and a windy 13.7 in London again. In the European Games at Athens, he was second behind the great Italian stylist Eddy Ottoz, who had won the bronze at Mexico. In 1970 David had his second 'big' games high hurdles win in Edinburgh, with a good 13.6 victory over Australian Don Baird. (He also won in 1966)

In 1971, David had no competition but decided, despite being rusty, to defend his 400 metres hurdles title at the 1972 Olympics at Munich.

Despite his pessimism, he was less than half a second slower than when he broke the world record in Mexico City. It took another World record, from John Akii-Bua of Uganda, to displace him as Olympic champion, and Ralph Mann pushed him out of the runner-up position by one-hundredth of a second.

As David recalled later: 'I went too fast too soon in Munich between hurdles two and three. I accelerated extremely hard at this point and paid for it when I reached the home straight. John saw me ahead and resurged after the sixth hurdle, then ignored the rest of the barriers and ran flat out from there. He deserved his new 47:82 World record.'

Akii-Bua's own account follows: 'David started building speed from the sixth hurdle. I changed to fourteens. Ralph Mann was caught at the fifth, then, when they were going for the sixth, Hemery went past him. We were coming up faster. I wanted to take the tenth with my right leg, and that is what happened. To the finish I had that nice body lean, and think I could have gone even faster if they had put me outside lane 1.'

How important was winning to David? 'It has taken a whole chapter in my book to try and explain this one. Before Mexico, I had come to terms with the fact that it would not be the end of the world if I did not win. I was desperately trying to win for my coach, my family and all my loyal supporters. I was trying just as hard at Munich, but Akii was in the situation of desperately wanting to prove that a Ugandan could be the best in the world, and would have been absolutely shattered if he had not won. Perhaps the adrenalin count of being terrified of not winning was different from just wanting desperately to win.'

Munich, 2 September at 16.14.

1. John Akii-Bua, 47.82, WR. 2. Ralph Mann (USA), 48.51. 3. David Hemery, 48.52.

How did he see his role in his athletic career that he had enjoyed so much?

'It had been one of the largest tools in my self-development. One learns a lot about oneself and life. It's a mini-world, and if you can learn to face up to your strengths and your weaknesses and work on them, sport is an excellent avenue for self-expression, self-awareness and personal growth. Also it makes one physically very fit, running being the most demanding of all sports.'

After his last non-professional race over 400 metres in Paris, a headline appeared in the *Sunday Telegraph* over Peter Hildreth's article, entitled 'The Last Flight of a Rare Bird.' A fitting tribute, and one that summed it all up.

20

RON CLARKE

Born Melbourne, 21 February, 1937. 5ft 11½ins/160lbs.

Interviews 1965 and 1970

The most admired distance runner from 5000 to the Marathon during the last twenty-five years was not Lasse Viren, Miruts Yifter, Alberto Cova or any other successful big Games winners, but Ron Clarke. The tall, suntanned Australian who set junior World best times for 1500/one mile and two miles in 1956 and then, in the 1960s, twenty-one world records, from two miles to 20,000 metres.

He took no less than 26.2 seconds off Sandor Iharos's world time for six miles, and when you realize that he ran 27:39.4 for 10,000 metres on cinders back in 1965, there is no doubt that he was ahead of his time and would be up there with the best if he was competing today.

His medal tally on the big occasions was scarcely insignificant either. A silver medal in the 1962 Commonwealth Games three miles in a strong field. (1. Murray Halberg, 13:34.2. 2. Ron Clarke, 13:36.3. 3. Bruce Kidd, 13:36.4. 4. Bruce Tulloh, 13:37.8. 5. Alby Thomas, 13:40.6. 6. Eddy Strong, 13:41.4) Olympic bronze in the 1964 10,000, silver medals in the 1966 Commonwealth Games at Kingston for three and six miles, plus another silver in the Edinburgh Commonwealth 10,000 in 1970. Yet cynics, much of the media at the time, and worst of all, some of his own countrymen thought of him, to a great extent, as a failure because he did not come away with a gold medal. But to use the title of this book, *It's More Than Winning*, that has gained Ron the respect he richly deserves.

In my opinion, Ron Clarke was one of the finest gentleman ambassadors of the sport. I am far from being alone in thinking that. Let us just take a small cross section of distance runners to back me up.

Dick Taylor – of the great Coventry Godiva club – who was National cross-country champion, bronze medallist behind Clarke in the 1970 Edinburgh Games, and who once beat Ron at Crystal Palace: 'Ron Clarke has got to be the greatest. You don't have twenty-one world records if you are not something a bit special. I would personally give my right arm just for one.'

Pan-American Games champion at 5000/10,000, Rik Van Nelson (USA) who ran in Mexico with Ron: 'I think Clarke was great at the 5000 and the 10,000. Kip Keino trained more on speed for the mile, while Clarke trained for the longer distances. You didn't often see Keino running the 10,000.'

Taff Davies, now fifty-three years old, and a world-class veteran runner, who has represented the Army about 105 times, retorted: 'I used to will him to win. I remember watching him going through agonies in the altitude of Mexico City, and I really was willing him to win then, even though I felt he was not going to. I think he was a "Gentleman" athlete and a great runner.'

Another 'Gentleman' athlete is the 1983 World and, Commonwealth Marathon champion Rob De Castella, and his attitude to his own countryman is interesting: 'I have admired a lot of Ron's approach towards running, and tried to model myself, to a certain extent, on some of those attitudes. He was a very honest, a very open sort of a runner. He would not go into a race and sell himself short. Every time he put his foot on the track he put himself on the line and ran a good hard race.'

Now let's go revisiting those days when Clarke was dominating the world's tracks. I interviewed Ron Clarke in 1965, the day after he smashed the world three-mile record at the White City track, and then again in 1970 at the end of the Commonwealth Games in Edinburgh. But before that I will tell you what inspired me to write again about this phenomenal Australian athlete.

One lunchtime in November 1983, I was running hard along the Embankment, trying to keep up with two friends. To my amazement, jogging the other way was the grey tracksuited figure of Ron Clarke. I shouted out: 'Ron Clarke!' The wave and smile from Ron was like a shot in the arm, I increased my pace and caught my two friends inside another half mile with the memories flooding back. Ron Clarke, the King of Pace, running away from many an international field.

How about the lack of sprint? Ron replies: 'I had never been with Temu or Wolde on the last lap when I have not been able to pick thirty yards on them. In Mexico they ran a ridiculous last lap of 57.4 – something they could never do at sea level. At other times I have entered the straight against Jazy, Keino and others who are all well-known sprinters, been behind them and thought myself beaten – then won the race on a last sprint.'

I asked Ron when did he feel he was at his best as a performer? 'The 10,000 metres in Tokyo. I think I ran that race as well as my fitness allowed – and that is really the aim of an athlete. For my state of fitness then, I ran more than forty seconds faster than I had done three weeks earlier. I got more absorbed in the real tactical battle than in any other race – before or since.

'What would have given me the greatest satisfaction of all, I think, would have been the 1968 Olympic race – if it had been at sea level. I was fitter than I had been in 1964. My fittest period – my "peak" – was between 1965 and 1968 inclusive.'

The two races that stand out in my mind were the 1964 Olympic 10,000 and his three-mile world record in 1965. At Tokyo on 14 October, the Olympic 10,000 metres was the most exciting race over that distance I have ever witnessed. The weather was cloudy, but the race was a sparkler.

Thirty-eight runners started. At 1000 metres the leaders were Gerry Lindgren, Billy Mills and Mohamed Gammoudi together in 2:42.0, just a step or two ahead of Ron Clarke (2:42.2) with Leonid Ivanov, Mamo Wolde and Tony Cook together a few yards behind. Billy Mills was leading at 5000 in 14:04.6, with Ron Clarke on 14:05.0, Mamo Wolde 14:06.0, and Mohamed Gammoudi in 14:07.0.

By the last lap there were just Clarke, Gammoudi and Mills left in it, each one stabbing for victory in that final lap, with Mills (28:24.4) just sprinting ahead of Gammoudi (28:24.8) and Clarke (28:25.8) in the last fifty metres.

Billy Mills was born in Pine Ridge, Dakota, half Sioux Indian: 'I started training last February (1964) and I thought, possibly, I could win then! When the race had started, I was under the impression that any one of ten could win the race. Of course, I was one of the ten. After dropping the pack and realizing that Murray Halberg and some of the other great runners were not with us – with only five laps to go – I was fairly sure of getting a medal and a great chance of it being a gold medal.

'I had made up my mind before the race started, to go with the leaders. I knew almost definitely that Clarke would be one of the leaders, and also counted on Halberg being there. Once Clarke moved, I was prepared to go with him. I was not anticipating quite such a fast first 5000, but once everybody else dropped and I was still there, I knew it was a matter of hanging on for a couple of laps, and it started coming "easy" again.

'I actually feel I was just as much in control of the race from the 5000 mark as Clarke, although he led for most of the time. In the last lap, I think Clarke found himself in a box, we were lapping a runner while I was at his shoulder, I think he momentarily panicked and he had three choices what to do. One, he could have stopped and come around. Two, was to speed up and go out, but I would not let him out because I had him on the inside – I was doing nothing illegal. His third choice was to push me out, and I think he momentarily may have panicked and did push. I was bumped and, to me, I think it was unintentional.

'I was bumped out, and Gammoudi had his momentum going so the only thing he could do was to break through or else stop dead.'

Second home was Tunisian Mohamed Gammoudi, a highly underrated athlete who achieved not only a silver in Tokyo but a gold and bronze in Mexico and a silver again in Munich! He talked to me in Mexico in 1968.

Mohamed was born 2 November 1938. His career as an athlete began at the age of twenty, when he was in the

Tunisian Army in Physical Education. Two years later, he made the Tunisian team at cross-country. He was 5000/10,000 Mediterranean champion before going to the Tokyo Games. 'I thought I would finish about fifth or sixth. I was very nervous and had not slept for three days before the event, whereas in Mexico when I won the gold for 5000, I felt stronger and more confident. At the bell in the final I knew I was going to win, though it was a tough race until the last stride.'

Thirdly, Ron Clarke's comments about the Tokyo race: 'I think the move that won the race was when Billy Mills got knocked back behind. Straight away he "hit the trail" on us. To my mind, anyone who comes off the bend with two blokes in front of him has a tremendous advantage. Billy was knocked when he was already going pretty hard for home, I think, and it put him behind in what proved to be the most advantageous position.

'We both later ran together in Oslo and talked about that point, but even now neither of us is really sure exactly what happened. I always looked forward to the next race.

'What people always say in post mortems is, "If . . ." If one had done this or that, so-and-so would have happened. That Joe Bloggs was unlucky, etc. etc. These are all ifs. The thing is that Bob Schul won the 5000 in Tokyo and Billy Mills the 10,000 and no-one can take their medals away from them. They have achieved something which is the greatest in athletics. To win a gold medal is an athlete's crowning achievement, his real ambition in life.

'I had not done it, but it was still an aim. I had not the burning desire to solely win an Olympic gold medal. I have a bronze, and my ambition was merely to keep improving – to keep running faster and faster. To my mind, there is only one thing certain in life and that is what is past, what has been achieved – one can only improve on that. For an athlete, the race is the fulfilment of his or her ideals, training is but purely for racing and nothing more. That, in a nutshell, is what track and field athletics is all about.'

My second race was when Ron broke the World three-mile record at the White City; the first man ever to run under 13 minutes for the distance, doing 12:52.4 on 10 July, 1965. Second was Gerry Lindgren, 13:04.0, and third, Lajos

112

Mecser, 13:07.6.

Talking to me the day after in Brighton, Ron candidly remarked: 'The training for that race can be calculated to have been building up over the last two years, not merely weeks or days prior to the event. One thing, though, is the fact that I had only been getting just about five hours sleep a night on tour in the days beforehand, and I had been feeling very tired since I arrived in London. When it came to the actual race, I didn't feel at all good at the start, and in fact felt more than usually tired throughout it.

'After the gun had gone, I just kept thinking of winning, and that alone. I was not out for any particular time, but to beat the field – and run faster than ever. I was very scared of what Lindgren might do during the race, and wondered also about Mike Wiggs. On the second lap I looked at Mike, and he didn't look too good, or seem to be running well, so I decided to go hard all the way. I had a couple of good hard looks at Gerry, to see how fit he looked, and decided to test him out.

'I was surprised to have gone through the first mile in 4:15.0. I knew it was fairly nippy, but I had Gerry pushing me hard and we were both committed to a hard run all the way. After the two miles mark I tried hard to shake him off, and was still worried about his presence a great deal. I heard the times for each lap, but in fact they did not really mean a great deal to me. I suppose they must be useful to someone who thinks all the while about intermediate times, and where he lost that second – worrying that he is going too fast, and so on. For myself, never training with a watch, and never analysing the lap times, I feel I run much easier not running for time, as so many others do.'

Let us now take a look at Ron Clarke's training. In 1965 he achieved world records at six miles (26:47.0), ten miles (47:12.8) and 10,000 metres (27:39.4). 'My daily routine (at home) runs something like this. My son Marcus wakes me at 6.00 a.m., when I go for a run of three to four miles and follow up with about fifteen minutes weight training and a shower. After breakfast I leave for the office and am at my desk by 8.30 a.m. When lunch-time comes around – I get seventy-five minutes break – I run about six miles before my meal, sometimes less.

'At 5.15 p.m. when I finish working, I go home and do the little things there are to be done around the house and, after turning out the children's lights, I prepare for my main session of the day, which usually begins at about 8.30 p.m. when the evening is fairly cool, and lasts for about ninety minutes.

'The lunchtime run helps me mull over the problems (he was a company secretary) I may come across during the course of my work. I think that most businessmen would benefit from a long walk of about an hour at midday; they would feel far more refreshed and ready for the afternoon's work, instead of a heavy lunch, drinks and cigars. I shall most certainly aim to do something of the sort when I retire from competitive athletics – as well as taking up golf.'

In 1970, when Ron was at the close of his career, he told me: 'The amount of my training has always been exaggerated by people. It's not their fault, it's mine, because when I have been asked, "How do you train?" I have given them my ideal training – four or five miles in the morning and twelve or fifteen miles at night – and they have automatically done their arithmetic, assuming that I have done that every day, and they come up with a total of about 140 miles a week. Two or three days a week I do not get the time to do anything like that. I may finish at business at 6.00 or 6.30 p.m. in the evening, and just not feel like training. I might go out and do eight miles hard, or I might do some speed work. My training has always contained the usual ingredients of any schedule and has always depended on how I felt, what my business or social arrangements were, when I was likely to finish a particular job and where I was working. It has never been as organized as I would have liked.'

In 1970 he said: 'I only trained in the lunch hour for a four or five week period some years back when I was helping my brother to get fit for his footballing. Other than that, I have never run in the lunch hour. For one reason, there is not enough time in an hour to fit in a training run and a good lunch, and for another I don't see the sense in running three times a day, three sessions are useless.'

Ron Clarke is now the managing director of the City Sports Club in London, and enjoys working in sport here and in Australia. Those of us who are Ron Clarke followers were worried when he had major heart surgery a few years ago, but now he is in good form and enjoying a healthy life again. After spotting him on the Embankment, I went back to my 1970 tapes and listened again to his account of his beginnings and his attitude to races.

'When I first took an interest in athletics at school, the system was that one automatically played cricket and football, plus cross-country running. One could also compete in athletics during the three weeks in which they staged the school sports.

'So, from the very start, at the age of seven or eight, I did all four things. I always ran the sprints in the school sports and won. That was as far as one was allowed to run at that age. Through the various growing-up stages my main interests always were cricket and football, right through to the age of fourteen; I followed the same pattern – cricket and football, some cross-country and always the school sports sprint races, which I continued to win.

'Then, on the first occasion I was allowed to compete in the "distance" events, I won those too, as well as the cross-country races. My brother had been a better runner than me (we since discovered that he had also run faster times, although we were never interested in actual times at that age), and was a better footballer than me.

'My next major step was when I moved to Melbourne High School for Matriculation. I found that they were much more interested in athletics there, and more aware of the values of performances and times; they even had records. I had no idea at the time how fast I was running, or what events I was best at, and when the school house sports came around, I competed in every running event from the 100 yards to the mile on one afternoon – and broke the under-sixteen 880 yards and mile records.

'That year I was having my best year at cricket, but at the same time I was becoming increasingly interested in running. So much so, that on one occasion when I ran a good race, Gerry Tickle (a good footballer at the school, who was also very interested in athletics) persuaded me to compete in an inter-club track meeting, and posed the problem of how I was going to combine the two. (My father

115

had recently given me a new cricket bat, and I was regularly playing for the school).

'I tried running in various inter-club meetings, as by this time my interest in running was increasing even more – I had won the local open school sports events, as well as the all-schools title. I would go down to the race then dash back to the school cricket match; I still did not train at all for athletics.

'In the end, because my running escapades were interfering so much with my cricket obligations, it became apparent that I had to make a decision as to which sport was going to come first. One example I can give of this interference was that one day I had promised to meet a girl at a club race due to be run at 4.10p.m. that afternoon; I was already batting for the school cricket team and had batted right through the afternoon. I tried my best to make that appointment, even to the extent of giving very easy catches, but they were all dropped, and I stayed at the batting crease.

'It was inevitable that some definite decision as to my future allegiances had to be made. My brother Jack did most of the persuading to ensure I was lost to cricket: "As you are the Victoria State Junior Champion, you should be a runner, not a cricketer", he said.

'I was convinced. But you see, Alastair, I might so easily have made my name as a cricketer instead of an athlete – it was quite on the cards. However, into athletics I went.

'I still did not do any training, and I had a bad arm action. Jack gave me the once-over, and said, "You had better not do too much training until you get a decent coach, because your arm action is so bad that if you do much training now, the movement will only become ingrained into your running action and will always affect your style."

'One afternoon, soon after this serious talk with my brother, I went down to see Percy Cerutty at Corfu racecourse. We did not have a car, and it took us about one and a half hours to travel all the way to Corfu by train. My brother and father came with me. Cerutty's reputation was on its highest at the time, and when we met him there he had a group of youngsters training hard. He told every one of them that they could all make world champion milers.

'That statement put me on my guard right at the start. I didn't like it very much, because I thought that as some people had such talent, others had not, and there would be some disappointed ones in the bunch. He said to me, "All of them can make it," then he said that all they had to do was increase their stride length by two or three inches a stride, and with the same amount of effort they would run 25 seconds faster.

'That seemed reasonable to me since, if you do increase your stride length added to your natural effort and you keep it going, you would quite obviously run a good deal faster. To demonstrate this, he said that I had a short stride – which I knew – and he said, "I've got a much longer stride, and I am half your size.' Then he went and made a mark on the ground, made me run over it to measure my stride length. Then he ran over it to demonstrate his greater stride length – but he went much further back from the line than I did and came tearing down over the line. Of course, he produced a longer stride, but, as he got to the line he did a sort of a jump. I thought, "There's something wrong here if he has to illustrate his theory in this way." So I clamped up then and said no more. I didn't see him again, although he did write to me later that year, asking me to go down to his camp and learn more.

'In the meantime, however, I had met John Landy and Neil Robbins. I decided after talking to them about running that I wouldn't go down and see Percy again. I think for a while he said that he threw me out for some reason or other. Since then we tended not to get in each other's way too often, although we were always fairly cordial to one another whenever we met.

'Christmas of the next year – after having played football that winter – was when I started training. I met Neil Robbins, and he took me for my first training session at Essdenden football ground, where my father was the groundkeeper. We ran some repetition 220s – about the only training session I can remember. I ran against Herb Elliot in the January, in Adelaide at the Australian Championships, and a very hot day it was. I was sixteen and Herb was fifteen years old – it was an under-nineteen mile

117

race. Herb beat me by about a second, 4:20.0 to 4:21.0 or something like that, after I got a bit of a break on him in the third lap. He caught me in the last lap and beat me in the run-in.

'The next year, when I was running better and went to Franz Stampfl for advice, Herb had an accident – he dropped a piano on his foot – and did not run that year, so I did not have a chance to race against him at the time when I was running well.

'I don't like to hear of young athletes deciding to switch coaches. Sometimes an athlete will start working with a coach and then, simply because someone else has succeeded with another coach – and they personally have not succeeded as much as they had hoped – they blame their coach and criticize his methods and switch. I like to see the athlete with a good, personal relationship with his coach, so that they can work things out between them, and the athlete respecting the coach who has encouraged and helped him.

'If you start with someone and have respect for his ideas, I don't think that you would lose that respect for him easily, no matter what happens – if you have made a proper judgement in the first instance. If you lose that confidence in him after all (perhaps you never really had it in the first place?) and you decide that a switch is best, then that may be all right – once – because in your immaturity you may have picked the wrong person. But if you find that you want to switch again – I would not hesitate to say, "It is you. You need to take a very good look at yourself, you are probably blaming the coach for your own weaknesses."

'The main thing is the progression – in speed. The shorter the distance, the better I enjoy it – providing the pace is fast and it's an honestly run race; I dislike intensely anyone who just sits in with a weak field. I think there is a place for every man in a race, and if a man with a fast finish can win by not leading at all and kicking at the end, that is correct tactics. It is thus up to the others in the field to try and burn him off. But when a man with a fast finish is running in a weak field, and just sits in, knowing all along that he can win the race, to my mind he is not using his ability fully, and therefore there must be some "kink" in his approach to athletics.

'My training consists mainly of long runs; sometimes I train alone, other times with Trevor Vincent and Tony Cook. Each Sunday there is quite a school of us training together. I used to run for Melbourne High School Old Boys, but switched to my present club in Australia, Glenhuntly, because there was a much stronger interest in distance running. I reckon we must have the best distance running club in the world for, besides myself, there is Pat Clohessy (now coach to Rob de Castella), Trevor Vincent, Tony Cook and John Coyle, all of whom can run inside 13:35 for three miles.'

As readers will know, in those days that was a very creditable three-mile time. Before Ron went to Mexico, where the altitude became a problem to nearly all the low country distance runners, he achieved a world record two miles of 8:19.6.

In that Olympic year, he won highly competitive races in London, Stockholm, Los Angeles, Oslo and Melbourne. That was just one of those years, from 1965 to 1968, when he considers he was at his peak. Even now, many people look back and say, 'There was a runners' runner.' A frontiersman opening up a pathway for others to follow. Many have come and gone, but it seems the magical exploits of Ron Clarke will live on, long after the 1992 Barcelona Olympic flame dies down.

21

JUHA VAATAINEN

Born Oulu, 12 July 1941. 61kg/9st 8lbs. 1.72/5ft 7¾ins.

Juha Vaatainen to some extent revolutionized the thinking towards future 10,000 metre running, because in his career he had been able to match strides with 400/800/1500 men in competition. That gave him the essential armoury to detonate the opposition in a last lap sprint in a Big Games 10 km final.

The flowing, blond-haired Finn ran a 54:00 to get rid of twice European 10km champion Jurgen Haase and Dave Bedford (who had led for twenty of the twenty-five laps) in the 1971 European 10,000 final in Helsinki. Vaatainen's last lap was nearly ten seconds faster than any of the other twenty-four!

Interview 1971

'The whole Finnish nation is sports-minded, from the youngest to the oldest, so it was quite natural that as my Mother and Father too liked sport a great deal, I would also be enthusiastic; for as long as I can remember, I have been running, skiing, playing basketball and so on, but it was not until I was sixteen years old that I actually began training for running.

'I lived with my family – including two brothers and a sister – in a little village named Haadavese, about 600 kilometres north of Helsinki; I was more interested in skiing than anything else really, and of course it is the national sport in Finland. I can remember the 1952 Olympic Games, which were staged in our capital, and especially Barthel of

Luxembourg; he was from a small country, and was so happy-looking after his victory in the 1500 metres. I can remember too, in July 1957, a great 1500 metres race in Turku, when Salonen ran a World record; Salsola was second, Vuorisala third and Dan Waern of Sweden fourth. These sort of memories always come back so vividly when thinking of earlier days, I suppose because they had such a great effect on my outlook at the time, and prompted me to take running more seriously. My standard of running at that time was 1000 metres in 3:46.0. I was absolutely nothing then, as I was smoking and drinking too much, and not training anyway.

'I have always been a loner in training. I did have a coach, later, but he is dead now. I started my running alone, and nearly always have run alone. Sometimes I do run with other fellows however, but not very often, because I always seem to be nervous when I am running with others; I find that my training goes the wrong way and I am tense, and always thinking about what my training partner is doing. It is essential to stay relaxed at all times as an athlete, and I am very conscious of this. Maybe you noticed the way I come into the stadium: I run differently to the others, running further round the track, and faster; my warm-up and everything is different: only one thing is the same . . . I run in the same race.'

You say you started training for athletics at the age of sixteen, and that your best performance at that time was 3:46.0 for 1000 metres. How did things turn out after a year of taking it seriously?

'Well, things turned out quite good for me. At the end of my first real season, I had clocked 12.0 seconds for 100 metres, 53.7 for 400 and 2:43.0 for 1000 metres; that was 1958, after having stopped smoking and drinking in the February of that year. I continued training and racing cross-country, developing a real interest in running, and was looking forward to my next season. Then, tragedy for me: I was involved in an accident with a tractor, and broke my leg. This put me completely out of running for the whole of the 1959 season. I did not lose my keenness, however, and started training again in the autumn, probably with even more determination to make up for the last year. In 1960, I

121

won the Finnish Junior intermediate hurdles title, as well as improving on my flat times – 11.1 (100 m), about 51.0 (400 m) and one 800 metres in 1:59.9.

'Next year I broke my knee, so did nothing. Then the following year, 1962, I went into the army for national service, and although I kept up a reasonable amount of training, I only competed twice, in relays. The following year I decided to concentrate my efforts on the 800 metres, and came sixth in the Finnish championships of 1963, with 1:52.0. In 1964 I had to have an operation on a broken achilles tendon, but after it was better I was running again. I suppose that once it gets in your blood, it doesn't matter what problems you have; you still came back to running, if you are able. Anyway I was still a relatively short-distance runner, I was competing too in six-kilometre cross-country races, and came second in the national championship.'

So now, at last, you seemed to be getting somewhere. How did things go for you the next year, 1966?

'Not so good. I was doing quite well in cross-country running though, and in fact raced as far as twelve kilometres. On the track I was relegated to third place in the Finnish 800 metres championship, but ventured into the 1500 metres, and came second. I had a coach then, and he was really good for me. He was a school teacher, Mr Meskaes. It seemed easy for him to know what I should do in training: he got to learn everything about me, not just the running angle, but my complete background – my home life, work, eating (and drinking!), social life – girlfriends and so on, and psychological needs. He insisted that I work out my own training programme, however, and only afterwards did he discuss it with me, advising what was right or wrong. I know that there are many coaches who discuss training schedules very carefully with their protégés, so that the athletes understand the rights or wrongs about training, and can see the commonsense in the schedules, but there is also the danger that many coaches can be dogmatic about their methods without the young athlete really understanding clearly what they are doing, and why. Meskaes and I worked on the first approach, but with me planning the basic work.

'In 1967, I followed up my longer work of the winter with

more speed work than I had done before, concentrating my efforts on improving my best performances. This worked out well, and I ended the season with times of 10.9 (100 m), 22.1 (200 m), about 48.4 (400 m), 1:48.0 something (800 m), and one 1500 metres of 3:46.0. Next year was Olympic year, and I desperately wanted to go to the Olympic Games in Mexico, but I was just not good enough for the 800 metres. My last 200 metres in races was always my strong point, but overall my times were not very fast. I had been lucky enough to race against people such as Arese, Szordykowsky and others over 1500 metres, and some of the World's best 800 metres runners, such as Kiprugut and Matuschewski; so many outstanding athletes come to Finland to compete, especially before the Olympic Games and European Championships, so I was lucky in that respect.'

Did it help you, Juha, in the longer-distance events to know that you had competed with athletes of such great standing?

'Yes, it did. But the change came when my coach died in 1968, and I found myself alone again. I thought long and hard about what I should do now, and decided that maybe I should try the longer distances, and I subsequently trained with that in mind, and in 1969 I competed in my first 10,000 metres. There's a little story behind that, which you might be interested in, Alastair. In Finland, the press, radio and TV people always show a great interest in athletics, because everybody in the country is interested in it, and so one reads and hears a great deal about athletes who are not just internationals, or World record-breakers. I was so confident in my own ability by now, that although I had not yet run a 10,000 metres in competition, I felt quite capable of competing in the following week's international match versus Norway, but the Finnish Federation said I could not, and this really made me angry, as I knew I was in good shape. I said on TV three days before the match that I could run below 29 minutes (our national record was 29:07.0, and Kuha the steeplechase World record holder held it), and of course many people thought I was crazy since I had not run a 10,000 metres before. Anyway, on the same day the international took place in Helsinki, and Risa from Norway won the 10,000 in 29.58, I raced in my home town over the same distance, and clocked 28.53 – on my own!

'In 1970, I got my 10,000 metres team place in the match against France, and did 28:19.0, and three days later won the World Games event in Helsinki, beating guys like Dick Taylor, Sharafetdinov, Andre de Hertoghe and Gaston Roelants; Taylor, ten days earlier, had run a fast 5000 metres in about 13.26, but in Helsinki we ran a slow early race, with Taylor making his effort with five laps to go. I was waiting the whole time, because I knew he could run faster (my best 5000 was only 13.43), but with 300 metres to go I was able to respond easily to his effort, and after going away from him won the race by a clear six seconds. But now, here we are in Helsinki, a year later, and with 27:52.8. . . .'

Tell me more about the training buildup to these championships It didn't just happen, did it? You must have planned and trained for a long time, to achieve such fine performances.

'Oh yes, I trained harder than before, and with greater variety, but still nothing but running: long-distance work, speed work, tempo-training; it would take me a month to describe it, and then it would only be training to suit myself, very individual training. I was not a born runner, you see. I was short, and fat, and had to work out special training, just for me.'

You met Lydiard at one time, didn't you? Did he influence you in any great respect?

'I met him a couple of times, yes. He was coaching in Finland for some time. But my contact with him was not concerned with running, purely social. I do not think that he was right as far as the Finns were concerned. He thought Finland would be like New Zealand, and tried to apply his methods directly to what was a quite different country. I think that we need to have our own system specially for Finland, and we have, and now you can see the results. England is different, New Zealand is different, and so is every other country in their special characteristics and personalities. I feel, again, that I need a system just for me; quite different to that for anybody else. I have found that long distance running has benefitted me most, and I enjoy it. I like sets of 200s and 400s (because I was earlier an 800 metres runner) and tempo-change training. Today anyway, my training is much different than it was a few years ago.'

You are a schoolteacher, but have recently spent some time in South America. This period was not solely for training, or was it?

'I was teaching in a small Finnish colony in Brazil. The children there can speak our language but cannot write it, as they speak Portuguese. I went there as a schoolteacher, specifically to help teach them to write Finnish, during their summer vacation. The whole experience was very good for my mind: it gave me time to think, and time to train in a quite different environment. I spent about two hours a day with the young people, and was thus able to train two or three times a day for the whole time I was there – from mid-March to mid-June – which I had taken as a holiday, although I was paid sufficiently to live during my period there. At home in Finland, I am a teacher in an elementary school in Oulu, some 600 or so kilometres from Helsinki, in Geography, Mathematics and all kinds of subjects.'

How many times a week do you train?

'About fifteen to twenty times a week. Whilst I am teaching in Finland my first session had to be at about 6 a.m. in the morning, and lasts for about seventy to ninety minutes. Then I must go to school, and from 8.30 I teach for six or seven hours and then go back home and I start my second training run from school; it lasts for about an hour, sometimes more, depending on how I feel, or what type of running I am doing. Then I have a meal, and go out again at about 10 p.m. in the evening. Usually this third session lasts about an hour, maybe less. Sometimes I am tired, naturally, but during my holidays I try to vary the sessions as much as possible: morning, hard; mid-day, easy; evening, hard. I prefer morning training and am much fresher, as more often than not I am too tired in the evening.'

You did a fast 10,000 metres before the Games of 28:12.8, which put you second in the European ranking list. Where did you do that?

'In my home town of Oulu. Tuominen was 25 seconds behind me, and Viren (whom I coach) was third. It was terrible weather, really windy, and raining, and I said I could run half a minute aster.'

So you actually coach Viren?

'With Viren, it is something more than just coaching, as he is my good friend. I help him and he helps me. When I make out his training programme, we usually adapt it so that we can adjust our programmes to train together: it is teamwork.'

Now for the 10,000 metres: who did you think your rivals would be, and who did you expect to be the most dangerous?

'I thought as far back as two years ago that Hasse would be my biggest rival, as I knew him very well, and knew a great deal about him. You have seen his running a few times, I expect. He is clever, and he runs like a machine; his running looks very nice, and he has an economical style. David is too young. Maybe after some months or years he can be champion, but just now he is too young, and he was too nervous. I was only really worried about Haase.'

Did you expect Bedford to surge, to run out ahead like he did?

'One never knows what to expect of one's new opponents. But his tactics were a mistake, because it does not help to just run hard ahead for twenty metres or so, it should be a longer sustained effort. He was nervous, and must learn to run longer and faster; this is why he cannot run fast last laps. He must learn to be easy, easy, easy – and relax; he was very tense.'

Do you think he is not capable of being able to run fast enough in the last laps?

'It is a difficult thing to say who is fast or who is slow, or how one will run a race. Nobody knows. It is, after all, twenty-five laps long!'

What about the 5000 metres? Did you think you would win?

'After 3500 to 4000 metres, maybe; with a lap to go, I was almost sure I might be able to do it again, but Wadoux and Norpoth are really good, and I thought – I must be careful of these guys. Wadoux is fast. I know him very well, in fact he is a good friend of mine, and has been to my home town three times, and tomorrow we are going there again together for some racing – and hunting wild duck. Perhaps I know him too well, for I can follow him in his last 500 metres or so, and I can beat him.'

What other things do you enjoy besides running?

I like to be with my family, and have a normal life. I like music and the things that most people do. I try to be as normal as other people; something other than just a runner. I like to be like my brothers and sister. There's one thing I must tell you, I had a telegram yesterday from America, congratulating me on my Helsinki performances, and offering me a scholarship for the next twelve months if I go and study in the USA at some University or other, but I am staying in Finland to teach, and follow my career in education here.'

22

DAVE WOTTLE

Born 7 August 1950. Home town, Canton, Ohio. 1.85/6ft
0¾ins. 63kg/140lbs.

Dave Wottle, who raced in a white golfing cap, was
nicknamed 'The Head Waiter' because of leaving his
stretch-kick till so late in his races.

In 1972, he went to the Olympics in Munich to compete
in his favourite distance, the 1500, as well as the 800, which
was the event he equalled the World record of 1:44.3 in the
American Olympic trials.

In the Olympic 800 he went from easily last after 200
metres, to fourth place on entering the final straight, then
the famous 'Wottle throttle' was in evidence as he accelerated, catching the favourite, European champion Yevgeniy
Arzhanov in the last few metres. His finishing time was
1:45.89. The man who led through the 400 in 52.3, Mike
Boit, was third (1:46.01), and Franz Josef Kemper next
(1:46.50). But, to the shock of those watching Dave Wottle,
he tried the same sort of tactics in the semi-final of the
1500, and got up just too late to qualify for the final, where
he would definitely have been a factor; still, the man with
the cap had already captured the imagination of the
athletics world. One of his good miles the following year
was winning in Oregon in 3.53 from that other character
Steve Prefontaine, who achieved a personal best of 3:54.6.

Interview 1972

How did you get into competition?
   'It was in my Freshman year in high school, in Ohio.

They were having a track meet, so I decided I would try something. I signed for the 100, 220 and 440. They were all sprint races, because I did not know anything about distances. I was fourteen years old at the time, and after a few workouts the coach saw I was not a sprinter but that I could stay up with the distance men in two-mile jogs. So he just put me in with the distance men, half milers, and my first race was an 880 and I ran 2.13. It was not too good, but I got third place.'

You must have been influenced by a coach, then?

'Our coach was basically a sprinter in college and he knew a lot about sprinting, but he did not know a lot about distance running and training in high school, so I did not really learn anything about training. I only put in twenty miles a week, and I ran mainly on my natural ability.'

What were your first championships?

'In my senior year in high school, I won the State Meet in the mile. I was basically a miler, I did not get to the "State" in the half, as I had been eliminated in the District Meet. My fastest was 1:59.3 at the time. In the mile I won the District, Regional and State. I ran 4.26 in the District, 4.22 in the Regionals, and 4:20.2 in the State, which was my fastest time in high school.'

As you were progressing, were you inspired by any of the top runners?

'I was not really a track fan. I did not know anything about track. I only knew the Ohio high school runners, and I had heard about Ryun. My mum was always reading out from the papers – Jim Ryun did this, Jim Ryun did that! So I kind of admired him.'

You must have had a breakthrough, then?

'It would be winning the State, because after that I was offered a Scholarship to Bowling Green, so I decided to keep it up. In that race I had to come from about twenty yards down in the last 220 to win right at the line. It was a pretty big breakthrough.'

Did you then meet a coach who was important to your future?

'It was at college that I met Mel Brodt, and I am still under him right now. He uses the "Moderated Marathon System" that Snell used, and he is a very good coach, very

129

intelligent about track. He plans all my workouts, and I have great faith in his judgement.'

You were seventeen in your first year in college. Have you any memories of that year at Bowling Green?

'I was really glad I got down in the lower teens, then I finally ducked under. Near the end of my freshman year, I ran 4:06.8. I still remember that one. It was in the Ohio Meet at Miami University. I ran my best half-mile in 1:54.9 the same day.'

Those times must have indicated to you at the time that you had more potential as a miler?

'Yes, that's right.'

What was your next good performance?

'My most memorable one is the first time I ever broke four minutes in my sophomore year in college, when I ran 3:59.0. I can remember almost every step of that race. I just followed Lee La Badie and Gary Bjorklund, who was a great distance runner, but injured this year. He hung right on La Badie's shoulder. It was more or less a three-man race the whole way. In the last lap, I took off right at the quarter mark, which I came through in 3:00.1. Hec Ortiz came up to my shoulder with 220 to go. He asked me how I was feeling: I said "Fine," and then started my kick. He landed up about ten yards behind me. Also the same year, I came second to Marty Liquori at the NCAA, here my kick fell short. I was about a yard behind him. He did 3:59.9, and I did 4:00.1.'

How did it go the following year?

'A lot of misery. I was all psyched up to run, but halfway through the cross-country season I got a stress fracture on my left foot an inch above the ankle, and that knocked me out for nine weeks. That was followed by bursitis in my knee, which was followed by a stress fracture in my right foot, so I was sidelined for a total of eight to nine months. Fortunately, I met my wife that year, which helped my mental attitude. At the time she did not know anything about track or that I was that good. She enjoys it now, and she is learning a lot about it.'

Do you enjoy cross-country?

'At Bowling Green we have a great team spirit, and I enjoy cross-country running because I am with these guys on our team, we have a lot of fun in cross-country. But I

130

know I have to run cross-country to get the strength, because I am not really that physically strong. I started on my comeback about May to June last year. When I came back to school early September, we did about 120 miles a week for the first two weeks, then we slackened off to where we had a base of ninety to one hundrd miles a week: Then when the Championships came, we dropped to seventy-five to eighty miles a week.'

At the end of the cross-country season, did you go straight into track?

'We took off about one month then started track – indoor running a lot, because of the type of running where I have the acceleration. You need a medium-sized or short stride, and you need to have quick acceleration because of the turns. I had a pretty successful indoor season once I started going, but I was a little out of shape at the beginning and I got beaten once – third in the Millrose Games in New York.'

That must make you sharp early on, but not too sharp?

'Not too sharp, but sharp. I ran two miles indoors (8.58 and 8.39) but I mostly specialized in the mile. I went in the 880 in the Nationals because of our team situation. I had also to go in the Distance Medley relay, and it worked out really well, because we tied for second place overall, which is unbelievable for Bowling Green, because we have never done anything like that. We have a fabulous close-knit team, including Sid Sink (American record holder in the steeple); he is the big organizer who really gets us going.'

What training did you do in the spring?

'In the spring, we more or less start peaking for our relay season, which is early April. We come to a peak and then slacken down again, then peak for the Championships. I would say a typical week would be seventy-five to ninety miles; it rarely varies during the season. Our workouts are a system of hard – hard – hard, easy – easy – easy, for a week.'

Would you explain your training methods?

'These are the things I would use if I coached, and I plan on coaching and teaching. Monday is a distance day when we do mile and two-mile repeats. Tuesday is a speed day; we'll do 440 stuff. Wednesday is a pace day; we will do various things from 330 to 660s. Thursday, we start slackening off. Friday, we slacken off. Saturday, we have a race. It's almost that way every week, because we have races every Saturday or Friday. At Bowling Green meets, I might do the mile and half, plus a mile relay. Maybe one meet I may just do a three-mile. I usually do the mile, half, and relay triple, because it gets the most points for our team and it does not really bother me that much, as I am used to running three races on one day. They are all within forty-five minutes of each other.'

It gives you a good re-charging of the batteries and stops you getting stale?

'Right, we schedule our workouts so that we have that ability; I don't like to go to a meet and run one race, I think it is a waste of my time! I feel lousy all week if I go into one race and lose it.'

When did you think you would make the Olympic team?

'I did not know for sure until the Trials were over, because no-one knows . . . anything can happen.'

Do you approve of the sudden-death-type trials?

'Some people don't like them, because if you are off that one day you are out, but for a runner like me it would have been a tragedy if they had had it any other way, as my fastest time in the half-mile till then was 1:47.2. I would not have made it in the half for sure, and I would have had a hard time making it in the 1500, where my best was 3:39.7 in the NCAA two weeks before.

How did the AAU championships go for you?

'Basically the same as all my races. I stuck behind, and simply kicked down the straight away. It was a competitive race for me, and I like that type of race when I can rely on my "kick". Not really much different to the trials: it was more or less just stick on the guy's shoulder till the last 100, then "kick" like crazy.'

Did you feel sharp when you came to the Olympics?

'No, I did not feel very sharp, because I had been out for a month with tendonitis. I got in only four miles a day.'

Did you manage any speed work?

'I got in a little bit, mostly I raced 800 metres for my sharpness! I did not feel sharp in races themselves.'

How did your 800 metres heat go in the Olympics?

'The first heat was okay. I got second and qualified, more or less eased it in. The semis were kind of hairy, because I

132

was boxed in with 100 yards to go. It looked very bleak for me and I thought I might have had it as I could not get out. All of a sudden, lane 1, which I was in, opened wide because the guy who was in front of me, Franz-Josef Kemper, went out into the second lane to move Plachy out, and he left the first lane open. I accelerated through the hole, and placed first in the semis (1:48.68). In the final, I was almost in last place the whole way, playing a catch-up game.'

It looked to me in the stand that you nearly left it too late.

'I almost did.'

Who were your big dangers in the race?

'Everybody was my big danger, because I did not feel that good coming down the stretch. I was more or less just trying to get a medal 100 metres out. With fifty metres to go I was trying to get second place, trying to pass the Kenyans: then twenty metres from the finish, I saw Arzhanov was slowing or tightening up, so I tried for the win. I knew it was going to be close.'

(I conducted this interview with Dave Wottle in the Munich Olympic Village, and it was published in *Athletics Weekly* on 30 September 1972. At that time, the cornerstone of the magazine was 'Jimmy' P.W. Green, who was both Business Manager and Advertisement Director. Mel Watman was the Editor, and Dave Cocksedge the Assistant Editor. Shortly after, a fine middle-distance runner from Invicta East Kent – Jon Wigley – became Assistant Editor before going on to a 'high-ranking' position in the IAAF.)

23

IAN STEWART

Born Handsworth, Birmingham, 15 January, 1949.

Despite not obtaining an Olympic gold medal or breaking a World record, I consider Ian Stewart as one of the finest and shrewdest tacticians ever to run the 5000 metres. Once a gun tester and now a sales executive, he was one of three children who eventually achieved success at middle-distance running. The other two were Peter Stewart, who was the 1972 AAA 1500 champion with 3:38.2, and the AAA indoor champion in 1970. The youngest of the family was Mary Stewart, who set her first UK best as a thirteen-year-old, 4.55 for 1500 in 1969, and went on to become 1978 Commonwealth Games gold medallist in Edmonton Canada with 4:06.3, a Games record.

Ian held the UK 1500 record at 3:39.1 in 1969, and 5000 with 13:22.8 in 1970. He ran 45.12 for ten miles on the road in the 'Michelin 10', as well as running some impressive legs for Birchfield and Tipton in the National road relays. He also won the National Junior cross-country one year. He took three National and two European indoor titles over 3000 and came back after a short retirement as a racing cyclist, with his third European indoor title in 1975, following it with a world IAAF cross-country championship win in Rabat the same month. Here are some of the names of the cream of the middle and long-distance running fraternity in his wake! He did 35.20, Mariano Haro (Spain), 35.21, Bill Rodgers (USA), 35.27, John Walker (NZ), 35.45, Euan Robertson (NZ), 35.46, Franko Fava (Italy), 35.47, Ray Smedley (Eng), 35.50, Klaus Peter Hildenbrand (FRG), 35.51, Hans Jurgen Orthemann (FRG), 35.55, Gaston Roelants (Bel), 35.57, Abdel Kader Zaddem (Tunisia),

36.00, Grenville Tuck (Eng), 36.10, Waldemar Cierpinski (GDR), 36.16, Emiel Puttemans (Bel), 36.17, and Frank Shorter (USA), 36.25!

I will single out three races from the interviews I did from 1969–73 for Ian and his coach Geoff Warr to talk about, but before that here is Geoff Warr, like Ian Stewart a man who did not waste words, talking about training in 1973. 'Without going into great depth, I think it is the track session that makes you. The performance you can do for interval running has got a more direct influence on your scratch time than the bulk, although Ian did bulk which compared favourably with other world-class runners, but I still feel it's the track session that is the intermediate stage between bulk and the race.'

About the buildup for the European 5000 in the balmy summer evening of 19 September, 1969, in Athens.

Ian Stewart remarked, 'I can only remember one or two track sessions. I was getting in forty miles a week, doing track sessions like sixteen quarters, averaging 62–63 seconds with a minute jog between. We did a faster session of quarters with two and a half minutes jog. My best for this averaged 58.3 seconds.

'Repetition halves – two sessions of those. One session was three with a five minute jog – 1.58 – 1.59 or repetition halves with two and three-quarter minutes to three minutes jog in around 2.04. Before the AAA we did progressive miles with five minutes rest – 4.19, between 4.14 and 4.15, the 4.11. Before Athens I ran 4.18, 4.14 and 4.08, and I was quite fresh. That was the last session before I went out. In Athens I did a session of four halves with some sprints, 60 to 150 yards with Clive Longe and Mike Bull, so I could run with faster sprinters than me.

'I trained a lot with my brother from the beginning, and I did a lot of the mileage and track work with him.'

What did Geoff Warr think about that night in Athens?

'It was warm but the heat did not affect Ian, even though it was very humid. I recalled when we started with Birchfield and he came to me. We had come a long way from Blackpool. I was with two companions, Len Orton, the Birchfield Secretary, and Joe Segre, the reporter of the Birmingham paper, very old friends. Quite frankly, they were far more nervous than I was, because I knew when it comes to it Ian delivers the goods, and he would not have a bad run. I had also been in contact with him in Athens, and I knew he was going well and there was no question that if he did not win, it would not have been a disaster or anything like that. I was not too worried the way the race went. He showed superb competence, in the sense that the pace was rather disappointing and this can lead to a trick-ending, a made rush to the tape and one would say, "Fancy that so-and-so winning".

'Ian quite properly took up the pace himself and, if you recall, they were messing about 67–69. Ian went into the lead and, without necessarily knowing it himself, he ran dead regular 66s, just enough to take the steam out of one or two of the boys and reduce the bunch at the front. He was so in control of the race that I was not too worried. Diessner, an unknown quantity, had not run too well in the big games, but he had got a faster 1500 time than Ian, so on paper one had to fear him. He was very close to Ian, but just after the bell he went very badly and it was Ian against this Russian, and I could not imagine the Russian outkicking a 3.39 runner.'

Ian added his memories; 'I was worried about Diessner at the time, but after the first two or three laps it was slow – too slow. "There will be a rush ending." I thought, "if somebody does not get out." Baxter made a bit of an effort but I could see he was not going so well, so I thought I would take a few laps. Off I went. Of course they all followed, and I could not really get rid of the lead after that. It was a case of having to stay out there, although I did not really mind, because while I was out there I was not getting bashed about. Sometimes I would run zig-zag down the straight and run wide for them to come through, but they wouldn't. I decided I had had enough of it and so I stopped, which took them all by surprise and it had quite a devastating effect, although I did not do it for the effect, just to get rid of the lead.

'That seemed to knock them about more than I thought it would, and once they started to go I was in a great position, sitting on the outside. I was not running very fast, and Puttemans went with two laps to go. I went again at 600 metres, but I only half went and at the bell I was leading from Diessner and the Russian, I think. I was still not running flat out, and coming down the back straight the Russian took me; I could see he was sprinting almost flat out and I was striding fast. I thought, "I'll hit him right on the crown of the bend to take him unawares." I thought he would not think I would come at him there. I was feeling good then, I was pretty confident I was going to win. I got past him on the crown of the bend. It was great!'

19 September, 1969, European Championship 5000. 1. Ian Stewart (UK), 13:44.8. 2. Rashid Sharafyetdinov (USSR), 13:45.8. 3. Alan Blinston (UK), 13:47.6, 4. Bernd Diessner (GDR), 13:50.4. 5. Dane Korica (YUG), 13:51.4. 6. Giuseppe Ardizzone (ITA), 13:51.8.

The following year, 1970, was the year of the Commonwealth Games, and Ian went to the States. 'I won one race and was second in a mile in LA and in Kansas on the boards. I was not in any great shape. But when I came back I caught up quite a lot – 3:57.4 for the mile. I edged out (brother) Pete in the Emsley Carr Mile at Meadowbank.

'I was training very hard, Pete got the afternoon off from college – he seemed to be hammering me in training, although I was as physically fit as him. I was depressed about that just before the Commonwealth Games, but Peter had always been basically a better miler. That is not saying if I raced him over a mile he would have beaten me!

'I was training to race over 5000 and I was racing him over a mile on more or less bulk work, and he had the edge on me. I ran the Emsley Carr Mile from the front, and he just came at me at the last bend. That was just before we decided to run for Scotland.

'I did not have a great winter, and it was after I came back from the USA that I caught up, and in the spring I got quite fit.'

Geoff Warr again: 'It is not a bad thing getting in the miles in the spring, because the weather is better and there are no important races until the middle of June and July. We found it a good time to knock in the miles in April, May time. I think the ace card is the transition from the enormous amount of training that has to be done way back, to the actual race. In other words, say you are running 100 miles. Obviously, you are not going to race at your best. I think everybody will accept that, but it's an art to know how to cut it down and how much track work to win is needed. There is a certain amount of guessing about it.'

The lead-up to the Commonwealth Games was recalled by Ian. 'I ran the East German match with Pete in the 1500, just before the Commonwealth Games, and ran 3.41 and beat Justus. The heats of the Commonwealth were no problem.'

The Commonwealth 5000 Final was one of the most exciting races that I can remember. The result in bald figures was: 1. Ian Stewart (SCO), 13:22.8 (European, UK and Games Record). 2. Ian McCafferty (SCO), 13:23.4. 3. Kip Keino (KEN), 13:27.6. 4. Allan Rushmer (ENG), 13:29.8. 5. Ron Clarke (AUS), 13:32.4. 6. Dick Taylor (ENG), 13:33.8.

Ian's account of the race: 'I was running well, there was no doubt in my mind at any time in that race that I was going to lose. I had psyched Clarke in Stockholm, and I did not think Dick Taylor would win it. I watched him run in the 10,000 (third), and he had more chance in that. With 800 to go, McCafferty took off and I went with him and Keino went with us.

'McCafferty broke the bunch; I remember thinking, "I'm glad somebody else has gone now rather than me," because I was thinking about it. Coming off the crown of the bend into the bell lap, McCafferty was leading. At the top of the 100 metres straight I took off with 500 metres to go.

'We thought that if we could keep Keino under pressure till 150 metres from the tape we would, possibly, get him. That was why I took off so early, to really make him have to run hard, rather than to let him decide "to go now". A lot of people watched him and waited for him to make a move.

'He liked to say, "Well, I'm Kip and I am going – you can do what you like." I took the bull by the horns and went at 500, going into the bell. Past the bell I was really shifting into the bend and up the back straight, it just got faster all the time. He tried to get round me with 200 metres to go, and I fought him off as I went into the bend and round the bend.'

Geoff Warr brings his wealth of coaching knowledge into

play here. 'You get this classic moment when the pursuing athlete transfers his attention to what is going on behind him, and if you watch him you know he's had it. McCafferty was still running well then, coming into the straight off the bend, and showed every possibility of catching Ian, but Ian picked up again and was going away at the finish.'

You might wonder if Ian felt any surprise at McCafferty coming again in the straight. 'I did not know he had, till I had finished. I thought it was Keino. I came out of that last bend put my head down and started to go. I picked right up and I was really shifting through the line. McCafferty died during the last fifty metres and tied up quite badly.

Just after Ian's race, I left the Meadowbank Stadium in Edinburgh and queued for a bus. Two came along, both the same number and not the one I wanted. I mentioned that to the Scotsman next to me. He said, 'They always do it in twos in Edinburgh, laddie!' Which I thought was very apt.

1972 Munich Olympics 5000

I remarked to Ian that it was interesting having the European champion, Vaatainen, next to him in the heat at Munich. Ian replied, 'It's funny that – I was running very well, and I was pleased with my run in the heat. (Vaatainen 13:32.8, Stewart 13:33.0, and Haro 13:35.4) If you watched Viren in his heat (first in 13:38.4, with Nikolay Sviridov also 13:38.4), you will remember he never showed his hand once. I did not believe in showing my hand at all, and let Vaatainen go past.'

I suppose that the Munich 5000 metres final was one of the most loaded races, talent-wise, that has been assembled. The end result was: 1. Lasse Viren (FIN), 13:26.04. 2. Mohamed Gammoudi (TUN), 13:27.4. 3. Ian Stewart, 13:27.6.

Ian Stewart carries on: 'In the final of an Olympic Games you can't ever say there is only one man. Especially that final, it was the most open final of the lot. For instance, in the 400 hurdles you could have said it was Hemery, Akii-Bua or Mann. Those were the ones for the medals. In the 5000, there were any of half a dozen who could have won it.

'One could look down the list and say Viren looks good, Prefontaine has some good qualifications, and so on and each one would have equally good credentials to be there and a right to win that medal. I thought Gammoudi would have won the 10,000 if he had stayed on his feet. I thought I should have beaten him in the final of the 5000, because I was only point one off him. I did not run well. It was not often I slipped up in a big Games but I did there, and I could have kicked myself for doing so.

'With 800 to go, I was on Prefontaine, Viren came past with Gammoudi on the back of him, and I could not get out. With 600 to go, I stepped out to get behind Gammoudi and get round Prefontaine. But as I tried to get round him, Prefontaine came out sideways and knocked me almost into the third lane and I lost a hell of a lot of ground – ten or fifteen metres; I pulled myself together, but they were still going a bit.'

'You see, this is three or four blokes running 3.56 miles,' Geoff Warr explained.

'I could give Dave Bedford ten yards with 600 to go,' said Ian, 'but not Viren, Gammoudi and Prefontaine. I came with 200 to go, I thought I was not going to get anything; when I came off the bend, I did not think I was going to get a medal. I would have liked to have had a watch on my last 100 metres!'

Ian Stewart once tried to sum up what athletics is all about for him. I was interviewing him in 1969, and I think his conclusions echo most runners' feelings.

'It's hard to explain. You get hooked on it, I think – it is like a drug. The more you do, the harder it is to stop doing it. It means such a lot to me. It is very hard to explain what it does for you. Whether you are a bum or whether you are at the top, nobody in the street knows. They pass you by just the same, it does not really make any difference. But when you are running well it satisfies you. If you have run, say, twenty miles, you feel you have accomplished something very great that day. You feel pretty good, but as far as what it actually does, it's very hard to say really.'

1964 Olympic champion Gaston Roelants the first man to
run inside 8:30 for 3000 steeplechase

Janis Lusis the 1968 Olympic Javelin champion – possibly
the greatest competitor ever in his event

Henry Carr – Tokyo 1964 – double Olympic champion

Lillian Board – Double European champion 1969 in Athens

Effortless movement of 1968 Olympic 200 metres
champion Tommie Smith

Miler supreme on his day – Jim Ryun

1964 Olympic champion Lynn Davies whose UK Long
Jump record of 1968 was still on the Books in 1992

The powerful stride of Lee Evans – winning the Olympic
gold in '68 in a world record 400 metres

Madeline Manning-Jackson the 1968 Olympic 800 metre champion leading

Ralph Doubell '68 Olympic 800 metre champion

Al Oerter four times Olympic Discus title holder and now a
veteran champion

Irena Szwinska winning the Olympic 200 metres in 1968
in a world record. Easily amongst the greatest of all time

David Hemery who shattered the world 400 metres hurdles record while taking the Olympic title in '68 to follow in the footsteps of Americans Rex Cawley (1964) and Glenn Davis (1956–60)

Double European champion in Helsinki in 1971, Juha
Vaatainen – a true stylist

Dave Wottle beating Yevgeniy Arzhanov and Mike Boit for
the Olympic 800 metre crown in 1972

Ian Stewart who won major championship titles over all
surfaces

Dick Quax, leading Lasse Viren to one of four gold medals
he achieved at the Olympics

No 724 Bronislaw Malinowski the 1976 Olympic
Steeplechase champion

Allan Wells the 1980 Olympic 100 metres champion in
Moscow

The incomparable Edwin Moses the 1976 Olympic
400m hurdles champion in a world record

1991 Dream Mile winner and Olympic medallist Peter Elliott – here leading Tony Morrell and John Gladwin – before going on in 1992 to win the Grampian Road mile in Aberdeen

The long lasting John Walker winning the 1976 Olympic
1500 metres

Seb Coe 80–84 Olympic champion

Dave Moorcroft winning an epic 3000 metres at Crystal
Palace in 1982

Abdi Bile world champion. 1500 champion of 1987 and
World Cup winner of 1989

John Ngugi winning the Olympic 5000 in 1988. He also
won four consecutive world cross countries

1988 Olympic 400 Hurdles champion Debbie Flintoff-King
in the lead in the home straight in Seoul

Double Olympic champion (1984–88) Roger Kingdom
with Colin Jackson

Paul Ereng 1988 Olympic 800 metre champion

Arturo Barrios, World IOK record holder (89) and 1991
Pan American 5K champion, on his way to victory in the
Midlands Run in Birmingham – 1990. No 3 is Paul Davis-
Hale and No 2 is Eamonn Martin

Darren Clark here winning one of four AAA's
Championship 400 metres from 1991 world relay gold
medallist Derek Redmond

David Bedford leading many of the rest of the best cross country runners of the decade in the National of 1971

24

ROD MILBURN

Born 18 May, 1950, at Opelousas, Louisiana.

Following in the tradition of outstanding American Olympic high hurdles champions, Harrison Dillard (1952), Lee Calhoun (1956–60), Hayes Jones (1964), and Willie Davenport (1968) came Rod Milburn, nicknamed 'Hot Rod', to win the 1972 Olympic title in Munich.

Renaldo Nehemiah, who ran so brilliantly in the late 1970s, early 1980s and was still amongst the best in 1989–90 talked to me about his inspiration:

'It was probably Rod Milburn who influenced me at the start, as he was about my height then of 5'9" to 5'10", and I parted my hair down the middle to resemble a Rod Milburn and we were both double arm thrusters (I am not anymore). We were both sprinter types. We were aggressive and powerful hurdlers.' Colin Jackson, the Olympic silver medallist, in 1988: 'Rod Milburn was the one I admired, because he was a good smooth hurdler, that was the major thing.' Guy Drut, the 1976 Olympic champion from France, talked to me in Edinburgh after winning the Europa Cup Highs in 1973:

'Rod Milburn is a very good athlete, he trains very well and he is very strong in the head.' Who then did he fear in competition? 'Nobody but Milburn.'

Rod Milburn ran a 13.00 over 120 yards hurdles in 1971 in the AAU championships in June, which was a World record, and besides winning the Pan-Am Championships that year he was undefeated in a host of good performances.

In 1974 he became a pro athlete and was reinstated in 1980. He then had a couple of years amongst the top ten hurdlers in the World again.

Interview 1982

Willie Davenport, the 1968 Olympic champion, once remarked about you: 'I doubt if I'll be able to win another gold medal. You see, there's this young fellow I brought with me here from Louisiana. He finished fifth tonight, but by 1972 nobody but nobody is going to be able to beat him. He's going to be the best high hurdler in the world.' Did Willie inspire you as a great hurdler?

'I would have to say so because at that time, of course, Willie was at Southern University and an exceptionally great hurdler, well-known throughout the world. I felt that by going to Southern I could kind of get some things from him, as he was the top at that time, and I think I made a good choice by doing that. He inspired me most because of the fact that he was one of the most fluent hurdlers with a lot of tenacity. He was just remarkable.'

Would you go along with the feeling that Davenport had tremendous talent rather than being a hard trainer?

'Yes, more than any hurdler I have actually come into contact with. I think if anybody else would adapt to his style of training, they would probably never be very competitive in a situation. He is, I guess you would say, a rare type that just had a good perception for timing rather than the result of a hard training programme. I would see him come out occasionally, maybe two or three times a month and get out and run a meet, expecially during the indoor season when he could do 6.9 or even 6.8 at times for sixty yards hurdles. It was remarkable.'

Dick Hill trained you at Southern University; was he a particularly useful coach for you?

'I would think he was very much a benefactor in my success, especially in my second year at Southern. His programme catered for short type workouts, so you would never really tire yourself out, but it was very, very effective. For example, we would work at times on things like train leg drills for a good while, then we would switch to the lead leg drills, working on these fundamental snaps and actually manipulating the biomechanics. At times we would work on strength and work out over maybe ten or twelve hurdles, not too many, maybe three or four times, and that proved to

142

be very effective.'

Track and Field News rated you in the top ten of their 'Athletes of the Decade' (1970–80), quote: 'Milburn became history's all-time greatest hurdler in his sophomore season at Southern University (1971), not losing a single race and chopping 0.2 from the hand-timed World record with his 13.0 to win the AAU. Those exploits earned him Athlete of the Year honours.' Which race from that year stands out for you?

'I think it was the World record race at Eugene. The field was Willie Davenport, Tom Lee White, Lance Babb, Leon Coleman and Ron Draper. I had a very good start and the track was a good surface. I must have cleared the first hurdle in two seconds flat minimum, and started accelerating right at the third hurdle, very aggressively. I was then really going on my own; by the fifth hurdle I was out there by three to four metres. I had been able to get out there very quickly and relax. When I was in my prime, I could always get out very soon, and from the third or fourth hurdle I would just get into my relaxing situation without nipping a hurdle or anything else. You relax much more when you get the field behind you. I had a very good recovery situation if I was to ever hit a hurdle.

Thomas Hill and Guy Drut must have been two of your main rivals for the 1972 Olympic crown. How did you see them as opponents?

'Thomas Hill was a very good hurdler, but at times I think he had a little thing you might call mental paralysis. He had very good potential, his technique was rather fair, but he was very swift over the hurdles. At times I would not have too much of a problem holding him off, but with Guy Drut it was really kind of different. He was very fluent, he had good smooth hip rotation and his body was pretty well upright, almost vertical, whereas other hurdlers go to the hurdle dipping. He was the only competitor around that time that I had very strong thoughts about, as far as defeating me was concerned. I knew if ever I made a mistake on him he would be up, and it could be all over with. You could not really recover with Guy Drut if you made a mistake.'

What is your memory of that Olympic final in Munich?

'Looking back at 1972, it was a very good year . . . and a not so good year. The reason why it was not so good was the fact that I got third in the Olympic trials – that was one of the most critical things that happened to me. I don't know the reason why I only managed to get third, but things appeared just not to be working right, so I barely made the Olympic team – which shook me a little. When I got to the Games, I said, "Put everything behind you and start again; work well, and be much more conscious of what is going on.' I did not know if I took the race for granted in the trials, or if it was just that my mind was not working in the right direction. But when I got to Munich I was able to relax and really get into the race, actually get a feel for the competitors, how they were running in trial heats, and so it gave me a pretty good base.

'When I got in the blocks in the final, I can remember it was a very good evening, the temperature was about 75 degrees, the stands were packed solid, which was very good. I could just feel the electricity; it was a great feeling sitting out there before 100,000-plus people and the millions that were looking at TV, so that in itself was a great support. I felt almost weightless. Into the starting blocks I went. The only thing I was actually focussing on was the gun sound. When I hear that sound, it is all spontaneous. I think I had a very superb start. We were together for the first three hurdles, then that was where I started to make some little moves. I think by the sixth hurdle I made a tremendous gap of about two and a half to three metres on the field. To my left, I had seen Willie Davenport up until that point; I had actually seen him and almost heard him. Going down into the seventh and eighth hurdles, I looked to my right and I could see Guy Drut vividly, coming through very strongly, so at that point the main thing was really just to concentrate and relax, move without clipping any hurdles – because if I was to clip anything from the seventh to the tenth hurdle I would have been in serious trouble with Guy Drut for sure, because he was the one coming very strongly for the second place.'

Guy Drut: 'I looked at the three Americans and Siebeck because he was the European Champion, and I wanted to beat him because in Helsinki he clapped his hands when he saw me fall down, and I never forgot that. Hill was good, and Milburn would win. I had beaten Davenport three months before in Italy but I had never beaten Hill, so it was between me and Hill for second or third place.'

1. Rod Milburn, 13.24 (World record). 2. Guy Drut, 13.34. 3. Tom Hill (USA), 13.48, 4. Willie Davenport, 13.50. 5. Frank Siebeck (EG), 13.71. 6. Leszek Wodzynski (POL), 13.72. 7. Lubomir Nadenicek (CZE), 13.76, and 8. Petr Cech (CZE), 13.86.

It was no surprise in that case for you that Guy Drut won the 1976 Olympic final then?

'Exactly, it was no surprise, and I predicted that he would win that next Olympics, and it was a very good time.'

(1. Guy Drut, 13.30. 2. Alejandro Casanas (Cuba), 13.33. 3. Willie Davenport, 13.38).

25

LASSE VIREN

Born at Myrskyla, 22 July, 1949. 1.80/5ft 10¼ins 61kg/ 134lb.

Lasse Viren will go down in athletics history like Paavo Nurmi did with his legendary exploits in the 1920s and 1930s. People will talk about Lasse Viren for at least another hundred years.

The fact is that he won the Olympic double – 5000/10,000 in 1972 and again in 1976. The latter was followed by a 2.13, 10.8 Marathon (at Montreal)!

He was back in the Olympics in 1980, running 27:50.05 for fifth place in Moscow, when Myruts Yifter won in 27:42.7.

Nick Rose, who gained a Commonwealth 5000 silver in 1982 and was a world-class short-distance road racer, cross-country runner and ran a 27:31.19 for 10km in 1983, had this to say:

'Yifter ran a fantastic performance in Moscow in the Olympics, and you knew that if he was just there with a lap to go that he was going to be hard to beat, but I would not say you could put him on the same level as Viren, as I think Viren is one step above.'

Another person who gave me his opinion on the 'All-time Bests' was Peter Hildreth, who had been several times to the major championships, both as an athlete competing and as the *Sunday Telegraph* athletics correspondent. In 1979 he thought: 'The most outstanding individual I have seen outside of the hurdles event must have been Lasse Viren. I would say that his victory in the Munich Olympic 10,000 was the most extraordinary single athletic achievement that I have seen. He fell flat on his face half-way through the

146

race, but still got back on his feet to take the lead, win the race and break the World record.'

Regarding the first part of his second Olympic double – the first four at Montreal were: 1. Lasse Viren, 27:40.4. 2. Carlos Lopez of Portugal, 27:45.2. 3. Brendan Foster (UK) (who was a Commonwealth 10,000 and European 5000 Champion), 27:55.0, and 4. Tony Simmons (UK), 27:56.4 (who ran the fastest heat, in 28:01.8). Foster remarked, 'I don't think I was really such a hot favourite because Viren obviously was the one. He had run faster than me and was in good form.' He went on to say, 'He is such a great athlete and such a tough competitor when he wants to be.'

Interview 1973

Secretary for the Finnish Federation, Pirkko Hannula, interpreted.

When did you start running?

'In 1967.'

Were you influenced by anyone?

'I decided on my own to start; there were no athletes who influenced me. I began at Myrskyla athletics club, running 1000 and 3000 m races.'

And when did you start seriously?

'Immediately I started to race!'

Were you with the Finnish team at the 1969 European Championships at Athens?

'I was a tourist there. I was training, but I didn't race at those Championships.'

But 1969 was a good year for you, and you progressed with your times?

'It was in 1969 that I won the Finnish championship for the first time over 5000 metres in 14:10.22.' Comment from Pirkko Hannula: 'I remember Lasse was very young at the time he won, and so it was then that all the Finns knew who he was.'

Lasse, you came seventeenth in the 10,000 in the European in Helsinki in 1971, and you were seventh in the 5000 final. How did those races go?

'I was pleased to get into the final of the 5000 metres. I fell over in the 5000 final, and maybe if I had not fallen I would have come fifth or sixth and got a point for Finland.'

Vaatainen told me in 1971 that he was coaching you.

'I have not got any training programmes from Vaatainen. Since 1969, Rolf Haikkola has coached me.'

Do you think your coach is the best, and if so, why?

'He is the best. He is like a father to me. We communicate very well. He is not only a coach, he is much more.'

Has your training changed much since the beginning?

'At the beginning it wasn't so hard, and it was not so much. I did not then need to train as I do now. I was training 120 kilometres (about seventy-five to eighty miles) a week then.'

What sort of ground did you train over?

'Usually on the road or cross-country. On the road in the winter, because there is much snow and one cannot get into the country, it is very cold then and we do not have races till April.'

What type of training do you like?

'Any kind of training is hard.'

What do you think has been the reason for your improvement over the years?

'One very important thing for me is that I have not had any troubles with my legs, and I have good health.'

What type of speed training were you doing when preparing for the 1972 Olympics?

'On the track I used to run 10×200 speed training in one day's session.'

How about your training in the winter for the Olympics in Munich?

'I ran 200 kilometres (125 miles) in a week. I think my best time to train was about six in the evening, and I trained about six in the morning as well. As a policeman, I work in the day. I travel about driving a police car, and I have to be in the office too.'

It has been said that people like you and Vaatainen train when you like, and that you do not have to work. What do you say to that?

'Okay, if someone does not believe I work they can come round and see the hours I do and check the hours I spend in my office. I work seven hours a day.'

After your heat in the Olympic 10,000, who did you think were going to be your toughest rivals?

'The most dangerous was Puttemans, Haro a bit, and there was someone else, but I can't remember who now.

How about your thoughts during the final?

'I had a good feeling, everything was going well. The main thing was for me to be in the leading group. When I fell over, I did not know what had happened. I realized somebody was falling over me, and I thought the main thing was not to be spiked, so that I could continue. I do not remember anything of what actually happened; I just wanted to continue. I caught the others, then went into the lead.'

When did you think you would win?

'About two laps before the end, I had the feeling I might win.'

Puttemans was near you?

'I was leading, so I did not see him.'

Heat 1 – Emile Puttemans of Belgium, 27:53.4, in an Olympic record. 2.Dave Bedford, 27:53.6.

Heat 2 – Mohamed Gammoudi, 27:54.8. Lasse Viren fourth in 28:04.4.

Heat 3 – Miruts Yifter, 28:18.2.

Final leaders in order per kilometre. Bedford one to five, Viren six, Yifter seven, Viren eight and Yifter nine. First six of fourteen finishers – 1. Lasse Viren, 27:38.4 (World record). 2. Emiel Puttemans (Belgium), 27:39.6. 3. Miruts Yifter (Ethiopia), 27:41.0. 4. Mariano Haro (Spain), 27:48.2. 5. Frank Shorter (USA) (winner of the marathon in 2:12.19.8), 27:51.4, and 6. Dave Bedford (UK), 28:05.4.

I feel I must point out here that Dave Bedford went on in 1973 to break that World record, without the high calibre competition, at London's Crystal Palace, reducing Viren's time radically to 27:30.80.

Back to Lasse Viren:

What were your thoughts on the 5000 final?

'I had planned after 3000 metres I would lead, then I would start to run fast, but all the other runners were around me so I did not have the chance to lead, and I had to wait. So it was with three laps left that I started to pass the other runners and make for the lead position. Prefontaine was leading. I knew all the time they were all there.'

Did it worry you that Steve Prefontaine would put in four fast laps?

'I knew Prefontaine was going to run very fast, but it did not work because I thought it was Prefontaine talking.'

The 10,000 was on 31 August and then came the 5000, Lasse had just pointed out. The kilometre splits were: 1. Nikolay Sviridov, 2:46.4. 2. Lasse Viren, 5:32.6. 3. Javier Alvarez, 8:20.2, and 4. Steve Prefontaine, 11:00.0. First four of thirteen finishers; 1. Lasse Viren, 13:26.4 (Olympic record). 2. Mohamed Gammoudi (Tunisia), 13:27.4. 3. Ian Stewart (UK), 13:27.6. 4. Steve Prefontaine, in 13:28.4.

The fourth Olympic gold medal that Lasse Viren obtained was in the 5000 metres at Montreal in 1976. Again, the field was loaded. The first six home in the final were: 1. Lasse Viren, 13:24.8. 2. Dick Quax (New Zealand), 13:25.22. 3. Klaus-Peter Hildenbrand (West Germany), 13:25.4. 4. Rod Dixon (New Zealand), 13:25.6. 5. Brendan Foster (UK), 13:26.2, and 6. Willy Polleunis (Belgium), 13:27.0.

To get another angle on that one, I talked to Dick Quax, the man who followed Kip Keino home in the 1970 Commonwealth 1500.

'I had a virus, which I actually got the night before the final of the 10,000. I had spent most of the night over or on the toilet. I still had not recovered properly from my flu or my stomach virus in the 5000 metres heat, but I was so fit'. (he won heat one in 13.31). Fastest heat winner was Brendan Foster in 13:20.4, which was an Olympic record, and Rod Dixon was just behind him in that with 13:20.6. 'It put pressure on me' said Dick Quax, and he then explained why: 'Because people at home said, "There goes Quax, he's blown again," as they did not know the full story, and I got a bit of a rubbishing from our not-so-knowledgeable commentators back home. I felt there was a little bit of extra pressure on me, as a matter of fact.

'In the final, my problem was I had all my confidence knocked out of me by my illness. I remember at one stage early on it was very slow, and in some ways I was thankful for that, because I think if the pace had been hard all the

150

way, I would probably have been dropped off, because I just was not strong any longer after my illness.

'After about five laps, Brendan Foster looked to me as though he was going to throw in a 59 or 60 quarter. He went for a half a lap, looked round and saw everybody still with him, and I felt he sort of threw it in a bit. I thought to myself – thank God! I felt if a break had been made at that stage, I probably would not have been in contention for much longer.'

Now for a little more on the man Lasse Viren:

What do you like most about athletics?

'It gives me satisfaction, which is the main thing, and it gives me the chance to travel all over the place, and you make many friends.'

What are your hobbies?

'When I have time, I like to hunt in the forest.'

Ian Stewart thinks you have the right approach, running here and there and not being bothered with finishing second, sixth or last. You are the Olympic champion, you've got what you wanted and you are enjoying it. What do you say to that? When do you like to race?

'I like to run, even though I know I won't get along very well. I like to race anyway. I don't care if I don't win every time.'

Looking back now in Edinburgh, after you ran to get a couple of points for Finland in the Europa Cup, which races have given you the most satisfaction so far?

'Of course the Olympic gold medals were very valuable ones, but a very important victory for me was when in 1969 I won the match for Finland against Sweden in the 5000. I was a junior then, and it was the first time I had represented Finland.'

26

BRONISLAW MALINOWSKI

Born Nowe, Poland, 4 June 1951. 1.81/68kg.
'Tough, rugged, with an excellent turn of speed (he's a
3:55.4 miler). Bronislaw Malinowski has been one of the
world's most respected steeplechasers ever since winning
the European Junior 2000 metres title in 1970.' That was
the comment made by perhaps the world's most outstanding athletics writer in his fifth' *Encyclopaedia of Track and
Field* (1981) – Melvyn Watman.

It was sad that a fatal car accident should have then
deprived 'Bronic' of being able to share with others memories
of a sparkling athletics career. His Olympic record alone was
impressive. Fourth in 1972 in 8:28.0 (first Kip Keino 8:23.6),
second in 1976 – 8:09.2, (behind Sweden's Anders Garderud,
who recorded a world record of 8:08.0), and first in the
Moscow Olympics of 1980 with 8:09.7, with clear early race
leader Filbert Bayi of Tanzania second in 8:12.5, and in third
place Eshetu Tura from Ethiopia, 8:13.6, and Domingo
Ramon of Spain fourth in 8:15.8.

Dennis Coates, from England's famous North-East club
Gateshead, who ran ninth in 8:23.0 in the Montreal Olympic
final after creating a new UK record of 8:19.0 in the heat,
talked about only one person who he considered the most
outstanding steeplechaser: 'I would say without a doubt
Bronislaw Malinowski, because of his all-round ability. He is
willing to have a go at anything. He's no sitter.'

Interview 1975

The interpreter was Alex Mineyko, a coach and runner
himself:

How did you get interested in athletics?

'My brother was a junior, running for the Polish National team in the 1500, and it was because of him that I started. One day my brother just said, "Let's go out training," and that was how it all began. It was in that first training effort that something clicked inside me, and that made me continue.'

Where did you first run, and at what event?

'I was born and lived just south of Gdansk (Danzig). When I started my training, the first races I did were over 1000 and 1500, the 1000 is very popular in Poland. At that time, I was no longer at school but in technical college. My club from the very start was Olimpia Grudziadz, and right from the beginning of my athletics, my coach has been Ryszard Szczepanski. I was not given any specific training to begin with, just general development, gentle running, plenty of warm-ups, even swinging from the trees and anything to give me a thorough basic fitness. I started running when I was eighteen, and trained then every day on my own. My time to begin with was 3.58 for 1500 metres.'

Did you look up to any particular athlete at that time?

'When I began in the sixties, the first cuttings that I kept were of Ron Clarke.'

What do you recall as your most memorable race in your early career?

'The European Junior Championships in 1970, when I represented Poland in Paris, winning the 2000 metres steeplechase in a time of 5.35. That was really memorable for me, as it happened to be the very first Junior Championship in Europe. My success in Paris influenced me in my decision to concentrate on the steeplechase, because up to then I was tackling a lot of events.'

What do you enjoy most about athletics?

'At present, at the level I am at, the thing that keeps me going is the enormous desire for a World record and some kind of medal in the Olympic steeplechase. When I was at a lower level, what kept me going – like so many of my colleagues in that part of Europe – was to do well enough to travel.'

Looking back at the Olympic final in Munich in 1972, how did the race go?

'I had the best result before the Olympic Games, and I thought I would win a medal. I shall remember that final for many years because Keino, who had never run the steeplechase seriously, came and won, and I think I lost a medal coming towards the water jump for the last time. Not only did I lose my balance, but in order to save myself being kicked in my "credentials" by another guy's foot, I had to support myself with one hand on the barrier, and by doing so lost at least two seconds. All that contributed at least to my not getting one of the medals. I shall always remember that as a race full of luck and misfortune for many in the race. It was not just the best guy winning on the day, or the best guy losing. In my view, the worst place you can ever achieve in an Olympic Games is fourth place!'

You were fourth again in the European 10,000 metres in 1974. Tell me about that race.

'It was a diabolical race for men, and perhaps the toughest I have had up till then. I had come to Rome after a heavy load of training in Font Romeu, and it was 36 degrees centigrade (97 degrees fahrenheit) with terrific humidity. My trainer wanted me to do that race to acclimatise before the steeplechase, to see how I was "clicking" after my hard training. If I had not done that thanks to my trainer, I would not have been equipped to win the steeplechase. In the 10,000 I lost at least a bronze medal, because I was blocked with 500 metres to go when Kuschmann struck and Simmons went with him. I wanted to go with them, but right in front of me was my Polish compatriot Legowski, and next to him was Boro of Norway (and by that stage there was much lapping), and I could not afford to get into the third lane. So I simply waited another 100 metres, till about the 300 metres mark, by that time the others were too far ahead, and in that way I lost at least a bronze medal. Mentally and physically, that race was so hard.'

There were so very many good runners in the race who were excelling around that time: Karel Lismont, Paivarinta, Jose Hermens and Franko Fava, but it was not from those names that appeared in the first few, in the result, from twenty-four brave finishers, but the following; in order: 1. Manfred Kuschmann (EG), 28:25.8. 2. Tony Simmons (UK), 28:25.8. 3. Giuseppe Cindolo (ITA), 28:27.2. 4.

Bronic Malinowski, 28:28.0. 5. Nikolay Puklakov (USSR). 6. Knot Boro (NORWAY). 7. Lasse Viren (FIN). 8. Mariano Haro (SPAIN). 9. David Black (UK) (who won two silver medals in the Commonwealth), and 10. Bernie Ford (UK).

Tony Simmons, who was a width of a vest away from victory, looks back on that one: 'The first mile was easy enough and it was just going through the motions of running, but when the pain really starts at three or four miles, then you start thinking of all the dedication and all the amount of work you have been putting in six months prior to the race, and when the pain is really on in the race you psychologically think, "that training session" was much harder than the pain you are going through at this present stage, so you just keep going through the motions. The pain was hurting for a couple of laps, then it seemed to go away and I could be relaxed again. I was getting prepared with 1400 to go, and I was thinking somebody would be running something in the regions of 5.2 for the last five laps, as they did in previous games, and I was prepared in my training and in the race to try to run that fast for the last five laps, but it did not come off, so I just sat in waiting for everybody. I had two good races that year, one against East Germany, where I ran 13.29 for 5000 and ran a very fast last lap, and then I went to Poland, where I ran fifty-five seconds for the last lap. I did run a few races where I was running last fast quarters, so I did not think there was anybody in the race I should be scared of, so I was content to run the way I was.

'You tend to watch different people, so when somebody comes from behind and shoots off in front, you don't think of anything you just go, and you never plan to run a fast last lap, it just happens that way. You just get excited and go right to the finishing line. With 200 to go, I was pleased to have a silver medal, and then I realized with 150 I could get a gold, then I started working with 150 yards to go.'

Bronic continues, as I asked him about the first of his two European Games victories (he also won in 1978, in 8:15.1). About his heat and final in Rome; how did they go?

'After my 10,000, I knew I was in superb form and very confident, so there were no problems, and I ran the least amount in order to get into the final. The race itself could have been won in 8:10, but there was nobody willing to run the first kilometre fast, and so that part of the race was very slow and there was no chance of a record. I felt Anders Garderud had ability well above mine, but it was basically a mental win over his good physique. Garderud made nearly a basic mistake, because he accelerated with 300 metres to go and I went with him, but after another 100 metres he slightly slowed down before the water jump. As Garderud changed into a lower gear and up a gear again, he was already adrift a little bit, and that was good enough for me as he could not get me then. I was particularly pleased to beat the guy everybody was quoting and thought was the absolute favourite, and who was considered one class higher than me, as I was basically regarded as a good average runner. So that was more satisfying than just a win.'

The first four in the final were: 1. Bronislaw Malinowski, 8:15.00. 2. Anders Garderud, 8:15.4. 3. Michael Karst (West Germany), 8:18.0, and 4. Franko Fava (Italy), 8:19.0.

This year (1975) you were first in the 10,000 metres in the European Cup semi-final at Crystal Palace, beating Tony Simmons in the process.

'On that particular day I felt truly good, and it was a happy day for me. I never thought I could beat Simmons, but once again another great runner has made a basic little mistake. He went with 500 metres to go when on that particular day he was able to sustain the effort for just a fraction under 400. Obviously I used his mistake to my advantage, although I am not saying no credit is due to me. I was delighted to beat such a great athlete as Simmons. I feel he is a class better 10,000 metre runner than me. It is not my distance. I will concentrate on the Olympic steeplechase and 5000 metres, because I am basically fast over 1500. I feel anyone who is going to run such a gruelling race as the 10,000 must have many years of general development of body and mind, and I have not got enough experience over 10,000 to concentrate on it yet.'

It would be interesting to note with reference to what Bronic said there, that some years later, in 1979, he came second in the World cross-country at Limerick in 37 minutes 29 seconds, and only nine seconds behind double World cross-country (78–79) winner John Treacy of Eire.

At Limerick, Bronic was followed home by Alexsandr Antipov (37.30) plus such stars as Nick Rose and Leon Shots of Belgium.

Bronic, having been second to Thomas Wessinghage in the European Cup final at Nice, must give you confidence to know you have that sort of speed when you are out on the line for the steeple? (He ran 3:37.4 in 1978 as a p.b.)

'Yes, you can say that I have got reasonably good speed over 1500, so it does give me some deep inside belief in myself when it comes to the steeplechase. However, I did not feel very well in Nice as I had only just about recovered completely from tonsillitis, and then I did some very severe training at Font Romeau to compensate, and I did not feel at my best. So, although I went for the World record in the steeplechase, there I was not fit enough or in my usual good rhythm. My best form was in early June when I ran 8.13, but the illness and condensed training had broken the continuity since then.'

What type of training do you feel has helped you?

'I do a lot of very hard training: twenty kilometres in sixty-five minutes – no messing about, never stopping, four times a week. I am very much an advocate of training at high altitude. I do my kind of training from December to the beginning of May, which gives me strength, but I must stress that it is after five good years of generally developing my body. I would not be inclined to recommend that powerful training to anybody.'

What do you like most, besides athletics?

'Women, good music in discotheques, good pictures, good soccer and other sports. My studies, which are taking five years, are quite tough, with bio-chemistry and other stuff. One very deep feeling – it's being rather sentimental – is that I would love to run in Edinburgh, where my mother comes from, and I would like to spend some time in England as I always admire the British runners.' Bronic added, 'My mother is completely Scottish, and therefore tough, both physically and mentally. I owe a lot to my mother, who has been living in Poland for the last twenty-five years. She is not only energetic, but has that zeal and no-nonsense attitude. The determination that I have inside of me in my blood, I owe to my mother. She helped me to win the European title in her whole attitude, and in many other tough situations she is the one who has been of most assistance to me.'

27

ALLAN WELLS

Born Edinburgh, 3 May, 1952. 6ft 0ins/12st. His wife
Margot was also an international sprinter.

'That race gave me a tremendous satisfaction because it
felt so easy, which is the way all good races should make
you feel. That whole year gave me great satisfaction
actually, and I was not having to try for the performances,
because they just seemed to be there, and to my mind this
is the way athletics should be.' Peter Radford, talking
about his World record 220 yards that he achieved back in
1960 at Wolverhampton (20.5), in the first interview I did
with him. Peter that year achieved a close third in the
Olympic 100 metre final in Rome, and the next UK athlete
to achieve an individual sprint medal was Allan Wells in
1980. I don't think Allan Wells, who came from the same
city as the talented 1971 European 400 champion Dave
Jenkins, had quite the fluent stride and initial talent that
Peter had, but through sheer grit and hard work he certainly deserved his Olympic gold medal in Moscow, and
went on shortly afterwards to defeat the top Americans
that were not at the Games over 100 and 200, to add to
Championship victories in the European and Commonwealth, as well as wins in the World and Europa Cup
finals. As far as the UK was concerned, he was strongly
challenged for his number one spot by sprinter Mike
McFarlane, but it was Linford Christie, after his 1986
European 100 win (when Allan came fourth), that one
realized that a new name had really emerged, to test the
world's best over the 100, and John Regis took his place
in the 200. But one might add, Allan Wells had had a good
innings by then.

Interview 1980

You were once a rather better long jumper than you were a sprinter. How do you think you would have got on in the long jump?

'For about six years I slogged away, and came up with quite a respectable long jump of 24′0¼″ (7.32). My best 100 metres time then was 10.9 windy, and on average I was doing 11.1. Now I have run 100 metres in 10.11, and if we work on that basis, it might surprise some what I could do now for the long jump! I have pulled Lynn Davies's leg about it, but I think if I really concentrated on it, I could come close to his British record of 27 feet (8.23) – as long as I could put the same amount of training into the long jump as I have into sprinting. It would need a lot of work; it's a case of making the muscles feel for the event again, but I think I've got the sort of control a long jumper needs on the runway. I honestly think with the speed I've got, the power and knowledge of long jump I've got that I could go twenty-seven feet. But I would really have to give up a whole season of sprinting to do it, which I'm reluctant to do. Mind you, say I did beat Lynn's record . . . I think he would come back to try and break it! Talking of Lynn, who was my idol, I think he is one of the most respected of all athletes and had one of the best physiques. He was an incredible athlete.'

Which of your opponents do you admire the most?

'I think the guy I have come up against most of all is Don Quarrie. He is an incredible ambassador for Jamaica on and off the track. He is really a gentleman of the highest quality. He's twenty-nine now and has done a hell of a lot, having been in it at the top for ten years. He deserves to be respected.'

When did you feel you were first breaking into world class as a sprinter?

'I think it came first of all when I did 6.68 for 60 metres indoors at Cosford at the beginning of 1978. That was the first breakthrough. The main breakthrough races, though, were in 1978, when I ran 10.29 at Gateshead and 10.15 at Meadowbank. They meant a lot more to me than just winning medals. The thing is that if I put my mind to something, if I get an inclination that I am going to do well, then I get involved in it one hundred per cent. We are looking for technically small things to make it better, and a lot of small things add up to a big thing.'

It must have been an important turning point for you when you met Margot and eventually got married, particularly as she is an international sprinter in her own right. Obviously she must have been one of those who have helped you a lot over the years . . .?

'You need somebody watching you all the time, whether it is a coach from outside or whether it is your wife, brother, uncle, whatever. You need someone there every day, not necessarily because you need them to coach you or anything but to talk to, to go over things with. It may sound stupid, but you really need them for stupid reasons. I don't know if it is a confidence thing or a back-up, or what. Margot has been a great help right through my career because we talk together. We are together all the time, so it is much easier to talk about technical things in training, and we look at it from a straightforward point of view. She might disagree with what I say, so when I listen to her, then I might disagree with that, and we come to a sort of happy medium. We could say, if I do this we are going to come off a wee bit better, and I think that is what I did in my training for Moscow. That is how I was able to come out in Moscow at a peak and run as fast as I did.'

Has your speedball training given you that speed of thought so essential to a sprinter?

'It is very hard to say what it does do. It is possible it strengthens your reactions; it holds the reaction for longer, so, instead of tying up at eighty, you will tie up maybe after 100. It probably makes the shoulders a bit more mobile. It does give this self-control right through the whole body. What I have done with it is probably the icing on top of the cake! I did a lot of leg work, not weights, but bounds and things like this to strengthen my legs a bit more this time. The speedball is not the only important part. The most important part is in the athlete's mind: whether he is doing it 100%, whether he is getting himself involved in it to the extent he is going to benefit from it. If he is doing it that way, he is going to get a lot back from it. If he is only kidding himself on, he is not going to get anything back from it.'

Can you give details of a particularly good training session that you have done this year (1980)?

'It is very difficult, as I can't specify them. We do press-ups in the gym. We do a thing called "Chinneys" – you are lying on your back in the gym, and you come up and bring your right knee to your left shoulder and you go down again and bring your left knee to the right shoulder, and it alternates like that. We also do squatting and the speedball. That is a gym session. I was training twice a day – I was doing leg work in the morning – and in both cases you warm up plus mobility exercises. I think I have concentrated on these for Moscow. It was a mental attitude to come up with the goods for Moscow, and that is how it paid off for me. I think if anybody wants to do athletics at an early age, at maybe eighteen, nineteen or twenty, then if they really want to make it to the top they have really got to concentrate – putting their mind to it as though they were going through their Highers, or, as you might call it in England, their A-levels.'

Do you remember a special session that pleased you before the Games?

'There were two or three days where I was running about half a yard faster than I had ever done in my life before, for sixty yards and over eighty yards. We tend not to run over eighty yards in training except when it comes to trials where we do a 100 and a 200 metres, but there were these three days about two weeks before Moscow when I was running well inside evens for sixty yards.'

You were getting very sharp already, then?

'I was sharp at the time, but I got a back injury. I am not quite sure what the problem was, but it kept me from actually running for two days, and the pain was so bad I could not even jog. It took me about one and a half weeks with four treatments a day at the West End General Hospital in Edinburgh to get rid of the pain.

'What has happened now is that I think it has gone into the sciatic nerve or whatever, because when I sit for reasonably long periods of time, this nervous thing goes down the leg, and it has been bothering me since before Moscow. It is something that has been a burden, but it has not kept me away from doing world-class times or obtaining Olympic medals. I have had a lot of problems down my left side, and my back has been giving me a bit of a problem, and that is something a lot of people don't know about. I got a problem with my hamstring in Moscow after the 100, when I was sitting in the dope-testing room. It had been warm all the time in Moscow, and it was even warmer in the dope-testing room. When I got up, I had just slight cramp in my hamstring, and although I stretched it out, it still felt as though it was there. Only now, at the end of the season, have I been able to get rid of it, without really doing anything. It is those problems people don't know about, because athletes tend to keep them to themselves.'

When you lined up for the 100 final in Moscow, you must have realized many people thought that, with his record, Silvio Leonard must have been the favourite, yet obviously that did not daunt you . . .

'It is all about peaking at the right time; in the quarter-final I ran a British record – it was the fastest in Moscow (10.11), and I think it proved to me that I could be the Olympic champion after that, as I did have it in my legs to run that fast. I knew Leonard had only done that time when it suited him, like when he had a wind behind him, and I knew he was not 100% mentally solid. I think in the sense that I felt that I was going to get at least a silver, and when it came to getting down on my blocks, there was no way I was going for second place. I was going for gold!'

It must have been difficult to judge the race, as Leonard was in lane 1 and you were out in lane 8?

'I was running up my lane with blinkers on, and I did not see anybody. The thing was for me to get the best out of myself at the time, and the thing that bothered me was that I was in lane 8. In Moscow, the wind was nearer the stands, and that was what I did not like. I would have been much happier if I had been in lane 1. In saying that, the Russians gave the wind as a plus wind, and that was ridiculous because it was a minus wind definitely. That time of 10.25 was really into the wind, so at the end of the day I ran particularly well.'

(1. Allan Wells, 10.25. 2. Silvio Leonard (Cuba), 10.25. 3. Petar Petrov (Bulgaria), 10.39. 4. Alexandr Aksinin (USSR),

10.42. 5. Osvaldo Lara (Cuba), 10.43.

In the 200 metres final, with thirty metres to go you seemed to have the race sewn up. Were you surprised with that late run of Mennea's?

'The race is never sewn up till you are over the finishing line for a start. People said, "Why did you run so fast on the bend?" The thing was, I did not run so fast on the bend. The other thing is that I spoke to Margot before the final, and I said to her that if Mennea comes at me with fifty out, then I will come back at him. I would physically try and come back at him, but when he came ten yards before the line it was just crazy, because it was too late to do anything. Another thing is the way I run 200s. When I am finished and over the line I am pretty well tired out, and if I was not like that in Moscow, then I would have believed I hadn't put everything into it. If I look at it, I can say it was a new British record, a silver medal. If I had come home with a silver medal I would have been absolutely delighted, and in fact if I had come back with just a bronze medal, that would have been a bonus for me really.'

(1. Pietro Mennea (Italy), 20.19. 2. Allan Wells, 20.21. 3. Don Quarrie (Jamaica), 20.29. 4. Silvio Leonard, 20.30. (Marian Woronin of Poland was seventh in the 100/200).

It must have been difficult for you, after gaining an Olympic gold medal, to motivate yourself to winning races after you had peaked for the Games?

'Just as you say, if you are going to peak for something and someone else is not peaking for that and he is not doing ten races in seven days or whatever, those guys are going to be much fresher, with a better chance of beating you. I have done quite well this time. The first race I had against Stanley Floyd (ranked No. One in the *Track and Field News* for 1980) and the other Americans I won, and it was more important to me winning that first one than, say, the third one. I met everybody who did not go to Moscow in the first meeting I had with them, and I beat them all.'

(Cologne: 1. Wells, 10.19. 2. Floyd, 10.21. 3. Mel Lattany, 10.25–10/8)

(200 in the Van Damme Memorial Meet, Heizelstadium: 1. Allan Wells, 20.26. 2. Mel Lattany, 20.27. 3. Stanley Floyd, 20.64 – Allan Wells went on in 1981 to win the

Europa Cup Final 100 metres in Zagreb in 10.17, beating the very good East German, Frank Emmelman, who recorded 10.21.)

28

WILLI WULBECK

Born 19 December, 1954, at Oberhausen, near Dusseldorf. 1.85/75kg.

West Germany's outstanding 800-metre runner in the history of the sport must have been Rudolf Harbig, who ran 1:46.6 for 800 metres in 1939, reducing the existing world record of the time by Sydney Wooderson (1:48.4) by a sizeable margin, and even today quite a few top races are not much faster than that! It took sixteen years till Roger Moens of Belgium set new figures of 1:45.7 for the record to be updated.

The German tradition in the event was not lost, as Willi Wulbeck, the consistent German, had the crowning achievement of his career by winning the first World Championship 800 metres in 1983. The names of the runners in that final in the famous Helsinki stadium, on 9 August, 1983: 1. Willi Wulbeck (FRG), 1:43.65. 2. Rob Druppers (HOL), 1:44.20. 3. Joaquim Cruz (BRA), 1:44.27. 4. Peter Elliott (GBR), 1:44.87. 5. James Robinson (USA), 1:45.12. 6. Agberto Guimaraes (BRA), 1:45.46. 7. Hans-Peter Ferner (FRG), the European Champion of 1982, 1:45.72, and 8. Dave Patrick (USA), 1:46.56.

Willi Wulbeck was ranked in the top ten in the Track and Field News, the USA's bible of the sport, in the following years: 1977 (third), 1978 (seventh), 1979 (fourth), 1980 (fourth), 1981 (seventh), but then in 1982, the year before his best competitive effort, he was not ranked at all, but he had some good races, beating Hans-Peter Ferner in the FRG Championships and also winning a 1000m in Cologne on 22 August in 2:16.95 from John Walker, who did 2:17.03. But he had a fairly disastrous run in the European in eighth place, yet he ran the third fastest ever 1000, with 2:14.5, behind Sebastian Coe in Oslo, so why did he do so badly in the final of the European?

Interview 1982

'First of all, in that race I was beaten mentally, as I was tired because I had only slept half the night for the two nights before the final. I felt really bad warming up for the final, and that made me feel a bit insecure for the race itself, and I did not feel good after 400 to 500 covered.'

Still, it was a different story for him in the GFR Championships on 25 July, when he won his ninth National 800 title, in 1:48.43 to Ferner's 1:48.48. What then happened to him in his lacklustre performance at the end of the season in 1982 at Crystal Palace, when he ran 4:03.55 in the mile at the Coca-Cola meet in September?

He told me about that race the night before.

'My season is over, I will not do well in that race. I look forward to the winter to train hard and do some indoor races and cross-country running in the parks, not racing over the hills. I will do the 1500 as well as the 800 in the World Championship year (1983), as that usually helps me bring my time down for the 800, which I feel I can do better at if, I do more 1500s. Looking back now, I realize that in the shape I was in in 1979–80, I could have gone below 1:44.0, but I was not in races fast enough for a 1.43, and the Olympics were in 1980, which, as a country, we did not compete in! Regarding the 1982 races in general terms, if I see that I lose contact in a race, like I did in the European final, and think I will not be in the first three or four, I tend to resign myself to not fighting hard.

'That is my problem! The reason why that happens is because I consider, over 800, I should always be in the first four, if not in the medals or to win the races outright. If that is not the case, I just can't raise myself to a good performance if I have fallen right away from the leaders.'

Taking into account that Willi Wulbeck was the Europa Cup Champion of 1977 (1. Wulbeck, 1:47.21. 2. Olaf Beyer (GDR, 1:47.29. 3. José Morajo (FR), 1:47.49), and third in

167

the World Cup of 1977, he must be qualified to give his opinion as to who were the toughest competitors he had come up against – Sebastian Coe or double 1976 Olympic Champion, Alberto Juantorena?

'I feared most Juantorena, because he looked so powerful when I ran beside him. He appeared superhuman, like a "Superman". He was the best 400 metres runner, and he had a big stride which made him so very powerful. He could play with the other athletes and the others could simply not follow, and that was very impressive. Sebastian Coe is small and does not appear so powerful with his strides, so he is more human-like to run against. It did not worry me so much, but when I was running beside Juantorena he was so huge, so he was more inspiring than Coe. I don't know who would have won in the Olympics, probably Coe when he was at his best, but Juantorena was somebody who could make the race and do just what he wanted, and I think he was also able to run as fast as Sebastian Coe. Those two are the best in the world.

'Now, looking back, there were several athletes who beat me when I was not in good shape and therefore I lost to them, such as newcomers Don Paige (*T and F News* rated top in 1980). There were Steve Ovett (Olympic champion 1980) and Olaf Beyer, who were certainly good. I admired Franz Joseph Kemper and Walter Adams, Harold Norpoth and also John Walker, all at the start of my career. Walker made races and won them from the front as he wanted to, and never got tired. I wonder how he can keep his shape over so many years (talking in 1982!).'

Willi started running when he was nearly sixteen, doing football as well. It was in the seventh and eighth classes that he turned to athletics. He soon found he was near the best in the school over 400 and 600 metres. His first minor competitions were over 800 and 1000, followed by cross-countrys. He found it was the sport he was best at and joined Oberhausen for five months, but he left that club because the athletes only treated the sport as a past-time, so he joined Oberhausen Rot und Weiss (Red and White), which was a bigger club. He then met Hans Raff at his new club. Raff was a long-distance runner back in the 1936 Olympics, and he trained Fritz Roderfeld to a

46:3–400 in 1967.

Willi explained: 'Raff advised me about training, and under his influence I improved from 2.03 for 800 to 1.45.'

How then did he improve so drastically under his coach's influence?

'My coach did not give me so much distance work; in the winter of 1981 I ran up to about twelve km in training, not more. I concentrated on things like 200, 300s and 400s. I would do five or ten of those, depending on what month. That was obviously a help. I did flying starts over 100 metres in 10.3. I think I am able to run 100 metres in 11.0 seconds. My winter season would be about perhaps 90, 110 or 120 kilomeres per week. In the summer fifty to sixty km a week. It depends on how many races I have to do regarding how hard I train. I do interval work, of course. I do test myself over various distances on the track, if I have not got a race too close. For the first few years with the club I trained with a group, but since then I have trained alone in the winter, which is a problem for me sometimes.'

Looking at his career through Willi Wulbeck's eyes:

1973

His first big breakthrough came in the European Junior Championships at Duisburg (1. Steve Ovett, 1:47.53. 2. Willi Wulbeck, 1:47.57). 'That race made the deepest impression on me, because I jumped into international class. I think it was one of my most impressive races; I led all the way until the last metre.'

1974

He improved his best to 1:46.3 in placing eighth in the European final in Rome, a race won by Luciano Susanj (1:44.7) with Steve Ovett second. To digress, here is what Luciano said of that in the Rome village:

'I thought of my wife and my son watching me on television, and that inspired me. In the first moment, I thought of the position I had. When I saw Fiasconaro go for

169

the whole 800 and do the first 400 in 50.1, I knew he must "die". I had thought Marcello Fiasconaro and Ovett would be first home in the race, but when I saw Fiasconaro's tactics I thought it was not possible for him to finish first, because he was too fast in the beginning.' Back from the Yugoslavian Champion to our subject Willi Wulbeck. It was in that year Willi gained his first West German title. 'That win in the West German Championship was a big advance for me. I was never in the final before.'

1975

His time progressed to 1:45.44 when he was third in the USA v Africa v FRG match at Durban, behind Rick Wohlhuter (1:44.12) and John Kipurgat. 'I did not think it was my optimum race, so I tried to run 1.44 that year, because the German record at that time was 1:44.9. But I did not get the record till 1979.'

1976

The Montreal Olympic Final was a good race for him. He finished fourth in a time of 1:45.26, turning the tables on Steve Ovett (fifth) and Susanj (sixth). Winner, Juantorena in 1:43.5, from Ivo Van Damme in 1:43.9.

1977

For the first year he did not improve on his time, but competitively he had a good season, climaxing with victory in the European Cup in Helsinki.

1978

He improved to 1:45.12, but missed his chance in the European Championships, when he failed to arrive in time for his heat. He cut over four seconds from his best for 1500, to 3:38.61.

1979

The year of his best time to that date of 1:44.65 – third in the World Cup.

1980

He was under 1.45 again, and placed seventh on the world year list for 1500, with 3:33.74, but there was no Olympic Games for him with a West German boycott.

1981

His best for the year was 1:45.34, behind Rod Druppers's Dutch record of 1:44.70 at Koblenz, and he notched up his ninth consecutive West German title.

1983

Willi Wulbeck became World Champion in a personal best time of 1:43.65 in Helsinki and became West German 800 metres champion for the tenth, consecutive time.

29

ED MOSES

Born Dayton, Ohio, on 31 August, 1955. 1.86/73kg.

There were some extraordinary athletic feats over the last one hundred years. American Jim Thorpe was one who was ahead of his time when winning the decathlon and pentathlon in the 1912 Olympics, before being eventually stripped of his titles because it was found that he had played some pro baseball.

Daley Thompson's gold medal performances in the decathlon put him as possibly the world's greatest all-round athlete!

For me, the most amazing talent was Edwin Moses, who strung together .a tally of 122 unbroken victories when running against the best in the world in the late 1970s and early 1980s, and, as I write this book in 1990, you can count on one hand those athletes who have beaten him in the intermediates, since he started the event in top competition in 1976.

Back in 1977, Gary Oakes, the 1980 Olympic bronze medallist who is now a Lloyd's underwriter, told me (when Moses had only been at the top for nearly two seasons) that he thought, that if John Akii-Bua, who ran 47.82 in 1972 for a World record, had met Edwin Moses it would have been a terrific race, as they were the only two athletes at that time capable of getting under 48 seconds!

Someone who competed against Edwin in those days and was amongst the top dozen in the world for several years, James King, the 1989 World Veteran Champion and age World record holder for both the 400 and 400 hurdles: 'I twice came close to surprising him. It can be done, but if there is somebody in the race with great potential to beat him, then he won't let that happen. Edwin is a smart guy. He did not come out in 1982 because he got sick; he got married, and I think he lost that concentration to get into racing. He would have had to really worry about his races in Europe and the States because there were too many guys out there who could come on in. I think he would have been hard pushed, but I don't think Edwin Moses's ability has really been tapped.'

James King continued in 1983, 'Edwin is a person you have got to catch off-guard, because he is always going to be ready when he gets into a race with someone like Harald Schmid or Andre Phillips. They don't really think about winning, because he is not going to give them a second thought.' Certainly in just one race in 1977, 'Big Harald' did catch him off-guard, but only the once!.

Regarding Andre Phillips, it took till 1988 at the Olympics in Seoul – (1. Andre Phillips, 47.19. 2. El Hadji Amadou Dia Ba (Sen), 47.23. 3. Edwin Moses, 47.56) – to overpower the champion or for Danny Harris to top the lists!

1987 World 800 metres Champion Billy Konchellah from Kenya had something to say about Edwin. 'I have lived with him in the same house. I still think he is the greatest guy on the track, and in his personal life he is a whole, rounded person. He is a person with a kind heart and hard-working, and he helps anybody in the position of wanting help.'

Edwin's World records read: Montreal 1976, 47.64; Westwood 1977, 47.45; Milan 1980, 47.13; Koblenz 1983, 47.02.

For me the most exciting race to watch was his World Championship win in 1983 in Rome, when the first three runners were locked in a titanic battle as they entered the straight. The end result: 1. Ed Moses (USA), 47.46. 2. Danny Harris (USA), who was runner-up to Edwin in the Olympics of 1984, 47.48, and third, his long-standing rival and a charming man, Harald Schmid (FRG) 47.48, with a consolation of a European record!

Interview with Lloyd Jackson, Edwin Moses's coach, in 1977

What times do you think Edwin Moses will be doing by the time the 1980 Olympics come round? (At the time of writing, the Games were ten years ago, and USA pulled out, although Moses was rated number one in the world that year).

'If he develops that twelve stride pattern between the second and sixth hurdle, he will bring the World record down to 46.2 – 46.5 for the 400 metres hurdles, and the highs he should be able to run in around 13.2, 13.1 or better. He ran 13.5 this year (1977), and beat Casanas and Davenport.'

Do you expect him to continue with the 110 hurdles, then?

'We always did both, even in the meets where the time span was, let's say half to three-quarters of an hour. We always did the high hurdles as a preparation and warm-up on the intermediates.'

Was it difficult for Edwin to use thirteen strides all the way?

'Not for him, because Ed has a nine foot (2.97 metre) stride. He takes 179 strides for 400 metres, and if you watch him run the 400 flat, it is just the same stride pattern, but he will employ greater leg speed. His stride pattern in the quarter hurdles falls into a thirteen stride category that enables him to get over the hurdles with the same stride pattern.'

Do you hope he progresses to a twelve stride pattern?

'We have been working on that for the last two years. He has been coming up on twelve strides between the second to the sixth hurdle, and alternating back to thirteen so that he can get the left leg lead to take advantage of the two feet around the run, and if he can't do any better than that, he will try for eleven strides, which would enable him to go around running the event all the way on a left leg lead. It is important you run a left leg lead, because you are closer to the line and you have two feet on each turn.'

What other hurdlers in the world would be tough competitors for Edwin (in 1977)?

'There are only two people who I would say can give him any kind of competition, but they really don't train: Wes Williams and James King. Wes Williams runs thirteen strides to the eighth hurdle.'

When do you first remember meeting Edwin?

'When I first meet Ed, I was at Atlanta University in Georgia. I was attending a theological seminary there, and I met Ed as he was working for me in a work study programme. I used to give him little tips, but I was out of track then. I was not coaching till the coach of Morehouse College quit, and the kids did not have a track coach. So what happened was, Ed and a few other guys came to me and asked me if I would coach them until they hired a coach. I felt as though I owed track a committment for what it had given me, so I volunteered three or fours hours a day to coach them, and that is what I have been doing ever since.'

What did you notice about Edwin's ability that made him stand out as an athlete at the start?

'When he and I met, he was only 150 lbs (68 kg), and he was running the 400 flat in 48 seconds and the high hurdles in 14.2. But the thing that struck me most about him was, whatever I told him to do he would never complain, whether he was well or sick. We just worked together, and finally he began to improve to what he is now.'

When did you see his potential as a top-class 400 hurdler?

'In his first hurdles race at Gainsville, Florida, he did the intermediates in 50.1, and also on the same day he ran a flat 46.1 for the 400, which also qualified him for the Olympic trials. We had something like ninety quarter-milers who had qualified and there were four days of heats, so we knocked that out because it was too much. In the high hurdles he also qualified, and there were 125 who had done that, which was too much, and so we knocked that out. We decided to deal with the 400 metres hurdles, because there were only about thirty people who qualified for that. Watching the world rankings, we saw that potentially he could win the gold, and we told people that back in March and May. Of course, they did not go along with it, but we knew what was going on. So what happened was, he steadily trained and I developed some workouts for him. Those workouts have given him a lot of strength and agility over the hurdles as well as the confidence in running the hurdles.'

In front of a 70,000 or more crowd in the Stadium, the World record in the 400 hurdles and the Olympic title in Montreal, went to Edwin Moses in 47.64. The supporting

175

cast was: Mike Shine (USA), 48.69; Yevgeniy Gavrilenko (USSR), 49.45; Quentin Wheeler (USA), 49.86; Jose Jesus Carvalho (PORT), 49.94. The others in the final behind that were Yanko Bratanov (Bul), Alfonso Damaso (Cuba) and Alan Pascoe (UK), but then Alan had run his best races with a splendid international career before that.

Do you thing there is no substitute for hard work, except that the medical back-up and facilities in East Germany might be that much better than the USA?

'The East Germans can use all the fanatical workouts, drugs, or vitamins and all that, but there is no substitute for conditioning. They probably do have better facilities, but the thing that I would like to stress is that the facilities don't make the person. It is what is inside of a person, the drive that he has. To get into the religious aspect, not only the drive – I definitely believe that we cannot do anything in this world unless God blesses us.'

Innocent Egbunike, who ran 44.17 in 1987 for a Commonwealth 400 metres record, adds to that comment by saying: 'I shake the hands of my competitors and give them my best wishes. God has already picked the winner, so I go there and do the best I can.'

Lloyd, looking back, do you think David Hemery was a great athlete?

'Definitely. I read up on him because when Ed and I started to talk about hurdles in October 1975, that was when we evaluated everything, and at the time I did not know a thing about hurdling! I knew how to condition a person for track, as I was a 400 metre sprinter myself, and did about thirty races over a period of thirteen to fourteen years. What I did was to buy some books and I talked to my coach, Leroy T. Walker, who was a very good friend, and he showed me and taught me things. So most of the hurdling that I know I learnt from him, and I just went on to a book called *The Hurdler's Bible*, written by Wilbur Ross, who was a fine hurdler and a coach to Willie Davenport, Elias Gilbert and Lee Calhoun among others. In his book he had some comments and a couple of pages on David Hemery, and I studied his workouts and just improved upon them.'

How do you see Edwin as a person?

'He is an intellectual. He likes to read and he likes

scientific things. He is not full of foolishness, he is serious, likes kids, likes solitude.'

Interview with Edwin Moses 1979

You told me how you liked to hear the crowd when you are out on the track, but what really gives you the most enjoyment in athletics?

'Just knowing the people and enjoying what you are doing. In my case, knowing that I am doing what I can do better than anybody else ever has; that is very satisfying.'

Which of the athletes you have competed with has influenced you most, firstly in hurdles and secondly in other events?

'I think Akii-Bua for my event. When I saw him compete in the 1972 Olympics, I thought that if there was any possibility that I could run that event, I kind of figured I would. For other events, I think Tommie Smith, when he won the 1968 Olympic 200 metres. I think that was one of the most dramatic shows of solidarity the black Americans had at the time. It was really a bad time in the US and just to be able to show the world that we existed and somebody cared was great, even though he made the sacrifice of losing his status for ever, along with all those other guys.'

You told me (in 1979) that your hardest year as a tough training period was the 1976 Olympic year!

'Yes, because I had to make the breakthrough from being an average college athlete to world-class, which I made in four months.'

You are not coached now, but did Lloyd Jackson have a great influence on your progress when he did coach you?

'He took me from being mediocre to being a champion.'

Lloyd Jackson considered that conditioning was important, hand in hand with a strong belief in God. Did that influence you a lot?

'I think it had a definite influence. Being in the position that I was, not knowing exactly how well I could do, or just going in hoping to become a champion. I think faith helped pull me through, gave me the energy and spirit at times when I did not think I could finish a workout.'

How many days do you train, then?

'Usually four or five days per week, sometimes even six or seven; it varies.'

Being up with the best in competitions over the shorter high hurdles must have helped your 400 hurdles?

'I have not run them at all this year (1979) except, for one I ran just for the exhibition. Next year I will probably start out running the highs again, as it gives me a break from the longer race, and when I do intensify training it really helps me out a lot with my leg speed.'

Since you started 400 hurdles, which race was the most pleasing performance to you?

(Up to the middle of 1979) 'I think the AAU at Los Angeles, Westwood, when I broke the World record of 47.45 on 11 June, 1977 – it beat the record that I had set in Montreal, although it was not really a good race. Knowing that I had run that time under those conditions told me that I was in terrific shape at the time. It gave me a sign which told me to keep going, as I could go under 47 seconds.'

Looking back again to some amazing performers, besides our subject, there were many who captured the moment of success so well. Mary Peters, who won the Olympic pentathlon in a World Record in 1992 at Munich. A really lovely personality, who had a stadium named after her. American decathlete Bruce Jenner who won the 1976 Olympic decathlon, had a major annual athletics meeting named after him and, was followed some years later by another future 'star' at his event in 1991–92, from the same country, by the name of Danny O'Brien, who won the decathlon in Tokyo and challenged the marks of Daley Thompson!

Also in 1992 Zambian Samuel Matete, the World 400 Hurdles Champion of the year before, came into the middle of the summer season of 1992 with a string of victories behind him, and as a favourite for Barcelona but, would find it hard to touch Edwin Moses' number of straight wins which had been punctuated with world records.

30

PETER ELLIOTT

Born at Rawnmarsh, Rotherham, 9 October, 1962. 1.81/ 1.67kg.

For as long as I can remember, athletes with potential as youngsters have been cast aside as 'also-rans' on the bumpy road to success for one reason or another, but in Peter Elliott's case, despite having been overshadowed in the news, particularly by his fellow-countrymen Steve Ovett, Seb Coe and Steve Cram, eventually came through and obtained a 'big' games gold for himself. He very nearly achieved that in the Olympic Games of 1988 in the 1500 (1. Peter Rono (Kenya), 3:35.6. 2. Peter Elliott, 3:36.15. 3. Jans-Peter Herold (GDR), 3:36.21). He persevered, and it eventually paid off in the Commonwealth Games in Auckland. It was on 3 February, 1990, with the result: Peter Elliott, 3:33.29. 2. Wilfred Kirochi (Kenya), 3:34.41, and 3. Peter O'Donoghue (Australia), 3:35.14.

He quickly followed that up with his first World record over 1500 (indoors), with 3:34.21 on 27 February in Seville.

In the summer, his build-up for the European 1500 in Split was badly effected by illness and injury; although he was out of the frame there, he came back with a British All-Comers record of 3:32.69, ahead of Steve Cram (3:33.03) in an enthralling 1500 at Sheffield on 16 September.

In Peter's case, I thought it would be interesting to go back in time to when he was a lad of seventeen, and the interview I did with him and Bill McRobb, who coached him then, before Wilf Paish and then Kim McDonald took over. It was in 1980, and he had won the National Youth cross-country championships at Leicester by seven seconds from Phil Hicken, with Jon Richards third (the latter went on to become Youth and then Junior champion). At that time, Pete was English Schools cross-country champion (1979), and held the UK best for a sixteen-year-old over 800 metres, with 1:50.7. He was very noticeably a down-to-earth lad with a lot of sense that success has not spoilt in any way.

Interview 1980

What do you like most about athletics?

'The sportsmanship amongst different athletes: there is no real hatred in it. Also I enjoy coming to meetings because it gets me about the country.'

Who were the people you admired at the start of your career?

'I was not really inspired, I just went down to the Harriers, and it started from there when I was about twelve years old. Of the people I admire, I think Brendan Foster is one, because of the things he has done for Gateshead and that area. Sebastian Coe has brought a name to South Yorkshire. I don't class myself as one of them like that, as I want to be an individual and make my own mark.'

Does your club, Rotherham Harriers and AC, mean a lot to you?

'Rotherham have pulled me through it all, and I could not have done what I did in the National cross-country without them. I have a team-mate called Glyn Davies, and we are always training together. Wherever you go, there is always someone from Rotherham there, so I am not by myself.'

Bill McRobb: 'I think the important thing about his comradeship with the club is that, although he has got the National title, he is still very much on the ground.'

Who has helped you, as far as coaching is concerned?

'Bill McRobb and Steve Moxon.'

Bill McRobb: 'He started originally with Steve Moxon from Rotherham. Steve at the time was coaching a pretty big group on his own, which tends to happen at a country club, if you like. Steve coached the middle-distance boys. I came in jointly with him, as I was coaching young athletes.'

What type of running did you give him to begin with?

Bill McRobb: 'Originally we gave him a pretty reasonable mixture, because you are dictated to by what he does at school. He has always done cross-country in the winter. It has been a pretty normal programme, with long steady stuff as well as fartlek. The facilities in South Yorkshire, when you start coming on to track training, are very, very poor. At last now we have the first tartan track in the area, so a lot of our training is done on parkland and on grass.'

Peter, how many days do you train, and what sort of mileage do you do?

'I train seven days a week, and my mileage is fifty a week.'

Bill McRobb: 'Perhaps forty of that is quality work. We have always made sure that we had the overdistance work in and we have always worked, through necessity, as we have not always had access to a track in winter, on grassland and uphill work.'

Which training do you enjoy most, Peter?

'Quality work. I like fartlek and hills, and I like circuit training, which I do once a week.'

Now you are seventeen and an apprentice joiner (1980), but, looking back to your school days, how did you come to do athletics as your main sport?

'First of all, I had the choice between running and football. I was doing them both, then running seemed to take over as I got more into my training everyday. It was then I packed in football, and have not looked back since.'

Which was the first race that really made you take that decision?

'The Northern Boys cross-country. It was a schools race with 700 in it, and I won that at Stockport. To win from 700, I felt, was great. I was fourteen then.'

Bill McRobb: 'We competed from then on in every major schools event, both on the track and cross-country. He has been the English Schools 800 metre champion at junior and intermediate level.'

Peter, if you could choose cross-country, road running or track at the moment, which one would you favour?

'I would choose track. Now I am training on a track programme, and I was only hoping just to get in the first ten in the National Youths at Leicester – I never thought I would win it!'

181

Bill McRobb: 'From the start of last track season, he disregarded the real competitiveness of cross-country running. It is crackers to say that, I know, but I think he made his mind up to stick to 800 rather than step up to 1500. He had that 1:50.7 last summer at the age of sixteen, and I think that was a big decision point.' (Incidentially, he was second in the World Championships in Rome in 1987 in 1:43.41, behind Kenyan Billy Konchella's 1:43.06, also a personal best. He improved to 1:42.9 for the fastest time in the world in 1990).

Back to the 1980 interview, talking to Bill McRobb. Bill, you decided to send Peter for training with National coach Wilf Paish. Why was that?

'We really took this decision just before Christmas. We talked about it for some time. With my business commitments, for one thing, I felt very much obliged to stick with the group of kids in the area that we are in, and there was a need for someone to be with the other kids. The other coach, Steve, felt he was having a lot of committments at home and that he needed to drift off the scene a bit. Although Peter has this affinity with Glyn Davies, the other lad training with him, all the way along the line, we felt that he really needed to get that extra edge in training too.'

How did that National Youth race go for you, Peter?

'There was no hurting at all until I got to the bend, and I was then feeling it a bit. Most of the people from South Yorkshire seemed to be gathered down the back straight, and I got into second place there, and they were cheering me on. I thought I could pull it off up the hill, and I could not see them catching me. The course was a bit fast, the pace was fast and to my liking.'

Bill McRobb sums up: 'Although there are various theories about weights and middle-distance running – Peter has always had a good appetite for shifting weights. He is a very strong lad basically. Forgetting about any running attributes, he is very strong physically.'

31

DON QUARRIE

Born at Kingston, Jamaica, on 25 February, 1951. 1.75/70kg.

Interviews from 1970–89

Don Quarrie was possibly the greatest championship sprinter over the longest period. Some would say he had not got the sheer power of Jesse Owens, Bob Hayes, Jim Hines, Leroy Burrell or Ben Johnson or even the blazing speed of Carl Lewis, Calvin Smith and latterly Michael Johnson at their best, but no-one could fault Don's consistency.

For instance, he was on the Olympic team for Jamaica in 1968 before he got injured, and then twenty years later in 1988 he was placed in the Jamaican Championship 200 metres, but was surprisingly left off the team for Seoul, even though he had tremendous experience as a relay runner – having been on the 4×100 relay team when Jamaica were second in the LA Olympics of 1984, etc. In 1988, he ran a 20.6 200 metres as well. It was also in 1988 that I talked to Grace Jackson about Don, as he was instrumental as a coach in getting her to crack the 22.00 second barrier and finish second in the Olympic final in Seoul in 21.72, behind Florence Griffith Joyner's 21.34 World record.

'As an athlete, he is able to relate to a lot of things, he knows what kind of pain it is, having been through the pain. I have a tremendous amount of confidence in him. He has helped me perfect my form and taught me how to run, and I also feel I have learnt how to win from his advice.'

She went on to say: 'I think he was really calm as an

athlete, and that was often the difference between him and his other competitors he raced against, so now when he says to me that I can run 21 seconds for 200, he knows what we have done and knows exactly why he says that!' In the light of what happened in the Olympics for Grace just a couple of months later, how very apt that all was!

1984 Olympic 100 metre finalist Mike McFarlane told me: 'I think it is Don Quarrie's attitude. I always admired the way he ran, his style, and his contribution to the track. If he ran well today, fine; if he ran badly today, it is just another race. You beat me today, and I'll beat you tomorrow. I think it is the right attitude to take; you don't expect to win every day of the week.'

Reflecting on the past in 1988 with Don on his whole extensive career in the sport, and touching briefly on his Championship victories in the Olympics, Commonwealth and Pan-American Games, which of those meant the most to him?

'I think the Commonwealth Games 100 in 1970 was one of my biggest highlights, because I came through on the international scene with those two wins (100/200) in Edinburgh. The Olympic 200 gold in Montreal in 1976 was a highlight as I wanted that, because in 1972 I had the misfortune of being injured, so I had that determination and everything was pointing towards 1976, and it came through just the way I was hoping and the way I had planned it. I would not change anything.'

I can often remember staring at a picture of Don Quarrie in the *ATFS Annual* of 1976. It was of Don running the bend in the 1975 AAU Championships that he won in 20.12, and I pointed that out to Don and asked if it was a memory for him?

'I do have a memory for the American Championships, because I won a couple of those. Some of the 200s I ran I knew I could win, and it was just a matter of staying in control and staying relaxed as I could, and it worked.'

From what Don has said there, I thought it would be interesting to reflect a little more on the two Games he mentioned in particular. He was a Champion sprinter at three Commonwealth Games, but it was the first one that stood out for him, so let us go back to Edinburgh in 1970, and Don takes up the story at the time.

'In the 100, I thought Lennox Miller would be tough. He had not been training for too long, about a month at the most as he had been in dental school and was studying hard, so I did not expect him to be in top form. With his experience I really had to watch out for him, as if he was really on his top form I think it would be hard to beat him.' (Lennox Miller of Jamaica had previously in 1968 come second in the Mexico 100 metres Olympic final in 10.00, with Jim Hines of the USA first in 9.95).

'In Edinburgh my start was my main problem in the 100. I thought, if I could start better I could really improve on my times. It was around fifty metres that I really started developing, and by that time everyone was gone. I really always come on strongly at the finish. However, near the tape I never gave up till past the tape. I was really pleased with the final because I was behind at fifty and Hasely Crawford was leading as he got out real quick, but at seventy yards I came right through.'

1. Don Quarrie, 10.2. 2. Lennox Miller, 10.3, and 3. Hasely Crawford (Trin), 10.3.

'In the 200 I was satisfied with the lane, but I did not run the race the way I wanted to. When I entered the straight, instead of gaining my form and lifting my knees, I was using too much leg speed and I tied up at the finish, but I kept driving right through. If I had been in lane 7 I think I would have won by a larger margin, but I was in lane 3.'

1. Don Quarrie, 20.5. 2. Edwin Roberts (Trin), 20.6. 3. Charles Asati (Kenya), 20.7.

Montreal in 1976 was obviously the highlight as he won the Olympic 200, but before that he was very much a factor in the 100 metres final. The first six were: 1. Hasely Crawford (Trin), 10.06. 2. Don Quarrie, 10.08. 3. Valerie Borzov, the 1972 Champion, in 10.14 for USSR. 4. Harvey Glance (USA), 10.19. 5. Guy Abrahams (Panama), 10.25, and 6. Johnny Jones (USA), 10.27.

Interview in 1976

'I was not really worried about anybody, so to speak, before the race. I figured, okay it is going to be between Crawford,

Borzov and Glance, and I was beside them. Crawford was way up in lane 1 in the final. I got off very well, even though a lot of people said I had a bad start, but I made a slight error about twenty-five metres, whereby I straightened up a little bit too early, which cut my stride for a period of time, so within twenty-five to fifty I had got myself back into that same rhythm, and that was when I started coming back on the field, and by then I could only see Borzov and Glance; there was nobody else because you don't look around for people and Borzov blocked my views, so there was no way I could have seen Crawford any earlier, so that around eighty I really made a second effort in order to catch him, and I caught him but just did not beat him.'

So often the wonderful success of one man on the big occasion is sorrow for others who were less lucky. In the 100 and 200 metres in the Olympics of 1976, Steve Williams, the tall American sprinter, would certainly have been a factor and amongst the medallists if he had not been so unlucky with injuries. I interviewed Steve the year after at Dusseldorf, when he not only won the World Cup 100 metres in 10.13, but was in the USA team (Collins, Riddick, Wiley and Steve Williams) who broke the world 4×100 record with 38.03.

Regarding 1976, Steve Williams's sad story: 'My coach and myself had spent a lot of time in preparation, and we did feel that we had not overprepared or anything. We felt we were coming along just fine. We had just run the hand-timed World record twice that year and we had run some very good 200s, but we really had not been putting out 100%, and the injury really disappointed me because of course all the work and time I had waited for – the fact that I got injured not doing anything in the first round of the 100 in the trials, which was really no stress at all, so it was something I had to live with for quite a while, and it is something I don't know if I'll ever get over. It made a definite change in my personality. People asked me what did I do when the Olympic final was being run at Montreal, and what I did was to go out and buy a car the same day, something to do. I never saw the 100. I did not see any of the Olympic Games. I think one of the really sorriest parts of what happened to me last year (1976) was that I could not imagine being in California as, in my diary, my little monthly planner had ever day laid out for the Games, and every day I had to open it to see what I had to do. I could not imagine that I would be where I was during that stage of the Games. I remember one night I was walking from a friend's house to my girlfriend's house in San Diego and it was a really hot summer night, every window was open in the block and every television was on the Olympic Games, and there I was walking down the street! Things like that have burned in me. The World Cup was nice as far as the world status of the event, but nothing will ever make up for the fact that I was not there in 1976. I feel I have an apology to make to the American people for not being there on my job, because, not that I do not have any respect for the people who did go, as far as the Americans are concerned, but for some reason I did not think that they were going to be able to stand there and have enough emotions to run Quarrie down who pulled in the finals of 1972. When Hasely had won the 100, people asked me about him. He had never beaten me in a 100 metres in his life, and yet there I was sitting at home!'

200 metres final, 26 July, 1976

First six: 1. Don Quarrie, 20.23. 2. Millard Hampton (USA), 20.29. 3. Dwayne Evans (USA), 20.43. 4. Pietro Mennea (Italy), 20.54. 5. Ruy Da Silva (Brazil), 20.84. 6. Bogdan Grzejsczak (Poland), 20.91.

Don Quarries's brief account of his training before the Games: 'Basically, a week's work-out when I am more or less in shape would be like this: Monday, I would do 330s (depends on what the meets are as to how many I will run); starts and 110s on Tuesdays, 220s on Wednesday. Thursday, I would run some starts and some 110s on Friday; if I don't have a meet next day, I would run a breakdown "3 to 1", but if I have a meet, maybe 2×150 on the Thursday and rest on the Friday.'

The race over 200 in Montreal

'In the final, Mennea was in 1 and I was in 2, while Hampton and Evans had two of the best lanes, 4 and 7, and

I don't think they wasted any time getting off the curve. I was not worried at all, because I figured if I was in lane 1 I was going to catch the field regardless.

'I have always run a good turn in the 200, and I figured that this time it was possible that I could get lane 1 and I did work a little bit on it, which got me prepared mentally for it.

'I am not really taking anything from them, but I was more conscious or more determined to win than to really run a fast time, because I came off the turn two or three yards ahead of them instead of going into my usual lift, where I would have gotten up and really stretched out. I just kept on running and I could tell, because I can run a 200 two different ways – can run one on the turn and keep turning over, and the last one's that I run the turn and get up and really stretch out, so in that one I ran, the turn came off ahead and I guess I was a little anxious, and so I just kept on turning over. I saw Millard Hampton coming, but I did not panic bacause I knew I was strong enough to hold him off, so I made sure instead of trying to drive away from him. I started pumping my arms a little more just to hold him off, but I was not going to try to pull away because I figured that I was strong enough to hold him off, as he was not coming that fast but, as I said, he ran very good after coming on the scene so late in the year. Regarding Mennea, I figured as he had got lane 1 he had not got a chance, because Mennea can not run a turn. If he gets lane 8, he will come off the turn last, but he will run. Lane 8 would have made him run the turn better. As he was in lane 1, at no stage of the game was he in contention, and by the time he had got into the home stretch he started running on, and by then everybody was gone.'

32

MIKE BOIT

Interviews 1975 and 1984

Mike Boit was born in 1949. He is 146lbs/5ft 10¾ins tall, a gentle and soft-spoken Nandi tribesman from Kenya, who ran 1:48.5 for two laps back in 1967 and ran 1:49.3 behind Olympic finalist Omar Khalifa when coming second on Steve Cram's Jarrow track on 9 September, 1984!

A glance at some of the fast times he has put up over the years is mind-boggling in itself.

His best time for 800 is 1:43.5 (1976); until 1984, that placed him third fastest of all time, behind Sebastian Coe and Alberto Juantoreno. In 1981 he ran 3:49.45 for the mile, which put him seventh on the all-time list. His best 1,000 metres time is 2:15.3 in 1977, put him again in the top seven in the world.

He ran five times under 1:44.5 in 1975. In 1977, he ran 1:45.1 or faster no less than ten times! In 1981 he was rated third in the world over 1500 in *Track and Field News*, with a best for that year of 3:33.67. In 1982, Mike ran 1:46.16/3:48.83, and in 1983 1:47.65/3:36.45. He turned forty on New Year's Day 1989, and on 10 February at Meadowlands, he broke Ron Bell's World Veteran indoor (forty to forty-four) record with 4:15.88.

Mike Boit started his education at the mission school run by Patrician fathers from Ireland, and then went on to Kenyatta College, about eleven miles from Nairobi, before going to round off his studies at Stamford University in America and Oregon University.

When you look back over your many years of inter-national competition, which of the great athletes stand out in your mind as tough racers?

'Of course there are different personalities. I have run against several good athletes, but of course the competition has changed a little bit now. Athletes are training more and more. They are getting to know more and more about their potential and capabilities, so that they can do a lot more than they originally thought they could.

'In the 800 metres, we go through in 49 seconds now and still keep going strong all the way. Things have changed now. I thought Juantorena was a great athlete. You saw him running in Montreal, and he won the double 400/800 metres. Very few have been able to do that. Rick Wohlhuter was a great competitor and mentally tough. The man I admire and who is still going strong is John Walker – I think he is amazing! But there are so many of them.

'Thomas Wessinghage is mentally tough – every time you get on the line with him, he is going to be very competitive. Adding to that, the English athletes, Steve Ovett and Sebastian Coe, although I have not been able to run against Steve Ovett very much. Steve Ovett's running is not the way I do. I like running more with Sebastian Coe, as he runs strong all the way. Steve Ovett has a really strong kick. When he is in good shape he stays back, then one or two laps to go his kick was always unbelievable.'

Your silver medal back in the Commonwealth 800 metres, of 1:44.4 in Christchurch in 1974, must stand out. At the 1972 Olympics in Munich before that, you gained a bronze medal in the 800 and were fourth in the 1500. Was it a disappointment that you did not get a medal for the 1500 at Munich?

'I think it was more of a disappointment that I did not get the gold in the 800 (1. Dave Wottle (USA), 1:45.86. 2. Yergeniy Arzhanov (USSR), 1:45.89. 3. Mike Boit (Kenya) 1:46.01), because I think I was capable of getting a gold in the 800 metres. I was stronger than Wottle, and I was stronger than anyone in the 800 at that time. The problem was with the coaches, and being a novice as I was, I did not have a good strategy. I never knew much about a world event. Coming off the turn, I had Robert Ouko ahead of me – coming into the final, Kenya officials had told me, "we expect a gold and a silver medal." Ouko took the lead, and was not a good leader. With 200 metres to go, he was really tired – I was up on his shoulder. It was a slow race – everybody was kicking hard – it was really very difficult to make up any lost ground.'

Will you continue with athletics in some way?

'I will continue to run, and I would like to be in the position where I will be able to help some young athletes with some advice. It would be a real pleasure to do that, because, as I know when I grew up, when I was beginning, I knew what I wanted but did not know how to do it. If it was not for people like Alex Stewart and also Bruce Tulloh helping me and giving me confidence, contributing a lot of time helping me to develop my potential, I would not have been anywhere. I did not think I was good enough, and if I was not good enough there was no point in wasting my time. I was good in school and I knew I would make it through in the Schools, but I thought running was not good for me if I was not going to make a good athlete. These people gave me so much confidence. Every time Alex Stewart told me I was as good as anybody in the world – at first I did not believe it.'

What do you lome most about running?

'One thing is that I have been able to make a lot of friends, able to meet a lot of people. I think it has developed my character. I was not that competitive, but as I went along I became more and more competitive. One reason why I did need so much encouragement was because I was just an easy-going person at the beginning. I think that made the big difference – I needed a lot of encouragement – these people wasted no time in making sure they really convinced me.'

Do you think the turning-point in your career was your improvement before the 1972 Olympics after some good short-term training methods?

'I think that may be what made me realize I had some good potential . . . I was probably one of the last to make the team with the qualifying mark. In the 800 metres there was such a strong field, I thought beforehand I had no chance of making the 800 metres team. I was at home, we had a long vacation. Alex Stewart had gone home. I went to Nairobi about May, and I was in poor condition and ran 800 metres in 1:49 or 1:48 in one of the trials, which was a tune-up meet for the Olympics, and 3:52 or 3:53 for 1500.

'Alex Stewart told me not to go home, but to come to his place, and we trained for three weeks. I was able to knock the 3:52 down to 3:40. Then I was able to bring my 800 time down from around 1:49 to 1:47.'

What sort of training were you doing?

'Mainly speed training. 300s, 200s, 400s, nothing more than 400 metres. Once in a while, I occasionally ran 500 or 600 metres, which I did not like doing. But Alex Stewart always made me do the long intervals occasionally. I always resisted. Before 1972, I used to train only three times a week. I did not think it was possible to train every day, so I had only trained three times a week.'

1975 was a noteworthy year.

'1975 was a good year, and I ran against Ivo Van Damme, I got to know him very well, and Luciano Susanj. I was really so much impressed with Ivo Van Damme, and we were very good friends outside of the track. On the track he was so competitive. He was a man with so much potential, it was really a pity that we lost such a young man at the beginning of a wonderful career.'

In 1976, you were shaping up well, but the bottom must have been taken out of your world as Kenya withdrew from the Olympics?

'I ran well in 1976. I had great frustration because I was not able to run in those Olympics. I had really a good chance, and prepared myself well. In 1972, I went just for experience, and it was not so important to me at the time, as I did not know what I was capable of doing, but knowing what I could do and having been ranked number one in the world in 1975, it was really very important as a year for me. I was doing well. I was able to run 1:43.79 (Zurich, 20 August).'

There are certain races that must have special memories for you. I certainly feel, from waching, that your 800 metres in the 1979 World Cup at Dusseldorf was certainly something a bit special – against a fit Alberto Juantorena. (1. Alberto Juantorena, 1:44.0. 2. Mike Boit, 1:44.1. 3. Willi Wulbeck, 1:45.5. 4. Mark Enyeart, 1:45.5. 5. Josef Plachy, 1:45.5) That race looked like magical half-miling, with you

192

and Juantorena coming round the last bend together, your long strides matched evenly in cadence.

'When I ran against him at Zurich he beat me by ten metres, when he ran 1:43.6 and I ran 1:44.6. When later I ran against him in Dusseldorf, I remembered the mistakes I made in Zurich, and to a large extent I was able to correct those mistakes. I was able to close the gap. I planned to win the race, and I had a lot of strategies. I had planned to be in the second or third position during the first lap and coming round the turn. After 500 metres, I was going to kind of fake trying to take the lead, to make him kick a little bit earlier, with 300 to go rather than with 200 left. I was going to settle and just follow him, and with 200 to go, I was to close the gap and start with my kick with 150 left. Which I did, but I think I waited a little bit too long for closing the gap at the 200. My strategy almost worked!'

In 1978 you won the Commonwealth gold over 800 – very easily it appeared – with 1:46.39 at Edmonton. That must have been a cherished gold medal after all your Olympic problems?

'It was a pleasing performance because we had the All-African Games – I came in last in the 800 metres. So you can imagine how happy I was, because I was having problems with my running at the time.'

What other memories would you not want to be left out?

'I think after 1978 the most important race was the mile in the Zurich meet, with me and Sebastian Coe – (3:48.52 WR). It was a good field, John Walker, Steve Scott and all the best milers – Gonzales, Deleze. I went with Seb right from the start, and we went through in 1:52. Everybody was beginning to realize that if you can run 1:52 and still keep going . . . I was having a great time, and I thought I should have been able to run a better time – I did 3:49.67.

'We had a problem, because Gonzales went between us and the rabbit, and forced Sebastian to run in the second lane all the way during the first lap and second lap. When the rabbit dropped out, then we were able to work a little bit faster. By that time Gonzales was tired, so we were able to go to the front and run more a relaxed race. In the third lap, I had a hard time trying to stay with Seb.

'On the fourth lap, Steve Cram came on my shoulder. It

was 1981, and Steve Cram was beginning to come through. He was right on my shoulder with 500 metres to go, and on the straight he challenged me, but I was able to stay away from him. With 200 metres left, he decided to settle behind me and stay close. With 100 metres to go, he challenged me again. I think the reason why I ran such a good time was due more to him than being able to follow Sebastian Coe. Because there was no-one else, I would have gone easily, so he pushed me. In Brussels I did not have the same thing. No-one was close to me, so it was the two of us, Sebastian Coe and me in the front. I pushed him with 200 metres to go and I was coming closer and closer to him, but with 100 metres to do I got a little bit tired and then I realized there was no one pushing me from behind, so I slowed up. I was still able to run 3:49.45, but I think if there was anybody behind I could have run under 3:49 easily!' (28:8.81, winner in a new World record, Sebastian Coe, 3:47.33)

You got married and had other responsibilities, yet kept at the top for so long. It must be a little difficult at times to make athletics a number one priortity?

'Oh yes, always. It has never been my top priority. I have always been going to school. I did my undergraduate degree in New Mexico – Physical Education and Biology, I took two degrees at Stamford, PE and Education, then after than I went to the University of Oregon, where I am now doing a further degree in Education. I have not always been able to concentrate so much on the athletics, and all along I have not had a full-time coach who has really coached me since Stewart and Bruce Tulloh. And they had different philosophies and a different approach – completely different from the American approach. Subsequently, I have not been able to get somebody whom I could really get along with the way I would like. So I have been on my own, and it is really very difficult to do things for yourself. It is much easier if somebody else is giving you the encouragement – I think encouragement is one of the most important requirements for you to reach your potential.'

Going back to the start again, were you from a big family, Mike?

'I am the oldest. I have four brothers and four sisters, and I was born in Nandi. That is where most of the Kenyan runners come from – Julius Sang, Amos Biwott, Julius Korir, Sammy Koskei.'

Did you have a particular person from that tribe when you were young that you looked up to?

'In the 800 metres, Kiptalem Keter from Nandi was the Kenyan champion for a long time from around 1960. He set a Kenyan record and East African record, running 1:49, and that was, at that time, really a great time. He was a good runner and a front runner, all the time. He stayed in the front from the gun to the finish, and no-one ever headed him, and until he retired he always ran from the front.'

Did you run barefoot or in spikes?

'I ran barefoot most of the time until 1966. I started occasionally running with spikes in 1964, if I could borrow them. We would share one pair of spikes between ten people, and most of the time they were not the correct size!'

In those early days, did you run in little groups?

'Yes, but I always liked to run barefooted, because I thought spikes would slow me down.'

You have used the best of your life to good advantage with your education and success at running?

'I could not have asked for more. I have been so happy, and to retire – not because I don't want to run any more, I would love to run all my life – but I think I will help some young athletes. I would like to be in Kenya and help. I can't help them while I'm in the States, but I can do that in Kenya. I want to give some young men the opportunity I have been able to get. It is very difficult coming up, if you have not got the confidence. A lot of them know me and respect me, I am sure I will be able to make a big difference to them.'

Did you ever think in those early days that you would do other sports, or was running more natural to you than anything else?

'There were other sports I liked – like playing field hockey – and everybody played soccer. I was not good at that, as I was too skinny. My father did not like to see me play, because I think he was a bit concerned that something might happen to me, so he encouraged me to run. I used to enjoy running in the evening when it was cool, and even at night-time, at dusk, I used to like to run at home and just run for fun.

'Most of the young boys ran to school and ran back from school. It was practical rather than training. I used to run about two miles, it was important to be on time!'

What age were you then?

'Primary school age – ten upwards. Most of the time we would not run round a track in those early days. It was a cross-country type run. They took people in a truck or a lorry to a race which was six miles away; and then we had to run back.

'I read an article, not too long ago, about the Nandi District. At one time they ran their first Marathon – in about 1930 – and they ran from one town to another town. They did not know they were running a Marathon or anything like that. They took them in a truck to the other town. "Okay, run down to that other town." And so they did that, the distance between the towns was about thirty miles.

'Something you might like to hear is that the Nandi people have always liked running very much, with competitions in running. When you ask them why the Nandis run so much, they will give a lot of different answers. I think the most popular answer is that they drink a lot of milk, and they associate drinking a lot of milk with running. I think it is a tradition that we have. The people grow up and see what the others do, and so they are more likely to do the same thing. It is tradition, like they have a tradition for skiing in Switzerland with the alpine climates, like they have ice-hockey in Canada and cricket in Great Britain.'

I know what it is like not to run. I feel terrible. If I don't run it really does affect me.

'I agree; but one of the things about the Nandis that I have a lot of problems with when I go home is regarding training. They think if you are good, you are good, and there is nothing you can do about it. They don't think about training all the time or exercising. They just think if you are good at running you are good at running, and they wait till the competition.

'When I went home after the 1972 Olympics, I met a lot of people, and they were kind of surprised that I had won a bronze medal in the Olympics, and they said, "Does that mean you can run faster than some of us?" One fellow asked me if I thought I could catch an antelope, and I said, "No, I don't think so." So they looked at each other and said, "Winning an Olympic medal must be very easy." Among us, we know that there are some people who can catch an antelope. They run after the antelope for a long distance till they catch him.

'I was in a boarding school, so I did most of my running at boarding school, so they never saw me training and never saw me running at home. They had never seen me hunting, and so they thought that as I could not get an antelope they were sure that it was easy to win an Olympic medal. Nandis generally are very competitive. I was at that time one of the people who were less competitive and did not like competition that much, but I knew I had the talent. I had to get annoyed and feel bad about losing to be competitive.

'At school, sometimes the teachers made us mad when they seemed to favour other classes, and we thought we were better than the other classes. We had an inter-class competition, and we fought hard for the school. To be able to run for the Nandi district you had to be the top, and always when you made the Nandi team you went to the Nationals.

'Making the Nandi team is as difficult as making the Kenyan team. We have Edwin Koech, Sammy Koskei and Julius Korir – Henry Rono!'

You are slim and tall . . .

'Nandis are generally lean and tall people, so we are more suited to long-distance running like tough Marathons, and we are not the type of people who do well in the field events or explosive sports. We have a great future as Nandis in 10,000 metres and Marathons.'

Mike explained some of the recent history of the Nandis.

'They would go and steel some cows from other tribes – Nandis are a very small tribe, surrounded by big tribes who out-number the Nandis by almost five to one, but the other tribes don't have the harmony. We never had a population census, so they never knew how many people were there. We constantly raided the people across the borders and brought the cows back for ourselves because, generally, we were not farmers. We relied so much on dairy products.

'There was nothing really destructive in this kind of "trade". Only the younger people took part in this. There was no animosity between ourselves and other tribes. In the day time we dreaded the sun, so during night-time the Nandis ran across the border to try and steal the cows, and occasionally succeeded in doing so. But they did not have to kill anybody.

'Occasionally there was some resistance. We had a hard time with the Masais – we belong to almost the same group as the Masais, who are very good runners too. They have different philosophies; the Masais thought the cow rightly belonged to them, and they think anybody else should give them to the Masais. The young men usually did their raiding during the day time – a sort of daylight robbery – and they just tended to kill the cows. If you resisted, they would kill you too, but if you let the cows go, they would not do anything. Their raiding was more destructive in that way than the Nandi raiding. The Nandis were far more sophisticated in their raiding. As they had to travel at night, so they had to be very clever in knowing the direction and distance, judging the times so you don't go too early or too late at night.

'You have to run at night-time and know all those things. When the British came to Kenya, they stopped the raiding as that could not be allowed! The older men said, "This is a sport for the young men." So they had to bring in a new sport to take the place of the oldest sport. They said, "How about running?" and that is, I think, how running started for the Nandis. The English Colonial Government was anxious to replace our old sport of raiding.'

33

JOHN WALKER

Born Papukura, New Zealand, on 12 January, 1952. 1.83/74kg.

When John Walker completed his 100th mile race inside the magic four minutes with 3:54.57 on 17 February, 1985, my mind went back to when I met him for tea in the Selsdon Park Hotel near Croydon in the summer of 1976. We recalled his start in athletics and some of his memorable races, and the time flew by, as it always does when you are with such a man.

There is no doubt that the figure of John Walker running around the tracks of the world, in his all-black strip with flowing blond hair and powerful stride, will be somthing greatly missed when he retires from the scene – middle-distance running will then be that much poorer. It is really hard to imagine a worthwhile mile or 1500 metres without John Walker somewhere up front in the field. He appears a self-assured and quietly confident man who carried that over into his athletics, and, it is no surprise to learn, he does not suffer fools gladly. Media comment from those who have not taken part in the sport would be of very little consequence to him.

There is no doubt that John Walker recently has used his vast ability and understanding of his event, primarily the mile, to such perfection that only a handful of men can ever get the measure of him. Perhaps the only weakness in the latter part of his career was the diminishing of his ability to sustain his thrilling finish up the final straight, but he is still capable of beating the majority of runners on his day. (1985)

The span of his career in the 'Blue Ribbon Event' of the

track is phenomenal, if you realize that in 1973 he ran the equivalent of 3:55.7 for the mile (3:38 – 1500), and yet, so very many years later in 1990, he did 3:55.19 for the mile, and had not retired then!

Long after setting his World mile record and becoming Olympic 1500 metres champion, he ran, in 1981, a good competitive World Cup race in 3:35.9, behind Steve Ovett's 3:34.95 and in front of Olaf Beyer, Mike Boit and Sydney Maree. It is interesting to note that in 1974, he became the then second fastest 1500 metres runner in history with 3:32.52, and some ten years later could still run 3:49.73 for a mile. He was also rated sixth in the world over the 1500 in 1984 by *Track and Field News*.

I met John again five years later, and we discussed media exposure. 'When I had the World record, people in New Zealand talked about Walker, Walker, Walker all the time, till it became a pain in the arse. Every time I picked up a paper I actually cringed, seeing my own name in the paper all the time. But you have got to look at it in another way as well; that the two greatest athletes in the world (1981) were in England, so, naturally, they were going to get written about. It just stands to reason, because they are national heroes. I think Coe and Ovett can motivate youngsters as well in the sport, which I think is a damn good thing. Athletics at the top is short-lived. You are as good as your last race, and if they are the best at that particular time they deserve to get all the publicity.'

Back in 1976, John Walker had some thoughts on who he admired at the start of his interest in athletics. 'People like Jim Ryun, Kuts and Zatopek, who were very great athletes. I think Peter Snell was one of the greatest. Elliott was a great athlete, but because Snell came from my own country, naturally I would have to admire him more.'

Who were the competitors that he had found hard to beat over the years?

'I have not run against Bayi enough to be able to say, we only had two races over 1500. One was in Christchurch, and one in Helsinki, when I beat him by forty metres. A lot happened in two years. Where everyone used to say it was a sort of revolution by going fast, we are now all doing it . . . 2:52 now is nothing for the first three laps, but a few years

200

ago if you went through three laps in 2:52, it was crazy. People ran three minutes, sprinted home and hoped to run under four minutes for the mile.

'Probably a very tough competitor was Rod Dixon; on his day he was as tough as anybody, he really was, he was one of the hardest racers and trainers around. Wessinghage is a tough guy, Boit is always tough, Bayi was a very good athlete. In fact, just about everybody I have run against was really tough, because until you cross that finishing line they were all creating a problem.'

What, shall we ask, did other people think of John Walker?

The man John Walker has so often battled, Ray Flynn, the Irish outdoor mile record holder said in 1983, 'I can remember back to John Walker, when he ran the Commonwealth Games 1500 in 1974, and how he was one of my heroes at that time. It is remarkable, really, when you end up running against him, after you have watched him at Secondary School like I did.'

Mike O'Rourke, who won the Commonwealth javelin gold for New Zealand in 1978, remarked, 'I get on well with John Walker. I can't say enough about John Walker, as he has done so much for athletics in New Zealand. You could never get a better ambassador, the work he has done to promote New Zealand athletics.'

How did it all begin for John Walker?

'My first race was when I was ten years old, running in a primary school cross-country meet. I won it, and virtually everything started from there. But I really never got interested or concentrated on running till I was about seventeen or eighteen.

In 1973, John Walker started to mix it with top-rated athletes, and ran a 3:38.0 1500 metres. 'I suppose it was a sort of breakthrough, because in that 3:38 I was against Jipcho and Dixon, and I beat Wottle and a lot of others. That was the starting point. But, unfortunately, I really had not had sufficient experience before the Commonwealth Games.'

John had started to show over 800 too, with a 1:45.3 in that year, and he ran a 3:55.8 mile on 9 January, 1974, in New Zealand, finishing second. It was on 2 February that the epic Commonwealth 1500 took place, but as a young man, despite the inexperience he talks about, he also ran a world-class time in an event he is not always noted for, and that was in the Commonwealth 800 metres.

Result: 1. John Kipkurgat (Ken), 1:43.9. 2. Mike Boit (Ken), 1:44.4. 3. John Walker (NZ), 1:44.9, and 4. Filbert Bayi (Tan), 1:45.3.

In 1976, John looked back: 'I have run so many 1500 metres over the last two years that I have neglected my speed and 800 metre running. Now I virtually only use 800 metre running for 1500s. I think if I had not got knocked out of my heat in the Olympics, I was ready for 1:44.5, as my speed had really quite improved. Where I was only running 39s for 300 in training, I ran 35.2 – which is not stopping around.'

In that aforementioned Commonwealth Games 1500 final, the first two runners were inside Jim Ryun's 1967 World record, and the first five ran into the top seven of all time for the event. What a loaded field it was: Filbert Bayi (Tan), 3:32.2; John Walker (NZ), 3:32.5; Ben Jipcho (Ken), 3:33.2; Rod Dixon (NZ), 3:33.9; Graham Crouch (Aus), 3:34.2; Mike Boit (Ken), 3:36.8; Brendan Foster (Eng), 3:37.6.

Now, uninterrupted by me, let us set down some of John Walker's opinions regarding that race. 'No New Zealanders picked me to be in a place, although my coach did. I was just happy to finish second, because it was really only my second international race. I blame our New Zealand system in a lot of ways; It's not like athletes in the UK, who get a lot of experience. I had two 1500 metre races before the Commonwealth Games event, and I think that if I had not been denied the chance to go to the 1972 Olympics, because of our selection policy, then I may have won in 1974. But you are right about the fact that I sat on Dixon, who at that time was the "great white god" in New Zealand. That was just inexperience on my part. Four months after that, in Helsinki, I raced against Bayi and beat him by about forty metres, but then I knew a little bit more.

'At the 1974 Commonwealth I had just turned twenty-one, and I did not know what it was all about. I had one short European season when I ran 1:46 and 3:38, and my coach kept telling me that I could break the World record,

202

but I just could not visualize five seconds improvement over 1500 metres. Yet I did break the World record at Christchurch – but unfortunately I finished second.

'You have to look back to those days to realize I was only running half miles and the odd 1500, so I was training for a totally different event. I ran 1:44.9 at those Games.'

In 1975, John Walker set new world mile figures of 3:49.4, beating Filbert Bayi's time of 3:51.0. Behind John's record in second place was Ken Hall of Australia in 3:55. Walker also ran a world best for the 2000 of 4:51.52 at Oslo on 30 June, in front of Karl Fleschen (5:00.4) and Klaus Peter Hildenbrand (5:00.6).

'I think breaking the World record for the mile and running under 3:50 would have to be the greatest thing that ever happened. The World record was virtually a time trial. Probably the greatest satisfaction was running 3:32.4 and missing the World 1500 record by two-tenths – but that was also a great disappointment, of course. Those were time-trials, virtually running against the clock. If I have to think back to my greatest race, the Olympics would be one of them because to beat the whole lot of them all together would have to stand out.'

But before going a little more into that Olympic final, there were other races in 1975 that show the great competitive spirit of John Walker. In Stockholm on 30 June, he beat (in 3:52.24) a good field which included Marty Liquori (3:53.62), Thomas Wessinghage (3:54.14), Anders Garderud (3:53.45). Behind these worthies were Tom Hansen (3:54.78) and Steve Ovett (3:57.0).

I can remember a warm evening in London 29 August, when, against a star-studded field at Crystal Palace, John Walker opened up with his sustained long sprint in the back straight and won the mile in 3:53.62, from Mike Boit (3:54.88), Rod Dixon (3:55.25), Marty Liquori (3:55.52) and Frank Clement (3:55.26). Earlier in the year, John showed how he also had a 'fair amount of ability' at longer distances when he ran into fourth place in the World IAAF cross-country senior Championships, won by Ian Stewart. Behind Walker were many established distance men, far more used to the cross-country scene.

'It was probably one of the hardest races I have run,

203

because I had not done any specific sort of training for that race. I had run in New Zealand and gone to America for the indoors, and I was running with Dick Quax and Dixon in training. They were just screwing me; I could not keep up with them on the hills, they were beating me on the flat, and I thought it was a waste of time me going to Morocco. I was very surprised as I was up with the leading bunch for about two and a half miles in that International, and then I got a very bad stitch and drifted to the back. But I fought back again, I got right up to fourth, and in fact I had pulled my muscle so bad that when I got back to New Zealand I had to have an x-ray of the stomach. I thought I had done some permanent damage, but fortunately it was alright; it was just a strain, yet it took seven to eight weeks to get rid of it.'

At Montreal, 1976, John Walker followed in the footsteps of All-Blacks Peter Snell and Jack Lovelock. 'I had trained specifically for a year. I had been in Europe to gain experience, and I learned to run from the front just in case Bayi did not turn up – I had two plans. When I heard he had withdrawn it did not upset me, but it did knock me back a little bit, for the simple reason that I thought, "Look, there goes the guy who could ensure the pace was fast" – I could not see anybody else leading! Wessinghage was one that surprised me by not making it. Coghlan, I had never run against before the Olympics; I had heard a lot about him, but the best time he had for 800 was only 1:48, and I thought if it was going to be a fast race then he would not win, and I thought maybe he might get third or fourth. Rick Wohlhuter was very fast and had very good leg speed, but I thought if he went through and ran three heats of the 800 and three heats of the 1500 then he would be very tired.

'I think when you have been sitting in the Olympic Village for two and a half weeks, facing four walls and criticism from reporters and finally you go out there – you run – then win – naturally it is going to be a hell of a relief. It'a all over – four years of really hard work. It is everything that a person has dreamed about, winning the Olympic gold medal, and that's it, it's all finished.'

Certainly there is no doubt that his coach Arch Jelly was a great help to John Walker, with his intelligent correspondence when he was away from home and his advice with training back in New Zealand, but there are two interesting aspects with which I would like to finish off this story. Firstly John's attitude towards enjoyable runs and then, secondly, his philosophy the year he won the Olympics.

One must not forget that in 1977 he was hampered by an injury, technically known as a popliteal entrapment, in his leg, but with great courage he got back and produced a mile time of 3:49.50 in 1982, followed by a lifetime best that year of 3:49.08 at age thirty. He again broke 3:50 in 1983 and also 1984, which says something for longevity of performance. One must not forget either that he gained a 1500 metre silver in the Commonwealth Games in 1982, and ran a 5000 debut when coming second to Eamonn Coghlan in 13:20.89 in the 1981 AAA.

'I think environment is a great thing. In New Zealand we have got so many open places that I can go and train in and just be completely alone, and no-one would bother me. I think pollution is also a great factor, and in New Zealand there is no pollution. I think as long as you have got an open road to train on. . . I think that probably 95% of my training is done on the road, the streets anyway – even though I do have all these open parks to train in. I think the biggest thing with athletics is boredom. A lot of times I will run from where I live in Auckland to my parents' place, about thirteen miles away; along the great South Road, and I'll run because the cars keep me company – as long as they don't bother me of course. That is what I do a lot of times.

'First of all, I love racing – that is prime. Secondly, being able to travel as much as I do and, thirdly, meeting so many interesting people. Naturally, I think athletes are a very good sort of people, they are clean-living, they all enjoy the same sort of thing, and it is a very healthy life. It is good to feel really fit. It is a sport that depends purely on the individual; he'll get as much success as he puts in. Naturally, you have to be born with some sort of talent, whether it is playing a piano, running or whatever. I think you have got to have the ingredients there to start with, and I think I was very lucky to have this because my father was a runner, and I have virtually inherited it from him. But I still had to work upon it and it has not been easy, though maybe I have had it a little easier than some people.'

34

SEB COE

Born Chiswick, London, 29 September, 1956. 1.77/54kg.

I had just finished running in the Surrey Veterans cross-country championships a few years ago, and as I started to walk back to the Ranelagh Harriers HQ at Petersham with my family, quite suddenly appearing over the brow of the hill in front of me came the figure of Sebastian Newbold Coe in full flow. I shouted out, "Hello Seb," and he immediately stopped, shook hands with my wife and my son, who he had not met before, said a few words and then continued his session. To break his rhythm in the middle of hill work, just to talk to anyone is the reason, to my mind, that he will continue to be popular in the public sector now that he has retired from the international scene.

A lot of Seb's true personality comes through in the interview I did with him in April 1984, when he was on the start of his hard comeback trail, to eventually achieve an Olympic gold in the 1500 for a second time.

Amongst his many outstanding results were the 1980 Olympic 1500 gold in 3:38.4. 2. Jurgen Straub (GDR), 3:38.8. 3. Steve Ovett (UK), 3:39.0.

Regarding that one, in fairness, Steve Ovett pointed out to me once, '. . . after winning the 800, it was coming to terms with the deflation after achieving an Olympic gold medal, and then re-motivating myself again.'

From that comment one could make a suggestion that it left the door open a little bit more for Seb's powerful finish in the 1500.

Seb's second Olympic gold medal was in Los Angeles in 1984 (1. Coe, 3:32.53. 2. Steve Cram (UK), 3:33.40. 3. Jose Abascal (Spain), 3:34.30).

Sebastian Coe's world records included an 800 in 1:43.33 in Olso, July 1979, and 1:41.73 in Florence, 10 June, 1981; 1000 metres, 2:13.4 in Oslo, 1 July, 1980; 2:12.18 – Oslo 11 July, 1981; 1500, 3:32.03 – Zurich, 17 August, 1979; Mile, 3:48.53 – Zurich 19 August, 1981 and 3:47.33 – Brussels, 28 August, 1981. Perhaps the most significant 800 victory, as far as Championship winning goes, was in Stuttgart in 1986, when he took the European 800. The reason I say that is that many considered him to be more an 800 specialist than anything else. 1. Sebastian Coe, 1:44.50. 2. Tom McKean, 1:44.61. 3. Steve Cram, 1:44.88. Cram went on to win the 1500. In the case of Scotsman Tom McKean, he turned silver into gold with a well-controlled tactical win four years later in Split and was coached by Tommy Boyle, who had such success with his fine middle-distance runner Yvonne Murray, a great talent like Liz McColgan.

There was no doubt that Seb had the armoury to win the Olympic 800, but it eluded him, particularly after two years of illness and injury before LA in 1984.

That brings me into talking about another favourite for the LA 800 – Earl Jones, who won the vital American final trials in 1:43.7. Jones told me in one of several unpublished interviews back in 1986, that the race he was most pleased about (not counting the Olympic final) was the TAC Championships, when he was third in 1985 in 1:44.58, after coming back from a 48.4 first lap! He also thought, with that in mind, that if he trained the following season for the mile, he was capable of stringing together two consecutive 1:50s, which of course would give him a very fast mile time indeed; but unluckily he was involved in a serious accident which forced him to retire abruptly, before he was able to prove his theory correct. Regarding the Olympic 800 at LA, in which the result of the first four was: 1. Joaquim Cruz (Brazil), 1:43.00 (Olympic record). 2. Seb Coe, 1:43.64. 3. Earl Jones, 1:43.83, and 4. Billy Konchellah (Kenya), 1:44.03 – Earl Jones said: 'Before the race, I just knew there was no other way that I could not take top three if I could stay up close. I was looking at how the rest of the runners were running. I knew Cruz was strong, very strong.

'As the race started, I knew if I could get on out and get a position without being boxed, I would be okay and be able to run my race instead of running everybody else's race, so it won't be tactical. I didn't get a chance to take it out real fast, but it went out fast enough. I got caught in the last 150, when I was boxed in by Coe and Ovett. I could not get out to keep the pace moving, but it still worked out right for me.'

Sebastian Coe retired from the international scene in 1989, and at the time was the reigning AAA Champion over 1500 (3:47.3), and ran his last major race at Crystal Palace in the McVities's Challenge on 17 September (1. Coe 1:45.70; 2. Ikem Billy 1:46.81; and 3. Tony Morrell 1:47.03).

Interview 1984

There is this feeling in athletics that when a person reaches the top, people can no longer identify with them.

'Sometimes. Of the people that identified with you as a good club runner, as a good National class runner or even as a successful international runner, there is a drop-out rate all the way through. A lot of people are actually almost afraid to come up and have a conversation with you, people I have known for a long time, that I would see at the Yorkshire championships. That Yorkshire meet was a lovely outing for me, as I met a lot of people who I never see that regularly anymore.

'I won my first Yorkshire title – either schools or AAA – back in 1970–71, and by and large I have won a Yorkshire title right the way through until last year. That to me is great – I have had a title on the track at every distance from 400 to 5000.

'Yet you don't change. This is the thing; obviously your breadth of experience expands and you get a greater insight into life. No doubt about that. You are more travelled and probably more worldly about the sport.'

It knocks the rough edges off.

'I think it does. It tempers the balance between realism and cynicism a lot of the time. Yes, it is a little bit disappointing when people find it difficult to relate with you, just because on paper you have done . . . there seems to be a watershed . . . you start travelling, and you are assumed

208

to be a different person.'

It must give you a lot of pleasure to be in the Haringey club environment – just as it was at Loughborough, where you were just another runner?

'Without getting too romantic about it, I consider Haringey has put two or three years on my athletics career. It is one of the smartest moves I have ever made. I still work very closely with Peter (father and coach), but I am back into club life again and suddenly start thinking not only about my own problems. For instance, in the Southern road relay, I thought it was bad news to hear that one of the runners had pulled out with a septic toe on the morning of the race. The captain is switching the team around, and you are not focussing on yourself quite as much.' (The runner was Adrian Stewart, once an international junior).

With Loughborough, you enjoyed road relay racing – having been in the winning Hyde Park squad.

'I love road running, and have always done. I was never a great lover of cross-country. You develop a track style which makes it very difficult after a number of years of concentrating solely on the economy of effort and style (to run over the country). Road running is closer to track, and I have always loved relays. I love chasing people.'

You have a love for both London and Yorkshire?

'I have this split personality, having been born down here (London) and having always come down here for long school holidays – I don't have any relatives north of London. I was born in Chiswick, but I was brought up in and around the Fulham area, and my parents were Fulham people. One set of grandparents were true cockneys, born in Stepney. It is a London family.'

Going off at a tangent, I mentioned Dave Moorcroft, who was at Loughborough during Seb's first year there. Dave had said of Seb Coe in 1980: 'It was fairly obvious that he had quite considerable talent, and he made good use of it.'

What do you think of Dave Moorcroft as a person?

'It is often a misused and misapplied word, but Dave is actually one of the "nicest" people I have ever met. I don't mean that in a weak, watery way, but the guy is genuinely nice. Dave I have got a lot of time for.'

Does he surprise you sometimes when he manages to get

something out of himself beyond normal bounds?

'I have always thought Dave to be an amazingly talented runner. People talk about his inconsistencies, but when you think of how long he has been around the scene, he has been as consistent as anyone and has a breadth of distances that is almost unsurpassed.'

Tim Hutchings is another Loughborough man.

'I like Tim for one simple reason – he has always been a very patient runner. Somebody who, I think, knows – whether it is this year, next year or the year after – he is going to find his niche at some distance. It is a very steady increase, a very steady improvement from year to year, and he also has a nice perspective on the sport.'

You must be pulled two ways, in that you obviously should not throw away your special ability at 800, but you are also capable of good 5000s?

I genuinely feel that I have a good 5000 in me at the moment. I think that the real problem is that people are inclined to talk blithely about athletics, with very little understanding of what is actually involved. It took Dave Moorcroft two or three years to perfect (5000 metre racing). John Walker is open about not liking the distance – it hurts. Steve Ovett has been very open about it, he does not like the distance.

'You are an 800 metres runner, then you move up and run a good 1500, possibly you run 3:36, and then go straight to 5000, and you are a 13:20 performer. I am afraid it is getting a little tighter than that now. Dave has totally changed all that now. 13:20 means that you are twenty seconds off the pace and 180 metres behind the guy! That is what Bayi did to 1500 metre running in that one run in Christchurch.'

A change occurred in 10,000 metre racing at Helsinki in 1971 (European championships). Vaatainen upped the pace from Dave Bedford's penultimate lap of 65.2 into a fifty-four-second sprint over the last lap, to hold off Jurgen Haase and Rashid Sharefetdniov.

Vaatainen was a man who could do 10.8 for 100, 22.11 for 200, 48.4 for 400 and 1.48 for 800, and he capitalized on those abilities in the 10,000. In reality, that changed the type of runner who was going to win the 'big ones' in future.

'I am afraid Vaatainen, in the course of one race, changed

10,000 metre running on that last lap with Jurgen Haase. It put it into a different area. These distances are no longer the refuge of the second-class runner. People moved up because they were not fast enough for 1500 or 5000. If I am not fast enough for 5000 I will give it a go at 10,000, but it is no longer like that. It is a specialist distance.'

It is sad for someone who is a front runner without a special kick, to see Alberto Cova or Werner Schildhauer not do any work in a race, then turn it on over the last fifty to a hundred metres and sprint away from the opposition. Romantically, perhaps, I hold that they won't be remembered like Ron Clarke or Dave Bedford.

'I agree with you in one respect. I have never thought the Olympics or a one-off championship to be a solid indication of an athletic talent at the end of a career. I know that some people will argue that Lasse Viren has to be the greatest distance runner of all time, because he won four gold medals in a four-year span. It is very difficult to argue against. But I could say that in a straight comparison of performances, that Brendan Foster was a far more exhilarating runner, and I hold his career in higher esteem than Viren's. That is not to say that Foster is a failure, as he was European champion and Olympic bronze medallist; but on the other hand, Foster will always be able to say: "I ran against Viren thirteen times and beat him twelve times, and the thirteenth occasion was the Olympic final.'

Another great ex-Loughborough runner, John Whetton, once said, 'I honestly feel there is more to life than athletics. If I am running, I don't mind staying up to one o'clock with my friends and getting a bit drunk. The next day I will be refreshed, ready – not for more beers – but for more running.' John plays an instrument and is very interested in other things. You yourself love skiing, watching Chelsea, and jazz, among other things.

'That's right. I am quite unabashed about it. I get more enjoyment out of listening to live jazz than out of anything. I have often said that I would give up athletics to be able to play a jazz instrument – and that is one of my greatest sadnesses. Like most kids, I bridled against practice. I will probably take up an instrument when I retire from athletics.'

Has joining Haringey changed your attitude at all?

211

'Yes. Don't get me wrong. It has not diminished my resolve to come back from last year and run, I hope, extremely well this summer, but on the other hand, it certainly eases the burdens by having a little bit of humour and a great deal of fun along the way.

'There is nothing funny about some of the track sesions that we are doing on Sunday mornings down there. They are very, very hard, and a lot of the lads are chipping in and working hard to help me through, to extend the distances. It is give and take, and I accept that fully, and that is what is nice about the spirit there. But on the other hand, it is also very nice when the session is over and we sit around and genuinely have a very good laugh about it.'

It must have been nice to have your father and family behind you?

'I think he is one of the most intelligent people I know. His profession as an engineer means he has a breadth of knowledge which I find staggering. He has an appreciation of the Arts, and of course my mother was in repertory theatre for many years, and was at RADA. That is where my sisters get their interest from.

'I would say my father had obviously been a very big influence. I could never overstate the influence that my mother has on the whole set-up. There is an element that she brings to what I am doing and what he is doing – an element of humour which can be very, very amusing and very crushing at times; it is a broader perspective which is very important.'

To the whole family?

'Yes. Especially when you have two sisters and a brother. There was a wonderful comment in one of the colour supplements when they did a feature, without checking up at all, on two children families. They said, "The Coes are a classic two-child family where the children are played off against each other. He is a top runner and the other a top dancer."

'We wrote a very nice tongue-in-cheek letter. "Yes, this is a very interesting sociological observation, but we would like to point out that there are another two of them in the family. Perhaps you would like to rethink your rationale and analysis'.

In your book you mention a friend at Tapton School in Sheffield, who was suffering from a rare form of juvenile arthritis, he could hardly walk, let alone run. That must have brought home to you just how lucky we athletes all are?

'It is a very important thing to come to terms with. There have been two people I have been quite close to, Danny and a little girl who I speak to a couple of times a week on the telephone. She was involved in a horrific accident, and she lost parts of a limb and parts of her face. She started ringing me up after the 1980 Games – she is fourteen now.

'You worry bitterly about an achilles tendon that is sore or a touch of shin splints, ligament or knee problems that keep you sidelined for six weeks – then you get on the phone to a kid like that, who is in the process of having a plastic limb fitted and her face remodelled and all sorts of inherent problems. That brings you down to earth. It's not a question of, "There, but for the grace of God. . . ." It is not that, it is just simply that you can lose perspective about your own situation. It is a very sobering thought.

'When Steve (Ovett) came out with exactly that comment a few years ago, about the work he does with handicapped kids in Brighton, I knew what he meant. It puts the whole thing into perspective. Other people who are around you or are close to you can find it very difficult to put it into that kind of perspective.'

There are two harsh contrasts in athletics. One is being 100% fit and going for something when you know you have the ability to achieve it. And the other is actually trying to achieve it when you are ill or just a little below one's expected form.

'For the last two years I have been running on mental strengths more than anything. Because of various injury and illness problems. I have not had the background, and that is a most soul-destroying thing. I was going into a season knowing that, by the standards I had set myself in training during other years, I was percentage points below what I should be. Yet you still have to go in against athletes who have had much better buildups.

'For eighteen months, I was running on no physical background at all, just the mental determination that I was not going to lose. I think you run out of that after a time. The nice thing this year is, to put an optimistic gloss on it, I am actually going into a season where since Christmas I have not lost any time at all. I have only taken time off because I have decided I had better things to do than train, or I wanted a rest day. I have not been at the point where I have been continually chasing against lost time. Thinking back to 1982, I lost most of the winter with a stress fracture of the foot, and then I finished the season with a glandular problem which cost me a lot of the winter.'

It's this pattern of high-powered training followed by breakdowns that has happened to Moorcroft and Ovett.

'We are asking more and more than I think, sometimes, we are capable of, year in, year out. There is another aspect to this as well. The physiologists and biomechanical experts can tell us that there are very definite periodisation and recovery levels – seventy-two hours after hard road running, or thirty-six to forty-eight hours after anaerobic training. We concentrate an inordinate amount of time on the physical, the skeleton, muscle biopsy, the breakdown of the gas analysis. . . . All that sort of stuff.

'Now, if you accept that you can't go through life saying: "At the end of the day it is the win-loss tally that matters." because, as someone once said, there would be a lot of unhappy people leaving the sport, if that was the sole criteria – it is then down to personal expectation.

'My expectation was that I was – I still believe – the best 800 metre runner around. That takes absolutely nothing away from Ovett, who won a good race. People construed my total disgust as a sort of arrogance. It wasn't, it was disgust with myself, it was not aimed at anyone. I make no excuses, I just ran a very bad race, there is nothing you can do about that. But the probelm is again that the media are inclined to judge an athletic career in terms of World records and Olympic medals. Probably more so by Olympic medals.

'Again, it is expectation. In 1971, when Andy Carter won a bronze medal in the European Final in Helsinki, Andy was held up as the great hope of British middle-distance running. Steve comes along and wins a silver in the 1974 Europeans, we get into an era when the public expect that a

British athlete is going to pull off a major title in the course of the year.

'I won a silver medal in the European championship in Athens, at the end of what was a dreadful season – you would have thought that World War Three had broken out. The headlines! The photographs of me walking afterwards!

'It was construed as a total disaster. We may yet have to adapt back to 1971 standards, because there is no guarantee that some of the performances we are throwing out in middle distances, sprints and some of the field events are going to continue.'

The 800 metres has proved to be the most unpredictable event in the whole of athletics.

'I could not agree more.'

If you analyse Willi Wulbeck's performance in winning the World Championship last year over 800, you realize he just happened to be behind two runners who were killing each other trying to win. He was in the right place at the right time, and Heaven's door opened for him.

'Don't you think it was a most remarkably close comparison between that race and the 1978 European 800 final, with Ovett and myself busily taking each other to the cleaners with a forty-nine second first lap, and Olaf Beyer strolling past us with thirty-five metres to go? Should Roger Moens have lost it in the 1960 Olympics?'

You are the Olympic 1500 metre gold medallist rather than the 800 metre, but it showed some metal to be able to get up off the floor for that 1500.

'It was a tough three days, a lot of soul-searching. We both had to sit down, and could have panicked.'

Your father, particularly in that case, must have played a valuable part, even though he was a bit chiding?

'He was quite right to criticize. I expect criticism from him where I won't accept it from other people. I know when I have run badly, and he certainly knows when I have run badly. The one thing that I am very proud about is that the battle plan for the 800 – which should have worked except that for various reasons I was just not running very well that day – was the plan we stuck to for the 1500 metres.

'Everybody was screaming, writing letters, telling me, "Go from 400 metres! 600 metres! 800 metres! Go from the gun!"' I have been told what some of the pundits in the press box said when they saw the dawdle for the first two laps. "The guy has not got any brains," was just one of them.'

But you have got to run the race the way the race is run.

'That's right. You go into a race knowing you have certain strengths, and if an opportunity arises, you grasp it with both hands. But you must also go in with the intellectual adaptability to know that there was no point in carrying a plan through, just to be a sacrificial offering over the last 100 metres.'

Which of your world records stand out for you? 1:41 for 800 metres is so very fast.

'Yes, but I am also very proud of running the 1000 metres record, which meant doing 1:44.4, then still hanging on for twenty-seven seconds over the last 200. I have never felt as bad as I did forty metres out from the tape that night in Oslo. Two nights earlier, I had run 3:31.9 for 1500 (Steve Scott second, 3:34.17).

'That 1000 metres stands out; I consider it to be one of the better runs, simply because I was taken into areas where it actually was hard and it hurt. I have a tape of that race, and my right leg actually stopped functioning about four or five paces from the tape and I was dragging it through like a dead lift. If I had been walking, I'd have been done for lifting.'

Going back down the years, when Rod Dixon won the Emsley Carr Mile at Crystal Palace, he told me that he was impressed with the young Sebastian Coe, who had run 3:58.3. You were only nineteen then.

'I was well down the field – seventh. I remember leading it for three-quarters of a mile, and taking them all through in about three minutes. Somebody said it was the best piece of voluntary pacemaking for a world-class race in a long while.'

People criticize World record-paced races, but they give people a lot of pleasure. To people who ask, 'Ah, but what would it be like in a real competition?' I always cite your World cup win or the Olympic 1500.

'My answer to that is really very quick and, I am afraid, a little bit dismissive. Nobody ever set a World record and lost a race. It sounds very simplistic, but the race has still to

216

be won. when I set the World mile record in 1979 (3:48.95), everybody except Steve (Ovett) was there – the first ten guys were inside 3.52. I ran 3:47.33 in 1981. Who was in the race? Coghlan, Scott, Walker, Maree. . . .'

It must be a bit galling when Scott comes to the Palace and beats you when you are not physically fit.

'But on the other hand . . .'

You did not duck it!

'I got some very funny criticisms last year. I was not very well, and I think it was fairly obvious. I was finding it very difficult to get through a day without feeling dreadfully ill. But they are not the kind of things you come out with. If you make excuses, then you should not be out there. You just get labelled as a whinger.

'I was trying everything and anything over the last few weeks. I would stop training for three or four days. The press saw us sitting on the running tracks having the most violent arguments, but we were at our wit's ends trying to figure out the best way to approach the World Champion-ship, having had the tatters of a season, but far from mentally shirking.

'I was accused of mentally giving up. A week before the World Championships, I went up to Gateshead, in front of 20,000 screaming Geordies, to take on Steve Cram over 800 metres. To take on a world-class 800 field after having been turned over at Crystal Palace in the Robinson's mile the week before. And people said, "You knew you were not going to the World Championships all along. You did not want to go?" I found that absolutely astounding – and a week before, I had trailed up to Gateshead in the hope that we would find something.'

I sometimes wonder if Scott could have been the World Champion last year over 1500 metres?

'I think it was Crammie's year, and it would have taken an exceptionally talented runner to beat him. We all have years when you can't do anything wrong.'

1981 was yours?

'81 was my year. 1982 was looked upon as a total disaster, but I had nine international races, only lost once and ran against the best athletes in the world that year.'

You really like running 800 metres, don't you?

'I love 800 metre running.'

But, of course, it is an event, as we said before, with a certain unpredictability about it.

'The classic example of that had to be in the European Championships in 1978. I went out, not what I considered to be an all-round performer; I still had a lot of strength to gain, I was only nineteen or twenty. I decided to play that race on my strengths. My strength at that time was that I could sustain a hard pace all the way. So I ran the first lap in 49.2 or 49.3, hoping that I would get rid of a few people. 'Peter was quite unrepentant about it. Peter said that, irrespective of whether I won, lost or drew, if I ran 49.22, he would find more about the metal of the people around me for the next year and the year after, than if I went round in 53 to 54 and lost it in 1:46.

'But we don't actually stop and think that if, every now and again, we break down physically, what is happening mentally? Why is the general assumption that Man will take care of himself. "Don't worry about that, you have got another season, surely that is motivation enough?" I am no longer accepting this as a fair balance. I think we grossly underestimate the mental strength of the situation.

'Why is it, when I had been out of training . . . and I am thinking particulary back to 1982. I lost most of the winter, I came back a little bit in the spring, and lost most of the summer. Prior to going to Zurich, I had effectively been twelve weeks out of training. I had very little track background . . . I stepped straight on to the track after two weeks of gentle training up in the mountains and, with some world-class runners about, won the race, pulling up over the last thirty metres in 1:44.48.'

The 800 metres World cup in 1981 was only won in 1:46.16, but, because of the publicity that was given to these things, people didn't realize that you beat a world-class field in a competitive 800 race: James Robinson (1:47.31), Wagenknecht, Hillardt, Khalifa, Cruz, Grippo and Kirov. It was a better field than in Moscow, and must have reinforced your belief that you could still win a competitive 800 at a big games?

'That's right. There is a general clamour of people telling me to move up distance, but what is the rationale behind that? To use John Mortimer's book title, "if there is any wreckage to cling to" from last season, it was simply that at the height – although I did not know it at the time – of my illness, I still managed to go out to Oslo and run 1:43.8. That may be enough to win an Olympic title, although I don't think it will be, but I knew that if I could do that in a season where things had gone so desperately wrong, I must be in with just as much chance as I was in 1980. I do have the one big advantage of having been through an Olympics before.'

Media presence has become so strong in the last few years that it is impossible for people not to notice athletes' reactions after finishing an Oympic final. Ian Stewart got a brilliant 5000 metres third place in Munich, 1972, but it meant nothing to him at the time, because he felt he could have won the race – and you could see it in his face. Any club man will tell you that a silver medal in the Olympics, whether you have run it from the outside, inside or backwards, is fabulous. But I am afraid the public did not look at it that way when they saw you with a sour expression on your face after the 1980 800 metres.

'We are really talking about expectation. We are talking totally about expectation here. When you are talking about the club runner, you are talking about something that is unapproachable. For the average person an Olympic medal, or even an Olympic Games, to an average runner is not on.

'But it's the unpredictability again. You go out, and you start running what turns out to be a first lap of 49.2, 49.3, and I am fighting halfway down the back straight of the first lap with Olaf Beyer, who is trying to get to 200 metres inside twenty-four seconds!

'Looking back in hindsight, had I had more tactical awareness and acumen at the time, I would have said, "Thank you mate, it's all yours. I'll latch on to you." But I didn't, I went on forcing it to the tape and still managed to get through – mind you, the world did start caving in a bit at 600 – but I learnt a lot more out of that one race than, I think, any other.'

For you it is almost as much fun going to watch Chelsea.

'Very nearly. There is a feeling of uselessness though, when you are sitting there and things are going wrong.

There is nothing you can do about it, but it is a safety valve.'

George Gandy has been a great help to you as a coach, a man with a sense of humour and a special brand of intelligence. Did he introduce you to circuit training and the ideal of keeping supple?

'Circuits, yes. I started doing them in 1976–77 with a large group.'

At the Southern Relay, I watched you stretching while talking to someone.

'I have got into that habit now, nearly all the time. Even when I'm watching television, you'll find me stretching. I find it dreadfully boring – stretching. I find I cannot put aside three-quarters of an hour a day when I will consistently stretch. What I tend to do is stretch all day. You can feel after a training run that the calves are slightly tight or you are a bit tight in the low back or the shoulders. You consistently work on breaking down the muscle areas.'

Where do you enjoy running most?

'The Peak District to me is the ultimate delight, and my family home is in Sheffield, just on the edge of the Peaks. In the summer it is lovely, and in the winter it's pure Wagner – very bleak, a bit bare at times. It is a lovely area to hide away in.'

It's a place for you to do that bulk work?

'I go out there in the winter and run fourteen or fifteen miles on Sunday.'

Would you get bored with just bulk work?

'Yes, but if I am going to put together seven races in nine days in August, there is no way around it. But just going out and running distance I don't get much pleasure from. I much prefer the discipline of a hard track session.'

35

DAVE MOORCROFT

There is no doubt that Dave Moorcroft was always one of the most popular middle-distance runners on the international scene. Ollie Flynn, the 30 km road walk champion at the Edmonton Commonwealth Games in 1978, told me that Dave was so well-liked that they queued up in the Games village to congratulate him on his 1500 Commonwealth victory.

Dave Moorcroft was dogged by injury and illness in his career, but he always came back to fight another day.

In November 1976, the year he made the Olympic 1500 final (seventh in 3:40.94), his coach, John Anderson, looked at his young charge as having an exciting future ahead of him. 'I started coaching him when he was sixteen, so that has placed us together for about seven years now, and I am impressed with Dave, not just in terms of his athletic talent but in terms of Dave Moorcroft the man. I have watched him grow up from a young lad, through the various stages of adolescence and then arrive at what I consider now to be the beginnings of maturity. He is now happily married, he has had the backing of his family of course all the way through, and a lot of friends. He brings lots of qualities that can't but help be admired. It has not been a dramatic overnight success, but it has been a clearly definable onward march right from the beginning. There have been setbacks and disappointments, but they have been used as spurs towards greater achievements, culminating this season with a place in the Olympic final and winning the Emsley Carr Mile. There are successful athletes, and I am sure we can bring a number of names to mind, who become egocentric and so self-centred that they disregard entirely anything which happens outside their own little domain, and who perhaps do not value contributions made by others. In the case of Dave Moorcroft, I feel satisfied that he is the kind of individual who recognizes the value of friendships and is totally reliable. He is resolute and has tremendous courage and a sense of perspective of life itself. To sum it all up is to say he is an extremely well-balanced individual who has many admirable traits as a man, who takes them into his athletics and adds on one or two extra ones in terms of sharp edge of competitiveness, a desire to be the best that he can be, whatever that may lead to.'

Dave Moorcroft's highlights include the 1978 Commonwealth Games 1500 (1. Moorcroft, 3:35.48. 2. Filbert Bayi (Tan), 3:35.59. 3. John Robson (Sco), 3:35.60); breaking Henry Rono's 5000 metres record in Oslo on 7 July, 1982, with 13:00.41 (pr.rec. 13:06.20), followed ten days later at Crystal Palace with a thrilling 3000 metres in 7:32.79 (w.r. stood at 7:32.1), with Sydney Maree (7:33.27) second and John Walker third (7:37.49), plus the Commonwealth gold for 5000 at Brisbane on 7 October, 1982, in 13:33.00, with Nick Rose (13.35.97) and Peter Koech, the future World steeple holder 13:36.95, third for Kenya.

It was interesting to see who he admired most in athletics back in 1976: 'The fellow who stands out in my mind, when I became a junior, was Brendan Foster, purely because – above all, I am sure – what he has got in his heart and soul is the thing that carried him through. I think probably the deciding factor in the long run is your psychological and spiritual make-up. That's something I believe in very sincerely. It is a combination of natural ability and the ability to use what you have got in the correct situation I think that is something Brendan has done very successfully.'

Interview 1982 After his 5000 World record.

If you could dream about being successful at one athletic event, which one would you choose?

'What I am going to say is not just because you are interviewing me here for *Marathon and Distance Runner* magazine – editor Geoff Harrold – but the answer is this. When I was twelve and joined Coventry Godiva Harriers, everything was geared towards Marathon running. All the heroes, all the people were Marathon runners.

'If they were not Marathon runners – people like Dick Taylor – then they were destined to be Marathon runners. Actually, Dick never became one, but that was the pattern.

'I am glad that I did not take up Marathon running as an event early in my career because, certainly, I have got a hell of a lot out of track running. But the dream that I had as a kid, and still get now and again is coming into the stadium at the Olympics, three minutes or something ahead and running the last lap knowing you have won the Olympic gold medal.

'That can only happen when you are running the Marathon – it is something special. In track races, you are down there running round and round in circles, it is predictable as it continues there and you can see it, yet with the Marathon, it is something special. It is almost like, even if no-one person is in the lead, there is that waiting, waiting and waiting! And then suddenly someone appears through the tunnel and there he is – the Olympic Champion.

'That is something that appeals to me and now, of course, with things like the New York and the London Marathon, there is something unique surrounding that sort of approach!'

Dave, I always believed you had the talent, since I first met you in athletics, but I found I was alone in many ways in that viewpoint. Now you have achieved a World record, everyone expects you to win every race you run. Yet you only have to look to as recently as last year, you had serious trouble in races, like when you did 4:01.7 in the Golden Mile. How then do you cope with the fact that people knock you or praise you?

'One thing you learn quickly in this sport is that people like me have got to get used to failure, and I think that you are very, very fortunate if you go through the whole of your athletic career with only a few bad results. I think the quicker you come to terms with that, the better. Now for some people, failure is a thing that means they are never going to be any good; in other words they don't use it as a motivation.

'I think if you can come to terms with your disappointments and use them for a spur to the future, then I think you have got the right balance. Also, in doing that, you can come to terms with other people's reactions to your failure: because, as nice as it is to be a World record holder – to be hailed as something special – you know full well that the day you fail is the day they will write you off.

'The media and people generally can afford to write you off because there is always somebody else they can turn to and then, if you run well again, they will be back saying, "Eh! Great! Smashing!"

'Really, that is just part and parcel of the sport. It is the price you pay for running well. I have no complaints. I am enjoying it, but I try to keep things in perspective.'

John Anderson always likes to keep you a little bit sharp all the year long, even if you have been ill or in the middle of a cross-country season. Is that something you feel grateful for, that John as a coach has instilled that little bit of edge into your running, so that you can bounce back at any time?

'I think that is very important. I guess this all comes down to specificity. That's John's key word. He sees that I am specifically a fast runner, that is a range from 800 to 5000 metres. Anything shorter or longer than that has its place, but it all revolves round speed within that distance. He believes for almost twelve months of the year you have to be working on your speed – a different emphasis at different times, but you have got to be working within that range twelve months of the year.

'The endurance period, what people would call the conditioning period, is still built round conditioning for speed, with a little bit more emphasis on endurance. And a person like me, who is not endowed with the greatest natural speed, needs to do it or I would lose it and become pedestrian and plodding.'

I was sitting next to John Anderson and Linda (Dave's wife), watching you in a two miles invitation event at Crystal Palace in 1980, between the two Olympic trials. I remember Filbert Bayi going into the lead, then the field was quickly strung out and you fell back, about forty metres off the front. You had been worried about great stiffness in the legs before the race. In the race you shook your head as you came round for the third lap, as though you had had it. Despite that lapse and your leg trouble, you then went up the field, joined Bayi at the front and went on to win.

'I had run the 5000 trials on the previous Saturday at Meadowbank, and as usual my legs had cramped up and I had had a bad week. I really was not recovered enough leg-wise to race in the two miles at the Talbot meet. But I had treatment, and before the race I went into the physio-therapy room and saw John Allen. I had a wee bit more treatment, went out and warmed up.

'I decided I was going to give it a go, but it was very, very sore early on for the first couple of laps. Then, once I got into the race, I forgot about it and it was okay, but, of course,it was really sore after again. That was the pattern with the calf.

'If I raced when the calf was still sore it improved slightly and, as I said, after a couple of laps I was okay; but it was holding me back so much in training and also in recovering from races that the operation that I had in September 1981 was really do or die. If I had not had it, then I don't think I would have been able to have a realistic hope of doing a heat and a final within a short time.'

You obviously enjoy 1500 metre racing, but having turned to 5000s, there must be a lot of learning, both in training and the adaptation to the new distance in competition?

'A lot of 1500 metre runners when they moved up found it difficult. I have, I think maybe Eamonn (Coghlan) has not had it all that easy on his way up, although he has obviously done well. Liquori was the same – brilliant one day, not so good the next.'

How does your 5000 World record of 13:00.42 go down for you as a memory? I would like to add to that John Anderson told me a week before your race that you would achieve new world figures within a short time. Could you in your dreams have said that?

'The race that made me realize I was in good shape was the mile in Oslo the week before (3:49.34 in the Dream Mile). John said that he thought I could break the world record and that I could run 13 minutes, but I did not believe

225

him, because he says a lot of things – mind you, he only says the truth. He has never been wrong yet, except when there has been a reason for it.

'He said in 1976 he thought I could make the final for the Olympic 1500 metres, and I did – I should not have done really. He said that I could win the Commonwealth when everything had gone wrong, and I did. He said I could win the Olympics – but I was ill.

'If I had run 13:05, I would have been chuffed. The pleasure of breaking the World record is enough to alleviate the frustration of not breaking 13:00. The difference over the old record now means a lot but, in the future people will talk about the person who broke 13 minutes.'

Was there a training session that pointed the way?

'Round about the time of the National road relay, I had done some good track sessions. 1000 metre reps and things, it had gone very well, also things had gone pretty well two or three weeks prior to the first Oslo meet and the second visit . . . but I did not really know.

'I knew that I could run faster than 13:20 and I was hoping I could break Brendan's record, but I never thought that I could go out at the front after two laps and run 13 minutes, that was the furthest from my mind.'

Don't you think, perhaps, you had a realization that you were fitter than you had been for such a long time, and you just took the bull by the horns?

'I had the confidence that, even though I did not plan on going to the front, once I was at the front I never hesitated.'

If you had raced a few months before or even at the same time at another place, might the time have been quite different?

'There are many, many people capable of running exceptionally fast times at different times of their career, but they were unfortunately unable to find a race or it was not the right time. The ideal would be to run that race in the Olympic final – like Beamon producing his long jump in the right one.

'It just so happened that on that day everything was right, and I happened to be in Oslo running a 5000 metres and so it produced the time. That night I could have been at Coventry Apprentice Sports invitation 3000 at the Butts, on

226

a crummy cinder track, and I would probably have run something like 7:45 or something. Which would have been remarkable and would have personally been very pleasing, but would have not meant anything because of the race it was. I was just lucky that it happened to be in Oslo that night.'

36

JOHN GILMOUR

Born Perth, Western Australia, on 3 May, 1919.

John Gilmour was not an Olympic runner or an international at a major games, so why have I devoted a chapter to him when I have left out so many stars of Olympic calibre?

The answer is quite simple. John Gilmour, in many ways, is the most courageous runner I have ever met in my life.

Firstly, he was a prisoner in a Japanese camp in the last World War, where the conditions were deplorable and where many of his mates died through lack of food and terrible beatings. John suffered badly with malnutrition while he was in prison, and it even affected his vision. But he had a burning desire that he would eventually get out and win a South Western Australian title. That strong resolution somehow kept him going with his struggle for survival.

If that was not enough, he had a serious car accident a few years ago that did affect his running, so the reader of this book may be surprised to know that at the age of seventy, in November 1989, he wrote to me telling me that he had achieved a 70–75 World age best by running 3:03:4 for the Marathon in Australia (88.20 at the half-way point), a time some 20,000 London marathon runners would be pleased with on the day!

John corresponded regularly with me, as well as with one of the most respected officials/writers of veteran's athletics, Jack Fitzgerald of Mitcham.

John wrote to me on his Christmas card in 1989: 'I am still running these days, but quite a lot slower after a bad car accident I had a few years ago, still I am happy to be able to compete and do well.'

228

I met John for the second time at the end of July 1979, when he was competing in the well-organized World Veterans Games in Hannover. His remarkable performances at sixty, over five days of competition were; age world records in the 800 – 2:19.3; 1500 – 4:32.5; 5000 – 16:54.9, and 10,000 – 35:07.7, and then on his final day he ran 2:52.8 for the Marathon.

Interview 1979

What do you say, John, if someone turns round to you and says you can't improve, and you'll kill yourself with all that running at your age?

'I have proved that even at my age I have improved that much, and I know it is only because the training is making my body that much fitter – otherwise I wouldn't bother to do what I'm doing. When I was released as a prisoner of war, I would have been about seven and a half stone (47 kg). I know that my body took a thrashing while I was a prisoner of war, but I have not lost anything through it. . . .'

I heard from another Australian veteran that you were challenged by your prison commandant to a race . . .

'I actually raced against a Jap over 100 metres and I beat him, but he put on such a show that I knew he was all upset about it, and so I made out I cheated and we re-ran the race, and I let him win. From doing that, he allowed us to have a weekend of athletic competition in the camp, because it really stirred them on to thinking they could beat us at athletics. When you were in the prison camp you did not know what was going to happen to you next, and I know the hardships I went through. If I had not looked after my body like I did, I would not be around today. A lot of the fellows are not here today because they sort of tossed it in, and it is the same with running. It is all in the mind. You have to think you are going to make it. Ten miles, fifteen miles, is not problem, but if you go out and say I don't think I can run fifteen miles, you won't run it. If I plan to run ten miles I run ten miles, I don't chicken out at six. That's what running is all about in my opinion.

'In the prison camp, I always had in my mind that if I ever

got home I wanted to run, and I never ever did anything that may have been detrimental to my health. I never smoked or drank alcohol even when I was in the army, and I still don't. I did not know if I was ever going to get out of that prison camp in Japan, but I still lived and hoped that one day I would get out and run again and win a Western Australian title. That took my mind off being shut up and maybe never being able to get out. And I did win the Western Australian title for ten miles on the road. I ran second the year I came back after being released, in 1946 I won the State Championship!'

How did you prepare for the World Veteran Championships in Hannover in 1979?

'In May I was doing an average of 106 miles a week; twelve miles in the morning, eight miles in the afternoon. Then I got my back and groin injury, and I was right down to walking, and it hurt me to even walk. The week that I left to come over to Britain, the furthest I had run was three miles on the Monday and three miles on the Tuesday, and that was at jogging pace. I was given two cortisone injections on the Monday, and luckily they took effect. It was that one month of hard buildup training that carried me through in Hannover.'

Which athlete do you admire most?

'Herb Elliott, without a doubt. Herb proved that the more you run, the better you get. He could run a four-minute mile twice a week, and still come up and run a world-class 800 metre race in the middle of the week, so it proved that the harder you train, the better the results. I still say Herb Elliott retired before we saw the best of him.'

Although Ron Clarke, another one of your countrymen, achieved monumental success as a prolific record-breaker, as well as being a fine ambassador for the sport, he did not achieve gold medals in the big games. What is your opinion of him?

'I think he was one of those guys who was unlucky. To me, Ron Clarke defeated himself in the "Big Time". I reckon with Ron that, had he gone out running his races the same way he did breaking the world records, making them chase him, I think he would have done a lot better. I was disappointed with the way Ron was beaten when it came to

230

medal time, but when there were no medals on him he ran fantastic times. Another guy in the same class as him was Gordon Pirie, in my opinion. I saw him run into the ground in Melbourne by Vladimir Kuts, but he should never have been. At that time he held the World six miles record, but once again he got dragged away by another bloke's ideas of running. Kuts was a believer in fast sprinting down the back straight, and Gordon Pirie had a terrific stride and could run lap after lap as even as you like, and yet he got sucked into running the same way as Kuts.'

What do you think of veterans athletics?

'I think it is a great thing because a lot of people today waste their life away by sitting around watching television. Television is the biggest bugbear in the home today, in my opinion. As soon as people get home from work, they switch it on and they even eat their meals in front of it. That goes on every day of the week, plus the fact that they are eating and drinking all the time with no exercise, whereas the beauty of veteran athletics is that you meet a lot of people and you get a feeling of competition between yourself and your own body. It is not the competition against the other guys, it is the fact that you know that you are doing something for yourself and improving your own health, which I think is the greatest thing about it. Lots of guys who I know who were sixteen to seventeen stone, and today are down to thirteen stone and they are wanting to run twenty-six miles. Before, they would even get in their car to go a mile to buy a paper. Now, with veteran running and this fun running that has come into vogue, I reckon it is making everyone that much healthier.'

37

ABDI BILE

Born 28 December, 1962, at Las Anod. 1.85/75kg.

I met Abdi Bile the day before he improved his personal best 800 metre time to 1:45.68, at Crystal Palace in the Peugeot Talbot meeting in July 1987. In the race itself, the winner was Tony Morrell in 1:45.58, third was Stanley Redwine (USA) and Phillipe Collard (France) fourth.

It was straight after that I went home to my house in Upper Norwood and immediately wrote an article to post to the then Consultant Editor of *Athletics Weekly*, Melvyn Watman, now, along with Randall Northam, Editor of *Athletics Today*. I began: 'Abdi Bile is a name very few are likely to have heard of, but out of the shadows of Africa comes a talent from Somalia that has already, since May of this year, started to test some of the world's best middle-distance runners.

'That may seem a surprising statement when one learns about Bile's background, which includes a catalogue of injuries after a very late start in the sport.' He takes up the story himself:

'I was eighteen years old and a soccer player in defence (2, 3, 4, 5 and 6 positions) in the National Junior team when, one day, I decided to go along to a small meet and, without having known anything about running, I entered the 400 metres and won in 56 seconds, just using the endurance and speed I had as a footballer. I had only gone down to compete for fun, but the people who knew about that said to me – You are a good soccer player but you can be a great runner!'

His friends and family continued to encourage him, and within a year he had achieved a time of 1:50.00 for the 800 and 3.45 for 1500 on dirty dusty tracks. He enjoyed running with a couple of friends in Somalia, before going to the States to George Mason University, where he studied Marketing. His coach at the University, John Cook, was the first one to give him a serious training programme, and on that Abdi explains: 'He gives us some cross-country running, conditioning, weightlifting, cycling and swimming as he believes in variety, rather than doing one thing which you would get sick of, if you did it all the time.'

He considered his coach a wonderful person to work with, as he was knowledgeable and helpful as an individual. With that in mind, how did Abdi Bile view athletics as a sport for him?

'I see athletics as very exciting. It is fun, and you enjoy competing with the rest of the world, not like soccer or football, which you are only going to do with a few clubs. Most athletes are really good guys. If they were not good guys, they would not make it in life. If you see someone doing well it has to be something otherwise, they don't make it in the first place!'

There was a hope that he had, back in July of 1987, before he really broke through on the world scene: 'I think I want a World record!' he said.

He points out about his progress:

'Before, in 1980, I was not a runner and I did not watch the Olympic Games and I did not know anything about the Olympics, and yet there I was in 1984 in the Olympic Games in Los Angeles, knowing that one and a half months before, I got a stress fracture. For one month I was in a cast not doing anything, just swimming, weightlifting and a little bicycling and yet I came to the Olympics and made the final with a 3.36 (3:35.89).

'Nobody knew at the time or expected someone to show up, and yet I made that Olympic final, although I was disqualified.

'One guy had fallen down, and they said I had pushed him or something like that. Even though I ran 3.36 out of nothing, as I had not any basic training before that one.'

There was no doubt that result in such a competition gave him confidence in his ability as a middle-distance runner, as he had got very close to good quality runners, but in 1985 and 1986 more trouble came. 'In all those years the problem I had was with injuries – I was injured for months both years. I was doing stretching, as I had a hamstring problem, and this year (1987) an achilles problem. I did not start training till 20 April, and after a week's training I ran 1.48.'

In 1987, even though he was still a dark horse for the World Championships, he improved his times to 1:44.47/ 3:31.71, which sharpened him sufficiently for his successful attack.

In evidence, for all the world to see, was the tall bronzed figure of Abdi Bile in his Somalian National colours of light blue and white, striding out ahead in the home straight to win in Rome in 3:36.80, followed by 1500 specialists – 2. Jose Luis Gonzalez (ESP), 3:38.03, and 3. Jim Spivey (USA), 3:38.82.

Despite missing the Olympics in 1988 with a stress fracture, he recorded a personal best that year of 1:44.42 for 800, and in 1989 he traded victories with 1983 World 1500 Champion Steve Cram, the man who back in 1985 ran a World mile record of 3:46.32.

Abdi Bile went on to add the World Cup 1500 title in Barcelona to his World Championship crown, with a time of 3:35.56, with three of the outstanding runners of the decade behind him – 2. Sebastian Coe, 3:35.79. 3. East German European Champion of 1990, Jens Peter Herold, 3:35.87, and Italian Gennaro Di Napoli, 3:36.65. The latter two were joined by Africa's next great 'Blue Ribbon' of the track specialist to come on the scene, Noureddine Morceli of Algeria, who set world-class performances in 1990 and broke Peter Elliott's indoor World 1500 record with 3:34.16 in February 1991.

38

JOHN NGUGI

Born 10 May, 1962, Nyahururu. 1.78/62kgs.

John Ngugi had a clear victory in the Olympic 5000 metres in Seoul in 1988, as well as winning four senior World cross-country championships, but he did not have the same type of meteoric success that such men as fellow countryman Paul Ereng had; from a very early age he knew he was destined to be a runner, as he pointed out to me in between his morning session and evening hour jog at Crystal Palace.

'I felt something good inside of me when I ran, I felt that desire to go out and run. When I continued, I wanted to be like my heroes Kipchoge Keino and Henry Rono. I thought I would try my best to do that.'

John Ngugi, a Kikuyu, talked about his early attempts at racing: 'I first started in primary school at Nyahururu near Nakuru in Kenya, and I continued to run and improve till I went into the Army. Then my coach Musheru trained and trained and trained me! I owe a lot to him, and also I can thank Mike Kosgie, the Head Coach of Kenya, for his help too. I would like to point out that the Army gave me time to train more fully.' He is a sergeant in the Army, but regarding his travelling to meets around the world, he stressed that he likes to rest when he comes away from all that!

Now for his progress: 'In 1978 I finished third in the district 3000 metres in 10 minutes something! In 1981 I ran sixth in the National 5000 Championships and then in 1982 I came second which, of course, was an improvement, and I continued to get better.'

As I talked to John I kept on picturing him, in my mind,

235

with his loping stride, running out ahead in the World cross-countries, and I told him that and he gave me a huge John Ngugi grin!

Looking back at those interesting results, to illustrate, here are the first two and the winning team in the world event, according to the usual invaluable information in the *International Athletics Annual*, by the Association of Track and Field Statisticians, edited by Peter Mathews.

1986 – 1. John Ngugi, 35:33. 2. Abebe Mekonen (Eth), 35:35, team Kenya, 45 pts.

1987 – 1. John Ngugi, 36:07. 2. Paul Kipkoech (Kenya), 36:07, team Kenya, 53 pts.

1988 – 1. John Ngugi, 34:32. 2. Paul Kipkoech, 34:54, team Kenya, 23 pts.

1989 – 1. John Nugugi, 39:42. 2. Tim Hutchings (UK), 40:10, team Kenya, 44 pts.

About that impressive little lot, John remarked: 'I enjoyed the last two wins the most, whereas the other two previously were very hard races actually.'

John Ngugi likes racing all the events he does, and sometimes does appear to enjoy cross-country and road racing most. He finds training alone the best experience. 'When I am feeling well I always enjoy training and I would say the track work was the best work for the 5000s.' He went on to explain, 'So far my favourite training runs were when I ran in the forests high up in Switzerland.'

Who did he consider his toughest rivals, then?

'Aouita, and sometimes in the past, Domingos Castro. For me, as I look at it now, I hope to run for another ten to twelve years and do the 10,000 in Barcelona, and then after the next five years the Marathon.'

In 1987, in Rome in the World Championships, when Said Aouita won the final of the 5000 in 13:26.4, back in twelfth place (13:34.04) came John Ngugi. 'I had an injury in that I had a cyst behind my knee, so I could not run well.'

The next track race of significance was the Olympic 5000 metres in 1988 in Seoul, and the result of the first six past the post was – 1. John Ngugi, 13:11.70. 2. Dieter Baumann (FRG), 13:15.52. 3. Hansjorg Kunze (GDR), 13:15.73. 4. Domingos Castro (Port), 13:16.09. 5. Sydney Maree (USA), 13:23.69. 6. Jack Buckner (UK), 13:23.85. At a 1000 metres,

John put in a 58.2 lap and that was the start of the damage he did to his rivals, who were unable to get on terms again. John ran through the 3000 point in 7:56.12.

'I thought I would front run for a good time only, but I did not expect to win the gold because of the races I had in Europe before, which I did not do well in.' In the race itself, things went well for him. 'It was in the sixth lap of the Olympic Final I thought, maybe I could win!'

In the Commonwealth Games in Auckland in 1990, John Ngugi had a hard fall in the 5000 final early on in the race and lost many metres, but when he got to his feet he went very quickly through the field, and the remarkable man looked set to win yet another gold. Unfortunately, he just ran out of steam, as the Australian Alan Lloyd took him in the final ten metres of the last lap, to win the race in 13:24.84, with John Ngugi timed at 13:24.94. Ian Hamer of Wales, in his breakthrough race, was next in 13:25.63.

On 4 September, 1990, in Koblenz, John Ngugi gave an indication to the rest of the world of his great potential over 10,000 metres, when he ran to an All-African record of 27:19.15, with 13:27.86 for the second 5000!

As 1991 came in John Ngugi was returning from injury and, was not prepared to be a contender for the World track championships that year in Tokyo. The winner of the 10,000 there was fellow Kenyan Moses Tanui in 27:38.74, with compariot Richard Chelimo (27:39.41) second. It was at that time I talked again to John at Crystal Palace, when he was staying near his manager, ex-international steeplechaser, John Bicourt. John Ngugi said then 'I have been injured but I want to do some personal bests this season.'

A man of his word, he ran a solo 27:11.62 for 10,000 in Brussels on the 13th of September which, was the third fastest ever run to that date and, he went on to win his fifth world cross-country title at Boston on the 21st March 1992. His time was 37:05 with Kenyan William Mutwoh (37:17) runner-up but, like John for the victorious team.

39

DEBBIE FLINTOFF-KING

Born Melbourne, 20 April, 1960. 1.71/57kg.

In Debbie Flintoff-King's case, it was not so much her ability as a sprinter that eventually got her Olympic stardom in Seoul in 1988, but more the fact that, added to a fine hurdling technique, she was a fierce competitor when it really mattered. Amongst her many medals and successes, she obtained Commonwealth gold medals in 1986 for both the 400 flat (51.29) and the 400 hurdles (54.94). Her most outstanding performance was in the second fastest time in history for the 400 hurdles when in Seoul (First six:– 1. Debbie Flintoff-King, 53.17 in an Olympic record. 2. Tatyan Ledovskaya (SU), 53.18. 3. E. Fiedler (GDR), 53.63. 4. Sabine Busch (GDR), 53.69. 5. Sally Gunnell (UK), the Commonwealth Champion of 1990, 54.03. 6. Gudrun Abt (FRG), 54.04.)

Interview 1988

Where did Debbie take up athletics?

'Mainly at Booroondara State School. I used to be good at school, but I never really joined a club till I was about fourteen, and that was Frankston in Melbourne.'

Did classwork or running take priority for her at the time?

'Running definitely! In fact, I can remember in my high school years that my maths teacher used to fail me because I was always out at sport. She did not like sport at all. I can remember her failing me in the fourth form, because she said I was never in, and I was always out doing sport.'

What turned her more to athletics rather than doing

other sports?

'My mum and dad asked me if I wanted to join a club, and it just sort of took off from there. I started off doing the long jump and hurdling, as well as nearly every other event. In fact, I did the penthathlon, which then became the heptathlon, before I even did the 400 hurdles.'

What then made her lean towards the hurdles?

'My coach at the time, called Henry Schubert, who was from Germany, advised me till I was nineteen or twenty. It was after that I decided whether to go for the hurdles or not, and I then, at that time, actually met my boyfriend, who became my husband – Phillip King. He sort of realized that I had the talent, and has coached me ever since 1980. He said that I was good at the hurdles and have a long stride, so "Why not try the 400 hurdles." It sort of went from there, and we started to train for them , and in eighteen months I went from 63.00 to 55.9.'

It was in the Commonwealth Games of 1982 that Debbie first won her 400 hurdles Championship title in 55.89, and it was interesting to see that she was one of the pioneers of the new event, for women on the international scene, as she admitted:

'It was relatively new then, and it was in 1982, the first Commonwealth Games they had it in, and in 1984, the first Olympics as well. It is not going to be long before they are all going to be doing 52s.'

The Russians, East Germans and Americans are starting to take the event seriously over the last few years, so I would think it would be an advantage for some of them to turn away from the 400 to do the hurdles?

'A lot of 400 flat runners, like the Russians, who could not make it really as good flat runners, decided to more or less go to the hurdles.'

Of course that started to change the event?

'Definitely and, in 1984 the World record was 54.2, and now it is 52.94 (Marina Styepanova, SU – in 1986) and that is in more or less within three years.'

Before the Olympic Games in 1988, did Debbie feel she would have to improve in other areas to gain an Olympic gold medal?

'My hurdle technique is not too bad. It is probably as

239

good as any of the hurdlers around, but my flat speed – I do a lot of strength work, and I am very strong and I come home well, but I need to work on my flat speed more, and that is why I will try to do some 200s and 440s.'

Looking back, she agrees that 1982 was a good year for her!

'1982 was a wonderful year. 1983 was a year when I was sick and injured, so it was not a great year. I ended up by getting into the semi-final of the World Championships in Helsinki. In fact we probably over-trained if anything, and we more or less thought, "Well, if ten sessions got us 55.9 maybe, fourteen sessions a week would get us 54.9 or something like that." but it was not to be, and I just got very sick and injured. 1984 was a funny year, because I did personal bests in everything except the 400 hurdles. We were probably too heavy-handed again on the longer work, and it was not really until 1985–86 that I started doing more speed work, and the results showed.'

Progress became even more rapid in 1986.

'In 1986 I ran 53.76 in my first race in Europe against Busch, who I beat, and I also won double gold at the Commonwealth Games 400fl/400hdles, the latter in a Games record of 54.94, so I had a good year that year. That was interesting, because I was injured with my achilles tendon problem at the beginning of that year, and had to stop all hill work or weight training, and I just did speed work on the track, and I think that was what helped me a lot really, and there was something to learn from that as well.'

In 1987, in the World Championships, Debbie came second, so her memories of that were quite vivid. The first four in the final were: 1. Sabine Busch (GDR) 53.62. 2. Debbie Flintoff, 54.19. 3. Cornelia Ulrich (GDR), 54.31, and 4. Sandra Farmer (Jam), 54.38. That World Championship final gave her vital experience regarding the lane draw.

'I had always had 3, 4, 5 or 6th lane but I had lane 8 in the heats, semi-final and final. It was quite an experience to run by yourself the whole way round, that I probably did quite well really.'

That was a good dry run for the Olympics, in case she was in the outside again?

'We are quite often training in lane 8 since then, just in

case it happens again. The problem mainly arises if you are chasing someone, you don't think if you are feeling tired, whereas if you are running by yourself, you may start to feel it a bit and start to think how you are feeling rather than just chasing. If someone said, "What is your favourite lane?" I would say 4 or 5, because it is in the middle, but to get any lane would not have worried me.'

Did she feel then that getting second in the World Championships would give her the determination and realization that she could go one better and obtain gold in the Olympics in Seoul?

'That is true. If you get the gold, you think, "Where do I go from here?" When you get the silver, you have got one more stepping stone to try and get.'

Which events do you like doing most?

'I love 4 × 400s, and that is something you can go for and chase the person in front of you, and I always run my best doing that. My best times overall are 50.78/53.76 – 400/400 hurdles, but my sprints times had only been 11.7/23.5, so that was something I was going to have to work on for the Olympics.'

Regarding her love for running, Debbie outlined what she derived from the sport:

'Probably the feeling of responsibility and just to be able to cope with things in normal everyday life, which perhaps normal people might find hard. The dedication you put into running just makes you a stronger person in all sorts of life. For example, I had a car accident a couple of years ago. I was so nervous and worked up inside, but I was so cool on the outside. I am sure that was because of the races. For those you are nervous on the inside, but you try to relax and keep cool. Just little things like that have really been helped by doing athletics, also I think my approach to life is much better for being in such high-level competition.'

Were there athletes over the years Debbie looked up to?

'I always used to look up to Raylene Boyle when I was wanting to be a 400 flat runner, when I was a lot younger. I don't really mould myself or look at anyone else. Obviously I look at Edwin Moses, because he had so many races and had done so well. I am sure I respect all athletes.'

It was prior to the Olympics that I talked to her, and

241

subsequently she decided to go on and compete in 1990 before retiring, but before the Games in 1988, she said, 'I really only want to go on till the 1990 Commonwealth Games, because that will give me three Commonwealth Games, two Olympics and two World Championships, and I think that will be plenty for me! (She did announce a comeback in October 1990). The reason for that is the way I train. I don't think I would want to go much further than that because it is so demanding, as I am sure it is with all athletes, and the time it takes. A few years ago I would just do the training, but now I have to do stretching and massage just because I am getting older and been running so much longer. It is really very time-consuming. People just don't understand. I have a part time job which takes four to six hours a day, and even that is a lot. I am Sports Promotions Officer for the Olympic Federation in Melbourne, but doing that and with training time taking up four to six hours a day with all that you have to fit in to it, with physio and massage and everthing like that. I am eating at 8.30 or 9.00 at night after leaving at 7.00 in the morning.'

She continues; 'I think when I finish I will want a break. Whether I would get back into coaching or something like that later on – I have learnt so much, and Phil and I have done training through trial and error, not necessarily books or anything like that. What we have learnt we can pass it on, considering I have kept a diary since 1981. We quite often look at what sessions we did when I was running well, and so it is really great looking back on them, and it's worth it.'

Finally, for the aspiring hurdler, it would be interesting to find out what particular type of work helped Debbie Flintoff-King in her striving for the number one 400 metre hurdles place in the Olympics.

'We have had sessions during the week, where we do a lot of repetition 300s and that sort of thing. My hardest session during the week would be a hill session. We do four of them, but they last anything between 45 and 55 seconds long, and they are really steep and we just walk back. That would probably be the most lactic session I have ever done. I literally can't walk after the fourth one, can't sit down, and yet when we came away to Europe before the Olympics of

1988, I did my best personal bests ever. My strength and endurance was there through doing these hills, and so we realized with that there we could really work on our speed for the Games and sharpen up for Seoul.'

40

ROGER KINGDOM

Born 26 August, 1962, Vienna, Georgia. 1.85/91kg.

The man who predicted before the Olympics in 1984 that a young Roger Kingdom could win the high hurdles in Los Angeles was the 1968 Olympic Champion, Willie Davenport.

Looking back now, it is interesting to note Willie Davenport's opinion on the hurdlers that inspired him. 'When I got really interested in the event, it was Lee Calhoun that I studied and read about all the time, then came along Hayes Jones (1964 Olympic Champion), so I just took it from there.' He continued, 'Lee Calhoun had a beautiful form and he had the speed to go with it, and a lean at the finish, a fantastic lean. Hayes Jones had that blistering start which one had to learn to live with.' Davenport's idol Lee Calhoun won the Olympic 110 hurdles titles in 1956 and 1960, and the only other one to do the double was our subject Roger Kingdom. The first six in each of his finals were: 1984 – 1. Roger Kingdom, 13.20 (OR). 2. Greg Foster (USA), 13.23. 3. Arto Bryggare (Fin), 13.40. 4. Mark McKoy (Can), 13.45. 5. Tonie Campbell (USA), 13.55. 6. Stephane Caristan (FRA), 13.71.

1988 – 1. Roger Kingdom, 12.98. 2. Colin Jackson (UK), 13.28. 3. Tonnie Campbell (USA), 13.38. 4. Vladimir Shiskin (SU). 13.51. 5. Jonathan Ridgeon (UK), 13.52. 6. Tony Jarrett (UK), 13.54.

Roger Kingdom remembers his introduction to athletics as a child: 'It was when I was a little kid, when we had moved to Florida from Georgia, where my parents ran up and down the street with us, racing us back and forth from our house to my cousin's house, which was approximately

244

150 metres or so away. As my four brothers, one sister and I grew older, we got into running competitively. We then started to compete against each other and for the school, and it became something big in our lives. We started to bring home medals, and we really got into it and drew a love for the sport.

'After that at Vienna High School, Georgia, my older brother and I started to play football as well as doing track and field. I was 6'1¾" then in height and was close to 200 lbs in weight, which was a pretty good size for football. I managed to win the State Championships my junior and senior year, in the hurdles, discus and the high jump. I did 148 ft in my junior year for the discus, and 164 ft in the senior year. Now, for the decathlon, I am throwing the discus 172 ft. In the high jump in my junior year, I jumped 6'9", which was a State record at the time, and the following year, which was my senior year, I did 6'10¼". I ran 14.07 for the hurdles in my Freshman year in college. We did not have a coach at the time that was handling the team, so I left spring football practice and went to the track meet and ran that 14.07 with no practice, and I was only running two meets that year – that was the reason I dropped down from 14.07 to 13.44 in one year (1982–83) – the progress speaks for itself after that.'

Obviously there is more to Roger Kingdom's ability than hurdling, as he says: 'I have actually been thinking or at least considering for the last four years (talking in 1988 prior to Seoul) to do the decathlon, but after 1984 my injury held me back. It was a setback for two and a half years, and I was not able to concentrate on the discus, high jump, or anything. My main goal was to try to come back and do well in the hurdles.'

In 1983 he won the Pan-American Games and NCAA high hurdles races, so it gradually became apparent that he had a chance to make the United States Olympic team for LA.

'Coming up for 1984, I really did not consider myself seriously as a potential Olympian until eight or nine months before the Olympic trials (trials, he was third behind winner Greg Foster and Tonnie Campbell). I was working with my coach then, Albert Kennedy, who was also

245

the women's coach at Pittsburgh University, and at the time I had decided I did not want to play football that season, so I could train solely for track and field. Within one year of that, with no football, I dropped from 14 seconds to 13.16. When I hit that time I felt really good about it, because I knew that in the years to come, knowing how young I was, that I had an opportunity to run the times that I am running now or come close to the record.'

There are certain similarities in Roger Kingdom's powerful hurdling with the 1968 Olympic Champion Willie Davenport, and also in another way to Renaldo Nehmiah in approach, and that prompted Roger to say: 'I admired Renaldo because he was doing it at a young age, and he was still older than I, so by him being able to do all those things at a young age motivated me. It gave me that drive to try to do it myself. He was that clean-type hurdler. He was aggressive and he had finesse, and I like that. I tried to run the hurdles clean and aggressive like that, but the aggressiveness I had, but the cleanness was not there, and that was because of football. Anyway, I idolised the guy because he was the best hurdler of all time in my particular event, and I liked that and I admired him.'

Coming from third in the Olympic trials to being Olympic Champion in 1984 obviously taught Roger Kingdom an important lesson, regarding never to count anybody out in an Olympic final.

'You have to respect everyone really in an Olympic final or in another such important race. You could be in the race with all the big names, Nehmiah, Greg Foster, Tonnie Campbell, Roger Kingdom and Colin Jackson, but then again "John Doe" might come up and beat everybody, so you can't take anyone for granted. You just have to make sure you prepare yourself. I think the thing that enabled me to do as well as I did was because they, so to speak, ruled me out and expected me to battle for the bronze with Mark McCoy of Canada, but being the competitor that I was, young and nothing to lose, I wanted to win! I always go in a race trying to win. I never say, "Well, I get second or maybe I get third!" If I had listened to the press and the media at that time, I would have settled for the bronze, and if somebody had a good day I would not even have got third

246

place. You have to always shoot for the moon, so if you fall amongst the stars then you can be content with that, but never satisfied, content.'

I felt, as Roger had won an Olympic gold already, that was to a great extent a surprise in 1984, that perhaps there would be less pressure on him despite being the favourite for Seoul, and he agreed:

'Whenever they started trying to pile the pressure on one by saying, "How do you feel about being the returning Champion?" I said, "To me it is very relaxing, and I enjoy it because, for one, I have what all these people are working for." Okay, it would be an honour and a great thrill to get the second one, but I could relax, because I have what they are working for, and any time they try to pile the pressure on me that is the thing I tell them. It might cause some aggression among the other athetes or animosity, but it is not intended to. In other words, it was just to get the pressure off my back that the press were trying to put on!

'The only meet I felt any presure on was at the Olympic trials, and that was because I was not doing what I was capable of doing, and I also was starting to think about running, a different way, than just relaxing and being Roger.'

In the 1988 US trials, he ran 13.14 in the semi-final and 13.21 to win the final from the Olympic bronze medallist Tonnie Campbell (13.25) and Arthur Blake (13.28). Despite being hampered by hamstring injuries in 1985–86 and even in 1987, Roger Kingdom started to flow over the hurdles quite early on in the 1988 season.

'After all that injury time, it restarted the motivation and it gave me that push. When I was injured, they used to say "Oh, man! he is the Olympic Champion!" but it did not feel really good to me because I was not doing it at the time they said that, because I was injured then, so naturally I was not performing well. When they said I was the Olympic Champion, I would say, "Oh well", but I don't know what happened since.'

In 1988, prior to the Olympic Games, his policy had been to run against most of those he considered would be his opponents in Seoul, keeping sharp and running the European meets.

'You have to, in a sense, stay relaxed and stay sharp. Before going to Seoul I was keeping at the top of my field, because I was competing against everyone who I considered composed the toughest competition for me, and if I continued to beat them, then that was playing a mental game too. It is programming in their minds, "Here he goes again," and I can say, "Look how many times I have beaten this guy," and I can go to the Olympic Games training hard, knowing that if I can run the times I have been running against this tough competition, that I will get the gold, so that is why I like to run against them, because the better my competition is the better I am going to be.'

I told Roger that I thought that was proved, because when Renaldo went to the World Cup in 1979, he won just about all his races, leading up to that victory over 1980 Olympic Champion Thomas Munkelt of the USSR.

'Right, so as good as the competition is, the better you are going to be. Specifically speaking of Renaldo Nehmiah and Greg Foster in the Zurich race (on 19 August 1981), I don't think Renaldo would have broken that record again, if Greg Foster had not been as close as he was to him (13.03). He was a competitor, and he wanted to win. Greg being a competitor too, he stayed right on Renaldo's hip.'

Regarding that, Renaldo comes in: 'I enjoyed the races in 1981 that preceded the World record of 12.93. *(Weltklasse)* Koblenz (26/8), Cologne 13.07 (23/8), – I ran those alone. Greg Foster was not in the race, there was no-one in the race except myself. In the World record performance, he ran 13.03 chasing me. So, I thought 03s, 04s and 05s were far more significant on behalf of my strength, power and dominance. I take great pride in those times rather than the World record; as I think, the World record was on the cards, it was supposed to happen. If a hurdler can run that fast by himself, get anyone close to him and push him, he should be faster. That year, the 13.5 performance in the United States against Alejndro Casanas of Cuba – he false started and they did not call him back, and I had to go and catch him and I ran a 13.5, that was an important race as well.'

Back to Roger Kingdom, regarding his races in Europe and the buildup to Seoul. 'Before the Olympics I was right at the top of my game, so if someone else pulled up beside me I think I could continue to run as hard as I possibly could and as aggresive as I could, to stay in front of them. If that came about, I knew the outcome might be a tremendous time.'

(Certainly looking ahead to 1989, how right he was, with the knowledge that Colin Jackson was in the World Cup race, 1. Roger Kingdom, 12.87. 2. Colin Jackson, 12.95 +2.51 wind 10 September; also again in the official World record race in Zurich, 16 August – 1. Kingdom, 12.92 (.01 wind). 2. Jackson, 13.12.)

His training for the Seoul Olympics: 'There are a lot of specific drills that I do in practice that other hurdlers might do, but they don't think about them in the same aspect that I do or go into it with the same mentality that I do. I try to go over the hurdle with a bent lead leg and step back towards the hurdle, as opposed to stepping outward, and instead of bringing the trail leg all the way round and up under the arm in the pocket. I just bring it straight through. I do a lot of close step/quick step drills in between the hurdles etc., and those things help me out and my quickness between the hurdles.'

The things that Roger Kingdom likes about athletics:

'The thing that I love most about athletics, period, is that it is the fact that it is individual and whatever you do, you are doing it on your own. If you bloop up or make a mess, then all the crowd and all the attention is focussed directly on you, that one person/individual. If you do great, it is likewise all the attention is focussed on you, the individual. When you come over to Europe, track and field is really big. A lot of Europeans say it is really down and they don't get much attention here, but let them try running in the States, where you get 2000 to 5000 at a big track meet. I like the fans in Europe, the competition and the places I travel to, it keeps me up and keeps me sharp.

'I would like to be able to compete in track and field for as long as I possibly can. It is great, if I can stay around to age thirty to thirty-five, I would love to do it, and I will try to go beyond that point.'

The man who tested Roger perhaps more than anyone in the late 1980s early 1990s was Colin Jackson, and Colin said, after running a UK All-Comers record of 13.09 on 20

July, 1990, (as a fitting finish to the chapter): 'Roger Kingdom's major quality is that he is a good competitor. One of the toughest I have had to race against. He uses his height, weight and his speed to his best advantage.'

41

PAUL ERENG

Born Trans–Nzoia, 22 August, 1967. 1.86/72 kg.

Paul Ereng was the first world-class athlete to come from the Northern District of Kenya called Turkana.

It was less than a year after he had run his first 800 in 2 minutes, encouraged by his West Virginia University coach, and, being curious as to how fast he could go over two laps, that he found himself on the Olympic podium, with a personal best of 1:43.45. He went on in early 1989 to be World Indoor Champion in a World indoor record time of 1:44.84 and claimed the indoor crown again in Seville in 1991 with a time of 1:47.08, but was second past the post, as fellow Kenyan and top-rated in 1990, William Tanui, ran 1:46.94, but was disqualified for breaking from his lane too early.

I talked to Paul Ereng the second time for *Athletics Today* magazine in London in 1989.

Paul Ereng takes up the story:

'At first I was not very interested in running, as at school they used to be crazy about volleyball. I was fifteen at Starehe Boys Centre, Nairobi, when I started to run, and realized then I had a talent for running, but I did not really start taking it up as a sport till I was sixteen to seventeen years of age. My two sisters had not been doing any running, so I was not influenced by them.

'The first time I ran 400 in 1981, I did 60.00 seconds. In 1983, I did 53 and in 1984 49.6, which I felt was a good improvement. I was expecting to drop down even more in

251

1985, and I did run 47.6 which pleased me, so I kept running more, as I had got third in the All-Kenya Secondary Schools Championships.'

Paul Ereng still had very little knowledge of the sport at that time, and yet he showed immense potential. 'I was doing it alone, because in Kenya we did not have coaches.' Having said that, Paul had been optimistic about his performances: 'That was the time I really got interested. I had done no training as such, except just jogging and stretching, that's all. I did not know anything about interval work then. In fact it was not till 1988 that I had a chance to run around the world to get race experience.'

Going back to 1986, he said, 'I was a little disappointed because one morning, when I was doing my normal jogging that year, I stepped on the pavement and sprained my ankle. I was trying to come back to the track, and it began to hurt more. I did not know anything about putting ice on then, as I did not have anybody to advise me. I was getting frustrated about the injury. I kept running but it got worse, till later in the year, when I ran a 47.0.

'In 1987 I was not injured, and thought I would go and do a little bit of training. I did my normal jogging and, for some reason, I found a place that had a gradual hill about eighty metres long. I used to sprint up that, ten times up and then walk down it.

'The first competition in the early season was in Nairobi University, but still no-one was coaching me. I ran in the 300 metres and was even left at the blocks, woke up running 36 seconds. I thought that was not bad, and a week later I ran 47.6 in about February. It was early in the season. A week later I ran 47.6, but I thought that was coming on too fast for me then, but it looked as though it was going to be a good year, then I struck, I ran 46.6 and I kept on running; I qualified for the All-African Championships, where the qualifying was around 47.5. I ran 46.6 and 46.3. I would like to point out that I lived at a place where there was no track to train on, but I still came up with a 45.6, which was quite okay, and nobody believed or expected it!

'In 1987 I was working for my track scholarship to West Virginia – I was blessed by obtaining one in September, and left Kenya.

'I was still a 400 metre runner then, but my coach at West Virginia, Fred Hardy, was willing to help me, and we went along very easily together with no fuss.

'What I was scared of at the time was lifting weights in the morning. I did not like doing that and tried to keep away from them, but it helped me a lot.

'Fred Hardy told me, "You can run a good 800, I think. You have got the speed. You just need some endurance to stay with the people, and when it comes to kicking you can out-kick them easily!"

'I thought – how can I run 1.48 even, when he told me that, but he always encouraged me, and I kept on trying. I ran 1.54 indoors, then 1.50 and 1:49.3. I found indoors quite uncomfortable because I am tall and the track was small, the curves being too sharp for me. I then pulled a hamstring, but I came back during the outdoor season. Fred Hardy then gave me interval sessions to do which I had not done before, of 200s, 300s, 400s, and once in a while, 600 too.

'The first time I ran outdoors I ran 1:48.08 in the Atlantic Coast Relays in North Carolina. I did not even believe it, as I did not think I could run 1.48, but then I did 1:47.9 at North Carolina University and 1:46.7 at the Paper Tiger Classic at LSU. I then took a break before coming back and running a PR at the Pacific Conference meet with 1:46.6. It seemed as though I was running a PR every week. I won the NCAA in 1:46.76 with a 1:46.24 during the heat. I felt confident I could run 1.46 again and again, but in the NCAA I ran a poor race and came back from thirty yards down with 200 to go, when I sprinted home to win it.

'After a week's break I then trained hard, doing 400s, 200s and 600s and ran 1:44.82 in Sweden behind Abdi Bile, who did 1:44.42.

'It was straight after running that time that I got a cold. That left me low for some time, and I did not run well in Lausanne, as I felt sick running a 1.46 still suffering. I then ran a 1:47.1 and a 1:46.6.'

After hearing all that, I was most optimistic about his future and possibilities for an Olympic gold medal, yet he was most philosophical about it all:

'Everybody wishes to do that, but you never know. You can get injured tomorrow. You enjoy it while it is there. When it's not, you forget about it. It is not a lifetime thing for me. It is a talent. Any time it can go. You can not really tell.'

At that point, I asked him about the Olympic trials and how the first European tour of his life had helped him.

'If I had gone home I would not have known what to do, whereas I have been able to see the mistakes I have been making, as I make them again and again, so I could rectify them as it takes time to correct yourself in preparation for the trials.'

The Olympic trial: 'As I said to you before, I had been trying to learn in Europe and use that knowledge in the Kenyan Olympic trial in August, but it was a race in which I made a lot of mistakes. I was in the lead at 700 metres, I was under World record pace, but because of the altitude I was suffering, and Nixon Kiprotich went by with twenty metres to go. I struggled to finish third in 1:45.1, but I made the team for Seoul.'

It was interesting to hear about his feelings as he entered the stadium for the 800 metres semi-final in the Olympic Games:

'I was seeded with the top runners, all of whom had faster times than me, and I realized that on time I would be placed sixth. But it didn't bother me. If they are going to out-kick me, fine, but I'll try the best I can. In a way I underestimated myself, as I found myself winning easily in 1:44.55, my best time.'

Then came the Olympic final in Seoul:

'It was a very, very hard race. It was the first major title I was fighting for, and everybody else was more experienced. I had only been doing the event for a few months, and there I was lined up with all the best people in the world. I ran the race in the way I wanted to. I thought that if they beat me they will have to run fast, maybe under the World record!'

Was it a plan for Nixon Kiprotich to go out so fast?

'It was not a plan. I thought it was a mistake. When he ran hard, I almost shouted at him to stop, because I thought it was too fast, but I feared to do that. I was not sure of what he was doing, but you never know whether someone is going to keep going. I thought then I might run a World record, and maybe lose the race.'

Result of the first six in the Final – 1. Paul Ereng, 1:43.45. 2. Joaquim Cruz (Brazil) 1:43.90. 3. Said Aouita (Maroc), 1:44.06. 4. Peter Elliott (UK) 1:44.12. 5. Johnny Gray (USA), 1:44.80, and 6. Jose Luis Barbosa (Brazil), 1:46.39.

Paul Ereng's post-Olympic year of 1989 went well on the whole. He won seventeen of nineteen important 800 races, and his fastest for the year was 1:43.72, but he also achieved a World Indoor record of 1:44.48 earlier in the year, on 3 March in Budapest in the World Indoor Championships, with a never-to-be-forgotten breath-taking last lap sprint.

How did he see the year then? 'I ran my indoor race from the back like the Olympics. The other races I have run in the middle, except for some of them when I have taken them on.'

42

ARTURO BARRIOS

Born Mexico City, 12 December 1963. 1.74/60kg.

Interviews in 1988 and 1989

Arturo Barrios must be considered as the world's best combination 10k road and track runner from 1986–92. Unlike a few stars, he never ducked a race, even if he knew that on the day someone he had lined up against was in world record-breaking form, and it would be very hard for him to win.

Here are a small collection of his better results in 1989 and 1990, to illustrate his great skill of turning from the road to the track or the track to the road with consummate ease.

He won the 9.3 km San Sylvester road race in Madrid on 31 December 1989, (25.57) in front of two good Spaniards on home ground, Jose Manuel Abentova (26.15) and Jose Luis Gonzalez (26.16) and yet, earlier that year, he went right down in distance to race over 2 miles at Crystal Palace in the McVities Challenge (on 15 September), and won in a thrilling finish in 8:28.06, against several who were faster milers on paper. Some of those in his slipstream included Charles Cheruiyot (Kenya) 8:28.29, Khalid Skah (Morocco's World cross-country champion of 1990–91) 8:28.06, Jack Buckner, Mark Rowland (who was a good second to Francesco Panetta in the 1990 European steeple). Ian Hamer, Paul Davies-Hale, John Docherty, Sydney Maree and Andy Bristow, to mention a few of the twenty starters.

In 1990 he again showed his special talent as a two surface racer, when he won the Festival of Bojan road race, on 25 Aguust in 29:02, ahead of a very strong Kenyan contingent. Only a few days earlier, on 17 August in a heavy downpour in Berlin, he ran away from an international field over 10 k on the track in 27:18.02. That was the fastest time for 10 k in the world that year, and in that he had dominated the proceedings, in the same way double European gold medallist Sicilian, Salvatore Antibo, did in Split later that month.

Arturo signed off his campaign in Europe for 1990 by winning the Diet Coke Great Midland run on 23 September, in 28:24, with Paul Davies-Hale next home, leading the UK challenge in 28:43.

Arturo Barrios: 'Basically to me, you have to be consistent. I am not impressed by people who run one good race just one time. I do feel you have to run a good race, and be happy with yourself even if you come fifth or seventh, as long as it is a good run, that pleases me. I am doing different things in races, taking the lead, coming from behind another time. For me it is important to run fast and important to win races, but if I lose, it is no big deal.'

Someone who said he had seen Arturo in training in Colorado was an old clubmate of mine from Highgate Harriers, Michael O'Reilly (a 2.11 Marathon man), and he spoke highly of the gritty Mexican.

'First and foremost, he wants to be the best in the world, so he trains consistently hard. Not like two or three months of hard training, a couple of good races and rest on his laurels. It is always out training the next day, doing that run in the morning and doing another run at night. I have seen Arturo knock out 15 to 18 × 400 at Boulder, when it is snowing, all on his own, and I admire that sort of determination in an athlete.'

Arturo was from a family of five children, two brothers and two sisters, but they were not interested in athletics. In fact, as a small boy with little money, he used to work in a gas station in Mexico City, and the only wages he got were the tips he was given, however generous. It was this wish, as a young teenager, to get fit and be healthy that drove him to run, away from the pollution into the local parks like Chapultepec Park. 'I started to do that, but running was no big deal in Mexico, as association football was the main sport, and people used to say to me, "You are crazy, running!" Running for what?'

He continued: 'I really started to take a little interest in competition when Juan Arroyo began to advise me in Aragon High School. I remember coming fifth in my first race, and I was placed because it was an under-eighteen five miles road race, and I was only sixteen at the time. In those days, I did not take it seriously until I went to Wharton County Junior College in Texas, but it was there where my troubles started.

'It was not good in Texas for me for some time, because everything was so different. The people were different, the life was different, also Texas has a high humidity, with temperatures of 95–105 degrees Fahrenheit in the summer, whereas in Mexico it is dry and 70–80 degrees Fahrenheit. I did not improve much from 1981–84. 13.40/28.42 were my times for 5/10, which was not really good enough to think of making a living out of the sport. I was just using my running to help me obtain a degree in mechanical engineering.'

Then came the turning-point for Arturo Barrios. 'In 1986, as it came in, I thought I will go all out for the athletics. If it does not work, I will go back to Mexico City and settle down.' He remembers some sixteen race results that were good, after he had trained hard, at around 110 miles per week. He won the Phoenix 10k road race in 27.41, which was a world best road time, and he finished ahead of World steeplechase record holder Peter Koech (27:47), Mike Musyoki (27:48), John Treacy, Steve Jones and Mike Nenow. He also won the Portland 15k in 42:36 from Ibrahim Hussein (42:44). By 1988, coached by Tavusz Kepka, he learnt a lot from his performances, and with that in mind one can admire his track times so close together in 1988: 27:25.07 for 10k on 2 July, three quick 5000s, 13:17.82 – 5 July, 13:22.71 – 8 July, and 13:23 on 10 July. That leads me into my second full interview with him (unpublished at the time of writing), which is in question and answer form. I was bound to say, after his good collection of race results in July 1988, that he might have been disappointed with coming only fifth in the Olympic 10,000 final in Seoul in September, in 27:39.32 and having come fourth in the World Championships the year before?

'I was not disappointed at all. The Olympic final is a bit strange, because it is only twenty-eight minutes! You can have the fastest time that year or you could be the big favourite going into the Olympics – it's twenty-eight minutes, and whoever is going to be running their best for twenty-eight minutes that one day, is the person who is going to win. It is just the way it is. Obviously I was not the one who was running well, but I think I did okay and I think I did my best.'

When I talked to you before the Olympics, you told me that you did not admire someone who just runs one good race, but rather someone who is consistent?

'I don't think you can win all the time. I like to run always decent times, and that is what I try to do.'

You have achieved world best times on the road and the track, so which type of racing do you prefer?

'All my training has always been for track and, using my training on the track, I can go to the USA and run in good road races from 5 k to 21 k. It is very important for me to run on the track, as that is what I have been concentrating on for the last three years, really.' (said in 1989)

In 1986 you ran the Marathon in 2:14.09, having done much mileage before, but although you were going well for the first three-quarters of the race and on shedule for a very good time, you blew up. Presumably that must have been a blessing in disguise for you, as you went straight back to your shorter distances that you run so well at?

'Yes it was, but what happened in 1986 was that I was not training for the Marathon but for the 5 and 10 k, because I had run 27.41 for 10 k on the road, so I thought at the time it was going to be easy to run the Marathon, but I found out that it was not that easy because, even if you run 27 minutes for 10 k that does not mean you are going to run 2.06 for the Marathon. According to the book, yes, you are supposed to run that time, but, no, it is not true! When I ran the 27.41 on the road, I was racing basically every weekend, so I did not really have a chance to train for the Marathon. I said to myself – well if I can run 27.41 then I can move up, but I found out it did not work out that way.'

Leading up to your World record of 27:08.23 in Berlin on 18 August 1989, where you took a chunk off Fernando Mamede's mark of 27:13.81 that he did in 1984, you had run very good road races during the beginning of the year?

'I ran five, and all of them were competitive (27.51 to 27.59 range), and then the 10 k in Boulder at altitude in 28.58!'

You ran a marvellous race at Crystal Palace in the Royal Mail Parcels Games, when you ran away from the field in the 5000, winning in a time of 13:07.79, which was a UK All-comers record. That race must have told you that you were going to do something special over 10,000?

'It was always my dream, perhaps it is everybody's dream, to go to the Olympics. I have done that. Another dream was being able to compete against the best people in Europe, and I have done that too. The third one would be at one point to get very close to the World record, or maybe – why not break the World record – and now I have done that. I think at my stage of my career (in the late Summer of 1989), in my case, there are two things missing. Two dreams missing. The first one would be to go out to the Olympics and try to win a medal, any kind of medal – gold, silver or bronze.'

In order to do that, would you make changes in your training or race a little less, but having put that question, I realize you seem to thrive on racing?

'I am going to keep doing the same thing. I don't see why I have to do something different. As I say, my next dream would be to go back to the Olympics in 1992 and try to win a medal, and if I can do that, I think there is only one thing missing, and that will be that I don't want to be remembered in my country, as the guy who broke the 10,000 metres record. I don't want people to say, "He is the guy who had the World record." I want people to say, "Here is the guy who opened the door for the new runners in Mexico. Here is the guy who went to Europe and ran for Mexico, and proved that Mexican runners can do it.' If I see Mexico runners during the next two or three years, or when I retire in seven or eight or even ten years or whatever, if I can see Mexican runners running in Europe, doing well, then I guess it will make me very satisfied and very happy, and say then I think I have done everything.'

As Arturo talked, my mind went back to great days in hospitable Mexico. I can remember the warm happy evenings with the friendly people in Mexico City and listening to the Mariachis playing in Garibaldi Square. I suppose those memories helped give me my special interest in Arturo Barrios, not just as a runner, but as a Mexican. Arturo continues, 'Mexico is a poor country and underdeveloped, so that is why people have to move out to go to someplace else. It is very sad you leave your country, but that is the way it is. If you want to do something, you have to leave. You see, in Mexico you may improve, but I think it is going to be a little more difficult, and it might take a little bit longer. We do not have quite the facilities that you might get in Great Britain. There is little support for the athletes money-wise, so that is why you have to find the support in a different country, and that is what I have done, that is the sad thing.'

But that fact makes you more hungry as a runner to do well, rather than if you were in a soft situation?

'In my case, yes, obviously, but I have no idea how the set-up is in Great Britain and how the system works, but in my case, coming from a poor country means that you really have to work, as I say, a little bit harder if you want something.'

I have to say, Arturo, that I enjoy all your races, as I know you give good value and I find that very exciting.

'Obviously I try to win every race, but it is not possible. I am always trying, and get first, second, third or fourth or fifth. I like to go out and kinda fight, not giving up right from the beginning.'

261

One other thing was, did your training change before the World record?

'Not really, maybe just a little bit. Obviously the difference was I was getting older and getting stronger, and I think you can see that with all the athletes, that every year you learn from knowing what you are doing, and actually if you have a good coach then you can improve every year, and that obviously means you are on the right track, and for me I have been able to do that. That is why I am able to run a little bit faster, and so I try to be consistent.'

To illustrate that point Arturo brought up about consitency, it is worth noting that he not only won the prestigious Sao Paulo road race on New Year's Eve in Brazil in a course record time of 35 min 58 sec, but clearly beat the man some had rated as a better road runner in 1990, Dionisio Ceron – and then, went on to achieve two World records on 23 March 1991 at La Fieche in Europe. They were 21,101 metres for one hour, going through 20,000 metres in 56 min 55.6 sec.

Even in years to come, people will look back at Arturo Barrios as having been a fine racer, not only because he held the World record, but because he was an exciting runner to watch, who gave a good account of himself.

43

DARREN CLARK

Born Sydney, 6 September, 1965. 1.75/76 kg.

I first met Darren Clark at the Queens Hotel, Crystal Palace, a week before the AAA Championships in 1983. I knew very little about him other than he appeared a friendly and strong-looking one lap runner who looked to be between twenty and twenty-one at the time. He told me he was going on after the AAAs at Crystal Palace that weekend, to compete in the 400 in the World Championships in Helsinki, where he eventually obtained a place in the semi-final. Nearly every day before the AAAs, I met him on my walk to the station, as he was training at the track, and we would have a few words. On the Saturday I took my son Andrew (then six), armed with a picnic to the Palace. The AAAs 400 metres final duly came up in the course of the afternoon. Mike Paul of Trinidad, the 1988 AAA Champion, was running, along with four Americans – Eddie Carey, Walter McKoy, Leroy Dixon and Mark Rowe. From the UK Todd Bennett and Kris Akabusi, who went on to become an outstanding hurdler, and who broke the UK record. Could Darren Clark have a prayer in such company, I wondered?

After the gun, away went Mike Paul into a good lead, with nothing much to choose between the next four, that included Clark. Round the last bend it looked as though Clark might have a very slight lead on Carey and McKoy, but then there was a gasp from the crowd as Clark pushed for home and held off his two more experienced challengers. That was not the end of the story, and as the announcer came across with the news that Clark had set a new seventeen-year-old World age best, I dropped my cheese sandwich with amazement! The times of the first three were Clark, 45.05, Carey, 45.52, and McKoy, 45.56. To think Darren Clark had only qualified as a fastest loser with a time of 46.09! He explains, 'In the heat, somehow I knew that the pace was fast, and I had seen the other heats. I can always tell how fast I am going, so if I want to go through in 21.5 for 200, I can do it spot on 21.5. I seem to be able to judge pace very well, as I therefore knew coming second that, I was 99% sure I was going to get through anyway. It might have looked as though I just scraped in, but one of the reasons was that I knew my time was good enough to get through, because I watched the other heats. My heat was the fastest, but I had gone through very hard, the same pace as I did in the final: 21.6 for 200, 32.8 for 300. I moved up fast on Carey and thought I had him covered. I did have him covered, but I slowed up and strode in with him stride for stride, and then he kicked, and as it was my first run for so long I tried to keep with him, but had not got the strength. As I eased up, it drained my strength and I lost my momentum. That accounts for the fact that I looked like I was struggling in the heats, as it was a pretty inexperienced thing that I did really, slackening off round the bend because I thought I had it won, and then I had to try and kick again. Any 400 metre runner knows that once you slow up you can't really pick it up again. In the final, I knew I was going to run my own race and take off and not slow up. I knew that once I did that, I would be on my way to a good time. In the final, the race went really well. I ran very comfortably up the back straight and finished very well, I thought, as it was my first race since May.'

How did it all begin then for Darren Clark, who overcame the deformity in his feet, and wore orthopaedic built-up shoes till he was seven?

'I started off in Putney Primary School, near Sydney. I was still playing Rugby League at that time, when one of my mother's friends said to her, "My son is in a little athletics club, why don't you get your son into one?" It started from there. I found myself having a fair bit of speed and being able to run quite fast. When I realized I had more talent in athletics, I gave up Rugby League, because of the injury problems that would have been sustained in the future, like torn thighs, so I decided to have a go at being an athlete.'

In 1980, Rick Mitchell from Australia was the silver medallist in the Olympic 400 in 44.84, and in first place in Moscow was Victor Markin of the Soviet Union in 44.60, so it was not surprising the Australian's performance had a place in Darren Clark's memory.

'When he ran in Moscow in 1980, it opened my eyes. I admired him because he got second and especially as he was from Australia, but I did not like his race strategy. He went out very slow and then came home hard, whereas I think it is better to go out fairly hard and finish just as strong to make a successful 400 metres.'

Three of the men who have been instrumental in his success are Alan Hawes, plus the encouragement of Reg Austin when he was a teenager, and recently, since before the 1988 Olympics, Mike Hurst, who has a scientific approach which has been of benefit, but obviously there are others who have encouraged him over the years too.

In 1989 I had the fifth or so interview with him, and we briefly went over some important landmarks in his career, that he considered the most satisfying performances.

'Most probably the Olympics at Los Angeles and Seoul, which were the biggest competitions that I ever took part in, and also the most enjoyable ones, and the AAA Championships for the first time at Crystal Palace was something special, then when I won it for the third of the four wins, because I felt a lot of pressure, as I really wanted to win that third title for personal reasons. After winning that, it made me feel very good as well.'

In the Olympics of 1984, Darren Clark came off the final bend ahead, having been timed by top statistician Bob Sparks as doing 32.3 at 300 metres; with fifty metres to go, the first of three came past him. The effort was fantastic for the young runner, and he did 44.75 behind Alonzo Babers (USA), 44.27, Gabriel Tiacoh (Ivory

Coast), 44.54, and Antonio McKay (USA), 44.71.

In Seoul in 1988, the result was fourth again – Darren Clark, 44.55. All the medals went to the USA – 1. Steve Lewis, 43.87, Butch Reynolds, 43.93, and Danny Everett, 44.09.

But Darren had a hard late buildup for the Games after injuries, and the Americans were peaking well for the trials and the Olympics.

Nowadays there is even more incentive, with money for the best.

'That helps as, if you can run under 44.2, you can start making a lot of money. They have got a lot of competition in America as well, which gives them an advantage. I had a few problems earlier in the year with hamstrings again in the Australian season, and I only had three races up to the Olympics, so it was a very short buildup, but I was happy with the end result. I ran a personal best in the semi-final of 44.38, so I was happy with that.'

A person who was a National coach for many years said to me that he thought drugs in athletics were rife, so with that in mind, I asked Darren if he thought that was true?

'Definitely. It is sad, but I think drugs are ruining the sport, and I only hope they clean the sport of this use of drugs. I must admit I have been tempted, of course, because if you can run 44.38 for the 400 without drugs, obviously you can run a lot faster if you want to cheat, but that is totally against my morals, and I am not the sort of person who would like to go out there doing that. It makes me sad. Out of all the literature that I have read, I am sure that athletes who are clean last a lot longer, and that's why I have been around since I was seventeen, and it is my seventh year (eighth in 1990) in a row of competing in Europe, and I have always ranked in the top six in the world for that period. I intend to stick around for at least another five years.'

Darren Clark told me after the last Olympics, his ambition then was to win the next Commonwealth final in Auckland in 1990, which is exactly what he did, after being second the previous time to twice European gold medallist Roger Black of the UK. About the 1990 race,

266

he said: 'I was in my favourite lane, 5, and I had had an injury-free buildup – for a change.' Result of first three: 1. Darren Clark, 44.60 (Games record). 2. Samson Kitur (Kenya), the 1990 All-African Champion, 44.88. 3. Simon Kipkemboi (Kenya), 44.93. As a footnote, Darren switched to Rugby League in the latter part of 1990.

44

'THE NATIONAL'

For as many years as one can remember, an enormous amount of the leading middle- and long-distance runners have used cross-country as an integral part of their buildup to their summer racing on the track.

During the winter months in the United Kingdom, the most important club event was and is, the National Cross-Country Championships, although that has been watered down a bit because the full UK team trial for the World Cross-Country has been recently held earlier in the year.

Two well–known international cross-country men of the 1970s were Graham and Grenville Tuck. Grenville remarked in 1975, 'In this country, the "National" is the event of the year, you run your guts out over nine miles, and then two weeks later you are running a completely different race over a flat, fast seven miles. It shows, because a lot of the runners have good runs in the "National" and are then psyched out; the International (World) comes a bit soon. When you have got such a big field, it's got to be nine miles.'

The two outstanding memories of the 'National' for me were:

1. The incredible below zero, very sudden freak conditions in the senior event at Sutton Coldfield in 1972, when Thames Valley Harriers' Malcolm Thomas won. I can remember vividly finishing in the driving sleet and bitter cold 658th of 887 finishers (according to *Athletics Weekly* recorded figures). There were quite a few who got a dose of hypothermia! Looking back now, I can remember a clubmate and supporter Pete White with the

Holland twins, who had the presence of mind to bring a bottle of whisky on to the train for the Highgate Harriers team, to revive them with! The next day in the *Sunday Telegraph*, Peter Hildreth had said that Napoleon's retreat from Moscow could not have been much worse than that!

2. The other memory was to hear the tremendous support for Tipton Harriers at the 'National' at Epsom in 1989, when Dave Lewis won his second 'National', and Tipton won the team award. In this book it would be difficult not to mention just a few of those Tipton Harriers who during the last ten years or so have done so much to keep the club at the top over the country and in road relays, often sacrificing a more lucrative career in the sport. They include such luminaries as Andy Holden, Tony Milovsorov, Allan Rushmer, Andy Wilton, John Wheway, Eddie Wedderburn and long-standing supporters coach, Bud Baldaro and Ron Bentley, etc.

It is often hard for runners to identify with the exploits of major games champions, but not so with the 'National' winner, because so many people have run the event. John Sullevan, who was a good club runner for Hercules Wimbledon and a coach, explains:

'How do you assess somebody at the end of the day? The ultimate assessment is with your contemporaries, not necessarily with your peers. Everybody recognizes what it takes to say finish in the first 100 in the 'National'. People see the Coes and Ovetts of this world, and they do run well in the given arenas, etcetera, but so many club boys have had a go at the 'National', and people recognize Dave Clarke's history in the 'National' really. Dave, the tall, blond runner from Hercules Wimbledon, won his third Senior Championship over a rutted course at Newark Showground in 1988, after taking the title in 1982 and 1987. The three previous runners to achieve a hat-trick were Jack Holden in 1938, 1939 and 1946, Frank Aaron in 1949, 1950, 1951, and Gordon Pirie in 1953, 1954, 1955. By the way, Dave Clarke also came second in 1986, second in 1985, second in 1983, second in 1981, twelfth in 1980, sixteenth in 1979, third in the National junior of 1978, and seventh in

1977! What then did it feel like for Dave Clarke, with just one and a half miles left to do, before winning his first 'National' at Roundhay Park, Leeds, in 1982?

'The most chilling thought I ever had was when winning that first time, looking back now. Looking round, all I could see were hundreds of athletes. All I had to do was fall over, and you could fall out of the team and fail to finish in the top twenty. It's a horrible thought, because between succeeding, i.e. being in the England team and not being in the England team, was not very big.' (1. Dave Clarke 42.17, with Marathon runner Hugh Jones second in 42.33; 1605 finished). In the 1987 race at Luton, Stevie Binns of Bingley was only 14 seconds behind him, but Dave went well on the last hill to draw clear.

Tim Hutchings, who was one of the fine Loughborough athletes, who ran for coach George Gandy's teams that were successful at University level, and before Tim went on to obtain medals at Commonwealth and European Games, as well as twice being a runner-up in the World Cross-Country. He talked about his two victories in the 'National'.

'Luton in 1983 did not really extend me. I won it feeling quite fresh, by seventeen seconds. Likewise at Newcastle, probably I was working harder than I felt, because the adrenalin was flowing and it was a big occasion.

'Before the event I was nervous, very nervous, but at the time, I felt very relaxed and got away. The only time I really felt extended was for the first couple of miles, when Micky McLeod was leading. From then on, I was striding along. I felt I was working 70% output, and I was not at the least bit pushed. Only during the last mile, when my left hamstring started getting knotted up, did I start getting worried about anything in particular. It was not fatigue, but just the fact that my muscle was tying up.'

There were two very notable runaway wins in the 'National' over the last twenty-five to thirty years, and both were are Parliament Hill Fields: Mel Batty with his second win in 1965 and Julian Goater in 1981, but some

270

of the most exciting have been the close ones, like when Ron Hill and Mike Turner fought a tremendous battle up the grass finishing straight, at Sheffield in 1966. Amongst the other ones were the 1977 race at Parliament Hill, when one of the UK's finest 10,000 runners, Brendan Foster, coached by Stan Long, won in 43.49 from Bernie Ford, 43.50, and Tony Simmons (the top UK cross-country veteran of 1988, 1989 and 1990), 43.53, with Foster's club, Gateshead, taking the team title.

Brendan Foster comes in here: 'The thing is Tony, Bernie and Dave Black and people like that are better cross-country runners than I am. I am not a very good cross-country runner. Had the weather been as wet as it had been at Gateshead this year, I would not have been able to win it. Basically I can run well on the country if the conditions are to my suiting, but if it is wet and sticky then I am not very good at it. So, realizing that I am not a very good cross-country runner, I hate to prepare for a race and come to the course and be ruled out and not have a chance because of the conditions, which happens. If it is flat I can run on it, but if it is mud and hills, then I just don't want to know. I have never trained for cross-country, and even for this year (1977) I did no training particularly for it, it was really a force of circumstance.'

Another very close one was the 'National' of 1979 when 1984 Olympic medallist over 10,000, Mick McLeod, the Elswick Harrier, coached by Alan Storey, beat Bernie Ford by two seconds, Nick Rose by three and Steve Kenyon by six. Michael McLeod: 'I have tried so many times to win it. In most "Nationals" I have dropped out, because I just got cramp in the stomach after the first three miles or so; I finished fifth last year, and this year I finally won it.' To emphasize how pleased he was to win the 'National', he said: 'I was over the moon with that race!'

It takes many years of cross-country running to mature to the level of being National cross-country Champion, and there are pointers along the way to indicate that form. In the case of Richard Nerurkar, who was advised by Dennis Quinlan and Bruce Tulloh, won

271

the senior 'Nationals' of 1990 and 1991 – earmarked the Gateshead Open cross-country of November 1986 (1. Richard Nerurkar, 20.39. 2. Darren Mead, 20.50. 3. Jake Harper, 20.50) – as his confidence-booster for the talented Bingley Harrier: 'It was the Gateshead Men's Open cross-country that caught people's attention and made me sit up and think, then maybe I am capable of getting near the top of British running. I suppose you aim at it just, but it became a much more realistic type of target to set!'

To round off the chapter Dave Bedford, the Shaftesbury Harrier, who was advised by clubmate Bob Parker, held the World 10,000 record of 27:30.80 in 1973, was a truly incredible cross-country runner. He won the 'National' in 1971 and 1973, and was the International (World) Senior and Junior Champion. He amazingly won the Southern Championships Senior and Junior races on the same afternoon one year at Parliament Hill.

His remarks were frank and therefore to the point, similar in content to the ones I had come to respect from World Veteran star and European Marathon Champion of 1966 – Jim Hogan. Dave Bedford, enter stage left: 'I am a runner, and if they held the Olympics up my bloody back stairs, in my back garden or anywhere, I'll stand just as much chance. When it comes down to it when you can run, you can run on any surface, in any conditions, at any time. Far too many people get uptight about conditions and that kind of thing. If you're good enough to win the cross-country on a nice flat course, you're still good enough to win it on a big muddy course.'

45

SOME ATHLETICS PHILOSOPHY

New Zealander Dick Quax obtained the silver medal behind Lasse Viren in the Olympic 5000 in Montreal in 1976, and also briefly held the World 5000 metres record with 13:12.09 in 1977. I asked him the following question. Is an Olympic gold medal the strongest indicator as to whether someone should be considered the best in the world?

'It shows the best man at that event on that particular day against that particular opposition, but that's all. It's unfortunate that is what, at the end of it all, everyone gets judged on. When, at the end of the day you hang up your spikes, this is what they say, "That is as good as he was".'

He added, 'Very few individuals get judged on anything else!'

Regarding winning or losing, Dave Bedford, one of the main people in the world to bring back the crowds to athletics in the 1970s said:

'If everything ran to form and the best person always won, there would be no point in doing sport. The whole excitement and interest in sport is because it's so unpredictable.'

Bernie Ford, Aldershot's fine road, track and cross-country international, was someone I put a question to in order to get an interesting reply.

Bernie, you must wonder whether Lasse Viren, having achieved four Olympic gold medals, was as happy as you, who achieved many more things on a weekly basis for a far longer period of time?

'I would swap places with Viren if I could, but I think

you have got to find out where you stand in the pecking order. Viren is unique really. He gambled an awful lot – I remember Brendan saying to me that it was a very big gamble to put all your eggs into one basket every four years, but the guy had such confidence in his own ability that he was going to be right on the day, that was why he won four gold medals.

'I prefer to compete all the time at a reasonably high level. I could not go away and hibernate for three or four years, but I think a lot of it was forced on him by circumstance, injuries, etc. I don't think he intended to disappear for three years each time. I think the circumstances dictated that was what happened, but he trained very, very hard and was a superb athlete.'

Training and Competing

In 1985 I talked to John Treacy, still at the time of writing one of the world's outstanding distance runners, who achieved amongst other things, an Olympic silver medal for Eire in 1984, Olympic marathon in LA (1. Carlos Lopez, 2:09.21, 2. John Treacy, 2:09.56, 3. Charlie Spedding, 2:09.58). John also won the World Senior Cross-Country Championships in 1978 and 1979. 'I have been in athletics fifteen years. It is a major part of my life. I enjoy competing, and I enjoy a good hard race where you push yourself to the limit and there is a great sense of satisfaction from that. When you do well, it is a great sense of self-satisfaction, and that makes it worthwhile, to strive for that, really. Plus, in athletics you have so many friends. That is very important.'

Eamonn Martin won the 1990 Commonwealth 10,000 gold medal in Auckland in 28:08.57, with a last 200 in 25.8, and he also ran 27:23.06 for the distance in 1988, but although he had been an English Schoolboy Champion, he suffered some terrible long-lasting injuries, that took him into the class of being an average club runner, but he persevered, and along the way achieved a national Senior Cross-Country Championship title, like his adviser Mel Batty did a couple of times in the 1960s.

About training he was very positive, as he was about his future races and training in the 1990s:

'I have never found running a chore. I am always the first there on club nights. I have got as much enthusiasm as anybody possibly, for training. Since being a junior, I have missed four complete summers, so I have always had four summers to make up. Some runners are racing at a high level till they are thirty to thirty-one, whereas I am going to go that four years longer. Someone like Carlos Lopez had a lot of injury problems, and I look at myself as someone like Carlos Lopez with regard to that, and I may compete maybe longer than people might think possible, so my objective is to look after myself generally and keep my enthusiasm going.'

Then the Basildon Athletic Club man proclaimed, 'The thing I love most about athletics is a sense of well-being. I am talking about the whole aspect of training very hard and getting this sense of well-being every day of my life. Coming in from my run in the morning or again in the evening, I really do feel healthy all the time. When running has been taken away from me over the last few years, I really do appreciate how I do feel. I might feel a bit tired if I train hard, but that feeling of well-being is with me all the time. It is not even the competition, just the sense of well-being every single day.'

Essex runner Dave Green, who is the son of Andy Green, the AAA National Champion for the mile back in 1967, told me back in 1989 he had been down to the track where Eamonn did his training, and he saw him improve to 20×400 metres in an average of 60 seconds, each with a 60 seconds recovery between, and another session – 10×1000 metres in 2:35, with 60 second recoveries!

Ron Hill ran 2:10.30 in the Boston Marathon of 1970 to win that in a downpour, and a few months later won the Commonwealth Marathon in Edinburgh in 2:09.28, which was the fastest time recorded for the Marathon that year. Ron's first big international medal success was in the European Games in Athens in 1969, and here was the type of weekly buildup he did for that particular victory. 'Monday morning, seven miles easy. Evening ten miles fast and slow, to include some speed work.

Tuesday: morning, seven and a half miles to work. Evening, twelve miles home from work – in the summer that is easy. Wednesday: morning seven and a half miles to work. Evening, twelve miles home from work, fast and slow running. Wednesday: morning, seven and a half miles to work. Evening, twelve miles home from work, fast and slow running. Thursday: morning, seven and a half miles to work. Evening, eight miles home from work. Friday: morning, seven and a half miles to work. (Midday, seven miles at lunchtime) Saturday: (a) If racing: five miles in the morning, and race in the afternoon. (b) If no race: seven miles in the morning and thirteen miles in the afternoon (fast and slow). Sunday: twenty and a half miles and that's it.'

Every Marathon runner is aware of how tired you can get by the extensive buildup of miles for the event, and it can turn into being more of a drudgery rather than an enjoyment at times; that was backed up by Rob De Castella, who was the greatest Australian long-distance man before Steve Monighetti came along and joined Gelindo Bordin and Douglas Wakiihuri in the top flight. Rob De Castella, the World Champion of 1983, said, 'A lot of the time, I wish I could freshen up for a few days so that I could enjoy some of my sessions. You are tired every day from the previous day's training, every afternoon from the morning session and so forth, and every now and again you do have a good day – it is a great feeling to go out and feel good for a change!'

Taking it a step further, one would imagine an ultra-distance runner might need that little extra mileage. In that department, perhaps, the supreme Ultra Man could be Bruce Fordyce, having won his ninth Comrades over fifty-four miles on 3 May 1990. He also won the London to Brighton in 1981, 1982 and 1983.

'In South Africa, all the beginners start out with a programme of races that lead up to the Comrades (Durban to Pietermaritzburg) at the end of May, in South Africa. They have a twenty-miler, then there is a Marathon, then they have a thirty-three miler. A lot of people come up to me after a thirty-three miler – the Two Oceans race is an example – they say to me, "Look, I finished it! This fifty-four kilometres or whatever it is, but I was nearly dead. How the hell am I going to carry on and do a 90 km race?" It is just one of those things, that when you go further you get tired later. I don't know why it is like that, but it is. I think anyone who can finish a Marathon reasonably comfortably will finish an ultra race.

'But there is a limit that you have to set on training. There is a point where your training would no longer help you go any further. The further the Ultra-Marathon is, you might think the answer would be to train further and further, each time for the challenge of going further and further, but I don't think it works like that. There is a point where you can do just too much, and it is better to rest, to go into the race rested. I think what is going to happen is that the sort of Ultra-Marathon runners that we get now are eventually going to be displaced by faster Marathon runners coming up.'

Race walking is another event that requires many hours out on the open road, and certainly that will be substantiated by my next subject, the UK's last world-class walker, who won Championship medals. In 1964, Paul Nihill was inside the old World best time when he came second to Italy's Abdon Pamich over 50 kilometres in the Tokyo Olympics (4:11:31.2 to Pamich's 4:11:12.4). Paul went on to not only win the European 20 km in Athens in very hot conditions in 1:30.49, but also beat three of the leading men of the day in Los Angeles – Valdimir Golubnichiy, the Olympic Champion of 1968, Nikolay Smaga, also from the USSR, and Ron Laird of the United States. His training for his European win in Athens was printed in *Athletics Arena International* magazine by the Managing Editor and Hon. AAA coach, Charles Elliott.

'Sunday – twenty-five to thirty miles at a relaxed pace (with a friend). We would probably be on the road for four and a half to five hours. I pick up my friend on the way home.

'Monday – eight to ten miles (when I get home from work).

'Tuesday – I use a track (usually Crystal Palace's tartan surface) for a session of interval work, 800 metres, etc.

'Wednesday – I do twelve and a half miles, with a

friend again.

'Thursday – eight to ten miles (depending on how I feel).

'Saturday – I will do a competition.

'Thus during the summer, my mileage average would be about ninety to ninety-five miles each week.

'In the winter, I might do only a fifteen miles walk on the Sunday, which cuts my distance average down to approximately seventy-five miles each week.'

Ex-amateur boxer, Paul Nihill from Surrey, England, added, 'I am a great believer in regular work.'

The Motivation to Compete

Berwyn Price, who was the Commonwealth high hurdles champion of 1978 and the World University Games winner in 1973: 'Athletics for me is a tremendous challenge. A physical challenge with a never-ending sense of purpose to aim higher and higher. In many respects it can be a lonely sport, and I am one who enjoys being on my own, racing for myself and, whether winning, as I did in Moscow at the World Student Games, or losing, as I did in the Edinburgh Europa Cup in 1973, it is always my own effort that brings the good fortune or the bad.'

Willie Banks broke the triple jump World record in Indianapolis with 17.97 metres, on 11 June 1985. He created a lot of interest in field eventing. 'The whole idea of having the crowd behind me and things like that, is that it helps when I am down, or when I can't get myself psyched up and I need something.' He said, 'That helps me more than anything. There have been times when I have gone out and I felt I just couldn't jump and did not feel like it, but when I walk out the crowd just starts clapping and cheering. Somehow it gets the adrenalin flowing and the juices of my body start working, and I feel much better and I am able to jump. Sometimes I get phenomenal jumps. In Barcelona (1985), I came out and felt there was no way I was going to be able to jump. I was jumping something like 16.40, 16.60, and the crowd really got into it. It seemed like they really wanted me to jump well, and the next jump was 17.71!

'It is those kind of things I look forward to; being able to be with a good crowd, with good competitors. Just the enjoyment of jumping.'

Pete Browne, the Thames Valley Harrier, who has loved running since he was a child, was a European Games 800 metres finalist in Helsinki and the National AAA Champion for the 800 metres in 1971. He went on as a veteran to win the World and European Veterans Games titles, as well as being the over-forties World Veterans 800 metres record holder. He talked about the motivation to stay around in athletics as a competitor for an unlimited time. 'Frankly, regardless of whether there were veteran competitions or not, I would be running now (in the 1990s) because I enjoy it and love the sport.'

Rosemary Chrimes, who has been an official and an International (Commonwealth discus Champion for Scotland in 1970 – 54.46, when she was married to Howard Payne, who won the hammer at the same games in Edinburgh. Rosemary also set many World Veteran Bests for over fifty-fives in the late 1980s), said in 1989, 'I think the most pleasant aspects of athletics just now are the juniors and vets. I have been involved with juniors over the last ten or more years, being their team manager and so very close to them, and I felt that there it was still pure – all for the good of the team, and fun and so on.

'All the unpleasant arguments that everyone knows about that goes on in international athletics – money, drugs, commercialism, etc. – switched me off a bit, so when I came back to the vets hope was renewed, seeing people doing things for the fun of it, encouraging each other and pleased for each other to do well. It is very good.'

'My Life and Athletics'

Tony Morrell, who is coached by Gordon Surtees, has been for several years one of the half-dozen leading 800/1500 runners in the United Kingdom. He gave a personal account of his life, which has not previously been published to date.

Tony takes up the story in 1988.

'My wife Lesley is not really into the sport, like, but she keeps me down to earth and detached away from the sport. She has got an outside opinion, really, where as everyone else is on the inside. It is quite good and, with my son coming along now, I have obligations. It may be a horrible thing to say, but the running still takes priority, as I want it to be the future. I don't want to finish my running and go back now to being just a pipe fitter/welder, but, having said that, if I got a major athletics medal, I would then be quite happy to go back to that, but I would not like to devote all the years to racing without any results. Of course, I can't have a wide-boy lifestyle and devote myself to athletics too. Both my wife and I have missed out a lot there, but you have got to have your holidays round your running, as the running has to revolve around that, but with the baby, I have got to be there at the house a little more often. But it does give you something more to go for really – wanting the best for your son. I am not going to hide it by saying everyone knows there is money in the sport, but I would still definitely do athletics if there was not, but that is one of the goals. It just comes along with the sport now. I did running all those years without money, but it just makes life a little bit easier, and it rubs off on your family and makes life a bit easier for them too. Hopefully, if you speak to me in five years' time, I will say I am quite happy the way it went!'

Craig Virgin ran 27:29.16 for 10,000 metres in 1980, the year he first won the World Cross-Country Championship. I talked to him while he was in the bath soaking an injured foot that he sustained in the Coke meeting at Crystal Palace the night before. (He won his second World Cross-Country title the following year.) Like Tony Morrell, he illustrated how he manages his athletics in his daily life. 'I have made my job (with Front Runner Inc., Lebanon, Illinois) so it fits in. My athletics interacts with my business, and my business interacts with my athletics, and I think that is the only way! I consider my athletics to be a lifestyle, and not something that I was just going to take and sacrifice for a few years and then give it all up. I am in public relations promotion and advertising, I do some radio and TV work in the United States too.'

The Coach

Coaching methods have always been subject to criticism in open debate, and there have been some outstanding coaches in the UK, like Geoff Dyson in the 1950s and Tom McNab in the 1970s, also some controversial ones like middle-distance coach Frank Horwill and field events man Ron Murray, but they have added something special as a positive contribution.

Ron Murray, has been coaching high jumpers since 1958, before that he achieved his 'Purple' (colours) competing for London University. It was with London Athletic Club that Sir Arthur Gold encouraged him to continue to coach the high jump, and he has had considerable success over the years. One of his athletes was Barbara Inkpen (Lawton), who was a silver medallist in the European of 1971 and Commonwealth Champion of 1974, and another, was talented, long-legged high jumper Geoff Parsons, who achieved a Senior UK high jump record.

Ron takes up the story: 'I wanted to give back to the sport what I had had a certain amount out of and enjoyed thoroughly. I felt it was my job to come back and give something to other people.'

How important then is a coach to the field eventer, and for a very positive answer, I asked Ralph Boston, the United States long jumper who won the Olympic gold medal in Rome in 1960. Talking in 1963, 'My coach at Tennessee University was Ray Kemp. Larry Snieder was my coach for the Olympics of 1960, and he was very good, but the coach on the European tour of 1963 was exceptionally good – Payton Jordan. He works on you from a psychological standpoint. He gets you to believe you can do something, and after you believe it, zap – no problem at all!'

Colin Jackson, the 1990 Commonwealth and European gold medallist for the 110 hurdles, agrees with Ralph Boston's sentiments when he talks about his coach, Malcolm Arnold. 'One of Malcolm's great qualities is that he is always able to get you right at the right time, and I think if you have faith in your coach to get you right at the right time, then you have no problems with him at all. That is one of his best qualities and I have supreme confidence in whatever he says and that it will work out and that is really it.'

Judy Vernon won the National Veterans 80 metres hurdles and 100 metres sprint in July 1990, yet back in the same country, Scotland, in 1973, she was runner-up to 1972 Olympic Champion Annelie Jans-Ehrhardt (GDR) in the Europa Cup final, in 13.31 to Ehrhardt's 12.95. The year after, also in the 100 hurdles, Judy became Commonwealth Champion (13.45). In 1990, she achieved an award for outstanding coaching. Like another world-class veteran Pat McNab, she had been advised by National coach Tom McNab. Judy, a self-motivated athlete, related how important for her competing and coaching fiften athletes was, in the summer of 1990.

'The nice thing about competing myself is that I know exactly how my athletes are feeling, and I try to get to know my athletes as people, and I realize, some of my athletes, you need to get angry with them, some you have got to use a softly-softly approach. It really depends upon the personality entirely. When I was an International, Tom McNab never ever had to come over to speak to me before a race, but there were other athletes he had to speak to before they ran.'

Fred Hansen won the pole vault final for the USA in an Olympic record of 5.10/16'8¾" back in 1964, beating three highly-fancied Germans, who were also inside the old record. In the Tokyo Olympic Village he told me, 'Several coaches have inspired me during my vaulting career, and I only wished they could have been here to see me win the gold medal.'

Sydney Maree, the South African-born middle-distance runner who now runs for the US and briefly

282

held the World mile record with 3:48.83 in 1981, considered coaching a factor right down to the race itself. He ran his best 5000 in 13:01.15, behind Said Aouita's 13:00.40 in Oslo on 27 July 1985, and spoke directly about that. 'Well, I was happy to be able to run that fast. I give a lot of credit to my coach, Tom Donnelly, who really helped me rise to the occasion that particular day. It was a matter of getting into a positive frame of mind and just concentrating on racing.'

I thought a very profound comment about coaching was made by Moroccan National Coach Aziz Daouda, a few months before the Olympics in Seoul and he added at the time, he was aiming to have six or seven medallists in Barcelona in 1992. Since we talked, there has been an upsurge of Moroccan potential world-class talent on the scene, besides the man he advised, Said Aouita. Brahim Boutayeb won the Olympic 10,000 in 1988, and Khalid Skah the All-African 5000 title and the World Cross-Country crown in 1990–91.

Aziz sums up coaching: 'The results of coaching are easy to see. It is like doing some artistic work, painting a picture or writing music, coaching is the same. When you have planned the training, anyone can see the results. That is very satisfying.'

The Official

Brian Hewson, the European 1500 metres Champion of 1958, in the same year ran Herb Elliott close in the 880 yards in the Commonwealth Games in Wales, was also a finalist in the Olympic 1500 in Melbourne in 1956, behind his great rival, Olympic Champion Ron Delany of Eire.

Brian, like his contemporary, Olympic 800 silver medallist Derek Johnson, has taken a very active part as an official. In Brian Hewson's case, he has managed junior National teams with Mike Farrell, and been President of Mitcham and Sutton Athletic Club more than once.

As many people know, perhaps the most valuable

283

person in athletics is the official, but it is often a thankless task. Here Brian Hewson completes my book by saying, 'I got such a lot of enjoyment and personal satisfaction with my achievements as an athlete, that I feel I want to still be involved, and try to put something back. I like helping at grassroots level and upwards, as it is nice to see athletes making the grade, working their way through from the bottom as club athletes.'

Incurable Optimists

Getting the better of Parkinson's Disease

Incurable Optimists

Getting the better of Parkinson's Disease

Published by The Conrad Press Ltd. in the United Kingdom 2022

Tel: +44(0)1227 472 874
www.theconradpress.com
info@theconradpress.com

ISBN 978-1-914913-90-7

Typesetting and Cover Design by: Charlotte Mouncey, www.bookstyle.co.uk
The Conrad Press logo was designed by Maria Priestley.

Printed and bound in Great Britain by Clays Ltd, Elcograf S.p.A.

Incurable Optimists

Getting the better of Parkinson's Disease

Michael McDonald

Contents

Foreword – Incurable Optimists

Many of us who live with illness, or alongside illness, are aware that poor health can transport us into another world. The critic Susan Sontag described illness as 'the night side of life', and famously went on: 'Everyone who is born holds dual citizenship, in the kingdom of the well and the kingdom of the sick.'

What is so wonderful about the many heartening stories in this collection is how they make clear that a diagnosis is never a one-way ticket from one to the other; that there are many ways of living well with illness. That on occasion, illness can even offer us new and valuable experiences which, though we might have wished we'd never had to face them, nonetheless bring consolation as well as their own rewards.

My work as a GP brings me into daily traffic between these worlds of the well and the sick, whether it's a young mother fretful over her feverish baby, an elderly man with terminal cancer, a middle-aged professional meeting a diagnosis such as Parkinson's, a teenager crippled with depression or anxiety. My work as a writer makes me keenly aware of how we humans understand the world through stories; though not all of them will have a happy ending, we each can have a hand in writing part of our own. I'm perpetually surprised by the creative ways my patients meet adversity, and often wish there were more ways for them to share their own solutions with one another. I hope there will be many more projects such as this book, which offer such a lavish wealth of sharing stories.

When Michael McDonald approached me to ask if I'd write these few words of foreword, he mentioned he'd read about a book of mine that concerned Recovery in all its guises, a book that made a plea for our society to restore respect to the process of convalescence. It called for us to reconsider 'health' as a balance, rather than as a final destination. I'm convinced that even with an incurable condition it's still possible to 'recover' in the sense of building towards a life of greater autonomy and dignity.

Michael described how the Covid pandemic pushed Canterbury's local Parkinson's Therapy sessions online, and how the initial frustration of Covid restrictions had allowed for a new kind of support to blossom instead. 'We all learned from one another and so the idea of a book came from the concept of Chaucer's Canterbury tales', he wrote to me. 'A group of pilgrims sharing a journey, telling their own tales as they searched for a miracle.' That the group was obliged to meet online offered a paradoxical freedom: many others from farther afield felt able to join, and soon the stories of the local Canterbury group were jostling alongside others from all over the world.

Just as Parkinson's has imposed restrictions on the lives of the many contributors to this book, it has also occasioned new possibilities and new perspectives. I'm deeply grateful to have read these tales, and hope they'll offer reassurance and encouragement for those who feel as if they are stumbling into the new and unfamiliar landscape of Parkinson's Disease. The border between the kingdoms of the sick and well is porous; these tales prove we can all find ways to move back and forth between them. The following pages offer so many inspirational words, but I will leave you with a phrase from the tale of the mountaineer:

'So I say: don't avoid the uneven ground! Take it and climb it. The hell with Parkinson's for as long as possible!'

Dr Gavin Francis, doctor of medicine and best-selling author
www.gavinfrancis.com May 2022

Prologue

During lockdown, our local Canterbury group for people with Parkinson's Disease stopped the usual in-person physical therapy sessions and started meeting online. We found that we opened up and shared experiences, far more than when we had previously met face-to-face for physical therapy, speech therapy, or music and movement. We soon started sharing our stories with each other about what life is really like with Parkinson's – the challenges and limitations, but also the hopes and enjoyment. In doing so we found out how varied our experiences and stories are.

Word got around the community of people living with Parkinson's, and soon we had gathered stories from all across the world. It was a diverse group of people from different walks of life – from a salesman to a mountaineer, a cartoonist to a nurse, as well as those who care for and support them. Some told stories, while others sent poems and songs which helped the individual to live with the condition. Everyone was on their own journey of discovery and learning, and for each of us the route is different. We all hope for a miracle and expect to be disappointed, but we have found it helpful and reassuring to learn about each other's experiences – through this book we hope that other people affected by Parkinson's will do so too.

We asked ourselves:

What was life like before Parkinson's?

What would I have liked to know then?

What do I know now?

What are the important things to remember?

What do I need to do?

We are sharing our answers and experiences in the tales contained in this book – our 'Canterbury Tales'.

The salesman's tale

When I decided to leave the then-biggest company in the world to become self-employed, my nine-year-old daughter asked me: 'Daddy, how will you know when to retire?' It was a great question to which I had no real answer, just a feeling that I'd know when the time came.

I didn't miss a day's work through illness during the next twenty years, but when you work for yourself of course, it's not a sensible thing to do. My clients were located all over the world – consultancies, IT companies and governments. All wanted help with their bigger sales deals. During one of my final weeks, I worked in Copenhagen on the Monday, Frankfurt on Tuesday, Vienna on Wednesday, then to Milan, and rounded the week off in Paris, the only day that I actually stopped for lunch.

Heading for home on the Friday evening, I paid my hotel bill and was going for a taxi when a pain exploded in my back. I froze. My body just said 'no more.' The retirement question had been answered.

Together with my wife we had decided that we would move house when I retired, as it would no longer be necessary to be close to Heathrow Airport. After a year of looking around the major cathedral cities, we bought a house near to Canterbury, Kent. This proved to be very convenient for heading over the Channel to our apartment in France.

My retirement had commenced. However, I had a persistent

problem, a painful back. Sessions with a physiotherapist seemed to have fixed it at first, but only for a few days before the pain returned. An effort to disregard it was not successful, and nothing seemed to alleviate the pain. It was impossible to work out what made it worse or what caused it to go away.

Eventually I went to the doctor to see if there was anything she might recommend that we could try. She listened and then said: 'How long have your hands trembled?' I told her that I hadn't really noticed, and she just replied 'I think you might have Parkinson's.'

I had been thinking that somehow I was ageing too quickly, so I was strangely relieved. The only thing that I knew about Parkinson's was it made your hands shake. She suggested that there was more to it than that and arranged for me to see a neurologist.

But I needed to find out about Parkinson's; I needed to talk to other people with it, and then I should be able to work out how to fix it. My top skill after all was solving problems that had eluded others. My methodology would be the same: first analyse the need, then identify possible solutions, and then test my conclusions.

It took very little time for me to accept that it wasn't as simple as that. I realised that my symptoms varied every day. I could feel fine one day and terrible the next. Some symptoms would require attention every day and the important thing was to deal with the one that was causing me the most trouble. There are so many different symptoms and levels of severity that no two PwP (People with Parkinson's) are likely to experience the same.

I had a problem I couldn't hope to solve. The only thing I

could do was to address individual symptoms as they arose and plan my strategy. It was then when I realised how complicated it could become. The only real way of doing it was to deal with the problem that was most urgent at any one time.

I called my plan 'the squeaky wheel'. Every day I would decide what was disturbing me the most and that would get the oil. It's all very confrontational; whatever is causing the biggest problem I deal with. If my legs are stiff, I go for a walk. If my voice is very quiet, I sing as loudly as the neighbours will permit. If I'm constipated, I sort it out. And so, we go on, if my feet freeze (meaning I can't move), I step backwards, or to the side. I try to tell my brain what I want it to do. When I spot my mask face in a mirror, I gurn at the image until it goes away.

If nothing is working, I go and lie down for thirty minutes or until my next pill is due. If I'm just feeling sorry for myself, I do something entirely unrelated to my Parkinson's. If I'm feeling brave, I try something new or different.

Lockdown was new and different. When physio exercise sessions, choirs and quizzes moved online, something unexpected happened during our local Zoom sessions – something valuable.

I'd previously encountered lots of people from the area with Parkinson's when we had met for physiotherapy sessions, dance classes, choirs or such like. What we had never done was to talk about our version of Parkinson's, how we cope and what works for us.

Now confined to meeting online, we started to open up about our experiences. As we did so, we realised that we all had such different stories that by sharing them we could help others.

The accountant's tale

I was born and brought up in Canterbury. At eighteen I went to university at Bristol. But after graduation I started to move east, back towards Canterbury. I spent the whole of my working life as an accountant in the City of London, the first ten years of which was working as an auditor for one of the 'big four' accounting firms, and the next twenty-two working in the Lloyd's insurance market.

By this time I had moved to west Kent. This, unfortunately, involved a lengthy commute into London each day. When combined with long working hours and a pressurised working environment, this meant that for a large part of the day I was away from home. I didn't notice many symptoms of Parkinson's at that time. The first I recall was shaking in my right arm when I pressed to get out of a chair or sofa.

I was first diagnosed with Parkinson's in August 2004. I was forty-eight. I was diagnosed by my gastroenterologist! I had an appointment because I was suffering from continual, painful wind. I had seen the same consultant some three years earlier but had to come back because the symptoms persisted.

At the end of the appointment, he stopped me and asked if I minded doing a simple test. I agreed and after he had laid a metre ruler on the floor, he asked me to walk across his office and step over the ruler. This I repeated two or three times, before he concluded by saying he wanted me to see a neurologist.

A few weeks later, after several simple tests and many questions, the neurologist pronounced that I had either Parkinson's or a brain tumour! A scan would provide the answer.

Whilst waiting for the scan I found myself thinking, which would I prefer? Not much of a choice, and I hadn't come to a conclusion when I sat in front of the neurologist again to be told I had Parkinson's. He passed over a folder containing booklets telling me all I needed to know. They didn't!

At least the scan did confirm, contrary to my friends' and family's beliefs, that I did have a brain!

Whom do I tell?

This was the first question. As far as my family was concerned, this was easy; I let all my close relatives know.

More difficult was work colleagues. I was working in the Lloyd's market, and at my latest job I had been fortunate enough to be invited to join two colleagues in a buyout of the company. I told these two colleagues the next day. But I didn't want to tell everyone. If they asked questions, I would tell them. But I didn't want to volunteer this. I didn't want sympathy!

Having accepted the diagnosis, my wife and I wondered what we should do first, given the limited amount of time my body would allow normal movement. On my bucket list, but not at the top, was to go skiing. I had not actually skied before, although I had worked in Switzerland in the winter months for several years, during which time I witnessed some of the delights of skiing. So, only five months after diagnosis, I was flying to Austria, to experience skiing for the first time.

It was also our last time – I couldn't ski!

It was, however, enjoyable and led to our determination to *think positively and make the most of every day.*

One issue that I recall thinking about at length at this time, was the longevity of the drug I was about to be given – levodopa. It seemed to be common ground that the average effective life of the drugs was about ten years. At the age of forty-eight, I would benefit from the drugs up to approximately age fifty-eight. I would therefore be approaching my retirement age of sixty without the full benefit of the drugs to control my symptoms and assist with movement. As my wife said, the drugs would help me continue to work, but when we wanted to enjoy our retirement, I would get no benefit from the drugs. To me, it was a simple decision to defer taking the drugs. My consultant accepted my decision gracefully, although I do not think he ever understood the reasoning.

It was shortly after this that we heard about an alternative therapy being practised in California. They claimed to have had some success with Parkinson's patients, whose movement had been improved by their treatment, sometimes quite dramatically. But they did not treat those patients who were taking drugs. I was a perfect candidate. We found a local acupuncturist and alternative therapist who agreed to read the background material supplied. This made sense to her and she could see that it could work – so off we went, with e-mail support from California. About four times a year a practitioner from California visited the UK and Europe. We attended their classes and received treatment from them. Very simply, the treatment focused on positive thinking, visualisation and following the flow of energy through the body, whilst all the time relaxing.

Did this work? This is arguable. I had managed to 'survive' for some five years after diagnosis without the use of any drugs, and in the first two or three of these years my movement was probably as good as it would have been, had I been taking the drugs. This period, therefore, had the effect of increasing the longevity of the drugs to around fifteen years. However, eventually I had to accept that my movement was deteriorating, and that I needed to take the drugs.

I do, however, continue to follow the positive thinking aspects of the programme. To this day I am convinced that I am moving better than I would have been had I not undertaken the programme; and my wife is pleased that I retain my smile, which many sufferers are unable to.

Was it a clever Californian scam? I cannot see that it was. The hourly rate I paid to the Californians was less than I paid my UK practitioner, who charged the going rate in the UK for an acupuncturist. From this the Californians had to pay for flights to and from Europe as well as accommodation. Not once did they ask for any money in excess of treatment times.

It was during this time that my commute to work started to become difficult. Initially, the walk to the office from the London mainline station had become a trip on the underground followed by a shorter walk and, eventually, it became a taxi ride. My resolve was challenged many times, but none more so than on one evening when I was walking, or maybe more accurately staggering, from my office to the underground station. Some lads passing in a car wound down a window and loudly accused me of having had a 'good' lunch. This offended me. I had not had an alcoholic drink at lunch, for some time, no matter how attractive this may have felt.

However much I amended my route from the station to my office, nothing could replace the walk from my carriage on the train across the concourse, to the exit of the station, and when this became too difficult, I had to accept, with a heavy heart, that I had no choice other than to work from home.

My colleagues were very supportive and helpful. Most office meetings were held by video, with my picture projected onto a screen at one end of the room. Whilst this was effective, as time went by, I was becoming more and more remote from the day-to-day affairs. This came to a head in 2009 when we received an offer to buy the company, and I retired.

Since we both enjoy travel, my wife and I decided to take the opportunity of my early retirement to travel the world. In the last ten years or so we have been lucky enough to visit Alaska, many beautiful South Pacific islands, Australia, and Japan, among many other wonderful places. We have circumnavigated the world, during which I have climbed onto the Great Wall of China, been up to the top of the Acropolis in Athens, and into the Blue Mosque in Istanbul. Not all of these were on my bucket list but they were places that we were told by various authorities we couldn't access by wheelchair. We didn't accept no for an answer.

One mantra we developed during our travels which we wished I had adopted sooner was that of positive thinking and making the most of every day. By this I mean dismissing negative thoughts, problems, and any other issues of a negative nature, and replacing these thoughts with solutions and choices, as I am convinced that this has had a most significant effect on my movement and the amount of levodopa I need.

After 2009 when I started taking drugs, my movement improved, as expected, but this didn't solve all my problems. I couldn't walk any distance unaided, so I needed the assistance of a wheelchair. Over the next five years, my dosage of levodopa was increased by my neurologist on a yearly basis. This was necessary to maintain my movement at that level.

But in the last six or so years, when I have been trying harder to follow the positive thinking regime and I have managed to complete a full circle by returning to Canterbury, my dosage has not changed.

In over six years!

And my movement is certainly no worse!

And I still have my cheeky smile!

Long may this continue!

Had I known this when I set out on this 'journey', would it have made a difference? As before, I don't know the answer to this, but what I feel I can say is I'm sure that my life would not have been worse.

The intrepid traveller's tale

It was one Friday towards the end of June and my final day at work had arrived. 'What are you going to do in your retirement?' I was asked. 'I'm not retiring. I've just decided to give up working. Retirement sounds like I'm going to sit at home doing nothing all day and that's not my intention,' I declared.

I was just a few weeks off my sixty-fifth birthday and had decided that, with a few financial adjustments and the income from my state pension, there was no need for me to work anymore. I'd like to travel a bit if I could, nowhere too exotic but now I would have the time to take in the sights and appreciate the surroundings. I may need a travelling companion, I thought. Little did I know I had already got one, and one that was uninvited to boot.

Meet my constant companion, Mr P.

Let us pause here a moment whilst I tell you a little bit about me.

I've had a very varied working life, be it in London, Kent or Italy. Although a lot of it has been spent in an office of one type or another, I did work in my father's shop in my late teens. I also did a stint in Harrods and before it became taboo, I worked one day a week in a fur showroom in Knightsbridge. I've done garden clearance, turf laying, window cleaning, assisting with junior tennis coaching and running a small tennis club, and worked at a supermarket checkout and the customer service desk dealing with complaints.

Whilst living in Italy for the best part of six years, I was employed by a private school to teach English as a foreign language to adults and juniors at various levels. This also included visiting a nearby air force base twice a week to teach English to the officers as well as to the commander of the base.

Just to round things off, I spent the last year of my sojourn in Italy helping my then-husband run a bar. I had never worked in a bar of any description before. In order to obtain a licence to trade, I had to study hard in preparation for my exams with the Chamber of Commerce. I am somewhat proud of the fact that I passed more exams than my ex did, considering I'm English and the exams were in Italian, his native language.

Some years later, at the age of fifty-six, I found myself newly divorced with a teenage son still in full-time education. At the time, I only had a part-time job in a supermarket to support the two of us. I knew I needed to retrain in order to obtain suitable full-time employment. Fortunately for me the EU was funding training courses at a local university, and I obtained a place on one of those.

During the first year I was required to do a work placement as part of the course. A position was found for me at an English-language school in Canterbury. This led to me being offered an initially part-time position at the school and then a full-time position the following year. Having completed two funded years at university I was encouraged to take a third, for which I had to take out a student loan. So, at the age of fifty-nine I graduated from university with a BSc in Business Studies and Marketing. Something I hadn't planned to do but which gave a terrific boost to my confidence.

'So, what has all this has got to do with Parkinson's?' you may be wondering. Well nothing actually, but it has shaped the way I approach life with Parkinson's. I've had to be very adaptable and resilient throughout my working life, so I'm learning to apply the same qualities in my day-to-day life now.

Now, let's return to my Parkinson's tale.

Looking back, I suppose the signs had been there for a while: the occasional sudden jerk in my right arm which would cause me to send the computer mouse shooting across the screen, the unexplained loss of weight and my work colleagues asking me why I was giving them strange looks (due to my facial muscles going on strike leaving me with a right stroppy glare), to mention but a few.

I made an appointment at my GP surgery and was fortunate enough to be seen by a very understanding doctor. She patiently listened to me saying 'I don't know what's wrong with me, but I know something is not right.' I then read off my list of symptoms. She gently told me she thought I had a movement disorder and referred me to a consultant neurologist.

I was diagnosed a few months later by the neurologist, who told me she was pretty sure I was suffering with Parkinson's. To tell you the truth it came as a bit of a relief, as I had begun to wonder whether I had a brain tumour or multiple sclerosis, so it was good to know what I was up against. 'It's life changing but not life threatening,' I explained to the friend who had accompanied me to my hospital appointment.

It was then and there that I decided that I had to remain positive and learn to cope with this illness, an illness about which I knew very little but was determined to learn about so as to make informed choices. For several weeks after the diagnosis, I would wake up in the morning and think: 'They've made a mistake. I feel totally normal this morning.' But of course they hadn't made a mistake; it was just that whilst I was still in bed and wasn't manifesting any symptoms.

Of course, I went through those soul-searching moments, those *why me?* moments, those *how am I going to cope?* moments, those *will my friends be too embarrassed to be seen out with me?* moments. In time, of course, I realised I hadn't been specially selected for Parkinson's. Nobody knows why I have it. I am coping with life, and I certainly haven't lost any of my friends.

Now here we are; it's 2021 and what have I learnt? Well, my travelling companion is still with me although, thanks to Covid-19, we haven't been able to do any travelling together. We sometimes get a little irritated with each other, but overall we have learnt to get along. Perhaps that is the answer.

I don't think about giving up or giving in. We've just learnt to get along with each other.

I try not to be shy about introducing my friends, neighbours and acquaintances to Mr. P. The more they know about how he affects my life, the better. I find most people know very little and tend to think Parkinson's is just having the shakes, which is exactly the way I used to think.

I cultivate contentment and appreciation for life today and what I can achieve.

I fight any temptation to dwell on past days and what I was able to do then, as even without Parkinson's the ageing process would have brought about changes in life.

I try to keep active physically, mentally and socially.

I have taken the opportunity to associate with and am pleased to travel on this journey with others who have Parkinson's, as they all have their own tale to tell.

Above all I keep a sense of humour and am grateful to God for each morning I wake up.

Yes, life is precious and definitely worth living, even if Mr. P wants to tag along for the ride!

The physiotherapist's tale

The beginnings

It was a bright and sunny day in June 1999 when I qualified, in Wroclaw, a city in the southwest of Poland. After four years of learning, finally the dream of my youth came true – I became a physiotherapist. I was full of hopes, emotions, plans and self-confidence in my physiotherapy skills, knowing little how little I actually knew.

Sometime later, I accepted my first job offer as a paediatric physio. I progressed to adult physiotherapy soon after, working with people with neurological conditions for the next few years.

The new beginnings

But my professional path was far from established. It was entangled in the socio-politico-economic situations of the early 2000s. Finally, in the late summer of 2004 on a hot sunny day at the end of August, I arrived at Stansted Airport. I was welcomed by a busy airport, a mixture of noise, people rushing in different directions, the smell of coffee and food. With £200 in my pocket and a backpack, I was ready to start my life and career in the UK.

In my first job, I worked with people with severe spinal cord injuries. This job allowed me to work in different places around the UK. I finally settled in Peterborough, working in the orthopaedic ward.

A few years later I moved to Herne Bay, Kent to work for the Intermediate Care Team. It was there that my interest in

Parkinson's has developed. By that time my knowledge and experience of Parkinson's were still rather basic and limited, which I realised relatively quickly.

But let me tell you how it all really began.

One day, on a clear but frosty winter morning, I arrived to work and began my usual duties. Suddenly, a colleague walked in and informed me that our line manager wanted to talk to me.

It was one of these moments when you think: 'Gosh, what have I done?'

Three minutes later in a bright and hot manager's office, I saw her sitting behind the desk with a big smile on her face, the kind of smile that makes you suspicious.

'Well,' she said, 'I need to talk to you.'

'Yes?' I replied, getting a dry throat and red cheeks. I am still not sure whether it was from nerves or the heat in the room.

'Do you know the space at the back of the hospital where we used to look after day care patients, and we sometimes use for exercises?'

'Of course I know it. I have been here for a few years now'.

'Well,' she said, 'we need to do something about it. We need to increase our physiotherapy activities there, and we cannot afford to maintain it without demonstrating good use of it.'

'One of your colleagues has started developing exercise groups for patients with multiple sclerosis and Parkinson's. Would you like to take over? As she will be leaving soon.'

It took me a while to comprehend the meaning of her words, but finally I said: 'Yes, of course, I would be happy to do it.'

At that time I was really considering a change of my usual duties anyway. Later that day, I entered the gym-to-be and thought: 'What do I do now?'

I hoped that there would already be some documents in place from the previous physio that I could use. But me being me, I decided to go my own way: I developed a new exercise programme, more ambitious and demanding. I was so proud, but not for long.

Together with an OT and PA (occupational therapist and physio assistant), we were ready to deliver this life-changing programme.

We finally delivered the first session. Afterwards, the three of us felt exhausted. It took a lot of effort to teach a whole group of new patients new exercises at the same time. We were getting sweaty and dizzy trying to explain everything to everyone all at once. We managed it and the patients were happy, but we knew we had to change it.

Our second attempt was only slightly better: we designed a circuit workout, so that the three of us could support patients at different circuit stations making it easier to explain and monitor the required exercises. Overall, this proved to be nearly equally difficult, mainly for us as the patients really enjoyed the sessions.

The journey

At that point, I realised there was time for some serious learning. I asked myself a question: 'what do I want from it? What am I trying to achieve?' 'Do I want to be stressed, tired, not enjoy it?'

I decided that I wanted to deliver world-class therapy to local patients, in a friendly, nice, and enjoyable way. A programme that would be research and evidence-based delivered in a most effective way, both for patients and therapists.

I dived into the internet, reading research articles, online teaching presentations and such. I had to solve the problem. I came across LSVT BIG, an American protocol designed especially for people with Parkinson's. I attended a two-day course and in the end received my badge, Certified LSVT BIG Clinician. It really revolutionised my understanding, knowledge, skills and practice of working with PwPs. Later I discovered other programmes, PD Warrior and PWR (Parkinson Wellness Recovery). I completed the level one and two PD Warrior course, gaining the title 'PD Warrior Trained Clinician'.

These concepts are based on recent science about under-standing the physiology of brain cells – what makes them grow, develop and connect to other cells creating networks and neural pathways, and what makes them deteriorate, disconnect and die. In one word, they are based on neuroplasticity – an amazing ability of the human brain to change and adapt if provided with appropriate stimulation.

I applied all my new knowledge and skills to developing the Parkinson's physiotherapy service in the Herne Bay and Whitstable area.

The transformation

My theoretical knowledge and practical skills merged and developed further. I started sharing my knowledge. I began co-operation with Parkinson's UK, with whom I later delivered a series of training sessions for local exercise professionals on working with PwP. With the help of one of the patients, we developed an evening exercise group in Whitstable. I was also asked to deliver a presentation at the conference for PUK at the University of Kent. I was later invited as a guest lecturer to Canterbury Christ Church University to deliver a teaching session to physiotherapy students.

My practice has progressed dramatically since I began. Now I truly understand how important physiotherapy, exercise and physical activity are for PwP; for brain health, function and maintaining a good quality of life; simply put, for making a difference in people's lives.

The message

The message I try to convey to my patients is: stay active, push yourself as far as possible but in an enjoyable and safe way, and engage with aerobic (cardio) training and Parkinson's-specific exercises.

The difficult part of the patient's journey is that Parkinson's is still a progressive disease and things will change. It is important though to try not to be too focused on the past, but rather explore and discover new ways of doing things.

Optimise your medication (with a neurologist's advice); optimise your exercise and activity plan (with a physiotherapist's advice).

Exercise a little bit every day, as it is much better than once weekly for two hours. Exercise at a moderate activity level as the brain needs it to instigate important chemical reactions that protect brain cells.

Challenge yourself, learn new exercises and movements. When you exercise try to add additional tasks (dual tasking) like talking, memory challenges and additional manual tasks. It stimulates the brain more and leads to better neuroplastic changes. Learn about your specific limitations from the physiotherapist and address them through your specific training.

Go for regular brisk walks, try gardening any other activities you enjoy.

31

However, you need to be patient and understand yourself at the same time. If you are not an exercise person at present, creating new behaviours will take time. It is best to find support from family, friends and health professionals to start and maintain a change.

The belief that 'nothing can be done' (poor outcome expectations) is one of the leading barriers to engaging with exercise programmes. Overcome it with support from others.

It is best to commence an individualised exercise programme straight after diagnosis – to use your good physical abilities to stimulate your brain to produce chemicals that protect it from deterioration, and to restore lost or limited function.

Of course the earlier the better, but it is never too late. However, in older age, people very often develop additional medical problems which can have an impact on mobility and ability to perform exercises. It all needs to be taken into consideration as exercises have to be safe and not put patients at any risk.

Find a therapist who understands Parkinson's and the science of neuroactive exercise. Engage with a local gym, Parkinson's network or charities.

Beyond the present

Finally, there is an enormous continuous effort in the research community to find the cure for Parkinson's. There are a large number of trials taking place every year. Exercise plays an important role in managing symptoms, potentially slowing down the progression as we wait for the cure.

The specialist nurse's tale

I was appointed as a Parkinson's nurse specialist in the autumn of 1995. At this time, I had limited experience of caring for people with Parkinson's, but I had done some research and was armed with twenty-two years of registered nurse experience and plenty of enthusiasm.

The appointment was new to the Trust and had been lobbied for by one of the three local groups affiliated to Parkinson's UK with support from the organisation. The initial funding was from Parkinson's UK and local groups. The person I was to care for was involved in the interview process and development of the job specification, which was to provide a service for those attending specialist clinics, those admitted to hospital, those living in the community and those in care settings.

The applicant was required to be a registered nurse with experience and a degree, a community nursing qualification and experience in nurse education. I have never met another specialist nurse who was required to have so many qualifications and experience, but I must admit these have all been invaluable. Most studies have put the prevalence of Parkinson's as 120 cases per 100,000 people. This Trust has a higher prevalence due to it being an area to which people retire.

The trailblazer for the Parkinson's specialist role was a nurse appointed years earlier in Cornwall by a consultant geriatrician with a specialist interest in Parkinson's. Following the success of this appointment, Parkinson's UK appointed a number of nurses that covered huge areas such as the midlands. I was fortunate to be supported by this group and in particular the local nurse.

There was no database of people with Parkinson's, so the consultant neurologist armed me with lever-arch files of neurology letters to sort through and identify those patients with a Parkinson's diagnosis. However, two local geriatricians with a specialist interest were better able to identify patients and start holding specialist clinics. I was able to attend clinics and learnt a great deal about the condition and how variable it can be. I soon realised the importance of specialist input, especially at the time of diagnosis and the importance therefore of being seen by a specialist.

A month after my appointment, a new consultant neurologist with a specialist interest in Parkinson's was appointed. This appointment made a tremendous difference to the treatment options available in secondary care. Previously people would be referred to a tertiary centre for complex treatments or second opinions.

I was encouraged to attend specialist clinics at the National Hospital for Neurology and Neurosurgery in London. It was at the National Hospital that I attended with a patient from my area who was to have an assessment of their response to the dopamine agonist apomorphine, which is administered by subcutaneous injection. This treatment is not suitable for all patients and specialist assessment is important. The patient arrived in an 'off' state having not taken medication from the night before; they were tremulous and virtually immobile making them especially anxious. After the routine assessment of heart rhythm and blood pressure the first injection was administered. After a few minutes there was a transient feeling 'something' was going to happen, but this came to nothing. After forty minutes the second and increased dose was administered. After just five minutes uncontrollable yawning occurred, then the urge to stretch limbs and get up.

This was the closest thing to a miracle I have ever witnessed. The patient was desperate to get out of the building. We headed to the gardens within the square where they ran and jumped over flower beds then, spotting a zebra crossing, headed for that, running to and fro. I was terrified we would be reporting that the treatment worked but the patient had been run down on the crossing, but fortunately that didn't happen. The desire to run to and fro was because Parkinson's can make crossing the road difficult due to 'freezing of gait or a shuffling gait'. Once efficacy has been established, a plan can be made for injections or other forms of treatment. For the next twenty-five years I was no less thrilled each time I did this assessment and also enjoyed seeing the reactions of other nurses.

It has been such a privilege to have had the opportunity to witness how people's lives can be transformed by treatment, but also what I have learned from people living with Parkinson's and how they cope in adversity with grit and determination.

Currently there is not a cure for Parkinson's, but finding ways to adapt and maintain a quality of life is essential. I knew someone with Parkinson's who painted the most exquisite miniatures, but tremors had put a lid on this. However, I was thrilled to do a home visit and see that all the bungalows in his close had beautiful, colourful murals painted by him on their garage doors. He described how his symptoms eased when he was absorbed in the activity.

It is vital people are diagnosed by a specialist, because Parkinson's can be a complex condition with many twists and turns. My philosophy has been to learn as much as possible, to share knowledge and work closely with experts. The health care team is vast, from specialist consultant neurologists and geriatricians to the wider community of physios, occupational therapists, speech and language therapists, general practitioners, the mental health team, social care teams and care homes. Listen to your patients; know them as people, their families, their interests, their fears and their joys. Parkinson's is a long journey, and everyone is different. The nurse should empower the patient and their family to maintain independence, being there when something changes as they progress from diagnosis to palliative care.

This specialist job has given me so many opportunities to share knowledge and learn. I have been able to attend international meetings where there have always been new people to meet and new things to learn. In 2006 whilst attending a movement disorder meeting in Kyoto, Japan, I got up early one morning to walk 'The Path of Philosophy'. The path follows a canal lined with cherry trees, which still held their autumn hue on this November morning. It is one of those paths with a fine coat of grit that crunches as you walk. I heard the sound of someone ahead before I saw the back of a gentleman. His gait put me in mind of the Parkinson patient with a shuffle caused by not lifting one foot clear of the ground. From behind I could see his lack of right arm swing and stooped posture, symptoms so characteristic of Parkinson's patients. Of course, this observation doesn't make a diagnosis, but I am often reminded of this image as I walk along a canal path. Now retired, I recognise the importance of 'mindfulness' walking as part of a daily routine.

Exercise is vitally important for us all and so is getting outdoors, so try to keep active and don't be shy about using a walking aid of any description. If walking is unsafe, consider mobility vehicles and wheelchairs as these are all means of maintaining social interaction that is essential for mental wellbeing.

When I retired in 2020, five Parkinson nurse specialists were working in the Trust. Since I took up the sponsored post, the Trust has fully funded these positions for over twenty-three years. People with Parkinson's requiring surgical treatment such as deep brain stimulation or Duodopa, a specialist medical treatment, need to attend a tertiary centre; otherwise, all care can be provided locally.

A tribute to our best friends

Anumber of the tales speak to the importance of the Parkinson's nurse. With a condition as multi-facetted as Parkinson's, access to an expert is crucial. The effect on one's life can change overnight and advice from an expert is the first requirement.

A Parkinson's nurse

The job title actually means a person who is:
Patient
Approachable
Resilient
Knowledgeable
Interested
Nurturing
Supportive
Open-minded
Negotiator
Sympathetic
Never negative
Unruffled
Respected
Sincere
Empathetic
Special

I'm very grateful
I'm having a consultation over the phone
Due to COVID pandemic, I'm all alone
But my Parkinson's nurse
Is happy to converse
And I'm grateful for the care she has shown.

Music mends and poetry pleases.

Music and melody medicate me
Better than pills for infirmity
I can recover, I must endure
For my condition, please hurry a cure
Shortage of dopamine fuddles my brain
Starting with shaking, ending in pain
I start to freeze, then I may fall back
But musical rhythm keeps me on track
Tunes hold the secret, in every key
Music helps movement whatever it be
My brain is complaining, more Mozart play
Beatles can help, imagine Yesterday
So come on Eileen and God save the Queen
Preferred by all of us to a vaccine
Tell me what this is, what can it be?
What is this swelling an abnormality
Causing such pain abdominal cavity
The only curative Bohemian Rhapsody
Tell me what love is, what can it be

What is this yearning burning me?
Can I survive it, will I endure?
This is my sickness, is there a cure?
First is obsession seizing my brain
Starting in passion, ending in pain
I start to shiver, then I'm on fire
Then I'm aquiver with seething desire
Who knows the secret, who holds the key?
I long for something - what can it be?
My brain is reeling, I wonder why
And then the feeling I'm going to die
By day it haunts me, haunts me by night
This tender torment, tinged with delight!
Tell me what love is, what can it be?
What is this yearning, burning in me?
What is this yearning, burning in me?
What is this yearning, burning in me?
Music lifts a baby's pain
Music mends a broken brain
Music eases the final strain
For music and melody are the medicine for me
Three times a day
With food
When needed
Before meals, rectally in suspension
Help, imagine all that happened Yesterday
Rach Three reminds me
Voi che sapete you who know
Chiropody one step at a time and did those feet
Dentist wider still and wider

Dietician white cliffs of Dover whale meat again
Osteopath head bone connected to the neck bone
Neurologist brain damage Pink Floyd nothings automatic
Gerontologist when I'm 64/84
Psychologists think about it
Cardiologist you've got to have heart
Oncologist I've got a lump on my onc

The carer's tale

My pre-Parkinson's situation was having a boss with Parkinson's whose diagnosis turned out to be Lewy Body Dementia. He exhibited hypersexuality (not to or about me!) so I saw some unusual aspects of the condition. I knew his wife who was secretary to the local Parkinson's branch.

I wasn't a carer in the usual sense, as my charge was a colleague with whom I had worked a lot, who from a few years after diagnosis lived in his own flat and then a care home. Then, every hands-on task involved a journey, and every written communication with the 'powers that be' required written approval from him or his attorney.

My colleague had retired early with a 'good deal' before his diagnosis, as his symptoms were making work difficult. When he was diagnosed with Parkinson's I contacted the local branch secretary and dragged him to a branch meeting where he sat like a frightened rabbit between two university colleagues. His first experience of being 'supported' was tea and cakes on doilies provided by very nice ladies.

He wanted to be more active and, as a computer buff, set up our first branch website. He later lived on his own and my role in 'helping' was more active.

Looking back now, if we had known then more about the symptoms (in his case a stiff shoulder and difficulty writing on a black or white board, and maybe even vertigo), it might have been better for him to apply for retirement on health grounds.

But symptoms vary a lot, and for my former boss, who had Lewy Body Dementia, they were very different!

I wish we had known more about drugs. At the time the advice was not to take more than absolutely necessary to maintain a reasonable life. My charge was prescribed four Sinemet a day by his GP who knew this was a standard treatment for Parkinson's, but the effect seemed like an overdose!

I wish I had known more about agonists, and also the effects of taking too much of any drug. My charge struggled with urgency problems, and needing suddenly to pee is not conducive to a normal social life! We coped with walks in the woods, and at least all the walking was helpful. He was so keen on the benefits he felt that we started walks, usually with a pub lunch, for the branch. At that time, exercise wasn't plugged by Parkinson's UK as it is now!

I should have tried harder to encourage him to contact the Parkinson's nurse and consultant and ask for a drugs review.

My charge was anxious to have an active life even if it was a shorter one, and I was only a 'colleague and friend', so many suggestions I made were rightly ignored. I wish I had thought of getting a vehicle that can carry a person in their wheelchair before you drop them on the floor trying to transfer from wheelchair to car! Another thing I wish I had done was to slow down and be realistic about what can be done.

I wish we had chased more things (in the care system) that weren't right. I have done a lot of that since, having meetings with hospital staff and phone calls with appointment bureau staff, best done one thing at a time so it is remembered.

We did learn not to rush things, to spend more time talking and discussing, and less time 'encouraging' to try yet more adventurous activities, thus having a safer life! We began to fit less into a day, especially in the later stages of the condition, when experience suggests it can lead to accidents! Accidents did happen and bones were broken. Any broken bone sets back someone with Parkinson's far more than others because the inactivity means loss of muscle tone and muscle memory.

Osteoporosis is a problem for many older people and the treatment is generally not compatible with the inability of someone with advanced Parkinson's, to sit still and upright for hours, or to chew calcium tablets without letting them coat the front of their clothes! However, we discovered (eventually) that there are treatments involving an injection every six months that work; his bone density increased again to 'normal', and he was very proud of managing to roll, in thick clothes in winter, on the pavement without hurting himself when a wheel of his wheelchair got caught in a rut.

We wanted his life to consist of more than hospital visits, so time was made for other things. It became clear that consultants do not have a perfect understanding of 'care' environments, and it was necessary to be clear and explicit about when carers were present and what they were allowed to do, so as to fit with a sensible drug regime. Once all this was explained to the consultant, he saw it was extremely helpful.

Being discharged from hospital, PwP living alone are at extreme risk. It was necessary to check everything. Information recorded on his discharge forms could be hugely inaccurate (for example that he is 'married' so his wife will look after him, when in fact he is 'separated' and lives alone, needing a 'care package'). Often medication sent home with him at discharge was inadequate or stuff has been left in a hospital fridge. We were obliged to 'borrow' from another PwP (strictly illegal!) when discharged with no apomorphine syringes.

We were nice to district nurses, even if they drove us mad and sometimes did stupid things. We had to make sure we knew what they had done, and when, for example vitamin B injections had been given (this is important if you don't live with your charge who is in some form of 'care'), as the chances are others won't know what the district nurses had done. When he was in rehab and needing physiotherapy, I found that the visiting nurse had inserted the needle for his apomorphine pump up and down his stomach so he couldn't bend (or do exercises!) We learnt that even experienced professionals don't have experience of everything.

We had to keep fighting and keep smiling or laughing! For example, at being almost folded up in his wheelchair to get in a lift to an appointment!

Why do they build new medical centres like Estuary View with lifts that you can't get a large wheelchair into, let alone a stretcher?

We wanted to get out there and show the public what is possible: wheelchairs on buses, and in muddy woods! We discovered that mud can be fun but did find a great contrast between the attitudes of two care environments; one complained of mud on their carpet after we'd walked in the woods, whereas the other was delighted that he'd had an exciting outing.

I enjoyed the fact that my colleague and friend lived for over twenty years since diagnosis and, even when wheelchair-bound and hoisted, said to the staff that he enjoyed life. One of our last trips was a push to a pub along a muddy riverside track, for a real beer from a real glass!

The mountaineer's tale

When the pandemic restrictions came into force in 2020, my planned climb of Ben Nevis had to be postponed for a full year. Although I felt impatient and frustrated, The Ben wasn't going anywhere. It was just there, ready and waiting for the time when I would be permitted to go.

I knew I was equally ready and waiting for The Ben.

Meanwhile I started to climb walls, do indoor bouldering, then had coaching to rock climb and abseil outdoors.

It's now 19 May 2021, and we are standing at the foot of The Ben. Me and my climbing companions. We meet Max, our guide, who issues us with spikes for our boots as he tells us that there's much more snow up there than is usual for the time of year.

Just breathe now.

Max is calm, so I am calmed.

Then we start our ascent. Up we go and we just keep going up and up. When we reach the snow, the spikes pin us into the ice, and we keep going up. We reach the summit, and the sky is clear. We can see forever, a view not everyone gets to experience from the highest peak in the UK.

Then it hits me.

If I hadn't been diagnosed with Parkinson's I would never have been here.

That revelation would take me some time to process.

I hadn't seen this coming.

This was not the retirement I had planned.

My life was full, busy, and easy. I had retired at fifty-five following a career of nearly forty years in nursing and had planned a life of entertaining and travelling.

We had moved to a new house in a lovely village. There was bedroom space where friends and family could come and stay. I would cook for friends and happily host all the big family gatherings and special occasions, Christmas dinner, lunch on Easter Sunday, birthday and anniversary celebrations.

I would go anywhere alone with confidence and without thought or fear.

I ate too much and probably drank too much. I was over-weight and rarely thought about exercise. After all, I could move without thinking about it. I didn't fall. I wasn't slow. I didn't freeze.

I often thought that I should lose a bit of weight, get fitter, but then maybe I'd make a start on that tomorrow.

I could have my grandchildren with me without another adult being present.

I was confident and secure and sure of myself.

I didn't take any medication and rarely saw a doctor.

I had the freedom to be spontaneous and I didn't worry about the future.

I felt young. That I was strong and healthy and in control.

Then everything changed.

I was diagnosed with Parkinson's in May 2018. Fifty-six years old, twelve months into retirement.

The neurologist I went to see told me to exercise, but when I told him that I walked in local woodlands every day he exclaimed in horror: 'No, no! You must avoid uneven ground.

You are a high falls risk.'

So I left the clinic, labelled, devastated, prescription in one hand, advice to exercise in the other... but what exercise? I had no idea of what or how or where to begin.

I began by reading and researching the condition, and the one positive message that kept coming through was that strenuous physical exercise could slow disease progression and keep medication doses to a minimum.

Then I found a physiotherapist who became my saviour! He taught me what exercise could do for me.

'Avoid uneven ground?!' he scoffed. 'You could climb a mountain if you wanted to!'

He worked with me to improve my fitness, my stability, my core strength and, most of all, my confidence.

Then I did start to climb mountains.

Snowdon twice, followed by Scafell Pike then Kinder Scout.

I reached the summit each time.

The ultimate challenge was always going to be Ben Nevis, and now I had conquered even that!

So I say: don't avoid the uneven ground! Take it and climb it.

The hell with Parkinson's for as long as possible!

The headteacher's tale

In 2005 when I was thirty-nine, I was appointed as head-teacher of a village primary school. I loved the job: I really felt I was making a difference to the lives of the children. The hours were long, between sixty and seventy hours a week. The school was graded outstanding by Ofsted, which was an amazing achievement for everyone at the school. I was asked to support other schools that were experiencing some difficulties, and for a short period of time I ran two schools.

My stress levels were high and gradually my sleep patterns began to change. In 2015 I had a chronic case of tennis elbow (which we now realise masked some of the symptoms of Parkinson's such as poor handwriting and keyboard skills). The tennis elbow was eventually fixed with numerous sessions from a physiotherapist. I had expected my handwriting and keyboard skills to improve but this was not the case. Staff at school often could not read my handwritten notes, so I resorted to typing and printing and/or emailing. It soon became noticeable at home as well and my wife convinced me so see my GP.

The GP did some simple tests concerning grip, finger movements and pen control. I explained I thought it was linked to the tennis elbow and an old injury (I had broken my right arm in a cycling accident). She disagreed with me and thought it was neurological, before referring me to a specialist. Due to the long NHS waiting list I was fortunate to be seen by Benenden Health Care, in the summer of 2015. The consultant made me walk up and down the room and do some finger exercises. He looked at my face, and asked my wife and myself if we had noticed the right side of my face had dropped. The answer from us both was no. His next sentence sent shivers down my spine. He told me I had either had a stroke, a brain tumour or that I had Parkinson's, but most probably Parkinson's. He would confirm this by a couple of scans which I had. I was then diagnosed with Parkinson's.

I went into complete shock, thinking about what I had to tell our children and families, friends and work colleagues. Thoughts were buzzing around in my head in no particular order. I felt I was too young to be diagnosed with Parkinson's. I had no tremor or shakes, and why did it have to happen to me? He said he would refer me to an excellent NHS consultant. As we were leaving, he gave me what I now consider to be the best advice, to keep active and take up Pilates. I followed his advice, and my wife and I have been doing Pilates for the last six years. Though at times I hit my pain threshold, I am always amazed by how flexible I still am. My Parkinson's appears to be invisible to most people as I suffer from rigidity and stiffness on my right-hand side. When I first met members of the local Parkinson's group a few asked me who I was caring for! I do drag my right foot when walking especially when I am tired. I wear a Parkinson's wrist band when I go out and I will happily tell people that I have Parkinson's.

Telling our children was difficult, mainly because of the possible impact on their later lives. Telling my mother was really difficult as she did not really understand the severity of the condition, as in her eyes I still looked okay! Our family, friends and work colleagues were, and still are, extremely supportive.

I was determined to carry on working and not let Parkinson's stop me. There have been some memorable moments. In the early days my tablet intake and dosage were gradually being increased, especially ropinole/Repinex. I had been warned it might make me drowsy. I was sat in a headteacher's meeting and I actually fell asleep! Luckily a colleague woke me before it was widely noticed. The solution was to reduce the dosage.

One of my most enjoyable jobs as headteacher was to give children certificates for excellent and outstanding learning. Once a child knocked on my door with their work. Secretly my heart dropped, as this child had the longest name in the school with a double-barrelled surname. I knew I would really struggle to write her name legibly! I offered some excuse about being in a rush and would write it later and gave her a sticker. Off she went happy, and I had to ask my secretary to write the name on the certificate. This became her job, while I gave out the stickers.

My keyboard skills deteriorated somewhat. I began to use voice recognition software to compose documents. Having a stutter did not help. It was the software to compose comments in the children's annual reports. One class teacher handed the reports back to me, laughing as I had made so many mistakes using it. I was never one to make these sorts of mistakes. My proof-reading skills improved dramatically.

At the end of one summer term I was climbing the stairs at home, and just before I reached the top step I froze and could not go up or down. My wife was already upstairs and came to see what had happened. She dragged me up the last step. We could have cried but we just laughed and laughed, then decided it was a good idea to consider moving to a bungalow, which we did post-retirement.

As time progressed it became clear that Parkinson's was having a greater effect on my life. I was diagnosed with sleep apnoea and was suffering from fatigue. I would often fall asleep by seven in the evening and my quality of life lessened dramatically. I would literally work and sleep and not much else. My legs suffered from severe muscle pain almost every time I lay down. This really impacted on my sleep patterns. I had weekly physio for a number of months to try to ease the pain. As the impact of Parkinson's on my life increased so did the number of medical appointments. In 2019 I attended thirty-one medical appointments, all during the working day. Parents began asking if I was okay, as I was often absent from work. My reply was I was working from home a lot more because of the pressures of the job. In my last two years as headteacher I worked from home at least one day a week.

During the latter half of 2018 I decided enough was enough and applied for ill health retirement, which was granted in 2019. What a difference that made to my life and that of my family. The sleep apnoea vanished almost overnight as did the leg pains. My energy levels increased dramatically, though I still get very tired.

So, what is life post retirement with Parkinson's? My sixteen tablets a day help me manage my Parkinson's. Adaptations and compromises have to be made. Days out, of which we do many, have to be planned with rest breaks, as do the more strenuous jobs around the house.

Problems arise often due to my stubbornness and not giving in to Parkinson's, which results in me dropping things, dragging my right foot (which really annoys my wife and daughter), becoming over-tired and falling asleep the minute I sit down. I also have, though I cannot smell it due to the inability to smell, a certain odour about me when I get tired. It is simple to deal with once I have been told by my wife – I just spray myself with deodorant. My speech is not always easy to understand because of my stutter, my repetition of words and my voice gradually becoming softer during a conversation. My wife and daughter will often look at me and I just know they did not understand what I just said. My handwriting is still very poor and my wife often has to complete forms for me.

One of the most uncomfortable developments has been the effect of Parkinson's on my bladder. I suddenly get the urge to go, and I have to go. Medication has not really solved the issue, but I am on a long waiting list for Botox injections which I have been told by many health professionals should alleviate the problem. In the meantime, I manage my liquid intake, have a radar key, a he-wee for the car and know where most public loos are!

My wife and I walk most days (an unexpected benefit from lockdown) and I have the time and the energy to enjoy family life again. I have become active in the local Parkinson's group and regularly meet other people with Parkinson's.

There is life with Parkinson's. My retirement is different to how I thought my it would be, but by accepting that I have Parkinson's and that I have to live with it, I thoroughly enjoy it. I have a huge amount of support, especially from my wife who is incredibly patient with me, my children and our extended family, my friends, the local Parkinson's group, and the various health professionals I see on a regular basis.

The wife's tale

Before my husband was diagnosed with Parkinson's we were both working full time. We were always busy with the family and were a huge part of a local Scout Group. We often talked about our future together. We had planned to retire early and buy a campervan in order to travel around Europe. We had also discussed a few long-haul trips to visit family in Australia, to trek along the Inca Trail to Machu Picchu and cruise the Egyptian Nile.

Looking back there had been signs. When I could smell the gas leak and he couldn't. When we walked holding hands and he would squeeze my hand so hard it hurt, but he had no idea he was doing it. When he dragged his right foot across the wooden floors so badly that his daughter hid his slippers. When his handwriting deteriorated so much, we couldn't read it.

When I finally convinced my husband to see a doctor about these symptoms, he was referred to an NHS neurologist with a five-month waiting list. Luckily, we were part of Benenden Hospital and were seen within the month.

The consultant at Benenden Hospital was able to test, scan and diagnose in one afternoon. I was embarrassed when I was asked how I hadn't noticed that the right side of my husband's face had so obviously dropped and drooped. My heart sank when my husband was asked to touch each finger to his thumb and was unable to do it. We were told it was one of three things: a stroke, Parkinson's, or a brain tumour.

Following further tests, it was confirmed that he had a form of Parkinson's in the left side of his brain which was affecting the right-hand side of his body. We both questioned how that could be when he did not obviously shake. We were unaware that there were different forms of Parkinson's. My husband's type of Parkinson's causes stiffness down the right-hand side of his body, hence the draggy right foot and deteriorating handwriting. My first question to the consultant was 'how long has he got?' My husband's main concern and first question to the consultant was 'will I still be able to drink alcohol?', which we now look back on and laugh about.

This Parkinson's diagnosis was a complete shock to us all. I was furious with my husband and bitter because he was just fifty years old, and I was still in my forties. We had talked endlessly about our many plans for our life, and I felt that had been ruined. I was angry because we had talked about our retirement and travelling the world, and I felt so selfish thinking none of that would happen and I would just end up being his carer. I was so cross because it just wasn't fair.

Currently my husband's Parkinson's is kept under control by sixteen tablets a day. Many people who don't know him well ask him if he really has Parkinson's as he is so independent, and his symptoms don't present themselves as obviously as they might do. As long as he keeps taking the sixteen tablets a day his symptoms remain under control. I know if he's forgotten to take any during the day as his leg or arm will now start to shake uncontrollably. When this does occasionally happen, he seems to be unaware of it until I point it out.

My husband has access to a wide range of people who support him. There is the Parkinson's advisor, the Parkinson's nurse, the doctor, the consultant, the physiotherapist, the speech therapist, and the local Parkinson's Group. At the moment this support is accessed by my husband, but I know as things shift and change in the future they'll be there to support me, the wife, too. One of the main things I learnt from all the initial support was to stay positive. There was no need to be scared…

Six years down the line we have learnt to laugh. We have laughed on so many occasions. He once came home from work about four years ago when we lived in an old, two-hundred-year-old cottage. He was tired and wanted to change out of his suit but was unable to lift his leg up the step to get into the bedroom. I remember hauling and pulling him up that step as we laughed hysterically because he just couldn't get his leg up that high. We have since moved to a bungalow and he's taken ill-health retirement which has solved that problem.

I will often find him running as fast as he can through the bungalow, shouting as he goes: 'I've got to go now!' When he needs a wee, he needs it immediately. There was the occasion when he desperately needed the loo and ran off leaving me in the middle of Prague trying to locate the nearest public toilet in order to find him. Hopefully, following an eight-month waiting list, he will be receiving Botox injections in his bladder to help resolve this issue. He has been given a radar toilet key and he has a stash of adult-sized pull-up pants hidden under the bed, has bought himself a he-wee for the car and we always have an empty water bottle to hand. We have also come to know every service station on the M25 intimately.

I vividly remember laughing so much when we tried to buy a BMW Z4 and I had to physically pull him out of the passenger seat and he ended up rolling out onto the garage forecourt in front of the sales rep. We have since bought a SUV which is so much easier for him to climb in and out of.

There have been many occasions when I have left him alone for a few minutes, such as in Morrison's when I came back to find an old man shouting at him because he had turned too quickly, lost his balance and nearly knocked the old man over. He now wears a Parkinson's bracelet and is not too embarrassed to explain his wobbles.

My kitchen cupboards are slowly becoming less full as he regularly knocks over a glass, breaks a favourite dish or bangs down a mug. Thankfully, it's always replaceable…usually with a plastic one! I'm regularly on my knees mopping up spilt tea, coffee drips and water spills, but that's fine. I'm losing the battle to encourage him to sit in one place while he drinks his coffee rather than walk around the house dripping it everywhere. We have a laugh as I get on my hands and knees and follow him around with the floor wipes.

My husband's Parkinson's symptoms can be very annoying, of course. He tends to drag his right foot which then clonks on the floor. Our old house had wooden, parquet flooring and you could hear him coming a mile off. His daughter, even six years on, still hides his flip-flops or slippers when it becomes particularly irritating as he paces around the bungalow. The physiotherapist advised me to remind him to heel-strike when it is bad so that he places his foot down correctly. Funnily enough, a few particularly annoying pairs of his shoes have mysteriously disappeared.

My husband's stutter and quieter voice is currently causing some hilarious conversations within our household, not helped, I must add, by my slowly deteriorating hearing or, as he puts it, 'I don't listen properly to what he's saying.' Sadly, his speech is so bad sometimes (usually when he's tired) we can barely understand what he's saying. My daughter and I often glance at each other after an incomprehensible muttering and shrug shoulders before we ask him to repeat what he has said. The speech therapy he has had in the past has really helped. He is currently on a waiting list to receive some more, and I must book myself a hearing test.

We have read on numerous occasions that exercise is a great benefit to people with Parkinson's. Even the Benenden consultant advised that my husband take up Pilates in order to encourage his body to stretch and become less stiff. This same consultant took one look at me and told me that I would probably benefit from it too. So, the pair of us take to our Pilates mats on the floor of the dining room every Monday evening (as it is now on Zoom), and we generally laugh our way through the hour session as he declares at every move that his body just doesn't bend or stretch like that. Our Pilates teacher is fantastic and adapts his moves so that he can participate as much as he is able.

I try to take him out for a daily walk. During our walks I'll be chatting away and suddenly realise that he's ten steps behind me because he can't keep up. I have learnt that I need to slow down and now go for a 'stroll' with my husband and 'walks' with my daughter and friends. We have also had to make sure our walks are over a much shorter distance. A few years ago, a three-mile walk to a country pub for Sunday lunch with friends rendered him completely and utterly unable to do anything for the following twenty-four hours. He fell asleep within half an hour of our return. He was unable to go to work the following day and rested until he felt strong enough to get up and continue as normal.

My husband gets incredibly tired. The Parkinson's nurse has explained that his body has to work extra hard to do the same things as people without the condition, thus making him more fatigued. Almost within a few minutes of sitting down he will fall asleep. When he was still working, he had to be woken up by colleagues during meetings on several occasions. He'll fall asleep every time he wants to watch a favourite film, a new programme, read a book or play Sudoku on his iPad no matter what time of day it is. I have now become an expert in recounting TV story lines, recapping film endings and elbow digs when he starts to snore in the cinema or theatre.

There are, of course, other, more personal things that have come about because of the Parkinson's. As his wife, these things are kept between the two of us as they are difficult, awkward, and embarrassing subjects to talk about to friends and family. These include, amongst other things, the yellow, oily skin secretions which meant our white towels and bedding had to be binned and replaced with darker ones. When he's very tired he has a very distinctive smell and as a wife with a very sensitive nose I have no option but to tell him, especially as he has lost his sense of smell with the disease. We have overcome this issue with a strong-smelling spray which I encourage him to use on those 'distinctive smell' occasions. Other, more intimate matters and concerns have been raised to his Parkinson's nurse and doctor and, thankfully, we're told there's always a tablet for that kind of thing!

Six years on, I really don't feel angry or bitter anymore. Our plans for our future together have somewhat changed.

He struggles enough to get a good night's sleep in our comfy, expensive bed at home, what with his painful, thrashing legs and flailing arms let alone getting out of it in the morning, so a campervan is out of the question. Our travel plans have been thwarted by the current pandemic, so we have been taking lots of short trips around Britain, even staying in a shepherd's hut for a couple of nights. (That was an interesting one with a very small bed you could only get out of one side of, and exceptionally steep steps to climb in and out of the hut!)

We recently made the decision to start living our retirement now. There seems no point in waiting another ten years. My husband's deterioration is slow but who knows what the future holds. I have given up work to spend quality time with him. We have learnt to manage his symptoms and adapt and pace our life. Most things are still possible. I am taking him kayaking next week and yes, we will have a really good laugh! I don't feel a nag when I can see he's tired and needs to stop and rest. I don't feel scared when I see a change in his abilities or new symptoms and ask him to contact the doctor or Parkinson' nurse. I certainly don't feel like his carer, even though I now do a lot more in our relationship than I used to, including helping him occasionally with a collar, a button, a shoelace or getting his right leg into a pair of trousers. I do, however, feel incredibly lucky that he is so positive and is making such a big effort to be as independent as he can be.

Yes! I get frustrated at times; he can be so slow. So slow to walk, to answer questions, to talk, to get ready to go out, but then I stop and try to remember why I married him in the first place… and I have a good laugh!

Nothing's automatic anymore

Since the doctor said, 'it's Parkinson's, I'm sure.'
Ever since that diagnosis,
This condition clearly shows is
That nothing's automatic anymore.
Yes, nothing's automatic anymore
When simple things have now become a chore
Whether opening a packet
Or putting on a jacket
Well, nothing's automatic anymore.
No, nothing's automatic anymore,
Simply sitting down and staring at the floor.
The doctor says I ought-ta
Be drinking much more water.
Even that's not automatic anymore.
Though nothing's automatic anymore,
When I speak my voice is quiet and obscure.
But when it comes to singing,
The rafters will be ringing
Automatic - Operatic - Even more.
Oh, my darling, oh my darling,
Oh, my darling dopamine,
You have changed my life forever
Bad and good or in between.
Though nothing's automatic anymore,
I can sing and I can play and furthermore,
I shake hands with my new friends.
Our hand shaking never ends
Change attitudes – join us – find a cure.

The writer's tale

Writing has always been important in my life. I was an academic child who went on to university – lots of writing – lecture notes, essays, exams; and a sheaf full of love letters to and from my husband-to-be. My first job was in the education department of a county council – and the chief education officer commented on my beautiful handwriting.

I don't recall using a keyboard much before the 1980s – I did occasionally borrow my parents' typewriter – but then we acquired a Commodore 64. I started to train as a social worker – more notes and essays, the latter now computerised. Even more significantly, it was now a necessity for work to keep up-to-date and accurate written records. Our children grew up and went off to university in their turn, the Commodore was replaced by an Amstrad and the letters kept coming and going.

I worked in the mental health field for twenty-six years, qualifying as a family therapist during this time (yes, you've guessed it – more essays – this time composed on an anonymous series of desktops). At work most of my notes were still being made by hand, although quite a lot of typing was involved as well. I also began to notice that the process wasn't as easy as it had been – I was getting pain and stiffness in my (dominant) right arm and shoulder. I thought I probably had repetitive strain injury.

Eventually I went to the doctor and got referred for some

tests which proved inconclusive. I made another appointment with my GP – and then I worried that I would forget to tell him all the details of what was worrying me. So, I wrote him a letter which I took with me and handed over... and he sat and looked at the letter and said: 'I think I know what's wrong with you...'

The internet says: 'Micrographia is abnormally small or cramped handwriting. It is a secondary motor symptom experienced by some people with Parkinson's. Micrographia is often an early symptom of the disease.' So that was how I got my diagnosis – about eight years ago at the age of sixty-two, when I was still working part time and also in the middle of a professional doctorate which required the completion of a 60,000-word thesis.

When I first started taking medication, I can remember keeping paper by my bedside and writing something as soon as I woke, to see if it was 'getting any better'. It was a long time before I noticed any difference and even today it varies enormously, as does my ability to use a keyboard. An early adaptation was to learn to use the mouse with my left (less affected) hand.

I worked in the NHS and my manager was very good about arranging support. She sorted an occupational health assessment, as a result of which I had voice recognition software installed on my work PC. If we are allowed to advertise it was a Dragon – how fitting a subject for a tale! My colleagues were extremely helpful in doing most of the note-taking if we were interviewing jointly. However, this process brought sharply into focus one of the complexities of being diagnosed with a disabling condition. I needed the help – at least some of the time – but in order to receive it I had to assume a 'disabled' identity – to which I was deeply resistant. I was very snappy with the occupational health assessor – and I didn't always use the software.

This ambivalence was reflected also in which of my friends and relatives I told about the diagnosis. The closest either knew even beforehand that I was worried or were easy to tell face-to-face. It was the ones at a distance geographically and emotionally – the ones with whom I was mostly in written communication by Christmas round robin – that were the problem. Making that distinction caused trouble – one friend was extremely hurt that she had found out third hand (and I was pretty annoyed with the person who had told the third party). I delayed sharing the news more widely for several years and then made it look as if I had disclosed it previously and they had failed to register it. Somehow putting it in writing makes it too concrete, solid, and inflexible (a bit like I am sometimes). The same goes for reading about Parkinson's. I don't very often – maybe when there is a specific issue like difficulty in medication supplies.

There is, however, an exception to this. I have a friend of very long standing (fifty years) with whom I have always communicated in writing – initially by letter, now by email. We hardly ever speak directly – I think this gives us time to reflect usefully on what we are saying to each other. This correspondence is a very precious conduit for my feelings and fears about my condition. She probably knows as much as my husband about what goes on in my head and certainly more than my children. Her slightly removed, sympathetic but realistic support is an enormous help.

I'm still writing other things – I've had several articles published and am working on another. I think the intellectual exercise is as important to me as the physical. This is mostly electronic though I can just about manage a handwritten page of A5, and it can sometimes be as beautiful as ever. I can't say the same about the water colour painting I've taken up since lockdown – after a break of thirty years – but I am learning to accept that it's the process not the end product that matters. I've gone back to knitting and embroidery as well – I hope it will help maintain my fine motor control. I'm still refusing to give in to the Dragon. This is one way I can feel that I am in charge of my story and how it is told. Writing this has been another...

The beauty therapist's tale

When I was in my thirties, I developed a head shake that other people commented on. I was unaware of it at that time. On a visit to the GP for something else, I mentioned it. He assured me it was just a slight tremor for which he could prescribe beta blockers. They would probably lower my blood pressure (it was naturally low), give me cold hands and feet (they were always too cold), and something else that I now can't remember! Because I was only trying to stop other people's concerns, I declined. Over the years it got worse, and I started to see my head shake. I realised that my neck ached when I watched an exciting film. It became clear that the shake was worse when I was excited or stressed.

When I was in my fifties I was diagnosed with an under-active thyroid. I had become very tired and short of energy and just didn't feel well. Lethothyroxine was prescribed and I gradually felt better.

My sixties were overflowing with problems.

I had a small lumpectomy on my left breast. The surgeon was not happy with it, and I had a second operation to have more cells removed. Even though it was a small cancer and detected early, I still had to have radiotherapy and Tamoxifen. The hot flushes were worse than anything else, on and off all day and night. I had been on a very high dose of HRT that had not only kept me feeling fit and well, but took away the arthritic pain in my knees. I was a badminton player, so I know that before and after the HRT my knees were very painful.

When looking for something else, it was discovered that my thyroid gland had cancerous growths on one side of it. I had the infected lobe removed and instead of regular check-ups, I had the other lobe removed a few months later.

I broke my right arm when I was sixty-three and a few years later I dislocated my right shoulder. The shoulder didn't recover, and I was left in severe pain for which the doctors could find no reason. I had two lots of surgery, but the cause was never found. Eventually I was given a replacement shoulder.

I had my right knee replaced the year after I turned seventy, and the left one was also later replaced. The subsequent pain in my right groin resulted in a replacement right hip.

If you've kept count by now, I have had ten anaesthetics. The cancer two (they had missed some cells!), thyroid two, the shoulder three, two knees and a hip.

The point of telling you about all this is the shaking.

Dressed in only a thin hospital gown going down to the theatre and having all the things that need to be done to prepare me for anaesthesia, I always shivered with cold.

The Parkinson's diagnosis didn't happen until 2017 (I was seventy-two), and only during the hip operation was it realised that the by now severe shaking was not just cold. It was the Parkinson's. When I had my right knee operation, the anaesthetist got quite cross with me for not being able to control the shaking. The doctors did not refuse the operation because I had Parkinson's, but they did feel it was necessary to give me a full anaesthetic. The nurses were helpful when I insisted on taking the Sinemet medicine exactly on time.

Now let us go back in time to clarify things.

My head shake was by now part of me, then one day I realised it didn't shake any more. Wonderful.

Then later on I felt my right arm quivering ever so gently. Over a short time (I can't recall how long) it got so it was noticeable, so I told my GP. He still said it was just an essential tremor. It was not done to make a fuss, so I lived with it. By now writing was becoming difficult. It started off okay then gradually got smaller and smaller until I stopped, took a moment, and restarted only to find it just kept getting smaller.

Remember I had a right hand that didn't always work due to the shoulder ops. I had slowly, over a few years learnt to do lots of things with my left hand to compensate, so this was just another annoyance from the damage I thought.

At the beginning of 2017 my husband had an appointment with a neurosurgeon. We have always accompanied each other when visiting doctors, so I was quietly sitting in whilst he was being attended to. At the end of his consultation, the specialist turned his chair to look at me and said: 'What are you doing about your shaking arm?'

'Nothing,' I said.

'Why?' I told him that my GP had told me that it was just an essential tremor. He then asked me to touch each finger with my thumb on both hands and then to circle my wrists. He then asked me three strange questions: 'Do you suffer from constipation?' 'Do you have vivid dreams?' and a third I can't remember. They all seemed so disconnected to my shaking arm.

When I answered yes to them all he said: 'I want to see you in clinic. Go and tell your doctor to make you an appointment with me.'

It was August by the time the appointment came through. By then I was so sleepy and tired all the time that we assumed our new, very firm mattress was stopping me getting any rest. So, we went and bought an expensive new bed! The day we chose it I could hardly keep myself from falling asleep in the store.

At the appointment there was a Parkinson's nurse present, so the doctor obviously knew what was wrong with me.

I don't recall much of that appointment except being upset, and how insistent they were that the tablets that they had just prescribed must be taken with a large glass of water and spaced out regularly at the same times every day.

I started to feel better once the tablets were in my system. The sleepiness was reduced to a reasonable tiredness. By the time I was writing Christmas cards, my handwriting was almost back to normal and most of the time it is now good. On bad days it is wobbly. My shaking arm only improved slightly. I now have a fidgety right foot that is annoying. Fortunately, the arm and leg don't often fidget together!

I was directed to the local hospital to join a group of fellow sufferers where we chatted jointly with the physiotherapist and then had exercises to keep us mobile. From there I was directed to a monthly meeting where I got to know others with Parkinson's and some of the Canterbury group committee. We had refreshments and chatted. I learnt so much about this disease and made some more friends.

Knowing what I know now, I feel sure I had had Parkinson's for many years before my diagnosis.

I have always had irregular bowels and lots of constipation. I have always been slower than friends and family at everyday tasks. I have had a memory that worked beautifully sometimes, but most of the time it feels as if I can't remember anything I'm told. My back has gradually curved over. I have always worked bending over clients in my work as a beauty therapist, then while making decorations for celebration cakes, and with my gardening hat on when weeding, potting on cuttings, and looking at the ground generally. Now I think it is also the result of this condition.

I have learnt so much about Parkinson's through the contacts with the Canterbury Parkinson's group. I try to live my life as it comes, being positive. Most of the time I don't feel like a sufferer, just the same me but with a few annoyances.

But I really don't like the prospects in the future. I'm a very independent person and I don't want to depend on others to help me to live!

The systems analyst's tale

I suppose that sometimes we all look back and wonder 'what if?'

What if I'd kept that old cheque? Would my life have been any different? In 1963 I was the student treasurer at Liverpool University going through a box of cleared cheques from the Union Dances of the previous year, to decide which groups we might want to book again. On the back of one cheque for twenty-five pounds someone had already written: 'Gone to Germany, need a drummer.' I wonder what happened to the Silver Beatles. I could have learned to play the drums.

What if I'd never become fascinated by computers? My life would certainly have been different. I started my working life as a systems engineer in the late 60s, in the early days of commercial computing before we became known as nerds or gadget heads. I was usually known as an 'assistant engineer', but that was simply because no-one knew what a system was. I was regarded as some sort of wizard when I got a computer in Liverpool to drive a printer in Reading. The customer asked me 'where will it all end?'

What if I hadn't spent so much of my life hunched over a computer screen analysing complex multifactorial problems and trying to devise solutions? Would I have had a pain free back?

My back was becoming a problem; I was getting older and spending too much time bent over a screen. It was no real surprise that it was getting so very much more painful all the time. The first time I saw my doctor he agreed and recommended some physiotherapy that seemed to make a difference – but the benefits didn't last. The physiotherapist said my pain was caused by my shoulder blades sticking to my rib cage. She was able to release them by massage and manipulation, but again it was temporary.

This went on for a year or more. The problem was painful but not disabling. The other thing was that I was fast approaching retirement when, in theory, I could start to take it easy and look after myself.

After I retired at seventy it did ease off for a few years, with physio when needed and more attention to posture whilst walking. It was during a brisk walk when a massive pain in my chest followed by an emergency ambulance left me in hospital after a suspected heart attack. But it wasn't a heart attack. The favoured explanation was something called costo-chondritis, an inflammation of the cartilage between the ribs. Not really worth worrying about.

But now I had unwanted pains both back and front, so I went again to the doctor. 'Is there anything we can do differently? The pains keep coming back.'

I waited for the diagnostic words of wisdom.

The doctor sat up straight and faced me: 'You might have Parkinson's. I've also noticed that you're dragging your feet and your facial expression seems very fixed like a mask. I'll arrange for you to see a consultant.'

I couldn't care less about a mask-like face as he described it, but I needed something for my back. On the way home, I was not best pleased with the medical profession, so I consulted Dr. Google.

Dr. Google seemed to think I was a very good match for the profile of someone with Parkinson's. I certainly seemed to be showing many of the signs. It seems Parkinson's affects men more than women. There's not much I can do about that, nor the fact of being over seventy.

I had noticed a loss of dexterity. I'd abandoned a model ship I'd been building. It was becoming too finicky for me. My voice deterioration was certainly real. I had been an enthusiastic singer, but I'd dropped out of two choirs when my previous range of three octaves seemed to have disappeared. My muscle stiffness had just got worse and worse over the years.

I did experience constipation, but I thought that could have been down to anything, and my sense of smell had never been much good anyway.

I did occasionally have a little tremor in my left hand, but nothing really noticeable.

As for a lack of facial expression, I wasn't aware that my smile had disappeared. However, when I looked back at the photographs of my seventieth birthday party everyone else was smiling at the cameras, but my face wasn't smiling. It didn't look good.

The letter arrived with the date for my NHS specialist consultation, a wait of six weeks.

In the meantime, I was about to complete on a holiday flat back in the northwest. So, I arranged a private appointment and shortly afterwards I was walking up and down a consulting room whilst a neurosurgeon tapped my knees with an antique rubber hammer. No blood test, no scan, no modern diagnostic methods, just a declaration that I had Idiopathic Parkinson's. I left his consultation room with my first prescription. He also missed out the classic doctor line. He failed to say 'if it has not cleared up in four weeks, come back and see me again.' He wasn't expecting it to clear up. It was my first encounter with the concept of 'it won't get better'.

In the meantime, we had completed on our flat, ordered furniture and were camping out in our new holiday home as beds, chairs and tables arrived.

Then a miracle happened. I went into the centre of the city to buy a paper when I heard the rattle of a collection box and made a larger than normal contribution to charity. It was for Parkinson's UK.

Six people, four with Parkinson's, were willing and happy to talk about it, and gave me great advice. What if I'd not met them?

As soon as you are diagnosed, I strongly recommend that you find someone with Parkinson's and talk to them. As soon as someone you know is diagnosed with Parkinson's talk to them, or, if you can't talk to them, give them a copy of this book. You might like to try to assess how you are affected and how many of the twenty plus symptoms apply to you. Are you able to identify activities and resources to ease your symptom set, or slow things down? Then assess your symptoms regularly, perhaps every six months, and modify your focus. There is an example in the back of this book of my symptom log.

PD doesn't necessarily mean just Parkinson's Disease; it can mean Provoke Delay. You may not be able to stop it, but you can certainly slow it down. This approach is perfect for a systems analyst – that is to say, address the symptoms according to their severity with a view to slowing down or even reversing the effects of the conditions that are causing the most trouble.

I found it useful to identify the list of my most common Parkinson's symptoms and score the extent to which they cause me a problem or require monitoring. As soon as I had my list of symptoms and my assessment of my current ability, I really began to feel I'd taken back some control.

The next job for me was to identify an exercise or activity which would improve my performance. This in itself was useful, comparing the benefit I felt from different approaches. The internet came into its own. I tried every version of the question 'how can I tackle Parkinson's?'

PD Warrior was the first thing I found on the web that looked useful. This is an Australian-based, ten-week challenge to complete a set of exercises each day, measuring your performance from day one to day seventy. After doing the challenge, I got a huge boost when I realised how much I had improved over the ten weeks. I now had my own evidence that the effects of Parkinson's can be slowed down and, in some cases, actually reversed. I still do at least one hour of PD Warrior exercises per week.

The second source was the local branch of Parkinson's UK and their support programme.

Every Monday, I spent an hour in the gym with two very motivated physiotherapists and five other PwP. On Tuesdays, I enjoyed an hour of singing and vocal exercise with the brilliant Skylarks.

Wednesday used to be a session in a hydro-therapy pool where we talked football. However, I realised I was capable of more strenuous exercise and so I joined a dance class which was totally brilliant. I can't recommend this more strongly. It would seem that dancing to strong rhythms with other people involves more parts of the brain than any other legal activity. Friday's option was the Gentle Gym, which is too gentle for me at the moment but has the best cup of tea!

Then I started looking for apps on my iPhone. I bought an app to measure my sound output in decibels and discovered I was speaking in a whisper, and I thought it was everyone else getting a bit deaf. I also found Voice Builder, an app I still use every couple of months to build volume, bearing in mind that vocal cords are simply muscles and, like everything else, deteriorate without exercise. I also came across the app Clock Yourself, which makes tightrope walking seem easy but really helps with balance.

In addition to all the above, I resurrected a stationary bicycle and an elderly rowing machine which are useful when I feel I need some exercise and nothing else is scheduled. The only problem with these is that it has proved so far impossible to find anybody to come and give them a much-needed service!

The Neuro Therapy Centre in Saltney, North Wales has done a brilliant job in creating Zoom classes for PwP and carers. Twice a week, to build my upper body strength, I do seated boxing sessions. Boxing needs much less courage when your opponent is online.

I would also recommend another site, which I found very helpful during the Covid lockdown, called Power for Parkinson's. It is online from Austin in Texas and provides great exercise sessions with friendly, positive people and a huge energy level.

For someone who loves solving complex problems, Parkinson's is the ideal affliction. I never did learn to play drums!

The historian's tale

Loosening a demon's grip

This is the first essay that I have written on Parkinson's disease, a chronic degenerative neurological illness that has governed my life for more than twelve years. Why have I devoted so little attention to it?

In all honesty, I welcome any escape from the grip of demon Parkinson's, and I find that writing is one of the best ways for me to do that. Unfortunately, its grip on me is growing tighter with each passing year. Despite my best efforts and those of a first-rate medical team, the disease is gradually robbing me of a once vibrant and fulfilling life.

I was diagnosed with PD in 2004 at age fifty-eight which put me in the unenviable category of 'early onset'. After the initial shock at the diagnosis, I learned that my service in the US army during the Vietnam War qualified me to be treated for Parkinson's disease at the McGuire VA Medical Center in Richmond, Virginia, one of only seven such centres in the entire veteran hospital system in the United States.

The result of the care I began to receive was almost immediate and dramatic. Thanks to the expertise of a superb medical team at McGuire, I was prescribed the medication and given the expert counselling I needed to slow the disease progression.

For nearly ten years I have kept the disease at bay. Friends seemed amazed by how many of the manifestations of

Parkinson's disease were reduced by the care I received. Most people I met for the first time never guessed I had the disease.

Gone was the blank facial expression of many Parkinson's sufferers. I start swinging my arms again and taking full strides when I walked rather than the stutter step so common with PwP.

My handwriting improved from a scrawl to a reasonably legible script. I felt fully confident around people. I was completely comfortable in my public speaking. My wife and I travelled extensively overseas, realising that we needed to take advantage of my relatively good health while we could. With my friends who have Parkinson's, we formed a support group that we needed. We called it the Movers and Shakers. Together we helped to raise five million dollars to establish a comprehensive Parkinson's disease centre at Virginia Commonwealth University, one that has begun treating patients with movement disorders throughout central Virginia and beyond.

I have spoken at many Parkinson's disease seminars and participated in a number of related fund-raising events. People began to refer to me as the 'Parkinson's poster boy of Richmond'.

It was a honeymoon of relatively normal living that lasted about ten years longer than it does for most Parkinson's patients I knew. However, the honeymoon had a time limit on it. Parkinson's is a cruel disease patiently taking its time to shut down its victims, playing them like a cat slowly but deliberately torturing a young rabbit which it has caught.

Little by little it began to age me and sap my ability to do things that once came naturally. I began to freeze and feel unable to walk through doorways, terrified that I would fall.

I would go to the grocery store at a full normal stride, yet halfway through the shopping, Parkinson's would suddenly take control of me. I would begin shuffling my feet, gripping the cart in fear that I would fall. When I got to the checkout, I would struggle to retrieve my wallet to pay for my purchases. I couldn't help but notice people staring at me, making me want to flee the store in embarrassment.

I am still able to drive a car without difficulty. Recently my children won't let me drive my grandchildren to McDonald's or the movies, fearful that they're at risk with me behind the wheel. It makes me sad. I can't blame them.

While most people think of Parkinson's as an illness that affects people physically, it can have profound mental and psychological consequences. Depression is one weapon in its arsenal. Fortunately, that weapon has failed with me, but another one bothers me no end – the loss of executive function.

Executive function is a skill that most of us have. It allows us to get things done such as to arrange your schedule for the day, organise your personal finances, remember where things are, multitask or analyse a complex problem and find a solution. At times, this has driven my wife to her wit's end.

I know that part of this is the ageing process, but hardly a day goes by when I can't find my keys or a bill I intended to pay. I get frustrated trying to find a memo I received from someone, only to realise that I have stuck it in the wrong file. I find myself putting off decisions until the last moment – something I never used to do.

People ask me what it feels like to have Parkinson's. Is there pain and discomfort? Not really but there's more of the latter. The best description I've heard it's like driving with your parking brake on. Every motion seems to go at half speed whether it is buttoning a shirt, tying your shoelaces, getting in or out of the car or typing. It is the last that has really bothered me.

I get great joy out of writing, which I have done initially on typewriters and then on computer keyboards. Although I've never been a speedster with my typing, up until a few years ago I could pound out words at a fairly fast clip. Although I have no problem in finding words, committing them to my computer screen comes more slowly now.

What can I do? I'm getting ready to take a big step to try to loosen the grip of demon Parkinson's.

Until a year or so ago, I was able to control the disease by taking increasing amounts of the wonder drugs that help control the disease symptoms and might actually slow its progression.

Unfortunately, I have reached the point of maxing out on these drugs. I am a veritable walking medicine cabinet taking nearly twenty pills a day. Their effectiveness and duration is changing little by little and lessening.

As a result, I will soon take another step on this journey – deep brain stimulation surgery (DBS). This is an operation that could take up to six hours. The surgeon will insert two thin, insulated wires through small openings in my skull and implant them in a targeted part of my brain. These wires will be passed under the skin on my head neck and shoulder connecting to a neuro-stimulator that will be implanted under the skin near my collarbone. Once turned on, the device will send out regular electrical impulses that will block the electrical signals caused by my symptoms. Assuming it works, I can reduce the amount of my medications and will experience a reduction in my symptoms. Are there risks? Yes, anytime one undergoes brain surgery, there is a risk of infection or excessive bleeding in the skull or complications associated with anaesthesia.

But I'm willing to assume the risks. If this procedure works, then I can anticipate a better life for years to come. Frankly, I'm tired of being tossed around like a young rabbit. I look forward to giving you a post-surgery report – a good one, I hope.

The human brain is an amazing organ. It accounts for only two percent of human body weight, but it consumes twenty percent of the body's energy. Every physical move we make, every word we utter, every problem we solve – they all originate in the brain. When the brain comes under attack these functions can be seriously affected.

More than a decade ago I began to suspect there was an assault on my brain when I started to show signs of Parkinson's disease. My wife and I were devastated when a family doctor confirmed that our fears were justified.

Parkinson's is an incurable neuromuscular illness which strikes the substantia nigra section of the brain, ruthlessly mounting a short, slow and deliberate siege on the mind and body. Little by little it ages and slows you down. It makes you feel chronically tired and awkward in public. Simple activities such as buttoning a shirt, keyboarding, tying shoes, rolling over in bed or getting in and out of the car, turn into major time-consuming chores.

Balance becomes a cause for concern, with many Parkinson's patients experiencing serious falls resulting in injuries. Although people do not die from the disease, they often succumb to other causes that it has exacerbated.

This catastrophic illness was named after an English surgeon and apothecary James Parkinson who officially identified the ailment when he published an essay on the shaking palsy in 1817. Parkinson classified the disease and for the next century-and-a-half doctors and scientist looked for a cure and ways to beat it and treat it.

Finally in the 1960s, with the introduction of the drug levadopa, doctors had the first weapon available to them that actually works in fighting Parkinson's. Most patients receiving levodopa experienced significant improvement in their condition.

Over the years other drugs were introduced to slow the progress of the disease and to further minimise symptoms. These medications have brought about a revolution in the management of the disease. But diagnosing and treating Parkinson's is a tricky business, usually requiring the skills of a well trained and experienced specialist. As an Army veteran I was fortunate to qualify for the comprehensive treatment of the Parkinson's disease centre at McGuire VA Medical Center. McGuire is one of seven VA hospitals nationwide to have such programmes.

The team of specialists there was able to prescribe just the right combination of drugs to treat me. Almost as soon as my neurologist put me onto them I felt better, and my Parkinson's symptoms were reduced significantly. People often expressed surprise when I told them that I had Parkinson's. Having a positive attitude and adhering to a rigorous exercise schedule contributed to my overall well-being. This was the case for more than a decade.

Nevertheless, Parkinson's has proved to be a relentless demon that can be slowed down but not stopped. Gradually the symptoms I had experienced when I was first diagnosed began to suddenly reappear – a slight tremor in my right hand and unsteadiness whilst on my feet, occasional falls and increasing difficulty in performing simple tasks that require some degree of manual dexterity. Realising that more drugs would no longer provide the help I needed, early this spring my neurologist and I began to discuss the next option: DBS, which is a major surgery that if successful could diminish my Parkinson's symptoms.

I am fortunate that one of the country's most experienced and accomplished neurosurgeons specialising in DBS is located in Richmond. Dr Kathryn Holloway, director of the DBS programmes at VCU Medical Center, has performed more than 500 of these complex surgeries. I was 510. My wife and I met her in early April and Dr Holloway explained that during the six-hour surgery she and her team would insert two insulated wires into openings in my skull and then plant them in a predetermined portion of my brain.

The wires would then be slipped under the skin on my head, neck and shoulder, and be connected to a neurotransmitter they would implant under my skin near the collarbone. When they turned it on, she explained this device would send out a steady stream of electrical impulses that would block the electrical signals that cause my Parkinson's symptoms.

If the surgery was successful, I could limit the number of drugs I was taking whilst enjoying a reduction of my symptoms. Dr Holloway warned me however that the operation was not risk-free.

Any time brain surgery is performed, the patient runs the risk of stroke, infection and excess bleeding in the skull or having a bad reaction to anaesthesia. Given the alternatives I decided to take these risks.

To qualify for the surgery, I had to pass a series of tests to determine that I responded well to my medication, that I did not have other ailments not related to Parkinson's and that I was not suffering from depression. I passed easily and was given a date for my surgery: July 26, more than three months into the future.

I had to wait in line for my turn for the DBS. The next three months seemed excruciatingly long. The closer it got, time seemed to slow down to a crawl. It reminded me of those few days before Christmas when I was a child and the hands of the clock seem never to move.

Finally, the big day came and a small contingent of family and friends took me to a hospital for my 06:00 surgery appointment.

In many ways the rest of the day is a blur, but here are some impressions of an exceptionally friendly and welcoming medical staff who helped ease any worries I had: endlessly repeating my full name and Social Security number, being told to count backwards from ten and not quite reaching five before the anaesthetic kicked in. Waking up to the voice of Dr Holloway and some of the team members and realising that they were in the middle of my surgery, hearing a strange fluctuating pulse in the background. I was told after asking it was the sound of my brain as Dr Holloway guided a probe to find the sweet spot to place my implant. I remember my neurologist commanding me to move my arms and legs at intervals to ensure that the implants had been properly placed and waking up in the recovery room, my head still foggy from the surgery and effects of the anaesthesia.

The total time for the surgery was a little more than six hours. I was then kept in hospital for five days including one for

Dr Holloway to place a stimulator device in my chest. She did so to ensure that there was no infection or other complications. I had to wait two weeks for the stimulator to be activated.

My wife and I went back for an appointment on August 12 to have me 'turned on'. As we made our twenty-one-mile drive to McGuire I thought again of Christmas during my childhood. What will be under the tree, a bright new shining toy or a pair of pyjamas and some socks?

Fortunately, my device was the new toy. After they turned it on, I soon felt like a new person: no more shaking hands, no more freezing when I came to the doorway, no more falls, no more having people stare at me as I stutter-stepped my way to the grocery store.

I know that the DBS has its limitations and that the time will come when it will no longer be as effective as it is now, but if I can have another ten years or even five years of the way I feel now it was well worth the effort, despite the risks involved. Thanks to a gifted surgeon and her team I've been given back the way of life I thought was lost forever.

They truly 'turned me on'!

The cartoonist's tale

"SHE WAS SHAKING HER PARKINSONS COLLECTION
TIN VIGOROUSLY"

DON

THESE NEW PARKINSONS T SHIRTS WILL MAKE US
LOOK RIDICULOUS

3

NO PARKIN SON.

The public health inspector's tale

I am a lecturer in public health in the UK and regularly speak in Europe. I am not a linguist, however I can make a reasonable job with some German and I am reasonably proficient in French. I managed quite well until the day when my host suggested that it might be better to stick to English. I had to admit that somehow that day the words that were coming out of my mouth sounded very garbled and indistinct.

I seemed to have lost all clarity of speech, then I remembered that I had not done my pre-speaking warm up.

I had a French teacher many years ago who maintained that speaking her language requires much more physical attention than English or, as she put it: 'You can't mumble in French.'

Her recommended exercise was to recite in French, with exaggerated pronunciation and much facial movement.

'Petites pommes, petites pommes, petites pommes, petites poires.'

This gives a good workout to disobliging vocal cords and the wakes up the muscles round the mouth and tongue, getting an English mouth warmed up enough to tackle French. However, it no longer seemed to work. No matter what language I tried, the result was quiet mumbling.

What was wrong with me?

Several friends suspected that I might have had a mild stroke, but no other sign of a stroke was evident.

However, due to my speech difficulty, I found that I could

no longer do my job reliably. Covid has also forced me to stop travelling, which is a pity because it was the part of my job that I enjoyed the most.

As I am now sixty-four years old, I decided to retire a little earlier and to find out what was really causing my speech problems. My doctor referred me to speech therapist who gave me exercises to do. I saw her once a month.

It was while she was taking her holiday, that a trainee took my session and she asked me 'how long have you had Parkinson's?' I told her I didn't have Parkinson's and she got very embarrassed. This was the first time it had ever been mentioned.

I was advised to see a neurologist who said Parkinson's was strong possibility.

I was also sent for examination by a throat specialist who poked around in my larynx, could find no physical problem, and agreed that Parkinson's was a possibility.

By this time my original speech therapist had returned from holiday and confirmed that she also thought Parkinson's was a possibility.

Why is there no clear test for this condition?

To correct my speech problem, I was enrolled in the LSVT (Lee Silverman Voice Treatment) speech therapy programme, a half hour session, daily for one month. I now know how long I can hold a note and what volume I can reach. After the programme my speech was much improved, and I now have a card with a selection of phrases that I declaim daily at full volume much to the annoyance of my cat.

I now must admit that Parkinson's is the most likely explanation. In fact, just between the two of us, I am sure of it. But my foreign language skills have not gone to waste, as the best exercise is still 'petites pommes'.

What next?

This is the intriguing bit – if I have got Parkinson's I'm going to start exhibiting other characteristics, so I'm watching daily to see if my hand is shaking or anything else is occurring.

I seem to be shuffling rather than walking, but for the moment I'm keeping it between me and my cat.

Another carer's tale

I met my husband in London in 2002, and we were married three years later in Bolton. Previously I had no idea what Parkinson's disease meant, but I discovered that Parkinson's won't kill you, so I decided to marry him as a challenge. And indeed, a challenge it has been. But in the meantime, we have strengthened our relationship and met so many interesting people through Parkinson's UK.

In Bolton, my husband became chairman of the local branch and I worked as treasurer. We were actively involved with the Parkinson's UK group and had a memorable time there.

When we returned south to live in 2010, we joined the local Parkinson's Canterbury branch. We also joined a singing group called Skylarks, which was being set up by Professor Grenville Hancox and Roger Clayton. At this time I started to learn piano, and we have enjoyed making music together ever since. It helped us both during the recent lockdown.

Skylarks now comes under the auspices of the Canterbury Cantata Trust. (There is more useful information on the CCT website.)

Music has such a therapeutic effect on everyone and singing opens the mouth and the lungs wide. This is really helpful to people with Parkinson's, particularly if they have speech and communication difficulties, but it also provides a sense of well-being. My husband really enjoys singing and when he enjoys himself, he forgets some of the difficulties he lives with.

As with many other conditions, how you live and fight with Parkinson's is unique, depending on your lifestyle and your body strength; I think, above all, physical and philosophical thinking is involved.

One good thing is that it is not an intensely painful condition. It's worth remembering that there is nearly always someone who is worse off than you. With all the challenges that Parkinson's brings, you have to deal with what you can and forget what you can't do. Frustration doesn't help anyone.

There are still many things to enjoy in life and supporting your partner in the challenges that you both face is not a bad way to live.

The golfer's tale

Between 1980 and 1985 I noticed that I had back pain. I had a problem with the fourth/fifth disc which was initially treated with physiotherapy and eventually with an operation. The surgery was not successful, and I had constant pain afterwards. I continued playing golf and damaged my left elbow which was thought to be due to tennis/golf elbow. I was treated with steroids for some years which did not work. Later I had the tendon to my elbow cut to relieve the pressure, but this did not work either.

In 1990 I had a routine appointment with my new GP. I told him about the problem with my left arm and he said I might have Parkinson's. I was referred to a consultant neurologist at the National Hospital in Queens Square London where the diagnosis was confirmed. I continued to work, in denial of my condition, but took the medication Sinemet.

In 2003 I retired from my job. I kept my daily life as normal as possible doing sports, golf, and intensive fitness. I have always been a strong believer that physical exercise is hugely important in managing my condition, and I am sure that this has been a key factor in my longevity after diagnosis.

I met my wife in London in 2002 and we married in 2005 in Bolton. She has been my rock and support since then.

Difficulties with speech and communication are common amongst PwPs, and singing is known to help. In 2010 we joined a new singing group, called Skylarks. This local initiative became a national and then international network, with groups established worldwide.

I really enjoy singing and while I continue to sing with the Skylarks, I also have singing lessons. Making music is particularly important for me, and the songs that I sing are reminders of good times in my life. My wife plays the piano, and it has helped us both to sing and play together during the recent lockdown.

Having Parkinson's is hard on those who have it, but also very hard for their partners to have to watch them deteriorate, and it seems vital to me that we should remember the good times.

The nurse's tale

I had my first symptoms in 1995 but was not diagnosed with Parkinson's until October 1999.

The first thing I noticed was that I had an uncontrollable fine tremor in my right hand whilst in a meeting. This recurred some ten weeks later. At the time, I was working as director of nursing in a 480-bed NHS Trust.

In 1996, whilst at an NHS Finance Study Day in London, I lost the use of my right arm for about an hour – it may of course have been a response to the somewhat boring subject matter of the study day! The arm returned to normal, and I went home and then to my local GP surgery the next day. After this I was fully investigated, but all tests came back as either negative or inconclusive.

At that time, I asked if I had Parkinson's and was told that my presenting symptoms were not typical. As time went by, I began to find it difficult to walk as far as I had been used to, and I became very stiff and had moderately bad backache. However, I played golf regularly at weekends and this kept me moving.

I retired from my job in July 1999 and went for a two-week trip with friends to the west coast of Scotland to play golf and do a bit of hill walking. On one of the days, we walked to Sandwood Bay. This was a five-mile hike over rather rough terrain. We spent the afternoon at the beach and then set off on the homeward leg. The wind dropped and as a result the midges started to gather and then bite. It was a nightmare walk that I will never forget. I could only walk very slowly and my friends soon moved ahead. I was unable to keep up with them. I counted every step and when I eventually reached where the car was parked, I looked as if I had a bad case of chicken pox.

When I came home I went back to see my doctor. He told me that he thought I had some of the signs of Parkinson's and said he would refer me to a neurologist.

A week later I saw Dr Pollock, who was to look after me for the next ten years. He asked me what I thought was the matter with me. I said that I thought I had Parkinson's and he confirmed that this was his opinion also. He was very kind, but I don't think I heard much more of what he told me after that.

For the first three weeks after diagnosis, I had a great black cloud over my shoulder, and felt really low and anxious. Then I moved into a hopeful, slightly unrealistic phase where I decided I would do something heroic like run the marathon or write a book about my problems – neither objective was achieved! Then I came down to earth and started to think about how I would cope with this major change to my life.

The one thing I was absolutely certain about was that it was important to keep moving. I played a lot of golf which was the equivalent of four weekly three-and-a-half-hour walks, and this was undoubtedly what kept me fairly fit during the first ten years. I also told my friends what was the matter with me. It seemed to me that if people knew why my hand was shaking or I was very slow at some things then we could all accept that this was now normality for me and we could forget it and move on. My friends were enormously supportive during this time and this helped me to come to terms and live with the effects of the condition.

I think I was probably in a form of denial at the beginning, and I didn't want to spend time talking to other sufferers about my symptoms and difficulties. I just didn't want to spend time talking about Parkinson's; I wanted to get on with my life and live as normally as I could. Now I really regret that I didn't meet with other people with the same problems, and I have come to recognise what enormous support PwPs give each other.

During the first three months I was told about the importance of the medication. I was started on Sinemet for a short period to see if I improved. If I did, then this would confirm the diagnosis, and I would then be changed on to a dopamine agonist and the Sinemet would be kept for a later date when I needed it more.

Three weeks before Christmas I was started on Pergolide, a dopamine agonist, which I was told not to stop under any circumstances. This produced very low blood pressure and made me feel very sick and dizzy despite the anti-emetics.

On Boxing Day I got into real difficulties. My GP surgery was closed for four days and the Parkinson's nurses were also on leave. Eventually I rang the on-call doctor who said that I ought to know better than to ring the emergency service over Christmas with such a problem and suggested that I should take the minimum dose possible and then ring the surgery when the holiday was over. At this point I was beginning to feel that if I took another dose I would probably die. Eventually I rang a friend who was a consultant geriatrician with an interest in Parkinson's and he told me to stop it at once and go back onto Sinemet until I could contact someone after the holiday.

I had a difficult first year as I reacted badly to most agonists that were tried. Some gave me a range of different side effects, one gave me no relief of symptoms at all and eventually I was started again on Sinemet and then I began to improve.

My movement improved considerably and other symptoms also disappeared. One such was that my hands felt very weak when I gripped anything. I would tell people this and they would say 'squeeze my hand,' which I did, and my grip felt very weak and shaky. The person whose hand I squeezed always said that the power of my grip felt normal. All I can say is that this was not my experience, but in any case after two months of Sinemet my grip returned to normal.

Six years ago, I joined a Parkinson's singing group and I found singing both enjoyable and therapeutic. We meet fortnightly and it always gives a lift to my week when the Skylarks get together. As well as being physically beneficial, singing with others provides a great sense of well-being in a very supportive environment.

If I think about the things I was told that I found helpful, the first is undoubtedly to keep moving. I think this could have been emphasised more. In my view it's essential. I also learned that constipation was likely to be a problem and I needed to be very careful about this.

The importance of recognising that the management of this illness would be between me and my consultant and my GP was also emphasised. The neurologist was very keen that I feel in control of my medication with guidance if required.

I went on a ten-week physiotherapy/occupational therapy course which was very helpful and gave me a lot of useful information about help available.

However, there are other things I wish I had been aware of. This includes the importance of taking your tablets on time.

It was suggested to me that dopamine was the equivalent of putting petrol in the tank. If you were doing more physical exercise than usual, you might need an extra one-off dose increase to cover that activity. This is not necessarily a view that all clinicians support, but it made eighteen holes of golf on a hilly course possible for me.

Absorption of Sinemet can be affected if taken at the same time or shortly after a heavy meal. I found that if I had a big meal my walking afterwards was significantly compromised.

Now I realise the importance of a good diet. Nutrition is becoming more and more recognised, and a healthy balanced diet gives us a head start in staying fit and well for as long as possible. There is a lot of work being currently undertaken to explore the value of probiotics.

It is only in recent years that I have come to recognise and value the support from other PwPs. It is so helpful to be able to talk to and laugh with people who have been there and who know what you're talking about. PwPs provide an enormous level of support to other PwPs and the wider Parkinson's community.

I wish I had realised how useful it is to keep a diary, so that I had a record of what happened, when, with an outline of any changes in treatment. Try remembering, when a new doctor asks you, when you last switched dosage of a particular drug. I usually find it impossible to remember.

Singing with other PwPs is important for its physical effects but also provides a great sense of wellbeing in a supportive environment. During lockdown the group have continued to meet on Zoom and this has kept people connected.

The help and advice that PUK gives to all members of the

Parkinson's community is exceptional. I had no idea at the time of my diagnosis, and afterwards, just how much support they provided in so many different areas.

And finally, the relationship with the Parkinson's nurses is crucial. No-one told me at the beginning how to contact them, though I knew how their work could provide much help and support to newly diagnosed people. They were, and have been, an enormous source of support to me once I linked up with them.

So, this is what I would say to anyone who is newly diagnosed with Parkinson's:

Keep moving – any exercise that you enjoy, or even if you don't. Keep going. If you don't use it, you lose it.

Eat a healthy well-balanced diet, with plenty of fruit and vegetables, especially green ones, and lots of fibre.

Deal with constipation. Drink lots of fluids, especially water. Your GP will advise on the best aperients.

Get into the early habit of taking your pills exactly at the right time. You need to do this from the beginning. Never leave home without the next dose in your pocket or bag. If you get delayed you must not miss the right time for your medication.

Keep a diary of events. Even if you only do it weekly it will give you a reference point if you need to give information about what has happened to you in relation to your condition. I have had Parkinson's for twenty-one years and it has taken this initiative to make me recognise the value of keeping a personal record of events.

The support that I have received from fellow sufferers has been immense and it seems to me to be vital that we share our knowledge and experiences. In particular the ability to laugh at the funny and absurd situations that we PwPs frequently find ourselves in makes some of the difficulties easier to cope with. So sharing is a good and positive thing. N.B.: this does not mean sharing your pills.

Join a singing group if you can. You don't have to have a good voice or pass any test to join. It really helps to keep the voice exercised in an easy and relaxed atmosphere, and the support of other singers and the leader is exceptional.

The Parkinson's nurses are there to help you. Use their knowledge and expertise whenever you need to. Make sure that you know how to contact them.

Consider yourself one of the team dealing with your Parkinson's – you have a unique knowledge of your illness.

Finally, and perhaps most importantly of all, celebrate the good things in life. the friends, the laughs, the small or great triumphs over difficulties. Accept that there will always be some bad days that we have to learn to live with, but overall life is for living. Life is for now – enjoy it.

The dance teacher's tale

My training as a fitness instructor began when a friend announced she was going back to college to learn to teach exercise to music and asked me to go with her. She was very nervous and wanted me to do the course at the same time. Without thinking it through I said I would be happy to help. I enrolled, duly arriving on the first day of training and scanned the room packed full of students for the face of my friend. She was nowhere to be seen. She never did do the course. Her fears kept her away, but I was there!

The training was tough. We all felt vulnerable, having to learn the art of fitness instruction, demonstrating our learning (or not) in front of each other, exposing our inevitable errors in timing, memorising and execution of moves. Every week I would anticipate the ridicule of other students, yet every week there would be nothing but heart-warming support and good humour that made me feel so happy to belong in my group.

Qualifying was amazing. The joy of discovering I could do it was worth all the days, weeks, and months of self-doubt. I came away from that training course grateful for the patience of my college lecturer whose belief in me enabled me to develop a new skill set.

A fitness teacher knows that it takes courage to turn up in the first place. A fitness teacher also knows doing fitness is a process that never ends. We keep learning all the time about what our bodies can or cannot do, making adjustments according to the physical needs of ageing, injuries, acute and chronic conditions, and learning about the interplay between physical and mental health.

Witnessing the struggles of every fitness trainee on that course made me see early on that exercise to music is for every single body that wants to give it a try. It just takes courage to turn up and patience to try and try again. So, with this attitude firmly in mind, when someone asked if I would become the dance instructor for people with Parkinson's, a condition which affected some of my family members yet about which I knew very little, again I really did not need to think it through.

I launched a movement to music class with minimal knowledge indicated by the following:

If I saw a person shaking uncontrollably on a hot day, I would assume that person had a condition known as Parkinson's. If I saw a person immobile at the entrance to the supermarket, a queue building up behind, but unable to advance, I would assume that person had a condition known as Parkinson's. It would be easy to assume that a condition which induces uncontrollable movement on the one hand and paralysis on the other (literally) would never be compatible with dance.

Well, making assumptions can be bad for our health..!

I found that my class participants embraced the varied dance styles with great enthusiasm (sometimes with a bit of grimacing: Street dance? Bhangra?) Everyone varied in the movements they found easier which brought them more joy – and in the movements they found more of a challenge which might sometimes feel more trouble than they were worth. This is typical of any class I have ever run. This makes a dance participant with Parkinson's no different to anybody else who has ever attended a dance class, with or without chronic conditions. It is illustrated very well by the frequent experience of not being able to distinguish between dancers with Parkinson's and their dancing carer (sometimes the carer is worse though!)

My knowledge of Parkinson's symptoms has become more refined as I learn how much they vary from person to person and vary for each person from day to day. I now appreciate just how much the unpredictability of Parkinson's leaves someone not knowing how they will be the next day, so how to plan ahead? How to retain a sense of control over one's diary?

My dance group, in spite of what could feel overwhelming, kept itself going with mutual care and support, immense sense of humour, real commitment. In a dance class environment, it becomes evident what people can give to each other and receive from each other in return.

Lack of self-belief is a great disabler in itself, and I have witnessed participants developing self-confidence and a vital sense of inclusion from being part of a group moving to music.

Dance engages mind, body, and spirit. This is never more apparent than in the Tai Chi segment. We connect with others in synchronising our movements to the music. At the same time, we connect inwardly with our own breath and the energy travelling through our own body. Tai Chi is sometimes called moving meditation. Using its inherent grace and concentration we strengthen our bodies and lighten our minds.

To be part of the group's creation of peace and well-being feels very special.

I have definitely been moved by all my Parkinson's dance participants – and I hope they would say they have definitely been moved by me!

The finance manager's tale

My story starts with my wife, Sue, getting fed up with my complaints about a painful shoulder. She encouraged me to see my doctor, who referred me to a rheumatologist. His assistant could not make any sense of my symptoms and sought advice from the consultant rheumatologist, who happened to be her husband. He simply felt my lower arm and said:

'See a neurologist.' I suspect that he knew that I had Parkinson's disease but thought that this was a matter for a neurologist.

I saw the neurologist in December 2006. He was running very late and I think he was tired because all he said, after a cursory assessment, was: 'You have got Parkinson's. Come back in six months.' I had hardly heard of Parkinson's and it came as a complete shock.

The next morning I went to the library and found a book about Parkinson's which made it clear that it was a neurological, progressive and incurable condition.

When I returned six months later, the neurologist told me that he was now uncertain about his first diagnosis. My excellent and feisty GP said 'up with this we will not put,' or words to that effect, and she referred me to the Institute of Neurology, Queen Square, London, where my consultant immediately diagnosed Parkinson's and patiently answered all my questions.

I have now been under her care for about twelve years, and she is excellent at selecting the best drug recipe for my

Parkinson's at that particular stage of the disease.

So what impact has Parkinson's had on me and my family, bearing in mind that I was certain that I needed to stay positive if I was going to live with its various challenges, which would inevitably come in the years ahead?

I regard myself extremely fortunate to be as well as I am, given that it is now over fourteen years since the first diagnosis. With the benefit of hindsight, I am convinced that during the last months of employment, although Parkinson's had not yet been diagnosed, it was affecting some of my decisions, not least the offer of a dream position which I immediately rejected with barely any thought.

Kids and genetics

My first concern was whether Parkinson's could be transmitted genetically, and I was pleased to be able to reassure my two children that it was highly unlikely that they had the gene. If I had been under sixty when I was first diagnosed, the answer might have been different.

The early years

I retired at the age of sixty and worked as a volunteer for four local charities, but made the mistake of giving up my involvement in three of them within a few months of being diagnosed. I had failed to appreciate that many people with Parkinson's can function satisfactorily at least for the first few years.

I should have asked about life expectancy of People with Parkinson's. According to the Michael J. Fox Foundation for

Parkinson's Research (in the United States), patients usually begin developing Parkinson's symptoms around age sixty. Many people with Parkinson's live between ten and twenty years after being diagnosed.

Main problems now

Some symptoms are motor ones and others are non-motor. Everyone with Parkinson's has an individual mix.

Fatigue

I take the Parkinson's drugs as prescribed, but often need to ask the consultant if she will increase my daily dosage, bearing in mind the possible side effects. Over the past few years I have gone from 200mg of Sinemet (levodopa) to 1000mg + other drugs for Parkinson's. I don't know if there is a ceiling on the quantity of levodopa which can be taken, before the side effects become worse than the symptoms. I assume that this varies from person to person. Curiously, when I get tired my brain does not think 'have I missed taking my drugs?' It is usually my wife who reminds me to take them.

Balance

This is a fairly new problem and I now frequently stumble, so far without causing myself any serious injury. I cannot walk upstairs without a rail to cling on which means that I often have to make two trips in order to take things upstairs for bedtime (book, radio, water).

I try to do daily exercises, as proposed by a physio who has a special interest in Parkinson's but, not surprisingly, these require thirty minutes each day.

Speech

My voice is now weak, especially when I am tired, which makes communication with my wife difficult or fraught. More about that anon.

Parkinson's often affects the throat and mouth muscles – a model of these parts of the body shows how complicated they are.

Poor sleeping

Sleeping has been poor for a long time. For some months I suffered from 'restless leg syndrome' which is a maddening condition, now mercifully largely controlled by drugs. I also have terrifying nightmares from time to time, and find myself on the floor, having hit my head on the bedside table.

Constipation

Breakfast comprising All Bran and prunes used to deal with this problem, but I now some regular medicine is needed. Embarrassingly, flatulence is now frequent and noisy.

Water works

I have a problem with my bladder/prostate. Parkinson's and

prostate problems together cause havoc, especially on motor-ways, as the urge to pee comes on very strongly with virtually no warning.

Hand – lack of motor control

My loss of fine motor control is a real nuisance. For example, I am right-handed but can only use my left hand to control a computer mouse. Also, I cannot read my own writing, so writing down, say, a telephone number is very frustrating. Buttons, especially on the cuffs, are a real struggle. Turning down the collars of shirts and jackets is almost impossible.

Mild cognitive impairment (MCI)

This is a tricky area as it is difficult to separate errors due to normal ageing from those caused by Parkinson's. These are some examples of the sort of tangles which I regularly get into:

I now find that I make more and more stupid mistakes. Many of these can be attributed to simply getting older, but others are due to my condition. I get in a muddle when trying to read a map. I sometimes hear something clearly, but simply do not understand what has been said.

I am only able to concentrate on one thing at a time, which can be very frustrating for my wife who finds that if she asks me a question while I'm reading, I simply blank it out and do not reply. On other occasions, Sue will ask me to buy butter and milk, and I will only bring milk back. This is extremely frustrating for her.

Sue is a marvellous supporter/carer/driver/minder – despite

having chronic pain arising from four failed back operations when she was in her thirties.

Our main problem is poor communication arising from my weak voice, my poor hearing (unrelated to Parkinson's) and my inability to think clearly. She has the patience of a saint.

Activities

I was extremely fortunate in finding two activities which have really engaged me, as a distraction from thinking about Parkinson's. The first was the challenge of starting, with a friend who is very talented musician, a singing group for people with Parkinson's and their carers, called Skylarks.

Further information about Skylarks groups is contained at the end of this book.

After eleven years Skylarks is still going strong. Each session concludes with us singing the famous jazz song 'Five foot two, eyes of blue', which sends everyone away in a happier mood than when they arrived.

I really do recommend that you join a Parkinson's singing group: it is a great way to make new friends, to be amongst people who appreciate the problems which PwPs face every day, and most importantly it's fun.

The other project I undertook was to compile a history of Fordwich, Britain's smallest town, where I have lived for many years. While it took up a lot of time, it was enjoyable. I must emphasise that I 'compiled' the book and did not write much of it myself. It sold out after three print runs and achieved its aim of raising a modest amount of money for Parkinson's UK and Skylarks.

Tips

I should practice what I preach!

Sing!

Take your drugs on time.

Do your exercises regularly.

Find a physiotherapist who specialises in treating patients with Parkinson's who will advise on the most appropriate exercises for you.

Go for a walk every day, however short.

Do not try to do too much; you will only get over-tired.

Buy shoes with Velcro fastenings.

Buy polo shirts to avoid buttons.

If you suffer from MCI, try to go more slowly to get your thoughts in order.

Be thoughtful and kind to your carer, who will doubtless have worries of his/her own.

And what of the future?

Despite all the resources devoted to finding the causes of Parkinson's, we have to accept that, at present, the disease is not only progressive but also incurable. Furthermore, in my experience neurologists will not, and cannot provide any guidance about how long a patient, for example, will be able to walk to the shops nearby.

So, I will try to live life to the full for as long as I am able, but also try to learn to accept my limitations as my Parkinson's develops.

Seize the day.

Find a cure

Find a cure to stop us falling backwards
Especially when climbing up the stairs
Some way to help avoid disasters
And cut down on the A and E repairs
Find a cure to save us from depression
And lift us from our melancholic state
Put a smile upon a face without expression
Hint – something alcoholic would be great
Chorus:
Now Billy plays no longer on the banjo
And Ali showed us how to fight the foe
So, Michael Fox please go,
Back to the Future, so
You can find the things we really need to know
Find a cure that could prevent us freezing
And coming of a sudden to a halt
While others stand around us disbelieving
We would be grateful if you'd fix that fault
Find a cure to stop our hands from shaking
And dribbling we could also do without
If you can keep us free from constipating
Then we would all remember how to shout
Chorus:
Find a cure to help improve our posture
To strut around more like a matador
There's a problem with my body's architecture
That means I seem to focus on the floor
My substantia nigra pars compacta

Would then overflow with dopamine
Like a thermonuclear reactor
Fired by chocolate-flavoured tyrosine
So then, we all will play the banjo
The fight will be as good as won
As Marty McFly,
Helps us demystify
How we can wave goodbye to Parkinson's
Yes, we'll all wave goodbye to Parkinson's
So, let's all wave goodbye to Parkinson's

The librarian's tale

I was diagnosed with Parkinson's in 1986, although there had been tell-tale signs for quite a few years. In fact, there is a remarkable video showing me as a twelve-year old strolling along with family members, but with an unusual gait showing me lifting my right leg to hip height. It was reminiscent of a John Cleese portrayal of a member of the Ministry of Silly Walks, although it was ten years before the TV programme.

There were no suspicious symptoms throughout my university years in Reading or Toulouse, or at least none that were commented on or observed by myself. In the early eighties, I became aware of weakness in my right hand. This became particularly noticeable when playing cricket. After batting for my innings, which usually didn't last very long, I had to do some umpiring or scoring. Umpiring did not appeal to me, as I risked the wrath of my teammates if I gave one of them out. So, I took on the less hazardous role of scoring. This should have been a straightforward task, but registering the scores in a neat, legible format proved to be beyond me and attempting to do this under the watchful gaze of colleagues was not much fun. I would make an excuse to get out of the chore, usually saying that I had jarred my hand when fielding, but there was definitely a weakness in my grip with my right hand.

So, I was persuaded to seek the advice of a professional, my doctor, Dr Andrews, who was in fact close to retirement. His years of experience persuaded him gently to suggest that the most likely diagnosis was Parkinson's disease and he referred me to a specialist, whose name I can't remember. Narrowing the range of possibilities, I was assigned to Dr Pollock, the neurological specialist at Kent and Canterbury Hospital, who was to be my specialist for over thirty years.

The first significant development was to send me for a week of tests at the Brook Hospital in southeast London. This was a dull hospital which was surrounded by other dull buildings. The ward mainly contained patients with serious heart conditions, so there wasn't much opportunity to discuss common problems. The tests were wide-ranging, but not very memorable. At the end of the week Dr Pollock did his rounds and attempted to sum up the week's findings. There was only one question that I wanted an answer to: 'What am I suffering from?' And also: 'Will I be out of this horrible place by Christmas?' His response to the second question was that I should be able to carve the Christmas turkey. I knew the answer to the first one of course, but Dr Pollock passed on the confirmation in the gentlest way he knew how, asking me if I was aware of the scientist James Parkinson.

So I returned to Canterbury with the knowledge that life would be different from now on. The first change came up sharply and demanded immediate action. Up to this point I had not taken any medication for my condition. However, I had been given some tablets in the hospital which took a couple of days to have any real effect, but they had a dramatic effect as soon as I resumed my normal life.

Sinemet was the drug prescribed and I felt better than before I took the tablets, but it had the effect of a substantial deterioration in my gait, forcing me to lean backwards after I had taken the tablet. This presented an immediate problem, as I walked two miles per day each way to work, and my new walking method made continuing to walk there impossible. So, I acted decisively and bought a car. I had been considering buying one anyway, as I had a wife and two daughters by this time and car ownership offered attractive possibilities for family holidays and general mobility.

There was another significant aspect to the medication. The Sinemet tablets only lasted about three hours, so I had to become dependent on this tablet timetable. The first one was taken at about 8:00 in the morning and lasted until 10:30. The next one saw me through until about 13:30 when I had my lunch. The period until 14:00 was a relatively good one, as it allowed me to move normally, since the effects of the mid-morning tablet took a little time to wear off and the afternoon tablet took its time to take effect.

The time management of the tablets is perhaps best illustrated by my weekly game of squash, which I managed to play between 1979 and 1999. Each Wednesday I would take my first Sinemet slightly earlier than usual, at about 07:50, then taking my second with a cup of coffee just after 10:00. This allowed the effects to wear off in time for my game of squash. The stiffness in my legs and the awkwardness of gait disappeared. These were replaced by a slight tremor and cumbersome movements when getting changed, but the looseness of limb I was experiencing in the game was tremendous. I completed the game, having competed well, and headed back to my office. The brief respite continued, as I strolled back to the library where I took my next Sinemet with lunch, returning to my medicated state, with all its stiffness but also the knowledge that I was now in a position to complete the day's work effectively.

As the years passed, Sinemet alone did not work well enough and I tried a variety of other drugs, including selegeline, cabergoline, pergolide and stalevo, some of which worked well, at least initially.

I also tried the controlled release versions of Sinemet, and for a long period took a dose of amitriptyline to help me sleep.

Eventually I was persuaded to try apomorphine, which was a somewhat messy solution. Involving a daily infusion of apomorphine from a needle to a subcutaneous area of the thigh. I had to rely on my wife to do the infusion.

Now is perhaps a good moment to thank her for the patience and support she has given me over the years.

One problem with apomorphine was that the infusion occasionally leaked. This necessitated the use of an injected dose of the drug from a pre-filled syringe. This drug worked reasonably well and got rid of one of the unpleasant side effects that had emerged when the medication was at its most powerful – sweating. However, the cumbersome method of infusing the drug was slightly difficult and the occasional need to use the syringe was slightly embarrassing. If I was travelling by train for example, the use of a syringe was a suspicious activity. One of the most amusing incidents occurred at Munich Airport after I had seen my elder daughter off to university. I sprinted as best I could, passing about ninety-nine gates in an attempt to catch the plane. The sympathetic air hostess saw me approaching and yelled 'here comes an Englishman about to board.'

I made use of this drug until 2008 when my condition deteriorated, and I felt that I could no longer contribute effectively to my work.

I had now become interested in DBS, Deep Brain Stimulation, which seemed to offer good results after an operation involving the insertion into my brain of electrons powered by a battery unit. The operation would be carried out at King's College Hospital and there was a considerable delay in preparing for it. I made several calls to the specialists and did not make any progress until I spoke to one of the secretaries who was able to get things moving. Eventually I was admitted and the operation took place. It was conducted under local anaesthetic so that I could be constantly monitored to see if there was any deterioration in my speech. The whole procedure lasted over five hours and I emerged from it without much hair. Two days later the device was inserted into my chest, connecting it to my brain. Friends now described me as the bionic man!

The operation was successful, although there was still some slight stiffness on my right side, and I was able to dispense with the apomorphine and replace it with a very small dose of Sinemet. I decided to take early retirement from work to take advantage of the freedom of movement and fulfilled a long-held ambition to cross the United States by rail with my wife, Sally.

The DBS treatment is still effective, although it is slightly irritating that I have to go back to King's for an overnight stay every three years to have my battery changed.

Well, that's my Parkinson's story. I have survived it for thirty-four years and hope to continue a bit longer.

The editor's tale

I have experienced an attack of the procrastinations. It is certainly true that my procrast... et cetera has caused me to forget the ends of certain words, more than me thingy Parkins. I have also experienced misplacement of words, although I have been like this for most of my life. Can't be bothered to work out why. My syntax has also suffered!

Grammar and parsing were things I just took for granted and they usually sprang, ready-formed, from my lips. Now this sentence must have taken a good ten minutes to key in! My favourite part of speech was litotes. I now know little about it but I'm sure it is quite un-tricky.

The symptoms are variable to say the least. I have less patience and far more annoyance. Remember annoyance? It was all the rage in the 1960s.

The only physical effects that I have identified are a few aches and pains and turning into the Gobi Desert, possibly moondust, but that's another matter entirely.

Another thing that annoys me is the name, Parkinson's. Not very descriptive and reminiscent of a chat show host and a philandering politician from the 1980s. I would suggest 'Premature Rigor Mortis' as being both descriptive and erudite sounding. A bit of Latin always goes a long way.

One useful side effect of my Parkinson's comes from a weakening left hand. It had been my stronger, but not necessarily strong, side. It forces me to use my left hand, left leg and other left-sided equipment far more than I ever did. The American humorist, William Widdershins, was heard to say: 'I would give my right arm to be ambidextrous.'

When I was diagnosed in 2018, I was already living a Parkinson's lifestyle – best defined as almost total inertia.

I was presented with my plastic watch (gold was too heavy, so my employer told me – how kind was he?) in 2014. I think it still works but it is extraordinary how, whenever I look at it, it always tells the same time. What are the chances of that?

From a small boy, I had a fascination with ships. Someone told me that whatever you were interested in at the age of ten, you would end up pursuing as a job. That certainly happened to me. At the age of nineteen I was an assistant to a well-known writer and illustrator in the world of merchant shipping. He had been producing shipping books since the 1930s. Eventually I was working on my own and continued to do so for around twenty-five years. Towards the end of my tenure of *Jane's Merchant Ships*, as the publication was entitled, an online database was developed which I used to edit. This was very unusual for those times, and it enabled me to work from home and submit material to the editorial team at head office.

From the age of four until seventy, I never went into a hospital for anything other than visiting or trivial procedures. Therefore, a condition like Parkinson's has never figured largely in the perception of my medical history. It sounds a bad way to consider a chronic illness, but it seems to help.

When I was told my diagnosis I didn't react either way. Perhaps this was because I hadn't had a chronic condition for nearly seventy years (osteomyelitis – a bone disease) and it suddenly struck me that there was little difference between my

Parkinson's and my previous existence.

I think that exercise is vital to keeping reasonably fit. I have two sessions a week and fill in with about a quarter of an hour of exercises myself. Often tricky to concentrate when Kathy Kirby and Ambrose were on the television.

I didn't start having medication for about one-and-a-half years after diagnosis. I had always had second thoughts and I know I had a stubborn streak when it came to pills. I have been taking the pills for three years now and I feel that they are keeping me stable.

The solicitor's tale

'I'm sorry to spoil your evening, but you have Parkinson's.' The consultant neurologist carried on writing his notes. I sat in silence for what seemed like an age but was probably only a few seconds. I had understood the words but could not grasp their relevance to me. Parkinson's? Surely that was something that affected elderly people. I was a physically fit and apparently healthy fifty-four-year-old. He was surely talking of someone else.

'You are in the very early stages, and it is unlikely to affect you significantly for some time,' continued the consultant. There were only the two of us in the room. As he carried on speaking, it began to sink in that he really did mean me. He went on: 'At this stage it is not necessary to begin treatment. I suggest that we review the position in six months. In the meantime, just get on with your life.'

I made my way home to my wife. We had both thought that my troublesome aches and the mild loss of coordination was something trivial, so she had not come with me to the appointment. We sat and looked at each other. Neither of us had had the faintest idea of the potential diagnosis nor did we have any knowledge of Parkinson's disease, as we used to call it. Despite that, we had a sense that with those few words our lives had changed forever.

And so it proved to be. My life is dramatically different from the future I had expected. At the age of fifty-four, I was the head of a large public body – at the top of my career as it were. Less than a year later, my wife and I had both retired and were starting to build a different life in the knowledge that I had Parkinson's.

It is now eighteen years since I had that diagnosis and I am now into my seventies. I still regard myself as basically fit and healthy. I have a good quality of life and there is very little that I cannot do now, that I could do then. Medication has largely kept pace with the progression of the condition, so I now have a cocktail of pills to take each day, which helps to keep me stable. But that is only half of the story.

Although drugs can help manage the symptoms of Parkinson's, they cannot halt the inevitable progression of the condition. It's not enough just to take the pills and assume that they will deliver an acceptable quality of life. Even with good medication, life is a daily battle to keep the progression at bay. I use the word 'battle' deliberately. Like many people with Parkinson's, I find it helps to personalise the condition and focus on Parkinson's as a virtual enemy which has invaded my body and wants to control more and more of it each day.

Parkinson's is progressive and, currently, incurable. Does that mean that there is nothing more that can be done other than to let the Parkinson's take its course?

I passionately believe that there is more that we can do, based on the experience of managing my own condition and of working within the world of Parkinson's for over fifteen years. Those who appear to do best in managing their condition and who enjoy the best quality of life seem to exhibit some of the following characteristics:

First, self-belief. A positive attitude and a strong desire to maintain one's independence are critical. It can be very easy to be shocked and distressed by the diagnosis. Without support at this critical time, some people with Parkinson's may sink into depression from which it is hard, and for some people, impossible, to recover.

Second, determination. Taking on the fight against Parkinson's requires a streak of determination. This might be categorised as pig-headedness, but it shows itself in a refusal to be constrained by the limits that Parkinson's wants to place on the individual's capacity to act. The most amazing things are done by people with Parkinson's every day, and no-one should feel limited in what they want to achieve.

Third, fitness. It is generally acknowledged that the single most important factor in modifying or slowing the progression of Parkinson's is regular exercise structured to the individual's needs. Personal fitness will underpin everything else. It may not be easy for someone unused to taking exercise, to come to it in later life, but it is never too late to start. Sadly, the availability of support by appropriately trained staff, although improving, is still very patchy.

Finally, learning and awareness. Every person with Parkinson's is different. They will have a unique portfolio of symptoms, will have a different rate of progression, and will respond differently to treatments. This means that the selection of medication is a matter for careful discussion with the consultant. The patient can play his or her part by becoming sensitive to the impact and side effects of the medication, how the condition is changing or whether the drugs are wearing off. The treatment programme is a collaboration between the consultant and the aware patient.

I hope that this does not read as though one has to be a

superman to deal with a diagnosis of Parkinson's. That is certainly not the case. With modest support, most people who are diagnosed can cope well – and do so instinctively. I have simply tried to give a flavour of those approaches which seem to help me.

It is fair to say that until recently, very little attention or priority was given to the therapeutic aspects of an individual's treatment compared with the medical. This is changing as we now realise that we have been missing a trick by not being more rigorous in emphasising the importance of having good access to physio and occupational therapies as well as less formal exercise classes such as yoga and Pilates. We should be aiming for early assessment and review of the appropriate therapeutic programme for the newly diagnosed. This sort of social prescribing should pay dividends in the long run, not only for the individual's quality of life, but also by reducing pressure on the NHS.

My message to those who receive a diagnosis of the Parkinson's is to be positive, plan for the future. Life will be different – but not necessarily worse.

The red sports car driver's tale

My life was going very well. At the age of fifty-six I had been running a very successful printing company for many years and had decided to take early retirement and hand over the reins to my two sons. During the previous few years, I had seen one or two acquaintances pass away and this made me more determined to get the most out of life that I could. Our two boys were married, and we had five grandchildren. We had bought a very nice cottage with a large garden of around an acre. I had become a school Governor and attended the local Methodist Church, and had several interests.

We were beginning to enjoy our retirement and I was organising our Golden Wedding Celebration. We had invited around sixty special friends who had shared in our life. Together we organised a luncheon where I was to make a speech. I was always good at speaking in public, so it came as quite a surprise to myself and my wife when I kept forgetting what I was going to say, even though I had my notes and had rehearsed it.

That Christmas we spent a couple of days with one of our sons, and he mentioned to my wife how slow he thought I seemed to have become. It is not easy to spot these things when you are living with someone day to day. I also had a slight tremble in my right arm, but as I was always keen to push a pallet truck when I was working, I just thought it was a permanent strain to my arm. After Christmas I was given instructions to make an appointment at our GP surgery to check out the arm and see what he thought, and the rest is history.

I was diagnosed in 2015 at the age of sixty-one. It was a complete surprise to me and at the time I was in complete denial, thinking that the GP and the consultant were totally wrong. I continued to be in denial even after the brain scans and other tests. I was also diagnosed with sleep apnoea at the same time, which I had also never heard of and thought that I was being picked on by the NHS. This was not to be and in the following two years, having refused any medication, I realised that I was becoming slower and stiffer. I eventually relented and reluctantly took the lowest dose of madopar that I could.

After about eighteen months I was becoming more under-standing of the condition and having (once again reluctantly) been encouraged to join the local Parkinson's branch, realised that there was life after a Parkinson's diagnosis. I then threw myself into the branch, becoming a committee member and joining in all the things 'men' like to do together. I found that I could relate to the other men in the group and together I formed a 'new' group of friends. We played golf, but to Parkinson's rules and we met together for exercise classes and had coffee together. In fact, for several years my Parkinson's really did not cause me too many problems.

My wife asked me at the outset what I would really like to have before it was too late, and the answer was a bright red sports car. So we finally decided to buy a new shiny one and, although I only used it in the summertime, I am so glad I had the opportunity to have it for seven years and drive it with the top down. I eventually sold it when I found I was unable to get in and out of the very low driver's seat, and another fellow Parkinson's member bought it from me. He has subsequently had to sell it but at least we both had a lot of pleasure out of it.

I had to give up my driving licence several years ago (the biggest blow I think I have had) and have to rely on my wife for driving. I was never a good passenger and we struggled for some time to come to terms with her 'different' way of driving. We eventually decided to buy an automatic car which seems to have solved a lot of problems! Having originally taught my wife to drive back in the 1960s I must not complain. We manage well and I am very grateful.

There are many things now that I would like to be able to do but I realise it is just not possible. Even trying to take a few days' break now is quite a task as we need to take such a lot of equipment with us, and then I am not able to pack and unpack or even pull a suitcase. Even getting into and out of a lift causes problems with my mobility.

Life now sixteen years on is much different. We sold our lovely cottage with the large garden and bought a bungalow, and have had it adapted to suit our needs. I felt sure we had moved too early but realise now that we did the right thing. We feel we have been lucky in many respects and were getting along very well until the pandemic struck. The lack of contact with other friends with Parkinson's during the pandemic has caused me to become much more isolated, although I have joined in the Zoom singing groups and had speech and language online as well. I have also had many appointments online which I find much less stressful than having to attend clinics.

My walking causes me some problems now and I do find I take a few tumbles as well, but I try to be as positive as I can. I also have the luxury of having a personal trainer who comes to the house once a week to keep me as mobile as possible.

When I had my diagnosis all those years ago there was very little mention of Parkinson's. Now there are so many places you can go to get advice and help, and the support of a Parkinson's branch is also a great help. Yes, you might see someone who is a little less mobile than yourself, but the friendship, positivity and support you get from a group will be amazing and will definitely help with your coming to terms with that diagnosis.

We are now preparing for a return of all our Parkinson's related activities: meeting with old friends, singing together out loud and having exercise classes with more than just the personal trainer. There is nothing better than friends, and when you have Parkinson's friends cheer you up when you are down, pick you up when you fall (which can be quite often nowadays) and are always there to care about you. It's lovely to have friends but it is even better to be a friend.

The doctor's tale

When I qualified many years ago my knowledge and experience of Parkinson's disease was very limited as with most new doctors. Unless you go on to have further training in neurology or geriatric medicine that is probably how it remains, despite Parkinson's being one of the commonest neurological conditions. I knew about the classic symptoms, the commonly used drugs, and the typical progression – there are many other things I would have liked to know then!

After general training I specialised in neurology. Parkinson's was one of a number of neurological conditions we commonly saw. After a couple of years, I moved to geriatric medicine whilst keeping a particular interest in neurology. PD is predominantly a disease of older people, so it was no surprise that when I became a consultant in Canterbury, I developed a special interest in that condition. This continued throughout my career.

What I know now is that the so-called classic symptoms are only a part of the management, and for many patients they may not even be the most important. Parkinson's comes in many forms, can have specific causes, responds differently to medication in different people and in the same person at different times and there is probably no 'typical progression'.

So, what are the important things for doctors to remember?

Symptoms such as tremors, stiffness, loss of dexterity need assessment. Slowing down is not just getting old.

Investigations such as scanning are often of limited value

and the diagnosis is usually made on history and examination.

Drugs for Parkinson's disease should only be started by a specialist.

When it comes to medication the maxim should be 'start low; go slow'. If there is not a significant response to drug treatment, then the diagnosis should be questioned. Is this Parkinson's disease? Is this even Parkinsonism? The difference should be explained by the specialist.

Consider symptoms of PD other than the best-known. There's a long list.

I think that the best advice for doctors to give patients would be:

Keep active. Walk as much as possible.

Don't over-obsess about timing of medication. This is important for some patients but can lead to unnecessary anxiety.

Be wary of misinformation on the internet and elsewhere in the media. Remain positive. There is no inevitability of gradual decline or disability.

Gain access to a PD nurse specialist if you can. They are probably the most valuable member of the team.

This is not an exhaustive list and is only my view, based on many years of experience with mainly older patients with PD.

A daughter's tale

At the time of my dad's diagnosis, I was too young (I was only eight years old) to understand what Parkinson's disease meant. I've grown up with it, so it just seems normal. Sometimes the tremor is noticeable when eating together but generally it hasn't made much impact on me.

Another daughter's tale

I was seventeen years old when my dad was diagnosed with early onset Parkinson's disease in 2015. It was a shock. I didn't know much about the disease at the time, other than that it usually occurs in people a lot older than him, causing tremors and eventually resulting in them being in a wheelchair. I vividly remember being worried that he might not be able to walk me down the aisle if or when I decided to get married later in my life, which seems incredibly random now looking back.

But I think that was because most of the information given about Parkinson's disease in schools or on social media is of the later stages, when it's most debilitating. At the time it would have been helpful to have some prior knowledge of how slow the progression of the disease is, even if that is due to medication, and that it can be completely unnoticeable to those on the outside. I was also surprised as my dad did not, and still doesn't have a tremor, probably the most well-known symptom of Parkinson's disease. The lack of communication about how unique Parkinson's disease is for each individual is an aspect that I still think needs to be improved, as this would have helped me to greatly understand more about what was going on with my dad at the time of his diagnosis.

Six years later, with a lot more understanding of how the disease progresses, we as a family notice his symptoms a lot easier. However, I still think that a complete stranger would have no idea that anything was even wrong with him. We have moved house, from a lovely cottage with a lot of steps that caused many issues for him, to a bungalow. This move was a big deal as it was a major step in changing our lives to accommodate my dad for the future, and to make living with Parkinson's as easy as possible for him.

He still loves to garden and go for walks but gets tired very easily. The walks take twice as long as they would normally, and that's not just due to the multiple wee stops he has to take! He sometimes struggles to get out of my Mini after a long day, and he drives me insane dragging his foot across the wooden floors in our bungalow! We have learnt to find humour in the small things he does since his diagnosis and look forward to the new challenges we will face as a family.

The friend's tale

I first met Tom in our first year of university, a vulnerable time for young people when loneliness and pressure to succeed make the support of a friendship group vital to well-being. Tom and I became firm friends. Once we left the university system our lives diverged but we always happily met up at our five-yearly university reunions. Time inevitably passed but, as is the case with people you have known from young, we never felt any older each time we met, although we were by now in our fifties.

The day of our latest reunion dawned, and we found each other amongst the wider group of friends. Walking down the street Tom and I were deep in conversation when all of a sudden Tom staggered, his left leg buckling beneath him. Instinctively I made a grab for him, and he held on to me, and we both laughed. Nothing more was said.

However, some months later, I was talking to Tom on the telephone and jokingly asked if he had fallen for anyone else recently. There was a long pause, then he said: 'I haven't told anyone else, but it has started happening more often; always my leg – it goes stiff and on a couple of occasions I have been close to falling. Since I last saw you, I have had sudden stiffening leg muscles and even occasional leg tremors.'

I asked if he had seen a doctor. He replied that he had told a doctor about his mysterious leg symptoms and had even-tually been referred to physiotherapy. This appeared to be helpful until it happened again: sudden cramp, wooden leg and desperately grabbing hold of the nearest support. A different physiotherapist suggested he might ask to see a neurologist. Following a referral to a neurologist, an examination resulted in Tom being given a diagnosis of Parkinson's. The irony of hearing this was not lost on Tom. After all, on this day he should have been celebrating because it was his fifty-second birthday. We continued our telephone conversation and Tom sounded angry: 'I've led a fairly healthy life, then at age fifty-two to suddenly learn that the rest of my time will be spent with a disease which can never get better, and which I can only delay getting worse. The only good news it seems is that you're expected to believe it doesn't affect life expectancy.'

Since receiving the diagnosis, Tom has dealt with it in stages. Following his initial angry reaction, he then coped by barely acknowledging the Parkinson's. He was aware of his persistent limp, but no-one else seemed to notice. When friends asked about his slowness, he said he must be getting old and left it at that. He did wonder if a company would still contract an IT specialist with limited mobility, but reckoned they still would. Tom dismissed Parkinson's as a condition that was not going to dominate his life in any way.

Gradually Tom admitted having Parkinson's to a few select friends. He said he did not want to be identified as having Parkinson's – at least not yet. 'If it can't be cured, what's the point?' he would tell me of the new symptoms when they surfaced. Sometimes he froze when walking. He was forced to touch tables and chairs as he walked past them to keep his balance.

Although Tom spoke a little more about what it was like

to live with Parkinson's he was not ready to listen to advice. For instance, I suggested he join the Parkinson's physiotherapy exercise class which had been recommended by his specialist Parkinson's nurse, but Tom really did not want to know. I tried to persuade him to tell more of his friends. He said enough people knew already. I asked if he was taking the tablets he had been prescribed. He said they cured nothing but only masked the symptoms. He would not agree to my telling other friends. In fact, he told me quite clearly, he did not want to talk about it at all and that if I persisted, he did not want to talk to me anymore.

I retreated in despair. Imposed lockdowns due to Covid-19 made things worse as Tom would not use FaceTime or Zoom. Communication became even more of a challenge as Tom's speech became affected by Parkinson's. Although I was Tom's friend, I felt useless as I did not know enough about the condition and what little help I had offered was being well and truly rejected by Tom himself.

And then Tom rang me. He talked about Parkinson's as the 'elephant in the room' and asked me if I knew how to eat an elephant. I replied that I did not, so he told me: 'There is only one way – a bit at a time.'

So, this is how Tom manages living with Parkinson's right now. We never talk about Parkinson's; it's too big and too obtrusive. We talk about which bit of the elephant is annoying him most. For instance, if it is balance, we research balance exercises. If it is a mask face, we pull faces at one another, which incidentally requires great skill to do over the ordinary telephone. He was thrilled to tell me he had joined a Zoom choir where no-one knew he was only exercising his affected vocal cords. Tom still does not identify as being a patient with Parkinson's. Instead, he has lots of little ailments. We can talk about them, and we can address them, or we can forget them for a while. But right now, we both know a lot more about Parkinson's than we did.

The tale of the person with Parkinson's, or is it Lewy Body Dementia?

I had been away on holiday when my husband met me at the airport, with the news that a medical friend had advised him to see his doctor because he thought he had Parkinson's. We were sent to a consultant who agreed with this diagnosis, and he was prescribed his first medicine. Subsequently he was prescribed different and higher doses of drugs, but medication didn't seem to have any effect on his condition.

As time went by, we found out more and more about Parkinson's but were puzzled by what was happening. He seemed to have many of the same symptoms as the other PwPs, but in addition he was plagued by dramatic hallucinations of strange people and animals.

When an eminent consultant gave a talk at a branch meeting of the local Parkinson's group, I asked him how to know whether my husband had Parkinson's or Lewy Body Dementia. He asked if he needed his medication to get going in the morning. I answered no and he said it was probably Lewy Body Dementia. His imaginary menagerie was another good indicator.

Getting a clear answer was more difficult as, at that time, appointments were continually being cancelled and put further and further back. I had decided to go with my husband to all his appointments because I felt it was important to try to convey what was happening. I felt that I was telling tales, but he always said it was fine.

We were referred to the mental health service for elderly people. I don't think he liked the appointments and found it demeaning. He was assessed as having probable LBD, something that can only be verified post-mortem.

There are many shared symptoms. Things like falling out of bed and hallucinations are caused by both LBD and Parkinson's. But my husband's night-time adventures included taking the bed apart looking for snakes and hunting for gangsters and burglars. The hallucinations were often unpleasant to the point where I became adept at rolling out of bed at the sound of his agitated voice to avoid arms and legs or being grabbed around the neck and throttled.

There were spatial problems too. Before LBD he could park on a sixpence but gradually his ability to park neatly had gone and he nearly mowed down an entire cycling team in France. However, he was very dignified throughout and thankfully gave up driving.

The condition seemed less and less like Parkinson's as his reactions to things changed. He took umbrage at random things, like the lilac-covered equipment at the gym and a salesman trying to sell us a car that he could get into more easily.

He was given medicines for psychological problems, but they didn't agree with him. It seems medication doesn't have much effect on LBD and the doctors didn't have the funds to help in other ways.

He had a very good job, but his executive skills were affected and he made some poor decisions and found himself unable to make others. At the time these were put down to other issues, but I am sure they were early signs of LBD.

A friend rang Parkinson's UK on our behalf to see how to get help. They told her how to contact the local branch, opening up a whole set of possibilities for support and activities for my husband and me to try.

We joined in singing sessions. He had a great sense of humour and registered us as Humphrey Bogart and Lauren Bacall. He got on very well with young and old. Before we were married (a second marriage for us both), he would say: 'We are living in sin, which is better than living in Herne Bay.'

We joined in a branch physiotherapist-led exercise group. One of the joys of this was the group of carers who sat around a table chatting while the physiotherapists had their charges doing exercises.

Other Branch activities included aquatic therapy, walks and pub lunches, all of which gave us a chance to learn from each other and share problems.

Knowing that I needed a break, he agreed to go into respite care at Age UK, but this didn't last long. He started humming *The Great Escape* and said he didn't know if he would escape via tunnel A, B or C. He didn't feel appreciated or understand whilst he was there.

When things became more and more difficult, it was suggested that I could arrange for someone from Carers' Support to look after my husband from 21:00 until 07:00. They would ring me and come when I was desperate. This was a godsend.

Such support is vital, and I don't know how we would have managed without it. We started a buddies' group to help people to chat about anything, share ideas and make friends.

This helped me enormously.

A tale of diagnostics

Or twelve missed opportunities to get a diagnosis of Parkinson's

(Diagnosis minus 400 days. Runny nose.)

I've gone to the doctor to see if he will refer me for some physio for my back. At the end of the appointment, I casually mention that I seem to have had a runny nose for ages, over a year in fact. I thought it was a cold, but I don't have any other symptoms that I would associate with a cold. To my surprise the doctor becomes quite animated about this.

'Over a year! Well, let's start with the most obvious things, try this nasal spray. If it hasn't sorted it out in two weeks, come back and we'll see if it's something more serious.'

'Okay, doctor, thanks, I'll give it a try.'

The doctor leans towards me and looks me sternly in the eye. 'I mean that – you must come back and see me if it hasn't worked.'

'Thanks, doctor. I'll do that.'

But I didn't. The nasal spray didn't work but I didn't go back. I mean, how serious can a runny nose be? It's just a runny nose after all.

(Diagnosis minus 320 days. Runny nose and dribbling at night.)

I'm slowly waking up in the morning. Sandra turns over and stretches and I move my head on the pillow. One side of the pillow is quite soggy. I've noticed this a couple of times before – I seem to be dribbling in my sleep.

'Sandra, do you find that you're dribbling in bed sometimes?'

'No, I don't think so. Anyway, how would you know?'

'Well, when I wake up, sometimes the pillow is a bit soggy. Do you get that?'

'Nope.' She rubs her hand over my pillow. 'That is a bit soggy though. Maybe you're too hot in bed. I was going to change the duvet anyway.'

(Diagnosis minus 306 days. Runny nose and dribbling at night and disrupted sleep patterns.)

I'm lying in bed staring at the ceiling. It's 04:20. I turn over onto my left-hand side, turn over onto my right-hand side, turn over onto my back. Nothing makes any difference. I'm awake. I get up quietly, pick up the glass of water from beside the bed and tiptoe down to the living room, taking care not to wake the dog in the kitchen. I turn on the telly and watch the news channels for a couple of hours, check my emails.

At 06:30 Sandra's alarm starts beeping and we sit down at the breakfast table.

'You were up early again today,' she says.

'Yup, 04:30.'

She chews this over for a minute. 'That's the third time this week, isn't it?'

'Pretty much. It was 03:15 on Wednesday.'

'Is the stress at work getting to you?'

'Well, yes, there's always stress at work of course. Hasn't got me up in the night like this before though.'

'Perhaps sleeping tablets would help?'

'Hmmm… maybe. Don't really want to get dependent on them though. They can be addictive. Let's see how it goes.'

(Diagnosis minus 280 days. Runny nose and dribbling at night and disrupted sleep patterns and dragging right foot.)

Sandra and I are walking the dog along the seafront. Every few steps my right foot scrapes on the ground. Sandra starts to notice this.

'Can you pick your feet up properly when you're walking? Scrape, scrape, scrape all the time, and it's not doing your shoes any good.'

I focus on lifting my right foot and placing it carefully. It stops scraping. 'I think I need new trainers. These are a good few years old now.'

'Yes, okay, we can have a look in the shops in Canterbury at the weekend. But if you just stopped dragging your feet that might sort it.'

We walk on. Scrape. 'There you go again! Pick your feet up.'

'It's my right foot. Maybe I've overdone it a bit – it does feel quite stiff.'

(Diagnosis minus 240 days. Runny nose and dribbling at night and disrupted sleep patterns and dragging right foot and stiff arm.)

Sandra and I are walking into town and she is watching me curiously.

'Why are you walking like that?'

'Walking like what?'

'Well, with your right arm hanging like that. It looks weird.'

'Remember I had that rotator shoulder muscle injury last

year? I don't think it's really healed yet. That's probably why my arm is a bit stiff.'

'That was months and months ago. Maybe you should get back to the physio.'

'Yes, could do. It'll probably loosen up though. I'll see how it goes.'

She walks behind me. 'Swing your right arm a bit more. Loosen your hand. Can't you swing it more, err, naturally than that?'

'I am swinging it naturally. This is just how it goes.'

'Well, it looks odd.'

Maybe I should have gone back to the physio. But I didn't.

(Diagnosis minus 180 days. Runny nose and dribbling at night and disrupted sleep patterns and dragging right foot and stiff arm and hand freezes.)

Sitting in a theatre, applauding wildly. After a minute or so, my hands are clapping quite softly. Then my right-hand stops moving completely. I'm looking at it as the audience rises for the third time. I'm asking it to carry on clapping, but it isn't moving. At all. I shrug it off as just one of those things. My hands must have got tired after clapping so much.

I really should have recognised that this was something very different from 'tired hands'. But I didn't.

(Diagnosis minus 140 days. Runny nose and dribbling at night and disrupted sleep patterns and dragging right foot and stiff arm and hand freezes and loss of sense of smell.)

Sandra comes through from the garden with a few roses to put in a vase.

'Look, don't they smell lovely?'

I inhale deeply. 'I'm not sure I can smell them, bring them over here. Hmm, quite a delicate scent.'

'Delicate! I wouldn't call it delicate, over-powering more like.'

'Really? Well, I don't think they've got much scent at all. I suppose I've never had a strong sense of smell.'

(Diagnosis minus one hundred days. Runny nose and dribbling at night and disrupted sleep patterns and dragging right foot and stiff arm and hand freezes and loss of sense of smell and illegible handwriting.)

Sandra is squinting at the calendar by the fridge.

'What does this say on the calendar?'

'Uh, I think it says 'Daisy vet appointment'. Does that look like a 'D' to you?'

'How should I know? You wrote it.'

'I think it's 'Daisy vet appointment, 10:30'.

'That squiggle is supposed to be the number ten, is it? How could anyone read that?'

'My handwriting has got a bit scribbly lately.'

'Well, you're not writing the Christmas cards this year; that's for sure.'

'Suits me.'

(Diagnosis minus eighty days. Runny nose and dribbling at night and disrupted sleep patterns and dragging right foot and stiff arm and hand freezes and loss of sense of smell and illegible handwriting and driving deterioration.)

We're driving to Canterbury. Sandra peers across at the dashboard.

'What gear are you in?'

'Fourth, of course.' The noise of the racing engine permeates my consciousness. 'Oh bugger, I'm still in third.'

'I thought the engine was straining a bit. And mind the kerb! '

'I can see the kerb!'

'Remember on the M2 last month you were stuck in third for a mile? I think when we change this car, we should get an automatic'

'Yeah, you could be right about that.'

(Diagnosis minus forty days. Runny nose and dribbling at night and disrupted sleep patterns and dragging right foot and stiff arm and hand freezes and loss of sense of smell and illegible handwriting and driving deterioration and short-term memory loss.)

I'm chopping up the vegetables to feed the guinea pigs. I scrape them into the food bowl and go over and wash the knife, put on the kettle, and go upstairs to get dressed. When I come down again, I notice the guinea pig food sitting on the side. I've forgotten to put it in their cage. I take it out to them and come in again. Sandra calls from upstairs.

'Weren't you making a cup of tea?' Of course, I'd boiled the kettle to make the tea. This kind of thing is happening a lot. I know, I'll give myself a test.

'What are you up to?'

'I'm just giving myself a little memory test. I seem to be forgetting lots of things lately. Getting old. You know Jen texted me yesterday to say I'd left the car boot open? And the other day I went to the shops and when I came back an hour later the front door was wide open? I'm going to test myself.'

There's a glass of water at the top of the stairs. I tell myself that I'm going to go upstairs, draw the curtains and bring the glass downstairs. Up I go, draw the curtains.

Sandra is there. I ask her if we need anything from the shops this morning.

'No, I don't think so. How much milk have we got?'

I go downstairs and check the milk in the fridge. Twenty minutes later I'm standing at the bottom of the stairs looking up at the glass of water, still at the top of the stairs. I tell myself that I'm going to go upstairs, start running a bath, and bring the glass back down with me. Up I go, start running the bath. There are a couple of towels on the floor that need to go in the wash, and I take them downstairs. Twenty minutes later I'm standing at the bottom of the stairs looking up at the glass of water, still at the top of the stairs, laughing at me. This is not good. Am I losing my mind?

(Diagnosis minus twenty days. Runny nose and dribbling at night and disrupted sleep patterns and dragging right foot and stiff arm and hand freezes and loss of sense of smell and illegible handwriting and driving deterioration and memory problems and tremor.)

I'm sitting up in bed reading. My right hand is shaking a bit.

'Why are you shaking that book like that? It can't help you to read it.'

'I don't know. My right hand shakes a little bit sometimes, especially when I'm reading.'

'It's okay if I hold the book in my other hand. Well, better anyway.'

147

I get up, go down to the laptop and Google 'shaking'. The word 'shaking' takes me down a fever route. Lots of questions about running a temperature and whether I've been in the tropics lately. Nothing relevant to what I am experiencing. I shut the laptop down and go back to bed.

If I had used the word 'tremor' instead of 'shaking' the results would have been very different, and more helpful. But I didn't.

(Diagnosis minus five days. Runny nose and dribbling at night and disrupted sleep patterns and dragging right foot and stiff arm and hand freezes and loss of sense of smell and illegible handwriting and driving deterioration and memory problems and tremor and friends telling me to go to the doctor.)

It's the lads' pub night and we're walking to The Ship. I can tell there's something on their minds. Sean speaks up.

'Look, mate, your arm. It's been like that for, what is it ... nine months now? And you're still doing that weird walk. It's not normal. You should see the doctor.'

'It's just not healed from the rotator injury I had last year. I think that's what it is.'

'Come on, that should have sorted itself out months ago. You've been doing this strange walk for ages. Go to the doctor and get it checked out, that's my advice.'

'Yeah, okay, I think maybe you're right. I'll get it checked out.'

(Diagnosis minus zero days. Runny nose and dribbling at night and disrupted sleep patterns and dragging right foot and stiff arm and hand freezes and loss of sense of smell and illegible handwriting and driving deterioration and memory problems and tremor and friends telling me to go to the doctor.)

So, I'm sitting in the doctor's, the doctor who saw me over a year ago. The doctor who had insisted that I come back and see him about my runny nose if the nasal spray didn't work.

I explain my list of oddities to him and at the end he says to himself: 'Well, it's very unusual, but...' and then takes me through a series of tests – handwriting, reflexes and rigidity in my right arm and leg, questions about sleeping patterns, smell, memory, walking. Finally, he says: 'I'm going to refer you to a neurologist. Do you have any preference for Margate or Ashford? QEQM Margate might come through more quickly, in three months or so.'

I still don't understand the implications of this. 'Okay, thanks doctor.'

He sees me to the door and gives me a straight look. 'In the meantime, you might want to think about Parkinson's.'

I had never in my life thought about Parkinson's.

Back home I go straight onto the computer and Google 'Parkinson's'.

And bing, bing, bing! Everything falls into place. An hour or so later Sandra comes home from work.

'I'm fifty-five and I've got Parkinson's.'

She cries.

A tale of diagnosis

The bones continued aching,
        The arm just wouldn't stop shaking.
The writing, different every day, smaller and smaller, oh what
does that say?
So, there I was a senior nurse with all those years' experience.
But not once did I consider the real possibility, how dense!
The GP, dumbfounded, back, neck or shoulder?
'Refer me to a specialist,' I said, suddenly becoming much bolder.
So…off we went, my friend and I, to meet the next in line.
Always being the optimist, the diagnosis would be just fine.
After much examination, surprise, he didn't know!
But knew someone who would, so off we go.
He introduced the neurologist, my jaw dropped to the floor.
A sharp intake of breath from friend, we couldn't take much more!
Many questions followed, lots and lots of talking.
There were no kind words or niceties when the diagnosis was
delivered.
A simple… 'you've got Parkinson's – surely this was considered?'
I looked across and saw her cold, uncaring stare…
'Not at all,' I said. I was totally unaware.
So, eight years on my life has changed, but not everything is bad.
Naturally optimistic, I try not to be sad.
With a cure around the corner, and friends and family there,
I keep a positive mindset and really don't despair.

The constipator's tale

It's 07:00 in the morning and the family is running smoothly through the morning workday routine. Sandra is quickly walking the dog before she heads off to work and Clara is re-doing her hair for the umpteenth time before going to get the bus to school. And me? I retired several years ago, pretty soon after I got my Parkinson's diagnosis, so my routine is not much of a routine at all, really. Today I'm eating toast in front of the telly watching the news, terrifying predictions about climate change illustrated with awesome pictures of Antarctic glaciers calving into the Weddell Sea. Huge chunks of embryonic icebergs crashing into the frozen water.

I carry the plate through to the kitchen and begin to wash up, previewing the day ahead in my mind. Lots of nothing, maybe a bit of gardening if the weather holds up. Sandra is sure to want the grass cutting. As I bend over to put the plate away, I get a sudden stab of pain in my guts. Ow! I know what this means, toilet time. I go upstairs to the bathroom and sit on the toilet but annoyingly nothing feels like it's happening. I give a push and 'aagh!'

Blimey, that hurt! Here it comes again... 'Ow! Aagh!'

I've had this experience once or twice before, but this feels like a bad one. I hear the front door open. That'll be Sandra coming in. She'll need to use the bathroom before leaving for work.

'Can I come in yet? I need to brush my teeth.'

'Sorry, no. This feels like it could be a long time. I'll pass your toothbrush out.'

I get up gingerly from the toilet, totter over to the door and pass the toothbrush out.

'Thanks. I suppose I'll have to use the downstairs loo?'

'Ouch! Aaagh.'

'I'll take that as a yes. Don't forget to get a birthday card for your brother and try to mow the lawn today. It's looking frightful, frankly.'

'Nnnnggg.'

'Pardon?'

'Anything else you might need from the bathroom? What about Clara?'

'I think she'll be able to manage, pass me her toothbrush as well.'

'Okay, hope you have a reasonable day at work. Actually, before you go, can you get the Nurofen? I think it's in the drawer by the bed.'

She passes the Nurofen through the gap in the door. I close the door, waddle back to the toilet, and take a couple of tablets. Oh, it's coming again. I grab hold of the towel rail and brace myself. 'Aaagh! Aaaagh!!'

It's agony. I relax. It waits. It feels like some enormous brick. I've been locked in the bathroom for twenty minutes now.

'Bye!'

I hear the front door close.

'Dad, can I come in?'

'No, not really sweetheart. What do you need?'

'I need a poo.'

'Sorry, you'll have to use the downstairs loo. Aaghh! Ouch. Ooooo!'

'You alright in there, Dad?'

'Ah, yes, don't worry, I'm okay, I think I'm going to be here quite a while though.'

I hear her go downstairs and ten minutes later the front door opens and closes. I'm home alone, with the dog and the brick. Again, I grasp the towel rail on one side and the sink on the other and try a tentative push. Aaagh! Oh God. It's some sort of massive, solid poo and it's wedged maybe half an inch out. There's no going back and there seems to be no going forward either. And the pain! I'm a little bit scared – I wonder if it's going to do some sort of damage. Another twenty minutes pass, I've been in the toilet for nearly an hour. Thank God the dog's behaving herself downstairs. I've got to try to sort this out. I stand up and walk around the bathroom.

Suddenly I remember the NCT classes we attended when Sandra was pregnant with Lara. I start adopting childbirth positions around the room: on my knees over the side of the bath; lying on my back on the floor with my knees up to my chest. I no longer care whether the brick comes out into the toilet or on the floor. I've just got to get it out. Once it's out I'll deal with it, wherever it's ended up. I get back onto the toilet. It's still there and it's still agony whenever I push or whenever it pushes.

Knock, knock, knock! Woof, woof, woof!

Oh, bloody hell. Jesus, Mary and Joseph, there's someone at the door. I'll ignore it.

Woof, woof, woof, grrrrrr! Ruff! Ruff!

Of course, the dog won't let me ignore it. Very carefully I pull up my pyjamas giving the brick as wide a birth as possible, put on my dressing gown and waddle downstairs. I grab the dog and open the door.

'I've got a parcel here for next door, can you take it? It says leave with any neighbour.'

'Hi, yes, of course, that's fine.'

'Can I have your name?'

'Roberts, Graham Roberts.'

'Great, cheers.'

'No problem.'

No problem! Ha! Back upstairs, back to my perch on the toilet, back to alternately pushing, gasping, walking, sitting. This is getting nowhere. And the pain is truly excruciating. I know why this has happened today. I've skipped my cereal and prunes for the past two days, just had toast. Big mistake. Actually, eating the prunes might still help. Maybe there's something in the medicine cupboard as well, perhaps some Ibuprofen. Another delicate manoeuvre downstairs, scoff the last three prunes. A rummage in the medicines box reveals a pack of suppositories, unopened. Hmmm. Well, this is going to be a new experience. But I've got to try everything, the situation is, after all, pretty desperate.

Back upstairs I cut one of the suppositories open and look at this small, jelly-like, greasy inch-long tube. I know where it's meant to go, but I'm used to things coming out of there – nothing has ever gone in there before. And how far in is it meant to go? No time for prevarication, I carefully ease it up. It's a bit messy and I have a real good wash before resuming the perch on my throne. The suppository drops out shortly afterwards. Maybe they should go further in. I try another, getting it further up. There are some drips around the floor now that need cleaning up. Five minutes later and the end of the brick has definitely softened, but otherwise no change, little movement, and lots of 'Aaagh!' I have another thought: beer! Beer can have a laxative effect, can't it? This is a cheerful thought and God knows I could do with some cheer just now. There's a bottle of celebration stout left over from Christmas. It's very strong, eleven percent. Maybe if I drink that something will occur. And if it doesn't, well, maybe I'll feel a bit happier anyway. I jam some toilet paper into the end of the brick to try to prevent drips and totter downstairs again. A few minutes later I'm sitting on the loo knocking back a very nice, albeit very strong stout at 10:00 in the morning. It's at times like this, on the toilet for two hours of agony, drinking eleven percent stout in the morning, that you can wonder just what you're doing and where you're headed with your life. I realise it's now been two and a half hours, God, when will it end?

Well, of course it does end. Everything ends eventually.

Whether it was the prunes, the suppositories, the beer or a combination of all three, the brick finally starts to budge. I wedge myself between the sink and the towel rail, grit my teeth and take the pain.

Images from the morning's news of Antarctic glaciers calving into the Weddell Sea come to mind as the wretched thing finally calves itself chunk by chunk into the toilet.

Twelve flushes and much poking and prodding later and the brick is finally gone. I emerge from the loo, nearly three hours after I first went in that morning, a bit shaken and wobbly. I must be about half a stone lighter. I make a mental note. I forget pretty much everything these days, but this is one message to myself that I won't forget in a hurry: Never, ever, ever skip your cereal and breakfast prunes again.

Not ever.

Getting there in the end

The doctor said 'it's Parkinson's – I've made the diagnosis,
It's slowed you down and life ahead won't be a bed
of roses.'

I used to be a spirit free – of life a keen partaker
But now I find I'm way behind – not a mover – just a shaker!
Look at me and you'll see just an ordinary person
And wherever I go I'm so slow – lost all momentum.

When baking cakes, the hand that shakes sends flour
into orbit.

And when I eat, I know I'll need to hoover up the carpet.
And the irritating life restrictions caused by this affliction
Sometimes make me feel I'm going round the bend.

But even though it may be daft –
Sometimes you've got to laugh
And then you know that you will get there in the end.
The problems caused by Parkinson's just make me rather
static,

I freeze a lot; I start and stop – excretion is erratic.
Stiffness a curse and balance worse – the problem's multi-focal
Handwriting's poor and what is more – not too hot on
the vocals.

Look at me and you'll see just an ordinary person
And though Parkinson's a bad disease, I might have had a
worse one.

But what you see is not the me who lived life in the fast lane

Though now I'm slow you ought to know I still have got a sharp brain.

And when I feel unable – I remember Aesop's fable
How the tortoise caught the hare on the last bend!
So finally, I reckon
That you've got to keep on trekking
And you'll find that you will get there in the end.

With Parkinson's I'm trapped inside a frame that doesn't function

Cos neurone A and neurone B don't synapse at the junction.
There is no doubt to sort it out should be our main endeavour
If we could only find a cure, the world would change forever.
Look at me – what you'll see is just an ordinary person
Who's lived a life as full as yours – an extraordinary person
Don't think 'cos I'm disabled now – I've never been a winner
I've had more nights of gladness than you lot have had hot dinners.

But it's difficult to hack it when you're stuck in a straitjacket
And you don't know the cause – or why – or when.
So, I believe we must make sure,
That we unite to find a cure
And know that we will get there in the end.
Yes, I know that we will get there in the end.

The cruciverbalist's tale

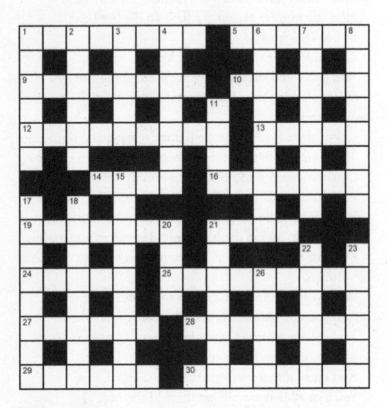

Across

1 Dribbling experiences? Pen's letters left a set of problems (8)

5 I see - speed back to the end of the earth! (3,3)

9 Making haste, preparing spicy food (hot for cold) (8)

10 Bellini's heroine left perpendicular (6)

12 What are stirred with a stick - stick stirred with coal. (9)

13 Editing Gore Vidal, less avid hack who stares lecherously (5)

14 Piece, prawn or penguin? (4)

16 Taking a practical view, the greatest boxers in dreamy sleep (7)

19 Shaking, I call Ray almost imaginative (7)

21 Lean in the elbow (4)

24 Enclosed area guarantees drunken guest will leave confused (5)

25 Average family - family member made a discovery (9)

27 University reflecting virtue finds complete agreement (6)

28 Party girl in note 'Am I number surrounded by drugs?' 17, 21, allegedly (8)

29 Measure a plum book (6)

30 Turned down, down... heading from the other end of road (8)

Down

1 Upsetting itches to reveal a code of morals (6)

2 Disturbed children lose pounds and pence yet make wealthier (6)

3 Call '1 across' for an underground chapel (5)

4 Giving voice, contributing to spiciness in ginger (7)

6 Clown takes heroin - dead enjoyable food! (9)

7 Moan about order, that's quite clear (8)

8 Travellers slip up - it's grim inside (8)

11 Gets a prescription; First things, usually Sinemet. (Easily remembered!) (4)

15 Shuffle home, ache after tea. (4,5)

17 Meadows surrounded by dog-mess - that's gratifying! (8)

18 Becoming stationary? - Liberate with spirit! (8)

20 Edges nearly spill over (4)

21 The Queen possesses gold: 'One's active substance' (7)

22 I leave Francis' place on the square to get help (6)

23 Mean me to end with National Trust membership? (6)

26 Annoyed comments on Trip Advisor?

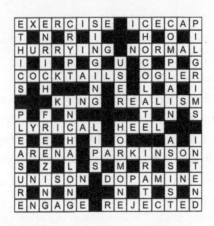

Across: 1 * (EXPERIENCES - PEN) , 5 I C + reversal of (PACE), 9 CURRYING with H for C, 10 NORMA + L, 12 * (STICK + COAL), 13 * (GORE VIDAL - AVID), 14 Double def - king prawn/king penguin, 16 ALI'S in REM, 19 * (I CALL RAY), 21 tHE ELbow; to heel is to lean, as a sailing yacht, 24 *(GUARANTEES - GUEST), 25 PAR + KIN + SON, 27 U + reversal of (NO SIN), 28 DO + PAM + IN + E; AM I N in DOPE; dopamine allegedly the 'pleasure hormone', 29 EN + GAGE (Chambers gives engage (6) book or reserve), 30 DEJECTED - D + R.

Down: 1 Anagram of itches ,2 * CHILDREN - L - D, 3 CRY (call) PT (exercise), 4 spicinesS IN GINGer, 6 H (heroin) in COCO + LATE, 7 C (about) + OM + PLAIN, 8 GRIM in PILS, 11 Acrostic - initial letters of Usually Sinemet Easily Remembered, 15 IN + CHA (tea) + LONG (ache), 17 LEAS in PURE (Victorian euphemism for dog-droppings as used in the tanning industry), 18 Charade of FREE + ZING, 20 Reversal of SPIL , 21 OR in HM + ONE, 22 ASSISI - I + T (square), 23 I + NT + END, 26 I RATE.

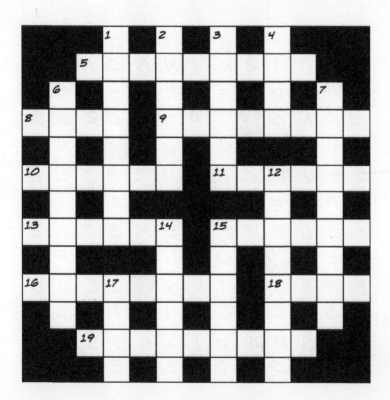

Across

5 Why we're here (9)
8 Going for a ____ (4)
9 Fitted (8)
10 Support (6)
11 Allowed on Zoom (6)
13 No lemons risk (6)
15 Makes you sick (6)
16 Cold not walking (8)
18 Suit (4)
19 Hands signal (9)

Down

1 Decorative plasterer (8)
2 Outline (6)
3 Unwell (6)
4 Dead as a ____ (4)
6 Young drivers (9)
7 Lovely clue (9)
12 Movement (8)
14 Hunters cry (6)
15 Motor (6)
17 Repeat (4)

Diagnostic quiz

How good would you be?
Match the complaint in the left-hand column with the diagnosis on the right.

'Doctor I have …..	Select your diagnosis
A beautiful Grecian God photographed	A broken rib
An early sign of pregnancy on the senior teacher	Snapped Achilles tendon
Batteries outside my house	Arm broken in three places
Noloc	A bump on the head
A damaged rubber vessel	Parkinson's
224 ounces of vinegar	Triple bypass
Complaints from back of the book	Twisted colon
Michael and Cecil	External piles
Three ways to get round London	Gall stone
Somerset ram Kent, Staffordshire	Grumbling appendix

An example of the way of managing Parkinson's symptoms, used by the systems analyst. He identified the most common Parkinson's symptoms that affected him and then scored the extent to which they caused him a problem or required monitoring. He then has a list of activities for each specific problem, a list to be improved as new ideas are tried.

Column one: a list of problems caused by Parkinson's symptoms scored by current severity in column two.

0 = not a problem

1 = not a current problem but needs to be monitored regularly

2 = definite problem needs regular attention (five-minute sessions to control)

3 = disabling problems needing attention three or four times a week

4 = chronic problems need to be addressed daily

5 = disabling, life changing (let's not go there)

Actions column lists a sequence of activity applicable to addressing the problem.

Many are self-explanatory, and others can be found in the exercise lists of PD warrior, Power for Parkinson's, and other programmes, but it is most important to identify the activities that provoke most change and improvement for you.

Problem		Actions
I've got Parkinson's	4	At least one hour each day of exercise from: Parkinson's UK local branch activities Neuro Therapy Centre, Zoom workshops Power for Parkinson's Texas sessions Skylarks Don't neglect any problem area/don't give up
Painful posture, stooping	4	Hold top of door frame and lean in Overhead pulleys working shoulders
Constipation	4	Water Senokot Glycerine suppositories Dulcolax
Bradykinesia, slowness of movement	3	Thirty-minute village walk Walk to marching music Exercise bicycle speed
Muscle rigidity and pain	3	Floor Pilates Scarf snatch and coconut crack (PD warrior) High knee march Walk
Loss of automatic movement, freezing steps	3	Stop look and listen routine Marie's wedding, 'step we gaily...' Body-toe taps (PD warrior) Clock Yourself app
Lack of strength	3	Boxing class (Neuro Therapy Centre) Rowing machine Squat and weights
Voice and speech	2	Singing (Skylarks) Voice builder app LSVT exercises Decibel volume app

Writing size and speed	2	Left hand exercise write poem monthly Typing, do slowly focus accuracy Handwriting, repeat both hands Compare previous attempts
Memory problems	2	Crosswords Recall challenges, things I used to know Zoom quizzes Duolingo
Mask, face expressionless	2.5	Pull faces Gurning into mirror
Tremor	1	Ignore Massage
Poor balance falling	1	Strength balance workshop (Neuro Therapy) Toe and heel rock Fast walking
Dribbling, drooling	1	Speech therapy LSVT exercises
Sleeping, turning in bed	1	Satin sheets
Low blood pressure	1	Check monthly
Sense of smell	0	
Nerve pain	0	
Urination / bladder	0.5	Take control
Dizziness, fainting	0	
Sweating profusely	0	
Difficulty swallowing	0.5	Research LSVT exercises
Depression, anxiety	0.5	Watch for signs Reset mood ASAP
Dementia, hallucinations	0	
Dyskinesia, writhing	0.5	Watch Research ways of controlling

Useful sites and searches:

https://www.parkinsons.org.uk

https://www.neurotherapycentre.org

https://www.powerforparkinsons.org

https://www.lsvtglobal.com

https://www.canterburycantatatrust.org.uk/our-choirs/
sing-to-beat-parkinson-s

https://www.michaeljfox.org

There are hundreds of sites that will tell you about Parkinson's, these are sites that help you do something about it.

Epilogue

In the mid-1960s I left university and did an aptitude test to get into the computer industry. In those early days computers were very simple, and most machines could do just one task at a time. If the computer was doing the payroll, the manager had to wait until it became free to run the invoicing suite. The early machines were very fragile and very unreliable.

A major advance was the introduction of multiprocessing with a fixed number of tasks, which allowed a computer to run up to three jobs at the same time.

The next major change was the introduction of multiprocessing with a variable number of tasks. A big breakthrough came in the 1970s with virtual memory this allowed the computer to decide how many jobs it would do at any one time, very much the way your current smart phone handles all your requests. Or your healthy brain works.

Having Parkinson's is a very similar evolution. It's the same process but unfortunately in the opposite direction.

Before being affected by the condition we can do lots of things at the same time. As the condition advances many of us lose the ability to multitask. It's known as executive dysfunction. On a good day I can still multitask. On a bad day I can only do one thing at a time, and I forget that anything else needs to be done.

That this book exists is in itself a triumph as many of the authors are, to a greater or lesser extent affected by similar problems.

We write to-do lists then forget about them. We promise to send emails and immediately forget. We file things away and forget them. We have days when the relevant part of the brain seems to have gone missing entirely.

Many people have senior moments. We have senior days, when our brain becomes very fragile and very unreliable.

But we did it!

Incurable Optimists -
compiled by those who know.

L ist of those authors and contributors who are happy to
be named:

Anne Broadhead

Charlie Byran

Colin Cheeseman

Roger Clayton

Jackie Crammond

Christine Endersby

Michal Widyma

Colin Gerrard

David Greenman

Tim Halling

Julie Halling

Megan Halling

Andrew Heller

Neil Hickman

Sue Hickman

Dave Hollamby

Junko Lord

Tony Lord

Wendy Mooney

Michael McDonald

Beatrice Shire

Paul Spackman
Isla Spackman
Nora Spencer
Anne Tanson
Janet Tripodi
Rosemary Vahid
Sarah Walter
Mike Wells

Special thanks to our editors Joe Mooney with Tim Halling, Mary McDonald, Wendy Mooney, Janet Tripodi, Sarah Walter and Mike Wells.

Thanks also to James Essinger, managing director of The Conrad Press and also to Charlotte Mouncey, our typesetter and designer.